MW01470497

LANGHOLM
AS IT WAS

John Hyslop 1827-1911

Robert Hyslop 1862-1943.
Photograph *circa* 1912

LANGHOLM
AS IT WAS

A HISTORY OF LANGHOM AND ESKDALE
FROM THE EARLIEST TIMES

By
John Hyslop, J.P.

Hon. President of the Eskdale and Liddesdale
Archaeological Society, Langholm

And his son

Robert Hyslop, F.S.A.Scot., F.R.Hist.S.

Editor of Transactions of the Sunderland
Antiquarian Society

Revised by Robert Hyslop's granddaughter

Dorothy Hyslop Booth

and great-grandson

Ewan D. Booth

Published in 2002 by
D. H. Booth & E. D. Booth
3 Raasay Road
Inverness IV2 3LR
Scotland

ISBN 0 9542635 0 2

Printed and bound by M. Downie and Son
Purdon Street, Partick, Glasgow G11 6AF.

This book is dedicated
with love and great respect to the memory of
John Hyslop,
the inspirer and principal author.

To his son,
Robert Hyslop, joint author,
who undertook the onerous task
of writing the original.

And to his grand-daughter,
Hilda McVittie Cooper
who perpetuated in her family
an interest in Langholm.

CONTENTS

APPENDICES

Index

ILLUSTRATIONS

Frontispiece
John Hyslop 1827-1911
Robert Hyslop 1862-1943, Photograph circa 1911

PREFACE TO FIRST EDITION

This Volume is the realisation of an ambition long cherished by my father and myself. For many years my father had been patiently accumulating the historical data here given.

It was with great reluctance that he was ultimately persuaded to write the Reminiscences which form Part IV. of the book, and I regret exceedingly that it has not been found possible to include all the material he provided. But another opportunity of publishing it may occur.

I frankly confess to a feeling of filial pride in this part of the Volume. For a man of 84 years of age to write what would in itself form a book of considerable size, and all of it with his own hand, was, I think, a noteworthy achievement.

His death, whilst the Volume was in the press, robbed me not only of the gladness which would naturally have attended the completion of our task, but also of the benefit of his counsel and guidance in many difficult matters.

In writing the book our aim has been, after consulting the most reliable authorities, to give a simple and unpretentious account of the History of Eskdale. Whilst we have endeavoured to relate the facts with only as much detail as we deemed essential, we have nevertheless felt assured that not even the most minute detail of the story but would prove of interest to Eskdale men and women, whether at home or abroad. The work has been to both of us a labour of love, and it is as such that it is now offered for the acceptance of our fellow dalesmen.

We had intended to issue a book of some 400 pages, which we hoped to have had ready last Christmas, but my father's death caused me to alter our plan, and to enlarge considerably the scope of the work. I feel confident the Subscribers will forgive the long delay.

My father's gratitude, frequently expressed in the last weeks of his life, and my own thanks are due to the many friends who have aided us in what, under the circumstances, has been an onerous task. Some of them, Dr Christison, F.S.A.(SCOT.), Edinburgh, Mr. Jas. Barbour, F.S.A (SCOT.), Dumfries, and Mr. J.C. Little, Burnfoot-of-Ewes, have also passed into the Unseen whilst the book was in the press, but I desire gratefully to record their interest and help.

To Mr. John Reid, Edinburgh, we have been indebted in a very special way. His historical and general information has been magnanimously placed at our service, and we have gladly availed ourselves of it and of his advice and assistance, in every section of the work.

Thanks are also due to Mr. Clement Armstrong, President of the Eskdale and Liddesdale Archaeological Society, who has most willingly given us the benefit of his researches, and rendered very acceptable help.

We have also been greatly indebted to Mr. George R. Goldsbrough, M.Sc., Sunderland, for his valuable Survey of the Stone Circles and his illustrative Map of Eskdale. Such assistance demanded both expert knowledge and a large amount of labour, both of which Mr. Goldsbrough has ungrudgingly given.

To the Rev. George Orr, Langholm, our sincere thanks are given for his unwearying help, both in furnishing historical information and in revising the proof-sheets, with such patience and literary skill.

The proofs have been also read by Mr. Reid, Mr. Armstrong, Mr. Goldsbrough, Mr. William Hyslop, Mr. J. James Kitts, Sunderland, whose extensive historical and archaeological knowledge has been of great assistance to us, and by Mr. Harry Goldsbrough, Sunderland, by whose care and intelligence we have been saved much arduous labour.

In special parts of the work we have also received valued help from Mr. J.H. Milne-Home, Irvine House; Colonel Irving of Bonshaw; Miss Dobie and Mr. Robert McGeorge, Langholm, who very kindly permitted us to quote from the MS. Diary of the late Rev. Dr. Brown of Eskdalemuir; Dr. David Woolacott, F.G.S., of the Armstrong College, Newcastle; Mr. Mathew Welsh; Mr. Robert Scott; Mr. Walter Wilson; Mr. James Morrison; Mr. S. McKune; Mr. R. Hamilton, M.A., B.Sc.; Mr. W.E. Elton, Langholm; and Councillor G.W. Bain, Sunderland. We are also indebted to Mr. James Smith's pamphlet on *Freemasonry in Langholm* for much of the material of Chapter XLVI.

We have also been permitted to make use of the MSS. of the late Geo. R. Rome, and of the papers read before the London Eskdale Society by Mr. Geo. Niven, Streatham.

The illustrations, not made from photographs, have been produced from pencil drawings by Miss Ethel Kitts, Mrs. Fred. Laws, Miss M.J. Bowmaker, Mrs. Robert Hyslop, and Miss Hilda Hyslop, Sunderland, to all of whom our cordial thanks are given. Acknowledgement is also made of the ready assistance afforded us by Mr. J.T. Burnet, Langholm, who has supplied plans and drawings.

It is not possible adequately to acknowledge all the help we have received, but mention must be made of the interest and assistance given by the following, to whom sincere thanks are offered:— His Grace the Duke of Buccleuch; The Right Reverend the Lord Bishop of Bristol; the Rev. Thomas Randell, M.A., D.D., LL.D., Rector of Ryton-on-Tyne; the Rev. James Buchanan, Langholm; the Rev. H.A. Whitelaw, late of Dumfries, now of Gateshead; the Rev. D.S. Boutflower, M.A., Vicar of Christ Church, Sunderland; the Rev. Jas. B. Macdonald, M.A., B.D.; the Rev. Robert MacQueen; the Rev. D.W. Inglis, M.A.; the Rev. J.A. Seaton of Langholm; the Rev. R.H. Kerr, M.A; and the Rev. John Jamieson, M.A., of Canonby; the Rev. D. Preston, B.D., Ewes; the Rev. John Gillies, M.A., Westerkirk; and the Rev. J.R. Macdonald, M.A., Eskdalemuir; Mrs. Bell, Castle O'er; the Misses Hyslop, Mount Gardens, Langholm; and Messrs. J.W. Allison, Langholm; Andrew Aitchison, Old Irvine; Messrs. Annan, Glasgow; Thomas Beattie of Davington; Jas. Burnet, Langholm; W.E. Bowman, Whitburn; S. Carruthers, Langholm; J.M. Elliot, Westwater; G.T. Elliot, London; W. Elliot, Westerker; Wilfrid Goldsbrough, Sunderland; R. Graham, Cote; James Graham, Wishaw; John Hounam, Gilnockie; H.M. Stationery Office, London; John Hyslop, Langholm; John Laidlaw, Langholm; James Little, Craig; Sir Norman Lockyer of the Solar Physics Observatory; W.S. Irving, Westerkirk; Jas. Malcolm, Eskdalemuir; Walter McVittie, Fiddleton; J.E. Miller, Sunderland; John Miller, Langholm; W.W. Moses, Sunderland; Director of National Museum of Antiquities, Edinburgh; T.S. Newton, Sunderland; William Park, Langholm; John Park, Sunderland; The Registrar-General, Edinburgh; Henry Sanders, Langholm; J.J. Thomson, Langholm; G.J.

Walker, The Observatory; Messrs. A. Walker and Sons, Galashiels; A.D. Raine, Sunderland; and W.R. Yuill, New Barnet.

A special word of appreciation must be expressed to Messrs. Hills and Co., Sunderland, and particularly to Mr. John Rutherford of that firm, for their interest and for the unfailing courtesy and patience as well as the artistic skill with which they have carried out their important part of the work.

5 BELLE VUE CRESCENT,   ROBERT HYSLOP.
SUNDERLAND.   *13th   June,*
1912.

PREFACE TO SECOND EDITION

When my grandfather, Robert Hyslop, published *Langholm As It Was* in June 1912 only 500 copies were printed and within three months of its publication the entire issue was exhausted. He was asked to issue either a second edition or to complete and publish a separate volume of John Hyslop's Reminiscences, which formed Part IV. These Reminiscences were expanded with further material, for which there had not been space originally, and in December, 1912 Robert Hyslop published *Echoes from the Border Hills*. In his preface he says that a second edition of *Langholm As It Was* must be postponed for a few years. Alas, it was not to be.

Always interested in history, he became involved with the history of his adopted home of Sunderland, and especially in the history of the churches. He wrote the original guide book to St. Peter's Church, Monkwearmouth, founded as a monastery in 673 and where the Venerable Bede received his early training, and several booklets dealing with the history of the various Presbyterian churches in Sunderland.

He was greatly in demand as a lecturer, especially with lantern slides. Woe betide any child who ventured into his study while a lecture was in preparation.

However, his affection for, and interest in, Langholm remained with him all his life and the annual visits to the Common-Riding are amongst my early childhood memories. Sadly, with advancing years and the death of his beloved wife, Annie, in 1936, that second edition was postponed forever.

Inevitably, since the original publication ninety years ago, changes have taken place in Langholm. Churches have closed, congregations have amalgamated, farms have changed hands, further archaeological investigations have taken place. Therefore there seemed no point in merely producing a facsimile of the original book.

In the first edition there is a list of errata and these have been incorporated. In Robert Hyslop's own copy of the book, which I inherited, there are several corrections written in the margins in his own handwriting, so these are recorded. However, in no way is this book a picture of **all** the changes which have occurred. The reminiscences of John Hyslop are not included as I had already, in 1991, brought out a new edition of *Echoes from the Border Hills*. I hope this does not cause disappointment.

For several years my son, Ewan, had been trying to convince me as to the feasibility of reproducing *Langholm As It Was* and this edition is entirely due to his organisation, help and encouragement. Without his knowledge of computers I would have found the whole project impossible.

Ewan has also undertaken the reproduction of all the maps, drawings and photographs. Where possible he has used either the original pencil sketches or Robert Hyslop's own glass photographic plates when these gave a clearer picture. In some instances we have taken new photographs when the original sketches were virtually impossible to reproduce. Ewan has also updated the terminology in the chapter entitled *The Geology of Eskdale*.

I am also indebted to my Mother, Hilda McVittie Cooper, only child of Robert Hyslop, who stimulated both my interest and Ewan's in Langholm and its history. She lived to be 101 years and her memory was really amazing. Thanks to her I have found letters from various people to my grandfather concerning Langholm. She kept a scrapbook of newspaper cuttings which I have found helpful and wrote copious notes concerning many of the people and places mentioned. She also wrote genealogical corrections in the margins of her copy. It is for all these reasons that I have included her name in the dedication.

I would like to express whole-heartedly my gratitude to my second cousin Marion McVittie Pool, née Hyslop, and her husband Alex Pool. Marion has been extremely helpful in finding answers to my numerous questions. Alex provided me with an update on the Eskdale Kilwinning Lodge of Freemasons. He also drove me around the area in order to take photographs and finally, after much searching, located the fallen Grey Wether stone for me. My sincere thanks to you both.

I would also like to acknowledge help from the following people and cordially thank them:—

Major T. C. R. Armstrong-Wilson.

Mr. Arthur Bell, M.B.E.

Miss Grace Brown who has allowed the original painting of the Langholm Coat of Arms by A. Brebner to be reproduced.

The Rev. R. Campbell, Minister of Canonbie United Free Church.

Mr. Alex Carruthers.

Clan Armstrong Trust who have re-published Robert Bruce Armstrong's *History of Liddesdale, Eskdale, Ewesdale and Wauchopedale and the Debateable Land,* originally a limited edition published in 1883, and on which the Trust now holds the copyright. The quotations were of course taken from the 1883 edition and have again been checked in my Mother's copy of it.

General Register Office for Scotland which supplied the population figures for the civil parishes of Eskdale since 1911.

Mr. George Irving.

Dr. J.C. Little of Morton Rig.

Mr. Alex McCracken, B.Sc., F.S.A.(Scot.).

Mr. John Packer.

The Much Hon. D. W. Paisley of Westerlea for new information on the Paisley families.

Miss M. Stewart, Editorial Assistant, The General Assembly of the Church of Scotland.

Mr. William Tait who, from his extensive knowledge of the history of Langholm, willingly answered so many of my questions. His death in January 2000 was a great loss to all his friends in the community.

Mrs. Doreen Thomson, née Hounam, for information on the Hounam family.

Mrs. Edith van Driel of Melbourne, Australia, who has supplied so much genealogical information on the Little families.

Dorothy Hyslop Booth,
3, Raasay Road,
Inverness,
IV2 3LR.

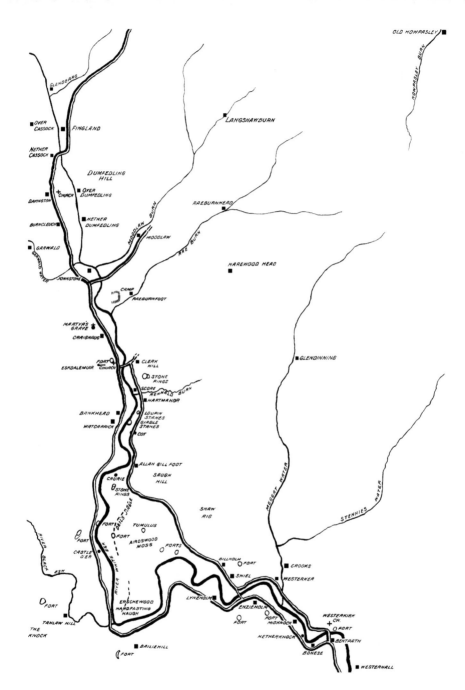

Map of Upper Eskdale

xviii

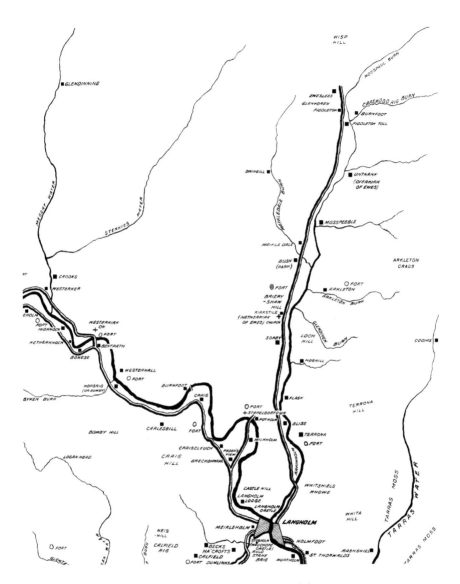

Map of Eskdale and Ewesdale

Map of Wauchopedale and Lower Eskdale

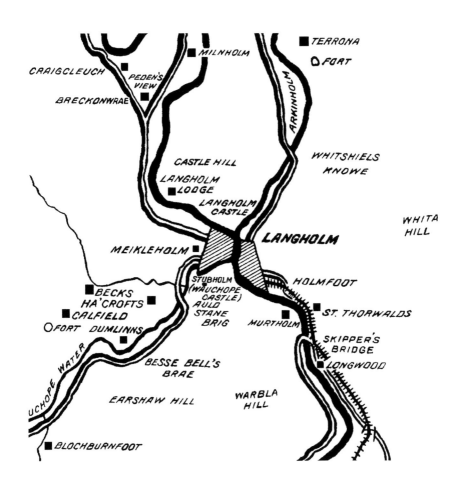

Langholm and Environs

CHAPTER 1

LANGHOLM

Langholm! A word of magic meaning to the sons and daughters of Eskdale, for whom, primarily, this book has been written, a name which awakens the longing and passion of us all who are her children. In our esteem, in our love, there is no place to contest its supremacy, and even comparison is often deemed unfilial. The remark that Scotsmen are "most at home when they are abroad" was the sneer of a cynic, and it fails entirely to apply to the people of Eskdale.

To the man who has lived all his days in the bosom of its hills, Eskdale has an attraction quite as potent and active as that which it offers to him who can only see these hills through the mists of distance and of years.

The causes which divide men and women into opposite parties — politics, religion, and the like — operate in Eskdale, where opinions and principles are tenaciously held, but to the valley itself, the common earth-mother which gave them birth, her children are drawn by one mighty common bond of affection. Probably this is true of a hundred other places, but our love for Langholm and for Eskdale seems a deeper and more intense feeling than even the common love of country.

Sitting by his fireside of a winter's night, far from where the Esk is perhaps rolling in flood, a son of Eskdale will suddenly get a glimpse of the home of his boyhood, its people, its hills, its woods, its lonely burns, recollections of far-off days crowd upon him, memories of men and women who lived their quiet lives among the Eskdale hills float around him, and that strange and subtle spell, which Home throws over us all, steals slowly upon him, even as he has seen the white mists fall quietly on the sides of Whita.

1

A man, who long years ago may have left his home in Eskdale, as so many have done, to find another in some thronging city where the call of the curlew is never heard, save in the exile's fancy, can see, as in a dream, the summer sun lingering on the brow of Whita, or he may catch the matchless trill of the lark as it soars above the hill on some bright summer morning, and there comes upon him that wistful longing which is only the mellowed reflection of a home sickness that was once prolonged and acute.

Or if these fancies and memories come to him when the heather is purpling round the Monument, which crowns so fittingly the summit of Whita, his eagerness to breathe again the heather scented air will probably determine him to return to Eskdale with all convenient haste. The heart of many a man beats faster as he recalls the song of the lark by Whita well, for a draught of whose cold water he ardently longs.

The affection which the Eskdale man cherishes for his old home is a potent influence throughout his life, an ever present passion which like the activity of radium, glows steadily yet wastes not away.

Wherein lies the secret of this magic power and influence? It lies not in any solitary cause, but adheres to every form or phase in which Eskdale or Langholm presents itself to its children, its charming natural beauties seen on every hill, hiding in every valley, its flexible and picturesque Scots tongue, its thrilling history, most of it preserved only in the old Border way of oral tradition, its men and women of vivid individuality, its humour, which pervades like an atmosphere all aspects of its social and public life.

Lies this power to influence in scenery, or history, in memories or associations? In all of these it lies, but not exclusively in any one, for we cannot dissect, analyse, or classify the most sacred emotions and passions of our lives. Light and shadow on the hill, green fern and brown bracken, splash of colour on the heather; cry of the curlew, whirr of the grouse; birk and hazel and hawthorn tree; the green and purple of the hillside broken by moss-covered boulder, primroses by the burn, blue hyacinths in wood and glade, snow on field and tree and hill, mist upon the brae, rain upon the moors with clouds lying low, trailing their white skirts along the sides of Whita; calm grey of a summer twilight, sunny fragrant morning when the woods are a waving chorus; Esk glimmering in the summer sun, or rushing mightily in flood when the November rains have fallen all day on the hills; a cluster of white cottages along the side of Wauchope, a winding and narrow street called Strait; memories of childhood, the music of one's mother tongue; these and a thousand other impressions concentrate themselves to a focus and we call it — Langholm!

Eskdale people meet out in the Australian bush, on the Canadian wheat fields, or in the great American cities and with unerring instinct they recognise each other as sons of the dale. They meet and talk the night long of Eskdale's hills and burns and glens; recalling some half buried memory of that Common-Riding long long ago. Their talk is of Home. That Home they left many years ago but towards which their longings are yet set.

The beautiful and varied scenery of Eskdale is, without doubt, one of the factors which has given to it a unique and unchallenged place in the hearts of its people. But not only its children have yielded to its spell. Not even the compiler of a gazetteer can look at Eskdale without allowing himself a few sentences of admiration.

Visitors become enthusiastic over its beauties, and indeed they discover beauty spots unsuspected or inadequately recognised by those long familiar with the district. Mr. Disraeli is said to have declared that the drive from Langholm to Canonbie was unequalled by anything he had seen in all his travels.

Pennant the great antiquary, looking rather for age than beauty, declared it to be great and enchanting, and added that it was "no wonder then that the inhabitants of these parts yet believe that the fairies revel in these delightful scenes".

Writing for Sinclair's *Statistical Account* about the year 1793, the parish minister thus describes Langholm: "The verdant hills beautifully skirted with woods which shelter it east and west; the Esk, overhung with woods, gliding gently along; the town appearing through the intertwining trees, and the hills and woods at a distance assuming a semicircular form, terminate this charming landscape, a landscape of which, as containing an assemblage of rural beauty and romantic scenery, it baffles the happiest efforts of imagination to give an adequate description."

The valley of the Esk indeed displays almost every aspect of scenery to be found among the southern uplands of Scotland. Geologists speak of the monotony of these uplands, but the term is scientific rather than impressionist. To the native or the tourist, who troubles less about

3

the geology of a district than about its climate, these hills and dales, and woods and glades present an unfailing theme of interest and admiration.

As the Esk tumbles down from its source among the lofty hills which border the counties of Dumfries and Selkirk, it creates some of the most varied and pleasing scenery, full of swift surprises, to be found in the south of Scotland.

For it is the river that has been and still is that master-sculptor, to whose bold and tireless chiselling the beauties of the dale are due. In the course of untold centuries it has cut its way through a tumbled mass of rocks whose summits are gaily decked with rowan or birk, and on whose green mossy sides wild violets and primroses grow. Now it slumbers in this dark pool, eerie with superstition, the haunt of the otter, the trysting place of fishers; now it glints and murmurs over some pebbly bed, seldom long in the one same mood, but to those who love it, it is always fair, ever fascinating.

May it not have appealed just in this way to the tribesmen whom the Romans found in Eskdale? Must it not have been such a love for his native vale as we have, that nerved the ancient Celt to withstand the shocks of the Roman legions? Thus, too, it would appeal later to the rude and troubled Cumbrian, slowly struggling into a crude civilisation, or a cruder Christianity, to the hardy Border raider who knew all the hiding places on its banks or amongst the hills through which it flows. Thus, too, did Esk make its appeal to those nearer forefathers of our own, who have transmitted to their descendants that love and admiration for its beauties which are so characteristic of Eskdale people.

But Esk does not reserve to herself all the charm of the district. Her many tributaries abound in those aspects of nature which leave their impress on every man of simple heart. Than the valley of the Ewes few more delightful places can be found. Even more than Eskdale itself, it has inspired the poet and the painter.

Of a different quality, wilder, lonelier, more rugged and indifferent to artistic form, with a weird, indescribable touch of melancholy upon it, is Wauchope, whose glory is in the past upon which now, alas only clouds and sunsets rest. Sunsets? If the reader wants to see a Langholm sunset he must climb slowly that old Peat Road which runs in straggling line along the northern side of Warbla Hill. There, when the sun sinks over the Calfield Hill and all the west is aflame with purple and gold, the tossed and scattered clouds waving red across the heavens like seas of grass on fire, and all the sky is brushed with hues too delicate, too beautiful to be other than short-lived; when the after-glow is lingering long on Warbla's side, though it has faded from off the other hills, touching the old alders, or ellers as they are called locally, and hawthorns with amber by a defter brush than that of the cleverest artist; when the brow of Whita is tinged with orange, and upon the distant hills there falls that wonderful purple haze which serves so well to set out those more vivid colourings of the western sky which is ever flashing into new gradations of tone and shade, changing momentarily but still remaining as a memory of the heart, then ought the reader to see Warbla and Wauchope.

THE PEAT ROAD

If, as the afterglow dies off the hill, the great full moon should climb over Warbla Knowe, so much more intense and more lasting will be his memory.

Esk, Wauchope, and Ewes meet at Langholm, and an impressive sight they make, especially when the winter rains have swollen the burns, and the waters come rushing and tumbling through the town. Over the head of Whita, and down in a picturesque valley of heather and birk runs the Tarras, the swiftest river in Dumfriesshire, scrambling over its great sandstone boulders, the wrecks of many a winter storm, which must have raged so long ago on that deeply scarred side of old Whita.

TARRAS WATER

Artists who come in sunny summer weather never tire in their eulogies of this lonely mountain stream. Then the anger of the water, and the absolute loneliness and weirdness of the moor are atoned for by the charm of its purple heather, and the greenness of its waves of bracken which shelter many a wild bird whose cry of alarm at your profane intrusion mingles with the plaintive bleating of the sheep, almost the only sounds one hears on Tarras side, unless, indeed, the thunder suddenly cracks overhead, for, say the people of Langholm, all thunderstorms converge into Tarras. In the burns which flow into Esk, up which few go save shepherds and fishers, are beauty spots of delightful variety. From Garwald Water, the rugged ravine, to Byre Burn, with its Fairy Loup, the valley of the Esk abounds in charms.

The hills on whose sides the town of Langholm is built form the larger segment of a circle enfolding the town. Thence they rise in ascending terraces to the sky line, spreading for many a mile far away into the uplands. The more scarred and rugged features of Highland scenery are wanting, but nature has provided compensations.

From the hill tops, so easily reached, what a panorama may be seen. In all directions seas of hills in vivid green, broken by valley and dell, the green speckled with the whitest of sheep, or patched with heather, whilst far away on the south-west like a silver ribbon drawn across the horizon stretch the waters of the Solway! Beyond it are the broken peaks of the Cumberland hills, and the less rugged hills beyond the Nith far down into the storied and romantic lands of Galloway.

GARWALD WATER

Probably it may be said of every place that it reflects more or less closely the different stages of development through which it has passed. Each stage of the evolutionary process leaves some evidence behind, and all these inheritances from the past generations unite to give colour and character to what the place is today. But this can be said with greater truth of a village or country town. There the colouring is sharper and wears away less quickly than where the population is cosmopolitan or changeable. It is eminently true of a town like Langholm.

To understand its present life aright we must trace back many a heritage. Many of the legends and traditions and superstitions which lived long in Eskdale, had their origin far back in those days when history was written in stones standing on hill tops, or in circles which today form topics of learned discussion by antiquary and archaeologist.

What the people are, what they think and say and do, is the aggregate of many influences which have coloured and modified life in these valleys during many centuries. This influence has exerted a cumulative effect, and it is traceable in certain well defined local characteristics.

In not a few of the customs of Eskdale the pagan influence or the Celtic may still be noticed. As we shall show later many of the place names in the valley are of Celtic origin. Similarly the influence of the Saxons and Norsemen, as they successively swooped down on Eskdale can be traced, not in names or words alone, but in the physical form and form and feature, and in the mental characteristics of the people.

Similarly one may note in the intense patriotism which pulses in every Eskdale man, the spirit of the Forest men who fought in many a fierce battle whilst yet the liberties of their country were insecure.

Perhaps, also, to this influence, born and nurtured in stern and long continued conflict, we may ascribe that resolute perseverance which strangers have noted in Eskdale folk, and have often called by less complimentary names.

In a religious connection one of the dominating influences in Eskdale was the Covenanting struggle. It left a deep mark upon the convictions and upon the religious and theological trend of the people of Eskdale, which is not yet obliterated, despite the tendency of the railway, the penny post, and the halfpenny newspaper to reduce even Scotsmen to a common denominator in politics and religion, as much as in dress, or customs, or laws.

Surely, too, their tenacity of purpose, their readiness to endure, their comparative disregard of personal comfort, which entered so much more into the mental makeup of our forefathers than they do into their feebler descendants, are directly traceable to those stirring days of Border feud and fray, when stock raising was a gamble and trading almost a skirmish.

So here in Eskdale stand those eloquent though dumb memorials of the past, stone circle, standing stone, cairn, fort or buried camp, Roman slab or coin unearthed by the plough, mound where old British warriors were laid to rest, tomb of the martyred Covenanter, bare and silent tower, fragment of masonry in kirkyard or field. All these remain to speak to Eskdale men of today of what the Eskdale men of the past were and did.

It is of these memorials and of those far-off days, when they represented all that was most active and powerful in the life of Eskdale, and also of the quieter though perhaps not less interesting days which afterwards dawned, and of the men and women who played a part in their tragedy and comedy, that we would try to tell in the pages of this book.

CHAPTER 2

THE STONE CIRCLES

The oldest archaeological remains in Eskdale are the Stone Circles. Originally these were styled Druidical Circles, or Druidical Temples, but in recent maps reference to the Druids has been dropped. Interest in the Stone Circles of Eskdale naturally concentrates itself upon those on the farm of Cote, or Cot, twelve miles from Langholm. Evidences exist that there were originally other Stone Circles in the district.

Writing in 1841 for Sinclair's *Statistical Account,* the Rev. James Green, minister of the parish of Westerkirk, mentions that "on a neck of land between Esk and Megget, and part of the farm of Westerker, there are several whinstones placed erect in the ground which have every appearance of the remains of a Druidical temple". No trace of this Circle can now be found, but evidently the stones were still standing in 1841.

There are also dotted about in various parts of upper Eskdale, what on the Ordnance Maps are called Stone Rings. This designation has been used to indicate that evidences of stone or masonry exist, but it implies no theory as to the nature or use of such structures. These Stone Rings do not seem to have any relation to Stone Circles.

The Circles at the Cote form a group which must at one time have been one of the most arresting landmarks in the valley. Their builders had apparently an appreciation of natural beauty as well as a keen mathematical sense. In Eskdale they selected as a site for their temples, a fairly level holm set in the midst of towering hills. Across the Esk there juts out the volcanic crag of Wat-Carrick, or Wud-Carrick. On the east the smoother hills behind the Cote rise abruptly to 1,000 feet. Higher up the valley the Holm Craig and Clerk Hill seem to meet to bar the way to the north, and on the west rise the Castle Hill and Over Rig.

Near to the Circles now flows the Esk which, when they were built, ran under the face of Wat-Carrick hundreds of yards away to the west. On a summer day a place of great natural beauty this, but on a day of rain or of swirling snow a scene of wildness and weirdness. It is not unlikely that both of these aspects of nature strongly appealed to the intuitions and superstitions of those old Circle builders.

The two Circles at the Cote are named:—

I. THE LOUPIN' STANES
II. THE GIRDLE STANES

Though now forming separate circles 600 yards apart, that they were at one time, though possibly not originally, parts of one scheme is clearly indicated by their relative positions and especially by the irregular line of large stones stretching from one to the other. Only two of the stones of the first Circle are now standing. One stands 4 feet 9 inches above ground and measures 12 feet 5 inches in girth. The other is also 4 feet 9 inches high but is only 7 feet 8 inches in girth. It is quite possible that some of the other stones composing the Circle are in their original positions, though they are now greatly weathered and broken.

The late Mr. Richard Bell of Castle O'er explains[1] the name *Loupin' Stanes* by a local legend. The young men of the neighbourhood were accustomed to exercise their athletic powers by jumping, or loupin' from one to the other of these upright stones, until an accident occurred, and one man broke his leg in the attempt. As the stones are eight feet apart the feat was one of some note even for a nimble schoolboy, to whom the off-chance of breaking his leg would no doubt prove to be an irresistible attraction.

This first Circle when built appears to have consisted of nine large stones, and was nearly 36 feet in diameter, or some 113 feet in circumference by inside measurement. Lord Avebury[2] has observed that the usual diameter of these circles was 100 feet, and says that a special significance attached to the number of stones composing the circle. Some had 12 some 30, some 60, or even 100.

In Cornwall, where so many ancient stone circles and other monuments still exist, the number was usually 19, but in other districts it was 9. Though the stones were often of unequal height they were generally placed at equal distances from each other, but this does not apply to the Eskdale Circles, nor yet to those at Keswick. Though the Loupin' Stanes had nine stones, the Girdle Stanes had about forty.

A little to the south-east of the Loupin' Stanes there appears to have been another circle also of nine stones, with a centre stone. Some of these stones have been displaced, and the contour of the circle is consequently broken. Nearer the Esk, and almost touching the Loupin' Stanes, are four single stones whose relation to the other members of the group it is very difficult even to guess.

Reference has already been made to the line of single stones stretching from the Loupin' Stanes to the Girdle Stanes. Though the line is not a straight one, and is broken, it seems to afford fairly conclusive proof that all these stones at the Cote are parts of what must once have been a prehistoric monument of considerable importance.

Naturally, the greater interest attaches to the Girdle Stanes Circle. This name is also of recent date, and was probably given because the Circle bore a general resemblance to the girdle, or griddle, of domestic use. This Circle is not complete. Nearly one half of it has been washed away by the Esk which, in the course of the centuries, has considerably altered its course at this point, creating a fine alluvial tract, but on the other hand, doing irreparable damage to this ancient monument.

Then the questions arise, what purpose was served by these ancient structures and when were they built? With the view of finding a reliable answer to these questions Mr. George R. Goldsbrough, M.Sc., of Sunderland, made, at the invitation of the writers, a careful survey of the Girdle Stanes Circle, and the results of his observations are given later.

Mr. Goldsbrough's calculations and conclusions have been submitted to Sir Norman Lockyer, the eminent astronomer, and Superintendent of the Solar Physics Observatory at South Kensington, and they have received his approval. We very gladly acknowledge Sir Norman's courtesy in permitting us to refer to this in these pages.

Some general considerations introductory to Mr. Goldsbrough's notes may here be set forth. There are hundreds of these circles scattered throughout the British Isles, whilst traces exist which indicate that perhaps larger numbers have been destroyed by the vandalism or the ignorance of later generations. In other countries these monuments are found in even larger numbers than in the British Isles.

The most wonderful of all, greater and more elaborate in design than Stonehenge or Avebury, is the group of circles at Carnac, in Brittany, a country singularly rich in such ancient monuments. In Denmark, in Egypt, and in India, stone circles are often found, a fact which in itself disproves the theory that the circles were Druidical, or that they were of Scandinavian origin. In Africa both stone circles and more extensive and elaborate relics of prehistoric times have been discovered and Dr. Livingstone mentions seeing such circles during his wanderings.

One may read with almost monotonous frequency in the Old Testament of stones being set up as historical monuments or as expressions of religious sentiment. These indeed were often single stones, but references are also made to the erection of groups of such stones both in Palestine and the neighbouring countries.

There can be scarcely any doubt but that the high places and groves which the inhabitants of Canaan so persistently set up, and which were so denounced by the prophets of Israel and Judah, were such circles of stones as we find at the Cote in Eskdalemuir. These high places and groves seem to have been an integral part of Baal worship.

These considerations indicate that the erection and use of these prehistoric monuments were part of a widely prevalent system of nature worship practised contemporaneously by many nations of different language and descent.

The most remarkable of such monuments in this country are at Stonehenge and Avebury in Wiltshire, and at Callanish in the Island of Lewis. Archaeologists are well agreed that all these monuments were built by the race which preceded the Celtic in the series of migrations to these Islands.

To Stonehenge, archaeologists, working entirely on the evidence furnished by the monuments themselves, by excavating, sifting classifying, and comparing all the data obtained, assign the approximate date of 1800 B.C. Sir Norman Lockyer, dealing with the monument from an astronomical standpoint, and examining the orientation of its axis, fixed the date of Stonehenge at 1700 B.C., a virtual agreement arrived at by strictly scientific methods applied along two different lines.

By the same method Mr. Morrow fixed the date of the Keswick Circle as 1400 B.C. The Girdle Stanes resemble the Keswick Circle both in the number of the stones and in the general astronomical plan, but in the latter the stones are considerably larger.

In his survey of the Girdle Stanes, made on Good Friday, 1911, Mr. Goldsbrough followed the method so successfully applied by Sir Norman Lockyer to Stonehenge and many other circles in Wiltshire and Cornwall. Subjoined are the conclusions arrived at by Mr. Goldsbrough, and it may safely be surmised that they will prove of great and lasting interest, not to Eskdale people alone, but to archaeologists generally.

THE GIRDLE STANES
Photograph May 2000

SURVEY OF THE GIRDLE STANES

"There is strong evidence to show that the earliest inhabitants of these Islands were sun worshippers. The circles of standing stones were their open-air temples where they conducted the rites and ceremonies of their religion. The nature of their worship and belief must of course be largely a matter of conjecture, for it must be remembered that the circles date back to periods long before the Druidical era. The forms and positions of the circles have, however, led observers to the supposition that they had not only a religious but a practical purpose. That practical purpose was to determine the seasons. It is probable that the hold of the priestly class over the common people depended very much upon the ability of the former to indicate the most suitable time to

"Plough and sow,
Reap and mow"

In our almanacs the year is divided into four quarters by the position of the sun in the heavens. Taking, the present year (1911) we have:—

Spring Equinox, March 21st
Summer solstice, June 22nd
Autumn equinox, Sept. 24th
Winter solstice, Dec. 22nd

At the equinoxes the days are of equal length, and the sun rises due east and sets due west. The day of the summer solstice is the longest day, and the sun rises and sets at its most northerly points. The day of the winter solstice is the shortest day, and the sun rises and sets at its most southerly points. These, the astronomical divisions of the year, could quite easily be determined by the early astronomer-priests by simply observing the position of the sun on the horizon as it rose each day. But they are of less practical value to an agricultural community than another set of divisions, the agricultural divisions, namely

Spring begins Feb. 4th
Summer begins May 6th
Autumn begins Aug. 8th
Winter begins Nov. 8th

These dates are, of course, only approximate. Their positions are midway between those of the astronomical year, and their value to the farmer is quite evident.

As the following calculations will show, the Girdle Stanes were erected in such a position as would enable the priests to fix these quarter days of the agricultural year exactly. Further, it seems probable that these quarter days were days of high festival, when the rising of the sun was greeted with great ceremonial observance.

In order that the priests might be prepared and have all their paraphernalia ready for the sun-rise, it would be necessary for them to know the time of night, or at least how near it was to sun-rise. For this purpose they used a warning star. A bright star was selected which would rise or set just before sun-rise, and so warn the priests to be ready for the appearance of their god.

The position of the sun-rise on each quarter-day and the place of rising or setting of the warning star were indicated, sometimes by outlying stones which could be illuminated when necessary, and sometimes by making use of the natural features of the horizon in hill districts. Both of these methods were used in the design of the Girdle Stanes.

Now, owing to the astronomical phenomenon known as the Precession the Equinoxes, the pole the heavens has changed its place, and consequently the warning stars will no longer rise or set in the places indicated. By noting the change to the present positions of the warning stars, we can form a very accurate estimate of the date when the Circle was set up.

The Girdle Stanes as now existing consist of 22 large stones forming an arc of a circle, standing on the left bank of the White Esk about twelve miles above Langholm. The Circle was obviously complete at one time, but a change in the course of the river has cut away the bank and carried off some of the stones, which can now be seen lying in the river bed. Some of the stones are upright, some recumbent, and some almost buried, while here and there are smaller portions, obviously pieces broken off the large stones by the action of frost.

The Circle is fairly correct. When the centre was found by trial, differences in radius of two or three links were noted here and there as the stones had fallen inwards or outwards; but no great irregularity was found. The diagram given on the next page represents the *positions* of the stones as indicated by the angle subtended at the centre. The distances from the centre are not shown on the plan.

The mean diameter of the Circle is 130 feet. About 140 yards away in a north-east direction on the slope of a knowe are two outlying stones just protruding through the turf. These stones are important, though their original position is somewhat doubtful. A rough estimate of the number of stones in the complete Circle gives 40. It is noteworthy that a similar circle at Keswick has 38 stones standing and two or three obvious gaps.

About a third of a mile away in a north-east direction is another complete circle of 9 stones, together with a large number of others somewhat indiscriminately scattered about, possibly the relies of one or more similar circles. The 9 stones form a complete Circle of 36 feet diameter. Two of them are under 5 feet in height, and the rest mere fragments, though clearly in their original positions. This Circle is

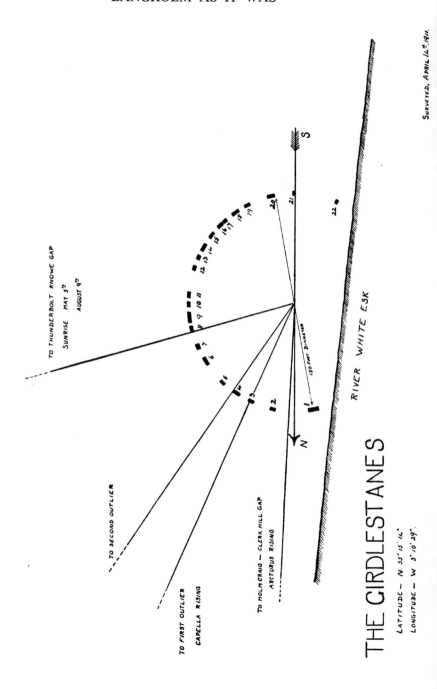

THE GIRDLESTANES

LATITUDE — N. 55° 15' 14"
LONGITUDE — W 3° 10' 29"

SURVEYED, APRIL 14, 1911.

TO THUNDERBOLT KNOWE GAP
SUNRISE MAY 5th
AUGUST 9th

TO SECOND OUTLIER

TO FIRST OUTLIER
CAPELLA RISING

TO HOLM CRAIG — CLERK HILL GAP
ARCTURUS RISING

130 FEET DIAMETER

N

S

RIVER WHITE ESK

The following are details of the stones, numbered as in the diagram:—

No.	Height in feet	Girth in feet	
1	6	12	
2	3½	13	
3	3	7 2/3	
4	3	10½	
5	3	9½	
6	5		Recumbent
7	5 1/3		Recumbent
8	2	8½½	
9			Recumbent
10			Recumbent
11			Recumbent
12	4½	12	
13			Recumbent
14	4¼	8	
15			Recumbent
16			Almost buried
17			Recumbent
18			Recumbent
19	2½	8	
20	3 2/3	10	
21			Almost buried
22			Recumbent

invisible from the Girdle Stanes, and therefore has no *astronomical* connection with them, though there may have been, and in all likelihood were, relations of some other kind. There is a course of 11 stones placed at intervals between the two Circles, rudely joining them, but not in a straight line. The last 4 of these nearest the Loupin' Stanes form almost a straight line in a direction S. 16° 34' E., but no satisfactory significance has been found for this line.

The meridian was first found by a double observation of the sun. Then the bearing of the two above-mentioned outlying stones was ascertained, as they seemed to be placed as special marks. Next, an inspection of the horizon was made. No specially distinct peaks were noticeable but there were two clearly marked hill-gaps — that between Holm Craig and Clerk Hill and that of Thunderbolt Knowe. The bearing of each of these was taken along with the height of the horizon. The observations, corrected for instrumental errors, gave the following particulars:—

	Alignment. Centre of Girdle Stanes to:—	True Azimuth.	Altitude of Horizon
I.	Holm Craig-Clerk Hill Gap	N. 2° 18' 52" E	1° 50' 10"
II.	First outlying stone	N. 24° 4' 58" E	3° 32' 30"
III.	Second outlying stone	N. 35° 7' 2' E	3° 37' 20"
IV.	Thunderbolt Knowe Gap	N. 74° 11' 42" E	8° 58' 0"

With regard to the weight to be attached to these azimuths the first and last are very accurate, as the Gaps are clearly defined and at a very considerable distance (between one and two miles in each case). The two outlying stones are only 140 yards away, and their original position is very indefinite. As only a small patch of stone is visible it is difficult to say within two yards where the base of the stone was intended to be. This implies a considerable error in the azimuths. However, it is noticeable that a line from the centre of the Circle to the first outlying stone passes through stone No. 3 of the Circle. We may consider this as strengthening the fact that we have a more trustworthy measurement for Alignment II. than for Alignment III. The latitude of the centre of the Girdle Stanes is N. 55° 15' 14". With this the above Alignments were then reduced to declinations and a probable interpretation put upon each.

	Alignment. Centre of Girdle Stanes to:—	Declination	Purpose	Date
I.	Holm Craig-Clerk Hill Gap	N. 36° 46'	Arcturus, warning star for August sunrise.	1290 B.C.
II.	First outlying stone	N. 34° 27'	Capella, warning star for February sun rise.	1360 B.C.
III.	Second outlying stone	N. 30° 3'	?	
IV.	Thunderbolt Knowe Gap	N. 16° 5'	Sunrise, May 5th and August 9th.	

18

The sun rises at Thunderbolt Knowe on May 5th and August 9th each year. In the centuries that have elapsed since the erection of the Circle there has been only the very slightest alteration in the sun's motion, so that what occurs to-day would occur then. This Alignment was then clearly intended to mark two quarter days of the agricultural year.

Arcturus rose in the Holm Craig-Clerk Hill Gap, just before the sun-rise on August 9th at the period 1290 B.C. Capella rose just before the sun on February 4th at the period 1360 B.C. As above mentioned, the angular measurements of the first outlying stone are subject to error, consequently the date 1360 B.C. will be inaccurate. A glance at the diagram shows that the line from the centre to the outlying stone passes through the middle of stone No. 3 but not exactly.

In the cases of other circles it has been noticed that the lines of direction often pass exactly through the middle of one of the standing stones. It happens here that stone No. 3 is one that appears to be in its true position, and though weathered down to about 3 feet in height, it seems to preserve its uprightness. Then if we *assume* that the alignment was intended to pass exactly through the middle of this stone, we may get a more correct value of the azimuth than is possible from the indefiniteness of the position of the outlier. But here again is a source of error, for the sides of the standing stones are very irregular and may not have been denuded equally. However, the assumption is worth considering. The true azimuth of the middle of this stone is N. 23° 26' 22" E. Taking the horizon height, as before, at 3° 32' 30", the declination is N. 34° 43'. This value gives 1310 B.C. as the date of rising of Capella before the February sun-rise. We may regard this as a strong confirmation of the date 1290 B.C. given by the more accurate Alignment I.

Alignment III., if it means anything, must refer also to Capella warning the February sun-rise at the period 2150 B.C., but without some confirmation we must refuse to accept this date, and conclude that the correct original position of the stone has not been found.

It will be noticed that there is a method of marking the May and August sun-rises, and warning the February and August sun-rises. In all probability there would originally be a mark for the November and February sun-rises, as the latter has a warning star indicated, and there would also be an alignment for the warning of the May sun-rise.

For the November sun-rise no warning stars have been found indicated in circles in other parts of this country. It is conjectured that this is because the misty and foggy weather prevailing during November would frequently prevent a warning star from being seen on the horizon. Of these missing marks nothing was seen when the observations were made. It is likely, however, that a special search in directions which could be definitely indicated might result in something more fruitful.

From the foregoing it will be clear that this Circle was erected about the year 1290 B.C. with a two-fold astronomical purpose:—

1. To mark the quarters of the agricultural year.

2. To give the priests an indication beforehand of the rise of the sun on these quarter days that they might have ready the appliances of their ritual for the sun's appearance.

The work of the astronomer-priests would be something like this:— each morning the sun-rise would be watched from the centre of the Circle, and it would be observed to creep northward along the horizon till it approached Thunderbolt Knowe Gap. With a little experience the priest would be able to estimate when the sun would exactly appear in that Gap on the following day. Then an all-night watcher would wait for the appearance of Arcturus in the Holm Craig - Clerk Hill Gap. In order that he, in the blackness of night, would know where to look, a stone with a hollow at the top in which burning oil was placed, would be erected as one member of the Circle. This member would be, as the diagram shows, between stones 1 and 2 where there is clearly a stone missing.

At the appearance of the star all the community would be called and everything put in readiness for the sun-rise, when a high festival would be held; and the announcement would go forth that this was the first day of summer of the agricultural year, May 5th. Then the sun-rise would travel north until Midsummer Day and return southward to Thunderbolt Knowe Gap, when there would be a repetition of similar events, the warning coming this time from another star and another direction, the mark of which has not been discovered.

This would be August 8th, the first day of autumn. The same would occur in other directions in November and February, so that the Circle of Stones with outlying marks would be sufficient for the complete determination of the seasons of the year, as well as the special requirements of their religious observances.

One cannot but admire the intelligence and ingenuity of the early race who, so long ago, erected a contrivance at once so simple and so clever. To arrange the Circle and put up outliers to mark special directions is comparatively easy; to put up a Circle in such a position that *one* of the natural features of the horizon may be used to mark an alignment is more difficult. But to find the exact spot where the irregularities of the horizon mark *two* alignments is a problem requiring remarkable penetration and acuteness, for in no other spot whatever but the one chosen could the Clerk Hill Gap and the Thunderbolt Knowe Gap both be used for the purposes indicated."

It will be noticed from the results obtained by Mr. Goldsbrough that the Girdle Stanes Circle had this peculiar and singular feature, that its builders, by their intelligent and careful choice of the site were enabled to utilise for their astronomical purposes, not one only but two of the natural features of the locality. Sir Norman Lockyer commented upon this unusual fact and desired to be furnished with more precise details. These were supplied, to Sir Norman's satisfaction. This indication of careful planning and selection considerably increases the archaeological importance of the Circle.

It is of interest to note that the worship of the May-year sun, indicated by Mr. Goldsbrough's investigations at the Girdle Stanes, was not only common to the builders of the early British circles but was also extensively used in Egypt, Babylon, and Greece. The earliest Temple thus aligned was that of Ptah, at Memphis, 5200 B.C.

The Circles, as centres of religious influence and also of legal administration, lasted into the Christian era. Churches were often built upon the sites of ancient circles, as in the case of the earliest Christian building on Iona. Possibly it was this which gave birth to the title of *The Stones*, as applied to a church. It is said that even into the 20th century, in secluded parishes, the question is asked, "Are you going to the Stones?" What we have later called *Circle-ism*, a strongly hybrid faith and practice, percolated down into the early Church, and very drastic steps had to be taken to stamp out some of the practices brought in by the converts.

Of these ancient monuments, whether in Egypt or Eskdalemuir, we now see but the architecture, and of it only a small portion, we guess and debate about the vanished. And so much has gone!

No longer does the gleam from the rising sun touch the stone of mystery, or, flashing upon a priestly emblem, is it hailed as a message from the gods; no longer is the "warning star" watched for up in the Eskdale hills, or the sun acclaimed as the only deity as it touches the Thunderbolt Knowe on some bright May morning, Temple and Girdle Stanes have lost their glory and are dead! Their ruins we see, but where are the thought and purpose that gave them form, the life that made each, not a silent relic of a far-off day, but an intense reality amongst sentient, intelligent beings?

What manner of men were those who, spurred by some commanding purpose or impulse, reared these stones? What they said and did, what they laughed or wept over, what hopes they nursed, what dreams they dreamt, what was their poetry or their song, what aspirations moved them to action, how they occupied the long summer days or the dark winter nights when the snow drifted deep on Eskdalemuir, what crises stirred them to passion-personal, tribal, or religious. All these would be of deepest interest to us now, but alas, we know not nor can know.

We gaze upon the ruins which Time has left us, and imagination alone can re-clothe them with the evidences of life and activity, after all enquiry and wondering they are still but Stone Circles among the quiet Eskdale hills!

CHAPTER 3

THE RELIGIOUS PURPOSES OF THE CIRCLES

In his notes on the Girdle Stanes Mr. Goldsbrough mentioned that the circles had a religious as well as an astronomical purpose. Various are the conjectures which have been made as to the object of those ancient builders. Most writers agree to the religious element, and various cognate purposes are suggested.

Lord Avebury[1] thought the circles were utilised for purposes of sepulture. This is not improbable, but certainly the suggestion does not apply to the Girdle Stanes. Nature itself has come to the proof of this, for the Esk, changing its course since those far-off days when the Cote was the centre of the life and light of Eskdale, has washed away nearly half of the soil on which the Girdle Stanes stand, tumbling the stones into the river-bed, magnificently oblivious to the ruin it made, but no evidence of sepulture has been revealed.

That, if the circles were not primarily designed for religious ceremonial, they were at least utilised in this way, is accepted by all writers of authority. The popular view that Druidical worship was afterwards celebrated in the circles is probably true in a general way.

Most of our knowledge of the Druids is derived from Caesar, and what he has not supplied has been ingeniously invented by writers whose gifts lay like those of the great physiologist in constructing a whole body from a bone!

For example, it has been confidently declared that these Nature worshippers had certain clearly defined views as to certain religious truths. The circle, these writers say, was used because it represented eternity,—without beginning of days or end of years. It is much more probable that it represented nothing at all beyond being an imitation of

23

the horizon which was so intimately related to the worship of the day. But the Druids did not flourish until many centuries after most of these circles were built, and we must look farther back into the misty past to discover the original purpose of the builders.

The elaborate design of many of the larger monuments, such as at Carnac in Brittany, Stonehenge and Avebury in Wiltshire, and Challacombe Down, where there had existed an avenue of upright stones of eight rows, three of which still remain, supports the argument that the circles had a religious and ceremonial significance.

That this was so with the great Temples of the East is of course known and accepted. The difference between them with their ornate architecture and the rugged plainness of the stone circles is one of degree only.

In purpose and primary design they were in harmony. Not only were those monuments in Egypt and Syria oriented to the sun or some prominent star, but so also were both the great British circles already mentioned and the smaller circles scattered throughout this country. It is a fair deduction, then, from their being constructed on the same astronomical and mathematical principles, that these small stone circles were meant to serve the same ends as the more magnificent piles.

THE LOUPIN' STANES
Photograph May 2000

Mr. Goldsbrough found no evidence that there had been any astronomical relationship between the Girdle Stanes and the Loupin' Stanes. From no point can one be seen from the other, so that any astronomical connection seems unlikely. The incomplete observations made at the Loupin' Stanes indicate that, in all probability, it was considerably the older Circle.

A simple and ready explanation of the two Circles being so near each other yet apparently unrelated, would be that the Loupin' Stanes having served its purpose or proved inconvenient, like some old kirk, was abandoned for a larger and better site some six hundred yards away.

But the evidences seem to indicate that, for some purposes, at any rate, there was a relationship between the two Circles. In many instances such monuments were double, and were often connected by a line or avenue of upright stones, which did not always stand in a line directly straight.

At Merrivale for example, the "avenue" has a distinct change of direction, what Sir Norman Lockyer calls "a kink".[2] Whether there was a single or double line of stones in the avenue between these two Circles cannot be said until a careful survey has been made. The theodolite and the link-chain have a curious habit of settling these disputed points and spoiling many a charming theory, without regrets or apologies! But this much may safely be said: if an avenue existed between the Loupin' Stanes and the Girdle Stanes, as appearances suggest, it was probably for ceremonial rather than for astronomical purposes.

The accompanying rough plan illustrates the relative positions of both circles and connecting stones. It does not profess to indicate the exact position of each stone in the avenue, but it gives, in the absence of a more careful survey, the general position of the monuments.

To the prehistoric inhabitants of Eskdale, as to other races geographically far removed from them, the celebrations to which Mr. Goldsbrough has referred as connected with the progression of the seasons, were the expressions of those feelings which to-day in ourselves assume the form of adoration, reverence, prayer, and spiritual rejoicing.

In other words the religious observances at the Cote were a phase of that Nature worship which in one form or another is common to primitive peoples. It was a mixture of Nature worship and Baalism, a hybrid compound of Phoenician and Assyrian religions with, no doubt, much of local paganism and perhaps barbarity superadded.

To many races, various in language and habitation, Baal, or some such deity, was   he representative of   the energising and fertilising processes of nature, and sun worship was the form it readily assumed.

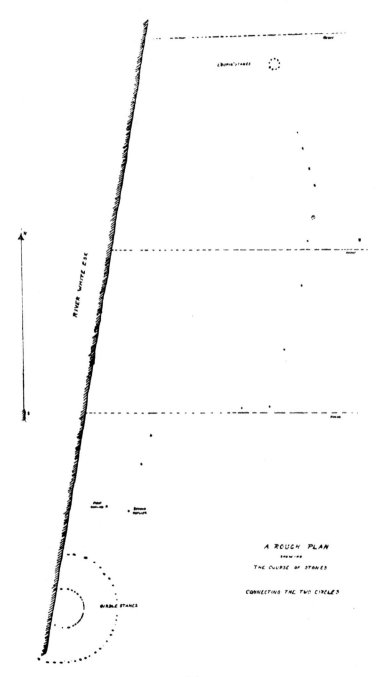

A ROUGH PLAN
SHOWING
THE COURSE OF STONES

CONNECTING THE TWO CIRCLES

Some of the superstitions and practices still lingering in certain districts of these Islands, such for instance as the oft-quoted Beltane ceremonies at Callander, are traceable to this Baal worship. Baal's-fire was associated with May Day, as representing the energy and power of the summer sun, and Mr. Goldsbrough shows that May Day was a high day at the Girdle Stanes.

Sir Norman Lockyer shows in his *Stonehenge* that the many legends, customs, and superstitions which have lived so long in Scotland, were in great part due to the rites and practices observed by the tribes who built these circles. These superstitions and customs survived through the Celtic age down into the early Church, which adopted many observances and gave them Christian symbolism.

The prevalence still in Scotland of a May-November year, Sir Norman argues, is a trace of a custom originated by the astronomer-priests in the religious celebrations at the old stone circles, and so are some of the observances and customs, which linger still in rural districts, connected with the seasons of the year, the sowing or reaping of crops, and the various celebrations of country life.

Associated with this worship of the sun and stars was the veneration of rivers, wells, and trees. One can readily sympathise with the impulse of an untutored race to regard the Esk as sacred, many Eskdale men and women of to-day tend to the same sweet faith. And in a district covered as Eskdale would then be, by great primeval forests, there would naturally arise a like impulse towards the veneration of trees.

The stone circles were generally erected beside a well or river and near the well, in later years at any rate, there was a tree on which the votive offerings were hung. This custom or rite belonged more to the Celtic era than the one under review, but the practice arose through the association of rivers and wells with the circles.

When the Druids rose to power the veneration of the oak was a part of their ceremonial, but in Scotland the object of veneration was not the oak but the rowan and the hawthorn. Without doubt the place these trees have taken in the romantic literature of country is the result of this ancient veneration. And to the same source may be traced the old custom of having a rowan tree near a dwelling house, from which it warded off the evil spirits that haunted wood and hill and glade.

CHAPTER 4

STANDING STONES

Our consideration of this branch of the prehistoric antiquities of Eskdale naturally forms itself along two main lines. First the relation of standing stones to the stone circles, and next, their significance as memorial stones or monuments. Standing stones are found in great numbers both in these Islands and throughout the world. They are very frequently found associated with stone temples or circles, to which they are related in a very important way. It is frequently found that comparatively near to almost every circle there is at least one large outlying stone, and various conjectures have been launched to explain its presence.

The Druidical theory of the circles embodied an assumption that human sacrifice was associated with the religious ceremonial. This by no means unlikely assumption, for it is little more, found support in the presence of these stones, and to them was given the designation of slaughter stones. Obviously this explanation could not include all such outlying stones even when found in association with circles, for some of the stones were obelisk shaped, and wholly unsuitable as slaughter or altar stones. If the latter were really a necessary part of the circle services, they would just as reasonably be placed in the centre of the circle. The slaughter stone theory clearly did not meet the requirements of the case, and some other explanation had to be found.

This has been supplied by Sir Norman Lockyer and others, who have demonstrated that these outlying stones near stone circles were part of the arrangements used by the astronomer-priests in their observations of the heavenly bodies. By them was obtained the alignment from the centre of the circle to a point on the horizon where, say, a star would appear at its rising. They served the same purpose as the foresight of a rifle and, it may be added, were always as accurately adjusted as it, for the desired purpose. Thus the standing, or outlying, stone was a very important factor in the determination of a date by the orientation method.

Lord Avebury regards the standing stones and stone circles as part of one common plan[1] most of them being tombs. Even those which were temples, he thought, were associated with interments. But Lockyer's theory has the merit of differentiating these various monuments, and of being supported by observations and definite astronomical results. There are very few of these standing stones extant in Eskdale In his survey of the Girdle Stanes Mr. Goldsbrough mentions two, both of which seemed to have been used to mark alignments from the centre of the Circle.

Two others may be mentioned. One is in the Thunderbolt Knowe Gap, and is seen just protruding through the turf. It was probably set up to emphasise the use of the Gap to mark an alignment. The other is a large recumbent stone in the garden at Cote, lying nearly south of the Girdle Stanes. Whether originally it also was used to mark an alignment cannot now be determined. Undoubtedly there would be other stones in a north-easterly direction.

Mr. A. L. Lewis [2], in his investigations of Scottish stone circles, found a great preponderance of outlying stones and of hill tops lying between the circles and the north-east quarter of the horizon. Probably owing to weathering and agricultural operations (the ground within and around the Girdle Stanes is under cultivation) some of these outliers have disappeared from the neighbourhood of the Eskdale circles.

Where the standing stones are near to circles their use for aligning is intelligible, but over all the hill districts there are considerable numbers of stones which could never have been put to such use, and to account for these some other explanation must be suggested.

The meaning attaching to most of these standing stones is that they are memorials of persons or of great events in the life of the district. And in this connection they are a most instructive and interesting illustration of the changes which the centuries have produced in the grouping of the population. Doubtless many of these stones were set up where they would be frequently seen by those to whom their significance appealed, and we receive the suggestion that what is now a lonely and deserted moorland must once upon a time have been peopled with considerable communities.

Standing stones set up to commemorate some notable event or achievement are common in all countries. David Livingstone, Mungo Park, and other travellers frequently noticed standing stones both singly and in groups or circles, in the heart of Africa. The practice was a common one with the ancient Jews and the Old Testament abounds in references to these memorials.

Between two and three hundred yards over the hill from the stone in the Thunderbolt Knowe Gap, as previously described, there is a somewhat remarkable stone. It stands erect about two feet out of the turf, though obviously its length when set up would be greater. In shape it is a rectangular prism, surmounted by a triangulated prism, and clearly gives the impression of having been wrought. It is quite invisible from the Esk valley, which fact dissociates it from the circles there. On one side of the stone are what look like markings, but owing to weathering it is now impossible to trace them with sufficient clearness to determine whether the stone belongs to the class, such as the famous *Cat-Stanes* found in various districts, set up to commemorate some great battle, (from the Celtic *Cath* meaning a battle), which Professor Simpson describes in his book on the inscribed stones of Scotland.

Apart from those near the circles at the Cote there are now very few standing stones in Eskdale. There is one within the policies of Castle O'er, a little to the west of Cleve Sike. Possibly it may have had some connection with the cairn on Airdswood Moss, about a mile away and almost due west. But we can only conjecture, the centuries have engraven no record of its meaning.

Another known as the St. Thorwald's Stone, a modern designation of course, stood below St. Thorwald's on the bank of the Esk, at the spot now known as Land's End. This was one of the most valuable archaeological relics in the district, but unfortunately it has been destroyed by vandals who probably found it in their way when building a dyke!

It stood until well within the memory of some still living, who speak of a curious practice in connection with it. Some old superstition had apparently attached itself to it, for children as they passed it deemed it a right and proper thing to spit upon it in contempt and derision, a custom whose origin it is now impossible to trace. If the legend be accepted that Thor the Long had a cell near what we now call the Thief Stane Quarry, then perhaps the stone became associated with him. Why this should create a superstitious dislike is hard to conjecture.

From the name of Standing Stone Edge being given to the eastern slope of the hills above the old Inn at Callister Ha', part of the ridge separating Annandale from Eskdale, we may assume that at one time a similar stone stood there. Near to it to the northward was Kitty's Cairn, and others un-named, and these, stone and cairns, would probably have some connection as we suggest there was at Airdswood Moss.

The best example of the standing stones in the Eskdale district is that known locally as *The Grey Wether* or *Wether Stane*. Weighing about two tons, the stone is the common greywacké, or whinstone of the Silurian series, rough and unhewn, about 5 feet high and its girth is 8 feet 7 inches.

THE FALLEN GREY WETHER
Photograph November 2000

It stood, from time immemorial until about 30 years ago, in the centre of a field in front of Meikledale House and could be seen from the road. However, a local farmer decided it was a nuisance and started to move it with his tractor, intending to take it down to the riverside. Fortunately he was seen and told that the stone was a protected monument. He then left it lying in its present position where it can no longer be seen from the road.

In 1981 The Royal Commission on the Ancient and Historical Monuments of Scotland reported as follows:—"This fallen standing stone lies in a field 250 m. SSW of Meikledale farmhouse". The stone is remarkably well preserved and the head of the sheep is easily distinguished.

The standing stones, as the centuries passed, were adopted by the early Church as Christian symbols. From the rough unsculptured obelisk was evolved the richly sculptured cross and the inscribed stone, and from them also came the idea of all our monuments, from the rude tombstone in a country church-yard, keeping green the memory of a simple life, to the most ornate memorial of the mighty dead.

In this connection we must mention the Ruthwell Cross, which dates to the ninth century, and to the Bewcastle Cros, two of the earliest extant Christian monuments in the British Isles, neither of them quite within the bounds of Eskdale, but both so near as to point to the important part taken by the district in the development of Christian art.

In after years of tumult and strife the standing stones became the points to which the clansmen rallied. Justice was not infrequently dispensed in open-air courts held at a standing stone, even as it was for long years dispensed at the circles.

As an example of this, reference may here be made to the famous Lochmaben Stone; an immense boulder probably dropped by the ice. It stands about a mile south of Sark Foot on the farm of Old Graitney, almost on the site of what is said to have been a stone circle. There, the Wardens of the West March held their courts and arbitrations during the troublous days that afterwards came upon the Borders.

Being a prominent land mark a standing stone was naturally enough chosen as a boundary mark, and in many an old charter or lease the limits of an estate are described by reference to it. It became the site of many sacred covenants, from the anointing of kings to the delimitation of boundaries.

CHAPTER 5

CAIRNS AND BARROWS

Not infrequently there were associated with the stone circles barrows or tumuli, or cairns. That these were often contemporaneous with, or even earlier in date than, the circles themselves, is shown by their having been utilised to indicate alignments from a circle to the horizon. This is especially applicable to many of the monuments in Wiltshire and Cornwall, and also to that of Stennis, in Orkney, where the alignments from the Stones of Stennis are obtained not only to outlying stones, but also to the large, chambered barrow, or tumulus, known as Maeshowe.

Archaeologists date the circles to the Stone Age, a view supported by astronomical investigations. Lord Avebury thought that most of the tumuli of western Europe were constructed during the same period.

These sepulchral monuments are found in almost all countries, and though they exhibit local characteristics they all belong to the same order. In Scotland they most often assume the form of stone cairns, though tumuli are also found. In all cases these cairns or mounds were places of burial, and far away in the misty years of the Stone Age the affections and regrets of people would cling around them.

To us they are but archaeological items. We examine their contents without sentiment, and hold debate over the poor skulls they contained, measuring them from *a* to *b,* and drawing conclusions on their measurements, comparing them, but generally forgetting the brain once contained therein, or the human heart that moved in harmony with it. We pull down the stones of the place of their sepulchre to build dykes and byres, esteeming the necessities of the moment of more import than these venerable relies left from a far off age.

Many cairns must have at one time existed in Eskdale, but few now remain. There was a very large one at Langholm close to where the roadway between Stubholm and Murtholm dips into the plantation, and almost on the old Roman road leading from Broomholm towards Calfield. Unfortunately this cairn was demolished and the stones were used to build some of the cottages of what is now Caroline Street. We have this on the personal authority of an old man who could recall the circumstances, and who remembered the building of the new town of Langholm between 1770 and 1800. Indeed the identical houses given in the illustration on page 240 were in all probability built with the stones from this cairn. It is said that an urn or cist was found under the cairn but there is no record of its contents if any.

Traces exist, too, a little to the north of Standing Stone Edge, near Callister Ha', of an ancient cairn. On the Ordnance Map this is named Kitty's Cairn and its situation is at the head of Kitty's Cleuch. The name is probably derived from the British *Cad,* or Celtic *Cath,* a battle place. Some years ago a flint spearhead was found. Near to the cairn is the largest of the three camps or hill forts which had existed in this neighbourhood, and it is possible that there may have been some connection between them.

On the hill to the west of Westwater farm three cairns have been found, but all of them had been previously disturbed. The principal one contained a cist, of which an illustration is here given, made of four whinstone slabs set on edge, and lying north-east and south-west. It measures three feet two inches in length, one foot six inches in width, and one foot three inches in depth. From these measurements it will be seen that any body it may have contained must have been buried in a sitting posture, as the ancient custom was. The Cist was very carefully examined by Mr. J. M. Elliot, of Westwater, but he only found a few fragments of calcined bone.

About one hundred yards north of this cairn are the remains of two other cairns, which had also been disturbed. A hill near the fort is called Raes Knowes, or Kings Knowes, but probably this name would be originally given to the hill on which the three cairns stood.

At the Camp-Knowes, near Fiddleton in Ewes, so called it is said, from its being a camping place of James V. when he was on his way to Carlenrig to entrap the Armstrongs, there was a stone cist found containing human remains, which crumbled to dust on being exposed to

WESTWATER CIST

the air. Flints, arrow heads, and stone knives were found near by, in considerable quantities, indicating that the discoveries were referable to the Stone Age.

The most important cairn of the Eskdale valley was undoubtedly that on Airdswood Moss, between the lands of Castle O'er and Billholm. It was disturbed in 1828, a new march-dyke between the two estates was needed, and this ancient landmark was demolished. It is useless at this date to censure such vandalism or the desecration that followed it. Similar outrages have been perpetrated all over the land, and the Government obtained its powers to preserve these monuments too late to save many from wanton destruction.

Andrew Brown, Esq., in a paper given to the Society of Antiquities of Scotland in 1829 states that "the cairn consisted, as usual, of a heap of loose stones surrounded by larger ones closely set together, forming a regular circle fifty-four feet in diameter. Its form, however, was singular. For about fourteen feet from the inner side of the encircling stones it rose gradually, but above this the angle of elevation abruptly changed, and the centre was formed into a steep cone.

Directly underneath this a cist was found, lying north and south, composed of six large unhewn stones and measuring in the interior four feet two inches in greatest length, with a depth of two feet. It contained only human bones, indicating a person of large stature laid with the head towards the north. But the further demolition of the cairn disclosed a curious example of regular internal construction on a systematic plan. From the four corners of the central cist there extended in the form of a St. Andrew's Cross rows of stones overlapping each other, like the slating of a house. At the extremity of one of these, about fourteen feet from the central chamber, another cist was found of corresponding structure and dimensions, but laid at right angles to the radiating row of stones. Another is said to have been found at the extremity of one of the opposite limbs of the cross, and most probably the whole four were originally conjoined to corresponding cists, but a considerable portion of one side of the cairn had been removed before attention was directed to the subject. Between the limbs of the cross a quantity of bones in a fragmentary state were strewn about. Such a disposition of a group of cists under a large cairn, though rare, is not without a parallel, and may perhaps be characteristic of a class." [1]

Mr. Bell [2] says that no fewer than 150 cartloads of stones were taken from the cairn whose site can still be identified. No mention is made by any of the writers of the shape and size of the crania of these skeletons, nor any details given which might enable the archaeologist to determine the approximate age to which they belonged.

The Airdswood Moss cairn was locally known as King Shaw's Grave. The tradition is that a battle between the Picts and the Scots was fought near by, and that, fleeing, the Pictish King was drowned in the deep pool, known since as the King Pool, at the junction of the Black and White Esks. His body, it is added, was afterwards recovered and was given a chieftain's burial — and the great cairn on Airdswood Moss was reared above him in honour of his deeds and renown, and that the Shaw Rig, one of the wildest hillsides in all the Esk valley, was named after him. An interesting tradition but, unfortunately, it will not bear examination. Pictish history records no King Shaw. The name is Norse rather than Celtic. The above particulars of the cairn do not bear out the story of the drowning.

To account for the name King Pool it would probably be nearer the truth to connect it with the visit to Eskdale paid by King James IV in 1504, when he came with a great retinue, partly to hunt, and partly to overawe the turbulent Eskdale men into submission to his royal will.

The name of Bailey Hill which, gaunt and bare, overlooks the Esk just round the spur of the hill, suggests the site of a town, where once an old British hill-fort stood. And Mr. Bell[2] tells us that on Handfasting Haugh the foundations of old buildings may still be seen. May it not then be that King James halted here in his toil-some journey and that the pool is named in *his* honour?

An explanation more probable still is that suggested by Mr. John Reid, that *king* is a corruption *of ceann,* the Celtic for *head*. *King Pool* would then mean the *head pool* of the united Esks.

There was also a cairn on the farm of Craighaugh. It, too, has been scattered and no trace left of its contents. In the Ordnance Map of 1861 the site is marked as that of a tumulus and there is also marked a cist at Garwald House.

There was another at Sorbie, south-east of Sorbie farmhouse, in the plantation near the Ewes Road, where the meagre remnants of it may still be seen, for alas it, too, was despoiled to provide the trustees with road metal. Whilst the spoliation was in progress it is said a stone coffin was found. Where it is now no man knoweth, probably it is, being utilised about some of the farm buildings!

Distinct from the stone cairns, yet possibly of equal antiquity, are the prehistoric mounds or barrows. In the Tarras valley there are two of these mounds. One, on the farm of Bogg, is a large symmetrical cone. It is called the Counter's Seat, there being a tradition that the old Border raiders were accustomed to halt here to do their accounting, which, one has often thought, must, in a large and successful raid, have proved a somewhat complicated and delicate undertaking. Conical barrows were, centuries later, adopted as meeting places. They were termed Moot hills. The name still lingers in the Moot Halls of some of our oldest towns, and in the word moot, meaning to discuss.

The other mound, this time oblong in shape, is at Rashiel, on the eastern side of Whita Hill, as it slopes down into Tarras Water. Whether these, like those at Airdswood Moss and elsewhere, were actually and without doubt places of sepulture, has not as yet been definitely proved.

The fact that these mounds at Bogg and Rashiel differ in shape, points to their having been made at dates considerably distant from each other. If the Rashiel mound should ever be found to contain human remains, they would probably belong to the Stone Age, whereas, if such be found in the round barrow at Bogg, they would refer to a later, the Bronze Age.

CHAPTER 6

THE HILL FORTS

Few branches of archaeological research have provided more interest, or excited more discussion, than the ancient hill forts, so characteristic of Scotland generally and of the Borders in a very marked degree. Next to the stone monuments these forts are perhaps the most definite indications now existing of the conditions prevailing in those early days. Our primitive forefathers threw up those strongholds mostly for purposes of defence. This defence was effective both against the wild animals which lurked in hill and wood and glen, and also against the surprises and incursions of invaders.

The position of some of these forts on the lower slopes of high hills has suggested the theory that defence was not their primary purpose, seeing they would be so open to attack from above. But this is an argument equally strong against their being the ordinary dwelling places of the tribes.

Our present subject touches the centuries immediately preceding the Christian era and possibly those following. This was an age when historical data became available, though not for some centuries yet were the materials definite or reliable. The inhabitants of the Britain of this period were Celtic.

The old settlers who had built the stone circles had gone, dispossessed by a later migration of westward moving peoples. It is to this early Celtic race that the hill forts are attributed — the race that opposed so splendidly the overpowering legions of Caesar.

It seems clear that, when the Romans came, they found that the Celtic tribes were not undisciplined barbarians, but that they followed certain principles of warfare and systems of offence and defence. These fortifications on the hills were amongst the latter, which afforded so many natural advantages to the people attacked.

The Romans themselves seem to have been considerably impressed by the fortifications of the Britons, which are referred to in the works of Caesar with something akin to admiration. This fact seems to indicate that most of the forts, at any rate, were British, but it appears natural and feasible that, as the Romans slowly forced their way into the Scottish lowlands, they would utilise the places of defence vacated by the vanquished, if for no other reason than this, that they occupied the best strategic positions.

They seem in this way to have utilised the great fort known as Lyddal's Strength, or, The Mote, near to Riddings Junction, one of the most important fortifications in the south of Scotland, corresponding in some degree to those at Castle O'er. Historians[1] tell us that there was an *iter* or *way* from The Mote to the Roman camp at Netherby, clearly suggesting that as the Romans drove out the tribesmen they themselves adopted The Mote as part of their system of fortifications.

So far as the Eskdale fortifications are concerned the principal of them are admittedly British. The evidences of any prolonged or effective occupation of Eskdale by the Romans are meagre. It was their custom to throw up earthworks, similar in nature to the British mounds, even if they encamped only for one night, but the fortifications of Eskdale, especially those in the Castle O'er area, are not isolated entrenchments hastily constructed, and as hastily abandoned, but form a large correlated system.

Few valleys show such a network of those hill forts and trenches as Eskdale does. The Ordnance Map shows no fewer than forty-one forts, none of them, as far as known, being of the vitrified type which has so puzzled both archaeologists and military writers. They are generally found to follow the course of the river valleys which they strategically command, defending not the main valley alone, but all the valleys tributary to it, as the distribution of the forts of Eskdale valley so well illustrates.

For the most part the forts in Eskdale occupy something like an acre in extent and are round or oval in shape. The exceptions to this rule are those at Eskdalemuir Kirk and on Old Irvine Hill, which are rectilinear. The general plan of the fortifications is usually modified by the nature of the ground. Where, as at Castle O'er, there is a steep declivity on any side, it has been utilised and regarded as a sufficient defence, no trenches or ramparts being made.

Writing of the Eskdale forts in general Mr. Bell says:[2] "They are of the same type, round or oval in shape and defended by one or more lines of deep trenches, the soil from which has been thrown up either on one or both sides so as to form mounds and ramparts, and so add to the difficulty of attack from the outside. These ramparts were probably still further strengthened by stockades, and all combined would offer a strong defence against an enemy armed with the primitive weapons in use at the time these forts were occupied."

Mr. Bell also gives a description of the principal of the eight forts at Castle O'er, which apparently was the key to all the fortifications of upper Eskdale. The main fort stands on the top of a hill some 884 feet above sea-level, and 296 feet higher than the dwelling house of Castle O'er, which is on the river Holm. It had consisted "of an inner stronghold defended by deep trenches, on the inner side of which had been strong stone walls, now entirely destroyed. The outer sides of the trenches are mounds or ramparts, formed as usual with the soil excavated from the trenches".

This stronghold, the most elaborate and impregnable in the Eskdale valley, "occupies the whole of the top of the hill and measures, roughly speaking, 510 feet long and 350 feet wide, whilst the size of the whole fort with its immediately surrounding trenches is close on 900 feet long by 750 feet wide". These measurements are unusual for this type of fort.

In his exhaustive work on *The Early Fortifications of Scotland*, Dr. Christison, F.S.A., gives an elaborate description of the forts at Castle O'er. We have the permission of Dr. Christison, whose courtesy we cordially acknowledge, to quote from this account and to reproduce the accompanying drawings of the forts and connecting trenches.

He says:— "The variety of forts in which the inner wall of dry masonry is girt by one or more trenches, with or without ramparts, is not common. Of the unusual length of about 900 feet over all, and broadly pear-shaped in form, the work is situated on a knoll, precipitous on the south-cast, that stands on the top of a broad ridge separating the White Esk from the Black Burn. The inner enceinte measures 320 by 170 feet inside on the Ordnance Map and is semi-oval, the form being regulated by the shape of the summit of the knoll, the edge of its rocky slope to the

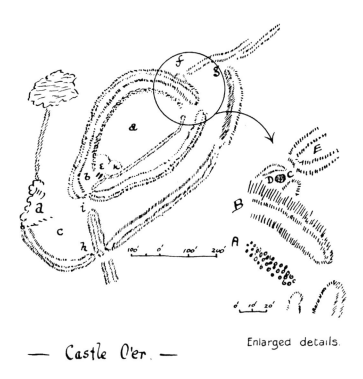

— Castle O'er. —

Enlarged details.

south-east being straight. On this edge there is but a slight vallum, but the curved side being more accessible has been defended by a strong stone wall. Outside the wall at a lower level, and somewhat retired from it, is a trench with a mound on the outer side, continued under the rocky south-east face and prolonged at the south-west end so as to form a forecourt *b* (see illustration) to the citadel *a*. A much larger outer enclosure *c* lies in front of this forecourt and is prolonged to the Northeast end of the work. It is shut in by an entrenchment which, after rounding the Southwest end, continues for some distance on the Southwest side, but ends abruptly on the rocky face of a knoll *d*. Beyond the knoll it is traceable, but soon ends in a marsh, so that this outer enceinte is altogether deficient at the north end.

A section through the apparent green mound of the inner enceinte revealed the remains of a wall, unfortunately so much ruined and plundered that no facing stones mained. Placed longitudinally on a bed of clay at the base of the wall near its middle, lay a log of wood seven feet long and one foot wide, black as if charred, easily going to pieces, and a good deal mixed up with the clay which rested on hard ground.

A slight excavation revealed on the Northwest side of the inner south-west entrance *e*, four stones of the first course of a built gateway still *in situ*. They were carefully laid, and measured seven and a half feet in total length. At least one more had evidently been torn from its place. This gives a breadth for the wall of at least nine feet.

A section through the inner trench where the scarp was eight feet and the counter-scarp five feet nine inches in perpendicular depth, showed a silting up of three feet nine, increasing the depth to above eleven feet below the top of the rampart and nine feet below the top of the counter-scarp. Allowing for the wash-down of ages the original height of the rampart must have been at least thirteen feet. Similar measurements were got in a section through the outer trench, and both trenches were found to be cut through solid rock.

There appear to have been two entrances, *f* and *g*, to the outer enclosure at its north-east end, one, c is dominated by the inner wall A and trench B, and it was found on excavation that it had been narrowed by a pit D dug in the solid rock on the west side, so as to form a counterpart to the cast side of the entrance. The pit was at least four feet deep, but neither its full depth nor lateral extent was ascertained.

The southern entrance *h* to the outer enclosure is divided by a little circular mound into two parts. From this entrance a strong entrenchment makes a straight line for the entrance to the main work, but stops abruptly short of it by fifty feet at *i*, the blind end being so neatly finished that it looks as if there had been no intention of carrying it farther.

Outside, the trench is continuous with one of those mysterious "catrails" with which the neighbourhood of Castle O'er is so abundantly provided, and another branches off from the north-cast entrance. Exploratory excavations in the interior of the fort disclosed nothing of note except that the oval levelled space *k* had a layer of stones very rudely laid only a few inches below the surface."

A very striking characteristic of the Castle O'er group of forts is the system of ways connecting them with the main fortification. Much discussion has been directed towards he satisfactory explanation of these ways. Local antiquities have regarded them as Roman roads, but in spite of the speculative nature of our knowledge of this branch of the subject, it seems clear that the ways and forts are parts of one and the same plan. A glance at the accompanying diagram copied from Dr. Christison's book, seems to establish this beyond any doubt. The principal forts in the Castle O'er group are all connected by these trenches. Respecting these Dr. Christison says:—"In the Parish of Eskdalemuir the strong fort at Castle O'er is surrounded within a radius of less than a mile by six others of lesser degree, and this in a purely pastoral district where the population is now extremely small.....

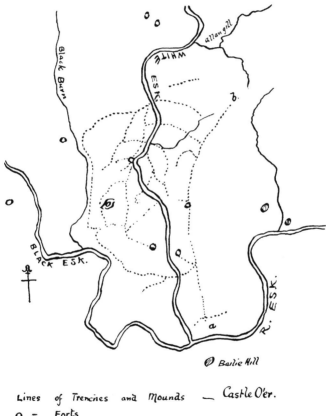

Lines of Trenches and Mounds ⎯ Castle O'er.
O = Forts

Perhaps the most remarkable example of lines connected with forts is at the group surrounding Castle O'er, Dumfriesshire. This example has been brought to light by Mr. Richard Bell, proprietor ot the ground, who has patiently traced out the complex network shown in the figure, the general accuracy of which can be vouched for by personal observation on the spot by Mr Lynn and myself.

The extraordinary number of the lines may be at once recognised from the figure. Indeed their very number is an objection to the road theory, as they would seem to be altogether beyond the requirements of primitive times in a district apparently never capable of cultivation. Nevertheless, as seen on the map they are more suggestive of roads than fences or boundaries, from the manner in which they cross the Esk at various points and join on the east side of the river the long line *a b* which Mr. Bell has traced from *a*, across the moor for five or six miles in the direction of Selkirkshire, and which he has been informed may be seen at various points almost as far as the Catrail.

The question now arises, what can we make of these long lines of mound and trench, so like the Catrail that Mr. Lynn calls them all catrails, and says that they must apparently stand or fall with it in any theory that may be found as to their object? The chief theories concerning the Catrail are:—

1. A military work for defence.
2. A road.
3. A boundary.

The first view is now abandoned, but the other two still hold the field, and whatever arguments are advanced in favour of them must apparently be applicable to the other lines of which we have treated, as well as to the Heriot's Dyke in the east, and the Deil's Dyke in the south west of the lowlands. Disregarding these last, however, as not yet sufficiently investigated, Mr. Lynn holds that all the others are roads. This in some respects is the most rational theory, but the objections to it are strong.

For instance, I do not know that roads of the kind, ancient or modern, have been met with in any other country. Again, it may well be asked: is a trench suitable to the purposes of a road? Would it not easily drift up with snow and become a wet ditch in rain? Another strong objection is that these lines, in crossing ravines, invariably go straight down and up, and sometimes so steeply that it is a hard scramble for a man making use of them, while they would be impassable for wheeled traffic or even to packhorses.

Mr. Lynn believes that the trench form was adopted in order to get down to hard bottom in the subsoil. It is in favour of the road theory that where the lines pass through districts with forts they wind about among them and give off branches as if to serve them, and that in the Castle O'er district after the forts are thus served, the line follows a straight course for miles through a country destitute of forts, as if to join the Catrail.

No doubt the boundary theory has also much to say for itself. The longer lines, such as the Catrail, may have marked the limits of principalities, and the shorter ones the marches of lesser chiefs, or of communities. But the Catrail cannot justly be compared with a Roman *limes,* backed as the latter was by a chain of fortified stations.

These intrenched lines are generally too extended, and too little subdivided, to be regarded as fences, for which they are also ill-adapted structurally. Even at Castle O'er, where the subdivision is so much greater, the enclosed spaces are very large compared with modern fields.

On the whole I do not think that the purpose or purposes of these long trenches have been clearly made out. Possibly excavations might help to solve the difficulties. Sections, which have never yet been made through them, as far as I know, might at least teach us their original form."

Mr. Richard Bell was of opinion that these trenches "were used as *hollow ways*, along which fort dwellers could move to and from the different forts without being seen by their enemies," though he admits the up and down formation even at the exceedingly steep scaurs is evidence against his theory.

On running a wheelometer over the lines of these trenches laid down by him on the Ordnance Map, Mr. Bell found that they extended to a total length of thirteen miles, and, were considerably within an area of 2,700 acres. The connection between the forts and trenches is complete as to six of the eight in the Castle O'er group. "At whatever part of the ground one enters a trench and walks along it", says Mr. Bell, "either to the right or to the left, he will find his way into one of the five minor forts or into the main fort, as he chooses."

On the opposite side of the river to Castle O'er is what is named on the Ordnance Map, *The Dell's Jingle,* a deep trench or hollow between hills or mounds, running due north and south for over a mile and then inclining to the Northeast. Mr. Bell thought that this *way* might be found to be connected with the famous Catrail, as it is noticeable at various places in this direction.

Before leaving the Castle O'er group of forts, mention must be made of one lying so close to the Esk that, through a change of its course, it has washed half of it away. This enclosure also is described as a fort, but this seems unlikely, lying as it does on low ground commanded on every side by steep hills. Mr. Francis Lynn, F.S.A., already referred to by Dr. Christison as an authority on these matters, considered it unique, both because of its peculiar position and because its floor is raised higher than the ground outside the inner trench. He suggested that it had been used for athletic sports.

Mr. Barbour, of Dumfries, thinks it might have been the cemetery or crematorium for the main fort, and excavations disclosed, under some logs of wood which had been used apparently for a floor, and under a heap of rough stones in the centre, a quantity of bone fragments, which to all appearance had been subjected to fire.

On their being submitted to Professor Struthers, of the Royal College of Surgeons, Edinburgh, however, he gave it as his opinion that they might be the bones of some lower animals, though he could not definitely say they were not human.

Mr. Clement Armstrong informs the writers that Mr. Bell himself was of the opinion that this was, as Mr. Barbour suggests, the ancient crematorium, a view also endorsed by Mr. Armstrong, though why, if this suggestion be accepted, there should be a double row of mounds and trenches does not seem clear.

Wat-Carrick kirkyard stands in an old oval fort, and Eskdalemuir Kirk is within a rectilinear fort similar in form to that at Raeburn, which is now proved to have been a Roman station. Possibly excavations at Eskdalemuir Kirk might show that it also was a minor and temporary Roman encampment. Other forts in upper Eskdale in addition to those mentioned are at Tanlaw Hill, Bailie Hill, Bankburnfoot (two), Sheil Burn (two), Lyncholm Enzieholm, Bonese, Westerhall (two), Stapelgortoun, and Craig.

In Ewes there is also a considerable number of forts, viz., at Footsburn, Loch Hill, Arkleton, Mosspeeble, Unthank, Eweslees, Meikledale, Rigsfoot Bush, Byke-foot, and Briery Shaw. Those at Meikledale and Rigsfoot Bush are in line with that at Mosspeeble, and the three were evidently intended to defend this, the widest part of the Ewes valley. The Briery Shaw fort is the only one in Ewes which is defended by two ramparts and a trench.

Other traces of camps and forts exist in Ewes, but these do not warrant any definite conclusion. Few of these exceed one acre in area, and some of them are less. Perhaps the most interesting of the Ewes forts is that on the top of the Loch Hill. The loch, unlike the large pond at Broomholm Knowe referred to later, is a natural basin, and seems connected with the camp, which is some two acres in extent, and is opposite the fort at Briery Shaw, of which probably it was a complement. The proximity of this natural basin may suggest some purpose for the artificial pond at Broomholm.

Reference must also be made to the turf Dyke which ran through the valley of Ewes, and can still be easily traced at various points. Commencing on the face of Tudhope Hill, though most likely connected originally with the Catrail, which, it will be remembered, runs across Teviotdale, not very far from the head of Ewes, the Dyke proceeds along, the hillsides above Unthank and Mosspeeble, past the base of Arkleton Crags, then over the heights of Glendiven and Howgill. It crosses Ewes Water near Terrona, goes over the Potholm Hill and straight over the Craig Hill on the other side of Esk, and then heads away towards the hills at the head of Carlesgill Burn. This, too, it is suggested, defined some old tribal boundaries.

In Wauchope there is a fort at the Schoolhouse, and another at Calfield, whilst several are to be found on the hills behind Westwater. That at Calfield is altogether different in construction from the others. There has been a building rather than mounds and trenches, and the masonry, both of the outer and inner walls, is clearly seen and is unmistakable. It occupies a commanding position on the steep hill side, and the Roman road running from Broomholm has swerved to avoid it. In this respect the Calfield fort is like that at Castle O'er, where Dr. Christison shows there are not a few indications of buildings, and also those on the Craig Hill and Old Irvine Hill, both of which retain unmistakable evidence of masonry. Probably these are later in date than the others, which have earth mounds as ramparts.

It is the opinion of some local antiquaries that the Old Irvine fort is Roman, but Dr. Christison is of the contrary view. There is also a small fort on the road from Wauchope into Canonbie, near to the Kerr to which it has probably given its name, *Car or Caer* being the Celtic for a fort or camp.

CHAPTER 7

GLIMPSES AT PREHISTORIC ESKDALE

Little trustworthy information exists to show what life in Eskdale was like between the building of the Girdle Stanes in 1290 B.C. and the Roman invasion of Scotland in the first century A.D.

Some glass beads and a stone whorl, both now in The Museum of Scotland, Edinburgh, were found at Mosspeeble in the years 1867 and 1869, and apart from the evidence supplied by the circles, the standing stones and the cairns, these are practically all that has been discovered of a tangible nature, dating from this early period of local history.

However, in the immediate neighbourhood of Eskdale, evidence is not wanting, to show to us something of what the primitive tribes were and what they did. From Lochar Moss, in Nithsdale, there have been dug up ancient canoes and oars and anchors, stone relics, bronze implements, and various articles of Roman civilisation and early art.

Few traces now remain of the dwellings of these ancient races. Eskdale is devoid of caves, and probably the variations in the course of the rivers may have helped to obliterate many traces of primitive man which would have helped us rightly to understand his life.

Reference has been made to certain traces of ancient structures now designated Stone Rings. These, it has been suggested, are the remnants of burghs, or Picts' Houses. In discussing the various types of the stone circles of Scotland, Mr. A. L. Lewis[1] arranged them into groups, each having certain local characteristics. The western Scottish type was either irregular or concentric in form, and the stone rings of Eskdale seem to show some features in harmony with these outlines.

The Eskdale rings are in four groups, two on each bank of the Esk. One group is a little to the south of Middleburn Farm on the left bank of the Esk, almost directly opposite Eskdalemuir Manse. It consists of two rings, both oval in shape. The smaller is held, as it were, in the northern arc of the larger, through which another course of masonry runs.

On the same bank of the Esk, a little to the south of the eleventh milestone on the Langholm road and to the west of the Saugh Hill plantation, there is a smaller ring in almost a perfect circle.

On the opposite bank of the Esk there are also two groups. These do not appear to have had any definite relationship to those just named, though the four groups form a rough sort of parallelogram, one of which is on the farm of Wat-Carrick. It is an incomplete ring with one of its limbs extended instead of being curved inwards to complete the circle. This may possibly be a suggestion of the concentric arrangement mentioned by Lewis.

Farther south, on the slope of the Castle Hill and almost directly opposite to Crurie, is the second group on this side of Esk. It, too, is formed of two rings. The larger, which is oval in shape, is incomplete in its northern arc, where it holds within its arms a second oval ring of smaller size. Whether these structures are the remains of Picts' Houses it is now impossible to say, but the suggestion is an interesting one.

We know[2] that the Celtic tribes had circular booths *within* their fortifications, the doors facing the east. There is a certain similarity between the rings thus described and the forts at Craig, Calfield, and Old Irvine Hill. Another suggestion is that these structures were the dwelling places of the Druids. It is not improbable, however, that these stone rings, if they were at any time parts of dwellings, belonged to the Saxon rather than the Celtic period.

The dwelling places of the common people would be either in the forests or on their outskirts. The negative results of Mr. Bell's excavations at Castle O'er point to the forts being refuges in days of peril or war rather than regular dwelling places. The forest homes would be rudely constructed of branches built round the trunks of trees and covered with moss and leaves, poor enough places, especially in winter, yet when attacked they were defended with patriotic courage. Such temporary dwellings accorded with the usages of the age, and when migration or flight became necessary they could be left without much inconvenience or loss.

The occupation of these primitive tribesmen would also be simple, befitting the stage of civilisation to which they had attained. The stone whorls found at Mosspeeble and elsewhere indicate that at a very early day spinning was known. A rude form of agriculture together with hunting and warfare, would embrace the bulk of the occupations of the people. Hunting became to the Celt both occupation and recreation. Quarry in plenty lay to his hand. The forests of Eskdale and Ettrick abounded in game of which we to-day know nothing. Species long ago extinct afforded sport and sustenance, both on the hills and in the great forests.

In his fascinating book on the wild life of Eskdale, *My Strange Pets,* Mr. Richard Bell mentions many animals and birds now extinct, but, at the time of which we write, indigenous to Eskdale. The wolf, the red deer, the wild boar, the brown bear, and the wild ox were amongst the fauna of Eskdale and neighbouring dales.

The abundance of such game would help to render the district a more exciting habitation than it is in these softer days, and would also develop that skill in hunting and in archery which, centuries later, shone out amongst the Forest men who fought in the Battle of the Standard, and alas! on the fateful field of Flodden.

Owing to his veneration of rivers the Celt abjured fish as a food, but when this superstition began to decline fishing would also be a source of wealth and amusement. But when the Esk and its tributaries were in the grip of a rigorous winter, when snow lay deep upon field and fell, other resources had to be found, and to what did the tribesmen turn then, when curling was unknown?

That they had domestic amusements seems fairly certain. Glass beads found at Mosspeeblewere possibly used for this purpose. These relics, indeed, may even date from the Stone Age, and it is suggested that they were used as counters in some domestic game, as well as for personal ornament. Dr. Wilson[3] thinks that the game of paips, or chuckie-stanes, so beloved of every Scottish schoolboy, is the lineal descendant of this game which the ancient Celts played with these glass beads.

If at any time the days hung heavily upon the Eskdale tribesman and he was in danger of becoming enervated, then probably a swift invasion of some other tribe or race would serve to brace him up to his wonted efficiency.

In war our tribesman was brave and skilled. Caesar vividly describes the methods of warfare of the Britons, and we may accept his words as applying also to the tribes of the lowlands. In the use of the war chariot the tribesman was an expert, and the Roman leader pays many an involuntary tribute to his dashing attack, his leaping down from the chariot and waging an unequal combat with the disciplined troops or the impressed auxiliaries of Rome. He writes admiringly, too, of their strongholds, excellently fortified both by nature and by art. Praise from Caesar is praise indeed.

In the days when the stone circles were built, the use of metals was unknown in these Islands, but, as the Roman era approached, the weapons of warfare would be of iron. Tacitus indicates that in his day the swords of the Caledonians were made of metal. There is evidence in Eskdale that the Celtic tribes were acquainted with the process of iron making. Some pockets of slag were discovered on Old Irvine Hill and also at Tarras Bridge. The largest deposit in Eskdale was found in 1911 by Mr. Andrew Aitchison on Burian Hill, about half a mile from Old Irvine farmhouse, at a height of about 400 feet. The main deposit is about 9 feet long by 3 feet deep. Professor Desch of Glasgow University, reported that these "were excellent specimens of two typical varieties of ancient slag".

The origin of the ore for this process of smelting is doubtful. So far as Eskdale is concerned it was probably imported, but in the north of Scotland a bog ore, a hydrated oxide of iron, readily fusible, has been found in considerable abundance. It is to be regretted that, excepting the slag, no other relic has been found near these ancient forges.

As already indicated, the religion of these early tribes was of an elementary character. The modified Baal worship practised at the circles developed into a secret cult, popularly associated with the Druids. The earliest Celtic races seem to have had native priests, but there is no indication that in their sacred places, whether these were the ancient stone circles or other structures, there was any visible form set up and worshipped other than that homage and adoration were offered to the sun.

It is from their religious practices, more than from any other characteristic of their age, that these primitive races have exerted a traceable influence. The religious instincts of the tribesmen found expression in forms and observances to which some of our own, though now apparently widely separated, can be traced.

These influences, indeed, still survive in not a few Christian rites.

Their veneration of wells, for example, was the origin of that position accorded to them by the early Christian Church, and the pagan pilgrimages to the wells were Christianised, and entered into the early religious ritual, and were justified by the medicinal value many of the wells possessed. To Langholm people it is interesting to note that to obtain the desired effect the pilgrimages had to be made in the early morning before the sun was up. It was doubtless this pagan superstition lingering in Eskdale which originated the annual visits to the Bloch Well, which were once regarded as part of the ceremonies attaching to the due observance of the Summer Fast Day

As always happens in nature worship, its doctrines became the superstitions of a more enlightened day and race. Their faith scarcely went beyond a profound belief in the agency of supernatural beings. Good or evil spirits, mostly evil, dwelt in every wood, well, or river. Charms, such as the rowan tree, were employed to ward off their malign influence.

Wizardry and magic, the evil eye, the potent power of witches, and the presence of fairies, brownies, bogles, and kelpies in every pool and in every burn, were accepted as truth by primitive man in Eskdale. Certain places were popularly thought to be the special abodes of these sprites. The Little Brig in Galaside Wood was said to be a favourite sporting ground:—

"Where 'tis said, the fairies ramble
And strange spectres nightly march".

The Bogle Gill in the Stubholm Wood was also held to be a haunted place, and brave was he who dared to cross it after night had fallen. In the name of Fairy Loup, given to the charming waterfall in the Byre Burn, we have an instance of the connection of fairies and elves with brooks and streams. Many of these places were regarded with fear by the inhabitants of Eskdale who would not pass such a place without using certain incantations or charms. The practice of carrying perforated or curiously shaped stones as charms against ill luck or disease is of course still observed. A generation or two ago it was also a custom much favoured in Langholm to have a large stone, a perforated one by preference, laid at the door of one's house.

It was these superstitions which gave to Hallow-e'en its unique hold upon the Scottish lowlands. On this evening the fairies held high festival, and the influence they were supposed to exert, especially over the relationships of the sexes, is chronicled in many a volume. The old ballad of Ettrick Forest, the *Tale of Young Tamlane,*[4] is characteristic of the beliefs of the people in the actual existence and magic power of these supernatural visitants.

A vivid conception of these superstitions is obtained from the prose and poetical works of James Hogg, the Ettrick Shepherd. Much of his literary work was expressly designed to preserve these old beliefs and superstitions. Such tales as *The Brownie of Bodsbeck* for instance, give us a clear insight into the eerie beliefs then current and not yet wholly dead amongst the lowland hills.

Fire festivals were among the most important observances of the early Celtic days. Cremation was largely practised, and was given as a mark of honour to a man of might, even as cairn burial also was. It was in this connection that the bonfire came into being. Originally it was banefire, the burning of the bones of the mighty dead, a practice which seems to have been the Celtic equivalent for a public funeral. From these fire festivals there arose such practices in the Christian Church, as the burning of candles and lamps. Candlemas which is a legal term in Scotland, even to this day, thus originated. Ash Wednesday, and such like festivals of the Church, are all referable to the pagan period.

In his Survey of the Girdle Stanes, Mr. Goldsbrough mentions the practice in connection with the sun-rise celebrations at the circles, of illuminating one of the outlying stones, and it is probably from this simple origin in the prehistoric age, that the various fire observances, both of the later pagan and the Christian eras, came into being.

Mr. Goldsbrough mentions, too, that at the date of the building of the Girdle Stanes the year began approximately on February 4th. In the centuries immediately preceding the Christian era, however, that is during the Celtic period, the year began on December 25th, our Christmas Day, and the event was signalised by a fire festival in honour of the sun and by the exchanging of gifts. This gave rise to our custom of burning the Yule log on Christmas Eve.

It is possible that the old northern celebration of Hogmanay originated in the same way and about the same time. Although its precise purpose and origin are obscure, it seems clearly to have been a special festival to mark the passing of the year.

Although licentiousness entered largely into all the pagan rites observed at the circles as part of the worship, in after years among the Celtic tribes there seems to have existed a well defined marriage law. Near to, and apparently in connection with, some of the circles in Cornwall, there have been found stones pierced with a circular hole. These perforated stones are said to have been used in the marriage rites at a very early date, the contracting parties pledging their troth by clasping hands through the opening.

Similarly, in Orkney, the Stone of Odin was so used. It is quite likely that it was a similar custom prevailing among the Eskdale tribes which gave rise to the custom of handfasting.

Handfasting was performed at Handfasting Haugh situated, appropriately, where the waters of the Black Esk and White Esk unite. This was a modified form of marriage, observed by the parties clasping hands in token of their mutual contract, of which the act of joining hands in the present marriage ceremony is doubtless a survival.

The marriage existed for a year, on the expiry of which either person could annul it, in which case due care was taken to recognise the legitimacy of any offspring and the one opting out of the handfasting was responsible for the child's maintenance. If the parties were mutually agreeable to the union, or had failed to have it annulled within the required period, the marriage was made absolute.

We have no record of the use of any perforated stone in Eskdale, but the custom itself was probably part of the old Celtic marriage ceremony. And it is no doubt due to these same customs that the marriage laws and customs of Scotland differ so materially from those of other countries.

CHAPTER 8

THE ROMANS IN ESKDALE

The first invasion of Britain by the Romans took place in the year 55 B.C. under Julius Caesar. This was only a reconnoitring expedition and the following year Caesar returned with five legions of soldiers. This expedition also returned to Rome for the winter.

After an interval of 98 years, in 43 A.D., there was another expedition under the Emperor Claudius, but it was not until 80 A.D. that the attempted conquest of North Britain was entered upon by Julius Agricola. In that year we read of him over-running the country as far as the Firth of Tay. The following year was spent by Agricola in securing his previous conquests and in building a chain of forts across the upper isthmus. In 82 he was in "that part of Britain which is opposite Ireland".

In 84 he defeated the Caledonians under Galgacus at Mons Graupius. This was the most decisive battle of the campaign and his victory enabled Agricola to penetrate even to the Moray Firth. After the recall of Agricola, two years later, little is known of Britain until the reign of Hadrian, 117-138 A.D.

It was during this period that the Wall from the Tyne to the Solway was built. Antoninus, the successor of Hadrian erected the barrier from Forth to Clyde on the line of Agricola's forts. Henceforth for many years one insurrection was succeeded by another, until, in 209, Severus endeavoured to compel the submission of the Britons of the north. After he had repaired the Wall of Hadrian, restored stations and generally improved the roads he marched against the Caledonians, but three years later he returned to York, to die a victim of disease and vexation.

The Romans encountered their most formidable difficulties at the

Borders. The bravery of the native tribes and their guerrilla tactics made the Roman advance beyond the Cheviots slow and arduous. The building of Hadrian's Wall from the Tyne to the Solway was itself a tacit confession that the Romans themselves deemed the task of subjugating the Caledonian tribes too great for their troops.

The occupation of Scotland therefore was never more than partial, and was finally terminated about the year 410 when the Romans relinquished the ambitions of half a millennium and withdrew their armies home to Rome.

During the first century the tract of country we now call the lowlands, lying between the Wall of Hadrian on the south and the Wall of Antoninus on the north, was peopled by a variety of Celtic tribes. These were all descendants of that common Aryan family which ethnologists conjecture to have come over about a thousand years or so before the Christian era, superseding the previous Iberian or Basque population. This Celtic occupation of the British Isles was one stage in that great westward movement of races, which is in operation to-day as markedly as it was two or even three thousand years ago.

The most numerous and powerful branch of this Celtic race were the Brigantes, who occupied the greater part of the southern lowlands. They were subdivided into tribes who peopled certain districts roughly defined by the watersheds of the country. Each tribe was ruled by its own king or chief, and here we have the germ of the clan system so characteristic of Scotland generally and its Celtic people in particular. Eskdale, indeed the entire county of Dumfries, was occupied by the Selgovae, from which the word Solway is derived.

The Romans never attained in Scotland the same influence they exercised in England. South of Hadrian's Wall they colonised the country and built their villas and their baths even as far north as Netherby. Further north their occupation was almost entirely military, and only in a few instances did it exhibit the characteristics of a permanent and civil settlement.

The discoveries at Newstead, near Melrose, and those at Birrens, together with the earlier finds at Duntocher, Cramond, Inveresk, Bar Hill, and other places, for the most part along the Wall of Antoninus, seem to disprove this claim, but these discoveries are indications of the camps of a garrison rather than the dwellings of a settled population.

It may safely be said that immediately north of the Borders the evidences point only to a military and not to a civil Roman occupation. Netherby being in Cumberland, now once again called Cumbria, does not come within the primary intention and scope of this work, except in so far as its history is of service in emphasising or illustrating that of the part of Eskdale with which we are mainly concerned.

The camp at Netherby seems to have been the key to the Roman history of Eskdale and an appreciation of its importance appears to furnish the correct perspective in which to regard the latter. The physical extent of the camp, and the number and nature of the discoveries made there, show not only that Netherby was a great military station, but also that it had a settled civil community of considerable repute and influence. Netherby, indeed, would appear to have ranked in importance with the large stations along the Walls of Hadrian and Antoninus.

The Netherby relics are many and varied, including altars, inscribed stones, tablets, carvings, and groups, as well as pieces of pottery, domestic utensils, coins and ornaments, and all the usual indications of a settled community, such as have been unearthed at Corbridge,the *Corstopitum* of the Roman legions. But in Eskdale not an inscribed altar, no trace of villa or bath has been discovered. Only meagre evidences of a temporary military occupation. Even these have not been found in such abundance as at Carlisle, Netherby, or Birrens.

NETHERBY MIDDLEBY , AND OVERBY

Archaeologists have assumed as a postulate in all their researches into the Roman period, that there was what curiously has been termed a trilogy of camps on the Borders. The camps at Netherby and Middleby were known. These two names implied a third place, Overby, and it was expected that here would be discovered the missing member of the group and reasoning from the similarity in the names the archaeologist placed the third camp at Castle O'er.

This assumption was logical enough, despite the fact that the termination *by* has of itself nothing to do with Roman camps. The three names are of Norse derivation, but camps having been located at Netherby and Middleby it was not unnatural that another should be expected to be found at Overby, and in the locating of it there has been much ingenuity displayed.

The generally accepted opinion was that the strong hill-forts at

Castle O'er constituted the missing camp. Castle O'er was regarded as Overby until in 1810 when Dr. Brown, the minister of Eskdalemuir, recognised in the earthworks at Raeburnfoot the usual rectilinear form of the Roman camp, and he therefore transferred the name Overby to the Raeburnfoot camp. Was he justified in doing so? It was to solve this question that the excavations at Raeburnfoot were made by Mr. James Barbour of Dumfries.

These excavations indicated conclusively that Raeburnfoot was indeed a Roman camp, though by every standard of comparison inferior to the camps at Netherby and Middleby. Mr. Barbour came therefore to the conclusion that Raeburnfoot was *not* Overby, and suggested that researches be made at other places in Dumfriesshire ending in *by* for the missing camp.

Mr. Barbour, it may be pointed out, *assumed* that the third camp would be of equal size to the others, but may it not easily have been that though not the place called Overby, Raeburnfoot may yet have been the sought for camp? It may have been garrisoned and fortified for part of the year, but not employed as winter quarters. Roman writers refer frequently to the troops going into tents, and these may have sufficed for Raeburnfoot, whereas stone buildings were required for such winter quarters as Netherby and Middleby seem to have been.

RAEBURNFOOT

In his book, *My Strange Pets,* the late Mr. Richard Bell argues that Castle O'er is the ancient Overby, and seems somewhat to resent Dr. Brown's change of opinion on his discovery of the rectilinear camp at Raeburnfoot, although he too hesitates to accept the opinion of General Roy that Castle O'er was the supposed *Uxellum* of the Romans. He quotes the late Dr. Macdonald, F.S.A., to support his plea that Castle O'er had "been known as Overby from time immemorial". It thus seems clearly established that the view of archaeologists that the third camp of the trilogy would be at Overby, has been proved incorrect.

It was to settle this point as much as to ascertain whether the works at Raeburnfoot were actually Roman that the excavations were made by Mr. Barbour. The second point seems thereby to have been conclusively settled, that is, that the rectilinear works at the Rae Burn were not early British, but were undoubtedly Roman.

In addition to the similarities discovered at Raeburnfoot to the large camp at Birrens, Mr. Barbour adduces further proof from Delph, in the West Riding of Yorkshire. The camps there are admittedly Roman, and the plan of the earth-works is so similar to that of Raeburnfoot especially the arrangement of forts inside one another as it were, that the report of the excavators at Delph, prepared by Mr. F. A. Bruton, M.A., of Manchester Grammar School, not only makes mention of the similarity of the two plans, but reproduces the plan of Raeburnfoot to illustrate their own discoveries. The plans are so exactly alike as to leave no legitimate doubt that they have been made by the same builders.

The Romans were regulated in their camp construction by well known military rules and specifications, and they sought uniformity not only in their large camps but also in less important works. With reference to Mr. Barbour's primary purpose in excavating at Raeburnfoot, he admits that he is forced to the conclusion that "Overby has still to be discovered".

The step succeeding Dr. Brown's discovery of Raeburnfoot in 1810, was not taken until 1896, when the Dumfriesshire and Galloway Natural History and Antiquarian Society, at the suggestion of Dr. Macdonald, decided to excavate. This was done in November, 1897, under the expert direction of Mr. James Barbour of Dumfries, who, afterwards, embodied his conclusions in a paper read to the Society in the following month. From that paper the following notes are taken with Mr. Barbour's kind permission, and the accompanying plans illustrating Mr. Barbour's paper are given by the courtesy of Messrs. Annan, photographers, Glasgow.

The Raeburnfoot camp is inferior in size and military importance to that at Birrens in Middleby. It occupies the tongue of land formed at the junction of the Rae Burn with the White Esk. It rises about forty feet above the holm lying between it and the Esk, and commands the valley of that river and considerable stretches of adjacent hill country. Its height above sea level is about 650 feet.

The camps at Birrens and Raeburnfoot present points of resemblance in some features, the direction of the major axis of both is N.N.W., thereby conforming to the Vitruvian rule for guarding against noxious winds. Each occupies a bluff rising in a hollow part of the country and skirted on its sides by running streams, the White Esk and the Rae Burn in the case of the Eskdalemuir camp.

The interior dimensions also correspond, by design, Mr. Barbour thinks, and the structural details have also much in common and both camps seem to have been laid down according to the well known established rules. The principal dimensions of the camp are:—

Including the ramparts and ditches the length is 605 feet at the east side and 625 at the west. The width, as far as it can be ascertained, is about 400 feet. With the fortifications the camp extends over five and a half acres, the interior area being rather less than four acres. The interior of the fort itself measures 220 feet by about 185 and contains nearly an acre.

Much of the form of the camp has been rendered indistinct, and occasionally completely obliterated, by ploughing and other agricultural operations, and through the same cause many relics have been lost which might have proved valuable data. Many of the stones used in the construction of the camp seem to have been appropriated for farm purposes, and thus another valuable piece of evidence has been lost.

The ditches are almost V-shaped, but the sides appear to be slightly convex in some cases. The outer one extending on three sides of the camp measures fifteen feet in width and five feet in depth. Those of the central fort are each ten feet wide and three and a half deep, and sixteen to eighteen feet apart between the centres of one and the other. The mound separating them is of a rounded section. The outer rampart was probably about thirty feet in width at the base. The rampart of the fort appears to have been about thirty-five at the base.

No indications exist of east or west gateways, but depressions in the rampart at the north and south mark where the entrances were at these points. The south gateway of the camp shows a roadway of gravel, level with the camp, but nothing remains to mark its width. The gateway on the north is similar but the gravel surface is wanting. At the south entrance of the central fort a good deal of cobble pavement surfacing is found, and several larger stones, which Mr. Barbour suggests might be for edging, also remain.

No certain vestiges of buildings were discovered by Mr. Barbour, but there were seen several pieces of stonework more or less regularly disposed. Pieces of undressed whinstone from twenty-four to thirty inches long were found covering a drain, about sixty feet in length, extendending southwards from the north gateway of the central fort along the west margin of the street at the point marked A on the

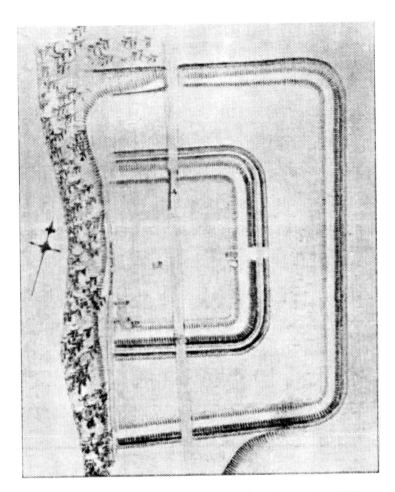

RAEBURNFOOT ROMAN CAMP, ESKDALEMUIR

accompanying plan. They were placed across the drain so as to fit closely together, and the top of the work which was on a level with the street had the appearance of a broad and well-set edging. Similar stones were found composing the side of the drain, and the subsoil formed the bottom.

On the east side of the fort, too, a structural piece of work was discovered where the tail of the rampart would be, nearly midway from north to south, marked C on the plan. It was composed of clay and

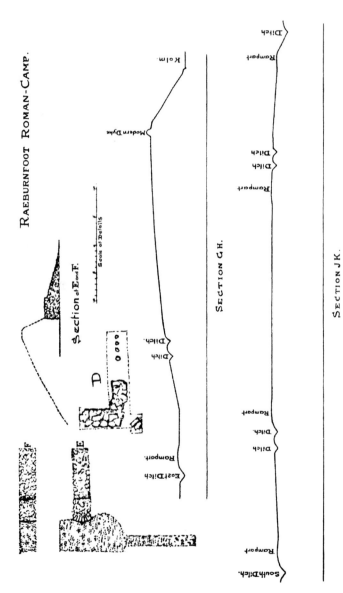

RAEBURNFOOT ROMAN-CAMP.

roundish whinstones about six or nine inches in diameter, put together in such a way as to resemble a mass of concrete. The outline was irregular, but the surface was hard and straight like a floor. It measured about ten feet from north to south and fourteen feet from east to west, and the substance was about two feet thick.

To the north of this there was a breadth of spread stones. To the west were fragments of cobble paving and a few stones together like a fragment of walling about a yard long and nine inches in height. These spread stones, Mr. Barbour thinks, are suggestive of a roadway, and probably the east gateway of the fort stood there, in which case, he thinks, the main structure described might have been a platform for the reception of the engine to be used in defence of the gate.

Another fragment of stonework lies under the tail of the south rampart of the fort near the west side, marked D on the plan. It is arranged in the form of the letter L reversed, and consists of a single layer of flat stones fitted together, and opposite the centre of the lower limb eastwards are four comparatively small stones placed in a row and at almost equal distances. No very certain evidence of a west rampart exists, but structural remains on that side at the south-west corner of the fort, marked E and F on the plan, favour the idea that the plan as regards the fort originally embraced such a rampart.

Only the one street or roadway has been discovered. It extends in a nearly straight line from the north end of the camp to the south, passing through the four gateways. It is surfaced with gravel but the width is uncertain. The four gates are opposite one another, and supposing there were a west rampart as conjectured, the street passing through the gateways would divide the fort equally in two.

The few relics found during the excavations consisted chiefly of fragments of pottery, very similar to those obtained at Birrens which Dr. Anderson considered to be of the Romano-British type. This pottery is a thick, coarse, yellowish ware, with parts of vessels of large size, one fragment being part of the handle of some vessel. Charcoal was found widely distributed, and also some pieces of glass and iron. Near the south gateway of the fort there was found a part of a socket stone.

From these evidences and from other proofs of occupation, Mr. Barbour concluded that the Raeburnfoot camp was Roman, not, indeed, a station like Birrens, but a camp of inferior importance.

These conclusions have received the assent both of Dr. Macdonald and Dr. Christison, both eminent authorities. It may be noted, however, that prior to Mr. Barbour's excavations Dr. Macdonald was of the opinion that the rectilinear earthworks at Raeburnfoot were merely a temporary entrenchment, thrown up by the Romans for the security of some punitive force sent out to quell the tribesmen. The camp is readily recognisable as of Roman origin, Mr. Barbour says, and is an interesting memento of the footsteps of the Romans in the county of Dumfries.

Further research during the 20th century has established that the Roman fort at Raeburnfoot is of Antonine date, circa 142-144 A.D. The fort, with its buildings, is the smaller interior structure. The outer enclosure seems to have been used to accommodate travellers.[1]

BROOMHOLM

The remains of the fort situated on the summit of Broomholm Knowe, about 500m SSW of Broomholmshiels farmhouse, were at one time thought to be those of an ancient British settlement, but aerial photography showed it to be Roman. Excavations during the 1960's uncovered the remains of a Roman Fort of the Flavian period, that is 1st century A.D. and could even be attributed to Agricola himself.[1] The Roman Fort appears to have been occupied at least twice between 80 and 120 A.D. In the earlier period the fort measured about 175m. by 100m. with an annexe attached to its south side. Both structures were initially enclosed by at least two ditches, but a third and possibly a fourth ditch appear to have been added later. This fort was eventually succeeded by a smaller one occupying the southern half of the original fort site.

GILNOCKIE CAMP

There is also a Roman camp at New Woodhead, a little to the north-east of Gilnockie Station. This was surveyed in 1897 by the late Mr. James Burnet, whose outline of the camp we here reproduce by the courtesy of his son, Mr. James Burnet, architect, Langholm.

The camp is in the form of a parallelogram, measuring about 506 yards on the sides and 285 yards at the ends, and enclosing an area of twenty-five acres or thereabout. Mr. Burnet was of the opinion that there had been six gates or entrances to the camp, two on either side and one at each end. There was a raised mound in front of each of the gates.

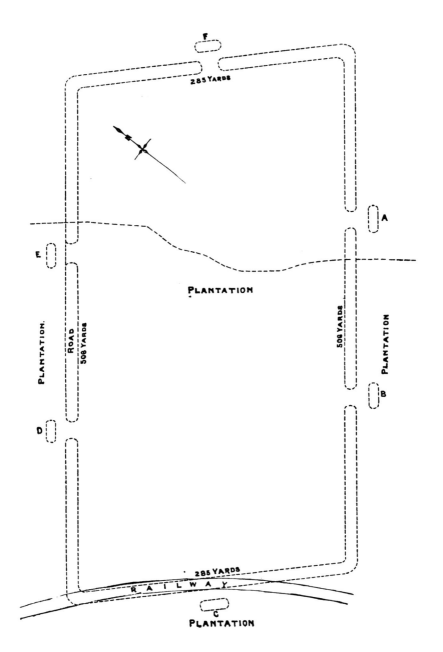

GILNOCKIE CAMP

The gateway at the west end of the camp has been obliterated by the North British Railway line to Langholm, and the accommodation road on the north-west side has destroyed the mounds and gateways on that side. The larger part of the camp is in the plantation and the embankment can be easily traced.

After the original survey there was some doubt about the Gilnockie camp being Roman. It was argued that there would not be a camp of this size so near to the large one at Netherby. But there is nothing inherently improbable in this. For military purposes the Romans frequently established subsidiary camps within easy reach of their larger stations, and this seems to have been done at Gilnockie.

Dr. Macdonald considered the camp of some importance and stated in a letter dated 21st September, 1897, to Mr. James Burnet, acknowledging copy of the accompanying plan, that in certain features it was distinctly Roman. However, it is now definitely acknowledged that the camp at Gilknockie is a typical Roman marching camp which may only have been occupied for one night, the area being large enough to have accomodated a complete legion. No Roman relics have been found so the camp cannot be dated but since marching camps were temporary structures they contain very few relics.[1]

ROMAN ROADS

Apart from the camps at Raeburnfoot and Gilnockie, and from certain relics mentioned below, the principal evidence that the Romans had been in Eskdale are the roads or ways traceable throughout the valley. These seem, however, to be not main roads, but tributary ways. One branch of the Watling Street of the Romans ran through Liddesdale, and the Eskdale roads would appear to be branches of that main road which, starting from Stanwix, ran through Dumfriesshire in more than one direction. The Eskdale road can easily be traced.

There seems little doubt that the Romans readily availed themselves of the strategic advantages offered by some of the old British hill-forts and the *ways* or trenches connecting them. This they seem to have done at The Mote of Liddel. General Roy in his *Military Antiquities* refers to a Roman road which, beginning at Carlisle, ran by Netherby, crossed the Liddel, passed by Nether Woodhead, and then ran along the Tarras side of Whita towards Teviotdale.

It seems clear that there were Roman military ways leading from Netherby into both Annandale and Eskdale. The principal of these can still be traced past Nether Woodhead and across near the camp at Broomholm Knowe It then heads towards Glenfirra where it crosses the Esk, reappears in the fields at the top of the Murtholm bank, and runs along the bottom of the fields lying south of Stubholm. Indications of it are traceable in the Stubholm Wood near the Bogle-gill, and it then runs over the Corsholm and crosses Wauchope at the Auld Caul.

Local tradition says there was a Roman bridge at this spot, and the masonry of the abutments can still be seen. Concerning the masonry there can be no doubt, and certain respected antiquaries consider the remains to be Roman. This bridge was still standing in 1793, but soon afterwards was demolished by the minister, the Rev. Thomas Martin.

In the *Statislical Account* supplied by him for Sinclair's series, he refers to the discovery of some Roman coins on the Corshol, but is silent as to the bridge. Tradition has it that he repented of his vandalism and discreetly left the whole subject out of his article. It seems scarcely conceivable that if this bridge had been built by the Romans it could still be safely usable in 1793. In the Kirk Session records of 1721 there is a reference to the bridge:—"April 1721, no sermon, the minister being barred by the waters. This occurred for 2 Sundays and application was made to have the bridge over Wauchope put right".

The name, the *Auld Caul*, given to the place where it crossed Wauchope, suggests that at one time, much later certainly than the Roman period, there had been such a structure in the river bed. Tradition speaks of an old mill lade somewhere about the foot of the Manse Brae, and it is said that the doorsteps of some of the houses in Caroline Street were made out of covers removed from it. Apart altogether from this bridge, however, there seems little doubt that the Roman road crossed Wauchope at or near this point. It is next seen on the northern edge of the Becks Moss as a well defined causeway running diagonally through a field towards the old fort at Calfield. Just at this point the Moss is thickly covered with stones, and within living memory, (early 20th century), the pavement was distinctly visible.

In the next field the form of the road has been obliterated. At the fort the road seems to wheel and can be seen stretching in a westerly course for nearly half a mile until lost on the Moss. It is next seen just behind Westwater running in a broad line straight up and over the hill.

Popular opinion gives another Roman bridge at Loganhead. Here some remains of masonry are visible, indeed, the bridge was standing until the year 1901 when it fell. In Pingle Burn there are also remains of masonry, as of the abutments of a bridge. Also existing is a well defined roadway similar to the one at Calfield towards which it also points.

ROMAN ANTIQUITIES

The memorials of the Romans found in Eskdale, apart from those in the Netherby collection, are very meagre. Undoubtedly the most noteworthy of them all is a tablet mentioned by Dr. Wilson in his *Prehistoric Annals of Scotland.* "The following tablet", he says, "thus oddly located in the Morton MS. belongs to the district of the Selgovae. This inscription is in a house of Jockie Graham in Eskdale, fixed in a wall, set up as appears, by the Legio Augusta Secunda in memorial of the Emperor Hadrian":—

IMP. CAES. TRA. HAD

RIANO. AUG.

LEG. II. AUG. F.

"Camden mentions an inscription the counterpart of this, dug up at Netherby, and Pennant describes another nearly similar (possibly the Eskdale tablet) which he examined among the antiquities at Hoddam Castle, Dumfriesshire" Dr. Wilson points out that "all the inscriptions transcribed at Hoddam were understood, where not otherwise specified, to be from the neighbouring station at Birrens, the *Blatum Bulgium* of Antoninus, and that the Eskdale tablet therefore forms an important addition to the traces of the elder Emperor Hadrian found thus far within the transmural province" that is, in the province of Valentia, which comprised that part of Scotland between the walls of Hadrian and Antoninus.

Doubt exists as to the location of this tablet. Some consider, on the authority of Camden, that though this is designated an Eskdale tablet yet it rightly belongs to the Netherby collection. Its being found in the house of a Graham seems to support this view. But Camden's story of the tablet at Netherby is not without its elements of doubt. His words are:— "and in the walls of the house is this Roman inscription, set up in memory of Hadrian the Emperor, by the *legio secunda Augusta:—*

IMP. CAES. TRA.
HADRIAN
AUG.
LEG. II. AUG. F

But when Horsley, the well known historian, came to Netherby and looked for this tablet described by Camden, it could not be found. He says:—"this stone is not to be found. Mr. Gordon enquired for and I likewise sought after it, but in vain, and part of the house is pulled down and altered, I doubt not this stone has been destroyed or lost in the ruins. However, this makes it evident that the Romans were possessed of this station in the reign of the Emperor Hadrian, and by the medals both of the High and Low Empire that have been found here, it seems probable they were long in possession of it"[2].

It seems very strange that if Camden *saw* this stone at Netherby it should disappear from Netherby and afterwards be found at Hoddam. It is true that small differences are noticeable between the inscription given by Camden and that given by Pennant, but these are in such general agreement that it appears probable that they relate to one and the same stone. The explanation seems to be that Camden was in error in ascribing the tablet to Netherby, and that according to the Morton MS the stone was found in Eskdale, as distinct entirely from Netherby. Admittedly the place named as "a house of Jockie Graham in Eskdale" is somewhat indefinite and its situation cannot now be determined.

There have been several discoveries of Roman coins in Eskdale. About the year 1783 some gold denarii were found on the Broomholm estate, viz., four *Neros, two Vespasians,* and one *Domitian. A Nero* was found on Cannonby glebe land by the minister the Rev. John Russell. From this it was argued that there must have been a Roman road there; if so, it might possibly be the continuation of the road at New Woodhead. On the Roman road running from Broomholm Knowe to Calfield where it crosses Wauchope some coins were discovered, viz., one *Otho* and two denarii aurei, which the Statist in 1793 said were in the possession of the family of Mr. Little, late baron-bailie of Langholm. A *Nero* was also found on the surface of the road at Craighaugh in Eskdalemuir, but probably this coin had been accidentally lost by some one.

CHAPTER 9

ESKDALE IN STRATHCLYDE

When the Roman legions were recalled home in 410 A.D. to further the purposes of the usurper Constantine and help to stem the ravages of the Goths, their withdrawal from the Borders produced something approaching to chaos. The tribes who had had a common purpose in opposing the invaders were left hopelessly divided and the balance of power, which the Romans had held, could not at first be assumed by any one of them. The influences of the Roman occupation were soon dissipated and the Borders were left to political chaos and to inter-tribal conflicts and jealousies.

One effect of the Roman invasion was that it planted in the Celtic tribes the rudiments of a monarchical government and these ideas tended to modify their clan or tribal customs. Apart from this, the influence left by the Romans upon the Borders was imperceptible, certainly in no way worthy of comparison with that of the later invaders.

The Saxons and the Norsemen, when they came , effected a much more potent change upon the language and thought and literature of the Celts, and, by inter-marriage, upon their features, than the Romans had done. The Celtic race seems to have slowly evolved into two main branches, the Gaelic and the Cymric or Welsh. This distinction still exists in the separation of the Scottish and Irish Gaels from those of Wales and Cornwall. It was to the Cymric branch that the tribes inhabiting Eskdale belonged.

What we now call Scotland did not, of course, then exist as a geographical expression. The land, was appropriated by various tribes of a common Celtic stock, but tending to develop along somewhat different lines, and gradually separating in purpose and sympathy.

The Picts occupied the highlands, the region beyond the Wall of Antoninus, a land of mystery even to the Romans. The Scots, who had come from Ireland or Scotia, as it was first named, occupied the Argyle district, which afterwards became known as the kingdom of Dalriada. The Damnii occupied Clydesdale. The Ottadini and Gadeni were in Selkirk, Roxburgh, and the Lothians. The Novantae held Wigton and Galloway. Dumfriesshire, which is of more concern to us, was occupied by the Selgovae. All these tribes were of Celtic origin but time and chance had drifted them into separate paths.

The tract occupied by the Selgovae extended like a wedge from the river Derwent, in the south, towards the Clyde in the north. In after years this developed into a more or less compact kingdom known first as Strathclyde, later as Cumbria, with Alclyde or Dumbarton as its capital.

At its southern extremity was the important town of Carlisle, one of the twenty-eight towns of any considerable size existing when the Romans left. It will thus be seen that Eskdale was almost the central valley in Strathclyde, a geographical position which was bound to give it considerable importance.

For a time the Strathclyde Britons were the dominant race in the lowlands. But to this native situation a new element was to be added which would exercise an enormous influence on the north of England and south of Scotland. This was the coming of the Saxon.

The precise date of the Saxon invasion is uncertain. Bede says 428, but Mr. Skene, whose authority in this field of historic research is unrivalled, says the Saxons were growing to considerable power before this, and fixes the date of their coming at 374.

It would appear that during the waning of the Roman authority the King of the Romanised Britons of Strathclyde invited foreign aid, and in answer to his appeal a mixed migration of Frisians, Angles, Saxons, and Jutes landed on these shores. Probably the Frisians came first, leaving clear a indication of their colonisation in the name of Dumfries, the camp or stronghold of the Frisians. Traces of their influence, too, are found in the dialect of that country and of Eskdale.

By the year 547 Ida, the Saxon King, had established himself as King of Northumbria, a tract embracing not only what we now know by this name, but also Berwickshire, part of Roxburghshire, and the Lothians. These territories were consolidated into the Saxon kingdom of Bernicia, which marched with Strathclyde, the boundary being probably the Catrail. Bamburgh was the capital of this kingdom of Bernicia.

At this date, therefore, Scotland and northern England as far as the Humber, were partitioned into four kingdoms inhabited by the Picts, Scots, Cumbrians, and Saxons. The history of the country, thereafter, was simply the story of the contests and warfare waged by these four parties for the choicest tracts of territory, or for political domination.

Constant warfare was carried on between the Britons of Strathclyde and the invading Saxon, who was ultimately to colonise the valleys of almost the entire lowlands, and stamp both his physical and mental characteristics upon the old Celtic race. It is these wars between Briton and Saxon, with their deeds of prowess, which provided the foundation for both the historical and the legendary tales of Arthur, the hero of so much poetry and romance. Many of the legends, of course, were added centuries later by Geoffrey of Monmouth and later still by Sir Thomas Malory.

Arthur was the representative of the Celtic church which, under St. Columba, was spreading the message of Christianity and was beginning to exert a powerful influence in the lowlands, especially amongst the Britons who inhabited Eskdale and the adjacent dales.

According to Adamnan, Abbot of Iona, in his *Life of St. Columba,* Arthur, born 559, was the eldest son of Aedàn who had been anointed King of Dalriada by St. Columba himself in 574. His mother was Ygerna (or Igraine) the High Queen of the Celtic kingdoms and this was accepted by the Celtic Church. Thus, through his mother, Arthur, on his sixteenth birthday, was anointed by the Celtic priests High King of the Britons.[1]

Many of Arthur's exploits are admitted to have been performed in the district of which Eskdale is the centre. His Twelve Battles were the outstanding features of his campaign. Though none of these great battles seems to have been fought in Eskdale itself, yet most if not all of them were fought in the Scottish lowlands. We have indications of this connection in such names as Arthur's Seat and Arthur's Oven and in the name Arthuret near to Netherby and Longtown. The name is the modernised form of Ardderyd, the scene of one of the determining battles of the early Christian period.

This battle of Ardderyd,[2] in 573, was fought on the west side of the river Esk, about eight miles north of Carlisle, between the Christian king of the Strathclyde Britons, Rhydderch Hael, and Gwendolew leader of the pagan tribes. The result was victory for the Christian party and Rhydderch was established as King of the Cumbrian Britons.

Two small hills here are called Arthuret Knowes, and the top of the highest, which over hangs the river, is fortified by an earthen rampart. About four miles north of this is a stream which flows into the Esk and bears the name of Carwhinelow, in which the name of Gwendolew can be recognised.

The battle seems to have been one of great ferocity if we may judge from the traditions of it handed down by the Bards. It lasted over forty-six days, and when "the war drum throbbed no longer" some 80,000 corpses, it is said, were left in the meadows between the vales of Esk and Liddel.[3] Of this battle the Bard sang:—

> "Guendydd loves me not, greets me not,
> I am hated by the chiefs of Rhydderch,
> For after Gwendolew no princes honour me,
> Yet in the battle of Ardderyd I wore the golden torques."

Amongst those who fought in this great battle was one, Nud whose name is found on an inscribed stone, *The Muckle Stane*, discovered in Yarrow. He was buried under a tumulus there.

Rhydderch Hael, King of the Strathclyde Britons, was killed in 603 near the Nine Stane Rig in Hermitage Water. After his death the warfare among the tribes occupying the lowlands continued without intermission, but the conflicting groups were not defined. They arranged themselves first into one combination, then into another. It was out of these groupings that the Scottish nation finally emerged, a result attained only after several centuries of faction and fighting.

In the see-saw of this fighting, with all its details of victory and defeat, we have only a partial interest here, that which is aroused by the part played in these civil wars and political evolutions by Eskdale or Strathclyde. At first the conflict lay, roughly, between east and west. The Scots of Dalriada and the Britons of Strathclyde united their forces to wage war upon the Angles of Bernicia, that long stretch of fertile country bordering the North Sea from the Tees almost to the Forth, and their vassals the Picts of Galloway.

Between the Britons of Strathclyde and the Saxons of Bernicia there was carried on a fierce and almost continuous warfare. Lying so near the boundary line between the two kingdoms, Eskdale would share largely in these conflicts. But its hills and ravines, and the Catrail itself, if this indeed were its purpose, proved only a temporary defence to the Britons, for the Saxons and Frisians spread themselves over Strathclyde in a persistent and successful invasion. The Celts were either put to the sword or became the serfs of the mixed Teutonic hordes who now filled the beautiful lowland valleys.

It was this invading race which was destined to give to us that language which, mixed with the Celtic and the later Norse, forms today the speech of the Scottish lowlands, a vivid, picturesque, and flexible language immortalised in prose and poetry, but especially in song.

On the death of Rhydderch Hael the leadership of the combined forces against the Saxons was assumed by the King of the Scots, and for a time the allies observed their offensive and defensive agreement. But within another generation the Scots and Britons were themselves at war. This conflict resulted in the Britons of Strathclyde, subduing the Scots, who thereafter yielded them allegiance.

This in turn gave place to the supremacy of the Angles, who thus secured under their domination, not only the Picts of Galloway but the Scots and the Britons as well. This overship lasted some thirty years and as the kingdom of Northumbria, virtually identical with Bernicia, and inhabited by Angles, was a Christian country under King Osuin, it must have left upon Strathclyde, and not least upon Eskdale, an impress which has lasted throughout all the succeeding centuries.

In 685 still another change occurred in the balance of power. On the initiative of the Pictish tribes Northumbria was invaded, and its King, now Ecgfrid, son of Osuin, was killed in the battle of Dunnichen. This battle was decisive, and its immediate result was to liberate nearly all those tributaries of Northumbria to whom reference has been made.

However, there were certain of the Strathclyde Britons who failed to break their serfdom to the powerful Angles. We read that the Picts of Galloway and the Britons residing between the Solway and the Derwent still remained in vassalage to the Angles of Bernici, and as the latter could only gain access to Galloway by way of the northern shores of the Solway, it would seem to follow that the tribes occupying the districts of Annandale and Eskdale may also have remained in subjection to their ancient enemies, though the records appear to indicate that the people of Dumfriesshire were amongst those liberated.

The tribes who, by the battle of Dunnichen, had gained their freedom from the Anglic sway, maintained it for a period of forty years. However, during these years considerable fighting took place between the Scots of Dalriada and the Britons of Strathclyde. Whether the Eskdale tribes participated in these conflicts does not seem clear.

In 731 the persistent Angles again asserted their dominance over the Britons. A few years later the old alliances re-appear, Scots and Britons sinking their differences to co-operate against the Angles and their Celtic allies, the Galloway Picts. After several years of desultory fighting, the Anglic King Eadbert, with his Pictish ally, Angus, led an army against the Strathclyde Britons, whose submission they succeeded in compelling at Dumbarton in 756.

So once again the tribes of Eskdale would be under the power and influence of the Angles and Saxons, an important factor in the evolution of the character, appearance and speech of the people of the district. The history of this period is admittedly obscure but it seems that towards the end of the eighth century, in 793, a new factor intruded itself into these swift alternations in the struggle for supremacy. This was the piratical and harassing raids of the Vikings who swooped down upon the northern coasts. These raids were almost incessant during the ninth century. In 875 the Danes again ravaged the east coast, laying waste not only Northumbria, but destroying the people of Strathclyde also.

Possibly owing to these frequent raids, the kingdom of Northumbria had fallen into a state of disorganisation. The domination which the Angles had exercised over the Britons of southern Strathclyde, or Cumbria as it had come to be called, came to an end. Giric, the King of the Britons, invaded Bernicia, or Saxonia, and restored Strathclyde, from the Clyde to the Derwent, to its old independence under a native British King.

In the year 927[4] Athelstan, King of Wessex received the submission of Northumbria. He also made pledges of peace with Constantin, King of Scots. However, in 934 Athelstan reneged on his oath and invaded Scotland where he defeated Osuin, King of Cumbria, and Constantin, King of Scots, and ravaged their territories. From these successes of the King of Wessex, efforts have been made to show that the Scottish lowlands lost their independence, but the people themselves do not appear to have so regarded their position, and a great united effort was speedily made to dispute this claim.

The Britons of Cumbria, together with the Danes from Dublin as temporary allies, who had probably landed in the Solway and travelled across Annandal and Eskdale, supplied a contingent for this supreme effort. In 937 [4] they crossed the hills separating Cumbria from the Anglic kingdom of Saxonia, formerly Bernicia, and in the great battle which followed, they bore their part in the fight for independence, a fight, however, which went all in favour of the Saxon Athelstan, who drove the Scottish and Cumbrian Kings back and slew most of their troops.

In 943 Malcolm I succeeded to the Scottish throne, and during his reign an important consolidation was effected by the cession of Cumbria to the Scots, the first of a series of events whose culmination was the formation of a united kingdom of Scotland.

The immediate occasion of the cession was that the Saxon King, Edmund, who had been incessantly harrying the territories of the Cumbrians, of which Donald, son of Osuin, was King, had granted these territories to Malcolm as the price of his vassalage. It is probably to this period in the history of Eskdale that we may ascribe a considerable share of that Saxon influence which made itself felt in the district.

These ravages of Cumbria by the Saxons continued, but were resisted by Kenneth, grandson of Donald, in whose reign the amalgamation of the Cumbrians and the Scots was effected. About this date, too, 1005, the Picts and Scots were united under Malcolm.

In the year 1018 Malcolm II, King of Scots, invaded Northumbria and fought a great battle at Carham on Tweed, where he defeated the Angles who ruled all the country from the Forth to the Tees. The most important effect of this victory by the Scots King was that the territory of Saxonia, as far south as the Tweed, was ceded to him.

Malcolm's kingdom of Scotia now embraced the whole of the present area of Scotland, except the lands in the western islands and in Caithness and Galloway, which were in the possession of the Norwegians, but it included that portion of Cumbria which lay between the Solway and the river Derwent.

After Malcolm's death in 1034 he was succeeded by his grandson, Duncan, (son of his daughter Bethoc), who was a minor when he came to the throne. According to the old system of succession a male of a collateral line could inherit, thereby ensuring that the new king would be of adult status. It was according this system that Macbeth claimed the throne although he may very possibly have had a better claim to it than had Duncan.[5]

In 1040 Macbeth defeated Duncan in a battle near Elgin in which Duncan was killed.[6] Macbeth reigned for 17 years and was well regarded. A reign of such length would suggest that he was a strong king. Shakespeare's version of the story is, of course, fictitious. At the time of writing, in 1606, King James VI, a direct descendant of Duncan, had succeeded to the throne of England as James I. Shakespeare could, by thus portraying Macbeth as a villain, expect to gain approval from the reigning monarch.

In 1057, Malcolm, son of Duncan, raised an army and, in a battle near Lumphanan, defeated and killed Macbeth. A year later, in 1058, Malcolm killed Lulach, a distant cousin but never the less another possible contender for the throne. Malcolm III, or Canmore, (big head), as he is often called, thus became King of Scotia.

When, in 1066, William the Conqueror seized the throne of England, Edgar the Atheling and his sister Margaret, as possible contenders to the throne, escaped by ship. A storm arose and the ship was wrecked near the river Wear, possibly on the notorious reef at Whitburn just north of the river mouth. Tradition says that it was here, "on the banks of the Wear" that they were rescued by Malcolm, who was evidently stravaiging around that area.. He escorted them back to Scotland. A year or two later Malcolm and Margaret were married. Margaret was destined to exert a most powerful influence over her warlike husband and his subjects, and was largely instrumental in Anglicising the Scottish Court and in extending the influence of the Roman Church, greatly to the detriment of the Celtic form of Christianity.

In 1070 Malcolm again marched into England and ravaged all the country between Tyne and Tees, burning St. Peter's church at Wearmouth, and carried back to Scotland many prisoners. These people settled in the lowlands thus further diluting the Celtic way of life. A Celtic king sat on the throne but the power was gradually passing away from that long line arising from the oldest Aryan colonists in Europe.[7]

In 1093 the Scottish King again invaded England but was killed in battle at Alnwick. As a result of this William the Conqueror gained the area of Cumbria which lay between the Solway and the river Derwent, with Carlisle as its chief town.

Malcolm had reigned for thirtyfive years, and at his death the kingdom had been welded into a fairly compact nation. After several years of unsettled government David, youngest son of Malcolm, came to the throne. He first reigned over the ancient territories of Strathclyde and Cumbria and the Lothians, and then in the year 1124 he assumed the sovereignty over the whole of Scotland.

David's attempt to add Northumberland to Scotland led in 1138 to the Battle of the Standard. In this decisive battle the Cumbrian forces formed one wing, together with the men of Teviotdale and Eskdale. David, however, was defeated, and the Solway, the Cheviots, and the Tweed were made the southern boundary of his kingdom. With the reign of David there began a new era in Scottish history.

CHAPTER 10

THE CHRISTIAN ERA

Even amidst all the wars and turmoils mentioned in the last chapter, a new light was slowly dawning amongst the Eskdale hills. The Christian faith, whose way had been prepared in the province of Valentia by the Roman conquerors, began slowly to influence the life of the tribes. The Britons of Strathclyde were regarded as the Christian party among the ancient Celtic tribes, and the great battle of Arderydd was in one sense, (a subordinate one certainly), a religious conflict, in which Rhydderch Hael, the British King, was the Defender of the Faith.

The Christianity of these early centuries in Britain was not an apostolic faith. Many of the observances of Celtic paganism had been incorporated into the new religion, as diplomatic concessions to the prejudices of the tribes and to the force of custom, to which even then our Scottish forefathers seem to have been wedded! During the sixth and seventh centuries rulers and church councils continued to denounce the pagan practices of some of their converts. Even in the eleventh century it was found necessary "to forbid our subjects to worship the sun, moon, fires, rivers, fountains, hills, and trees".

The Norse invasions of the eighth and ninth centuries were disastrous to both the early Christian communities and to the civil liberties of the people and Norse paganism infected the entire thought of the age. It is seen, indeed, even to the present day in the names we attach to the days of the week.

The source of Scottish Christianity, apart from any lingering influence from the Roman occupation, was the Irish mission on Iona, established by St. Columba about the year 563. It ought ever to be remembered that the introduction of the Christian faith into Scotland was separate from, and independent of, the mission of St. Augustine to England. The two movements were in no way associated. The early Church in Scotland was independent of both Rome and England.

The monks of Iona had established a mission at Lindisfarne, off the Northumbrian coast, and it was they who converted Northumbria to the Christian faith. The Lindisfarne community remained subordinate to Iona for many years. Not until the Synod of Whitby, presided over by the Abbess Hilda in 664, did the Northumbrian Church submit to Rome. It was twenty-four years later when events, largely political, produced a like submission of the Christians of Strathclyde.

The earliest Christian community in the south of Scotland was established at Candida Casa, or Whithorn, among the Picts of Galloway. As Eskdale was, partially at least, Christianised before the Roman demission in 410, it is not improbable that it came within the sphere of influence of Whithorn, though, we admit, there is no evidence supporting this suggestion.

The founding of the church on Iona by St. Columba, and his twelve companions, has ever possessed a unique interest for the student of ecclesiastical history. To the people of Eskdale and of Strathclyde generally it is of equal, if not greater, interest to note that St. Patrick, who became the patron saint of Ireland, was a native of Strathclyde.[1] His influence seems to have been more potent in the Dumfriesshire area than even that of St. Columba himself.

We cannot claim St. Patrick as an Eskdale man, yet his birthplace may have been in the shire. Judging from the evidences found in the place-names, St. Patrick appears to have left a greater impress upon Dumfriesshire, than upon any other part of Scotland. We have Kirkpatrick-Fleming, Kirkpatrick-Irongray, and Kirkpatrick-Juxta. His name appears, too, in the place-names of Eskdale.

In an old thirteenth century charter delineating certain boundaries, reference is made to the fountain of St. Patrick[2] in the neighbourhood of Stapelgortoun, one of the many holy wells then existing, but its site cannot now be identified. Such dedications indicate the popularity of the Saint, and they usually point to his having laboured in that district. It may also have been due to the influence of St. Patrick that there existed a friendly intercourse, if not indeed an organic union, between the early Church in Ireland and the Christian communities of Strathclyde.

In this association St. Bridget, or St. Bride, as she was popularly named in the lowlands, had also a share. St. Bridget was the Virgin Saint of Ireland. Contemporary with St. Patrick, she was renowned for her faith and works of charity. She exercised a gracious influence upon the imagination of the early Church, both in Ireland and Scotland, and excited the admiration and imitation of its adherents.

Kildare church was dedicated to her, and became the mother-church of all similar foundations which bore her name. In the eighth century a chapel at St. Andrews was dedicated to her, as was the famous old church at Abernethy. In the highlands and islands of Scotland dedications to her were frequent. What was probably the earliest Christian church in our area was dedicated to St. Bridget and the name lingers still in St. Bride's Chapel and St. Bride's Hill in Wauchopedale.

The site of this chapel seems to have been on the top of the hill separating Westwater from Cleuchfoot. The first building would be a very simple. structure of timber and wattles according to the custom of the Scots so often mentioned by Bede. This in time would be replaced by the usual stone building. R. Bruce Armstrong[3] mentions that in 1220 it was agreed by arbitration in the dispute between the Bishop of Glasgow and the Abbot of Jedburgh "in regard to the Church of Walleuhope that the vicar . . . . should have five merks uplifted in the said Church".

This no doubt was the Chapel of St. Bride which would be in the diocese of the Prior of Canonby Probably the only relic left of this second church is a large stone, known in Wauchopedale as *The Chapel Stane*, lying on what the Ordnance Map marks as the site of St. Bride. It is a sandstone of the district measuring nearly seven feet in girth and weighing approximately eight hundredweight. It is rudely worked and has evidently been used as a receptacle for holy water, possibly as a font for baptisms, or more likely still, as a porch stone.

Near to St. Bride's Hill are the Chapel Grains and Chapel Cleuch, indications that St. Bride's had once upon a time been a centre of the life of Wauchopedale.

In Cumberland there is a village of Bridekirk, which contains the famous baptismal font whose inscribed runes, said to be Saxon, have occasioned so much learned discussion amongst archaeologists. The date of the founding of this Cumberland Kirk of St. Bride is not known, but from the fact of the Saxon runes it may be inferred to be not much later than the seventh century. There is also a Bridekirk in Annandale in the parish of Hoddam and it may be that it was one of the early foundations of the See of Hoddam, established by St. Kentigern. The private chapel of the Douglases, founded in the thirteenth century, was also dedicated to St. Bride.[4]

The name of Columba stands pre-eminent as the apostle of early Scottish Christianity, yet it is not so much to him as to St. Kentigern that the veneration of the people of Dumfriesshire has been given. St. Kentigern, or St. Mungo as he was affectionately called, — Mungo meaning dear friend in the Ancient British language, — left upon the whole district of Strathclyde an influence that was deep and lasting. To the people of Dumfriesshire it is a matter of interest and pride that his first diocese was at Hoddam in Annandale. There can be no doubt that his diocese embraced Eskdale, for in that era of transition the ethnic boundaries were generally also the diocesan boundaries, and the people of Annandale and Eskdale were of the same kith and kin.

Old documents show that over 300 years ago there existed, apparently somewhere between Calfield and Westwater, a farm known as Cross-Mungo. This is an indication that there had existed one of those wayside crosses set up for the devotions of passers by, and who had associated it with the venerated Saint.

St. Kentigern was followed by St. Cuthbert who left a deep and permanent impression on the early Church, both in the south of Scotland and north of England. St. Cuthbert's sphere of influence is seen by the dedication to his memory of the Over-Kirk of Ewes, founded probably in the early part of the 13th century, and situated at Unthank where the graveyard still exists.

There is no dedication to St. Cuthbert in Eskdale, a fact which indicates the separate part played by Ewesdale in the early days. Ecclesiastically Ewes was under Melrose which was first in Saxonia, the scene of St. Cuthbert's early labours, but was afterwards transferred to Glasgow, whose diocese embraced the whole district of Strathclyde.

The church founded by St. Ninian at Whithorn in Galloway had been dedicated to St. Martin of Tours. The dedications to St. Martin in Eskdale are, first, in the twelfth century, the Priory of Canonby, and next, founded about the thirteenth century[5], the ancient church at Boykin, or Byken, in Westerkirk. Though the Over-Kirk of Ewes had been dedicated to St. Cuthbert, some influence of the earlier dedications to St. Martin seems to have lingered in the valley. We have a suggestion of this in the placename of Martinhope, which was contiguous to Unthank.

We have another indication of the early days of the Christian Church in Eskdale in the name of St. Thorwald. The derivation of the name is not easy to trace. The name *Thor* is not infrequently met with, e.g., in the village of Torthorwald. Probably the name in both cases relates to Thor the Long, a Saxon settler, who on the invitation of Edgar, son of King Malcolm, established a religious settlement at Ednam, or Edenham, on the Tweed.

It is related that there, in the twelfth century, a church, in honour of St. Cuthbert, was built by Thor the Long. The name and fame of Thor may have extended to Eskdale and the dedication to St. Cuthbert of the Over-Kirk of Ewes may have been due to the influence of the Saxon devotee. The addition of *Saint* to the name of Thor may have been a popular rather than a canonical recognition of his generosity and many virtues.

THE NEW WOODHEAD BROOCH

At New Woodhead, Canonby, there were discovered in 1864 certain relics of the early Christian Church in this district. These were held to be treasure trove and were deposited in the National Museum of Antiquities, Edinburgh, but now in The Museum of Scotland which opened on 30th November 1999. The find consisted of brooches, rings, and beads, together with some silver pennies of Edward I and Edward II John Balliol and Alexander III.

Most interest attaches to the brooch shown above. "It is circular in shape, formed of a rod of silver, 3 $\frac{1}{8}$ inches in diameter, ornamented with six rosettes alternating with six ornamented knobs"[6.] The pin of the brooch was missing. A second brooch, also of silver, 2 ¾ inches in diameter, was inscribed "IHESUS NAZARENUS REX". A third was imperfect, with "lozenge shaped ornaments covered with diapered pattern".

There was another brooch similar to the first, but broken. Also found were some finger rings and jet beads. These discoveries at New Woodhead dated, approximately, to the early part of the fourteenth century. The lands of Woodhead were in the possession of the Priory of Canonby, and were included in the Barony of Tarras, erected in 1606.

That the entire district bordering on the shores of the Solway Firth was well advanced in Christian civilisation, even at an early date, is well attested by two remarkable specimens of Christian art, the two Crosses, one at Ruthwell, in Dumfriesshire and the other at Bewcastle, in Cumberland. It is probably to about the period of the ninth century that these monuments must be assigned.

After much learned controversy, it seems to be clearly established that the Ruthwell inscriptions are not in northern or Scandinavian runes, but in Anglo-Saxon, and this indicates as the approximate date, the time when the Northumbrian Church was missioning the whole of Cumbria and Bernicia. The Bewcastle Cross is akin in design to that at Ruthwell, and the two are representative of the Christian art of the early Church.

Situated as it is between these two districts, Eskdale would come under the same influences, though no similar relics have been discovered there, but in the old church at Hoddam stones engraven in runic characters were found in 1815. Many of the symbolic details of the Ruthwell and Bewcastle Crosses have been made use of by Mr. C.C. Hodges, architect of Hexham, of the beautiful Caedmon Cross at Whitby, and the Bede Cross at Sunderland.

CHAPTER 11

THE ETHNOLOGY OF ESKDALE

Our knowledge of the races inhabiting the British Islands in the prehistoric ages is vague and uncertain. It is impossible to say definitely when, in the great series of migrations, one race disappeared and another took its place. These movements are generally gradual. The fusion of one race with another, the changes of form and feature or of language, are only slowly effected. Especially is this so during colonisation. Then the modifications are brought about by individuals and families, and extend over several generations. When, instead of colonisation, there has been war, tribes are exterminated and the changes are sudden and swift. Both of these agents have at various times helped in the ethnic movements in the Esk valley.

Elsewhere we have indicated that, at the date of the building of the Girdle Stanes, about 1290 B.C., the inhabitants of Eskdale were of the Iberian race. We say this without committing ourselves to either side in the great ethnological discussion which ever gathers round the word Iberian.

But, where history is silent, archaeology has come to our aid, and we may assume that the builders of the stone circles of Eskdale were at least of a non-Aryan race, whether Iberian, as so many authorities suppose, or Semitic, as Lockyer seems inclined to believe. It is not possible on our present information to determine absolutely. We cannot even say that this was the first race to inhabit Eskdale. The valley did not come into existence when its people began to build stone circles, and no doubt there were people living there whose antiquity makes even the Stone Age seem a modern era.

All the processes of evolution have been at work in Eskdale to produce that type to which its present inhabitants belong. Each succeeding race has left its legacy in colour of hair or of eyes, in cranial shape, in stature, in feature, or in language. The blending of many and varied traits of character, the modification of old forms and the production of new, extend themselves over long periods of time.

It will be most convenient for our present purpose to assume the history of Eskdale as beginning about 1290 B.C., the date, ascertained by Mr. Goldsbrough, of the erection of the Girdle Stanes. The dates given in the following paragraphs are of course only approximate.

THE IBERIAN

1290 B.C. Of the race who set up these circles very little is known. Ethnologists speak of them as dark and small of stature, but these features are also held to be characteristic of the succeeding race, who dispossessed the Iberian. By certain authorities in ethnology it is accepted as proved that about the time of the Roman invasion these Islands were inhabited by two types of people, one fair in complexion, the other dark. The latter are considered to have been the Iberians, the former the Gauls or Celts.

If this be correct, then we must assume that the Iberians had persisted from the Stone Age down to the Roman period, despite the evidence of the barrows that, after the Celtic migration, there was a swift modification and merging of races. The researches in the most ancient barrows point to this early race having been long skulled, and Dr. Thurman, one of the chief authorities on craniology, attributes these long skulls to the Iberian race of the Stone Age. Lord Avebury thinks that the race succeeding this long-skulled people also belonged to the Stone Age, and archaeology shows that this was probable.

In Eskdale this supposed Iberian race left no traces of its life, excepting the stone circles, and possibly some of the standing stones. It is said that they buried their dead, yet no trace of any of their burial places exists if, as we assume, the cairns and cists all belong to the succeeding or Celtic age.

Had any record been kept of the skull measurements of the skeletons found at Airdswood Moss or Westwater, some indication at least would have been given which would have enabled the archaeologist to form a surer opinion than he dare now offer. Nor is there any trace of

Iberian words in the language of the people. The Basque language, spoken in the north of Spain, is believed to be the lineal descendant of the Iberian.

In a previous chapter reference has been made to the stone rings of Eskdale, and the suggestion noted that these might have been Picts' Houses. The recent discovery of a neolithic village at Fewstone, in Yorkshire, suggests the idea that these rings might be remains of the hut-circles of a people who inhabited Eskdale during the earlier or Stone Age. The smallness of the number of these stone rings may be compensated for by the large number of hill-forts, suggesting that at that date the people of Eskdale were not so much a pastoral but a warlike race, dwelling in the forests in times of peace, and in war betook themselves to the hill-forts.

THE CELTIC

1000 B.C. The discoveries in the oldest, or long, barrows, point only to a long-skulled race. But in the round or conical barrows and mounds there are indications that the long-skulled people, probably by colonisation and intermarriage,developed first into an oval, and later into a round-skulled race. No round skull has ever been found in a long barrow, but long skulls have been found in the round barrows.

These facts, together with the discoveries of flint and other implements, suggest a migration of a new race into these Islands during the later Stone Age, and this migration Mr. Read, of the British Museum, places circa 1000 B.C. This race was Celtic, a round headed curly haired, dark complexioned people, for the most part, though some branches of the race were light haired, tending to red. It was this race that built the cairns and made the cists, whose stone implements have been found at Westwater and Camp-Knowes. It contributed very markedly too, both to the complexion and physical features of the present Scottish people. It left as a legacy many superstitions and legends which have entered into the religious notions and literature of Scotland.

THE BRYTHONIC OR CYMRIC

300 B.C. Whether there was one Celtic migration or two is another point upon which ethnologists differ. Mr. Read, one of our greatest authorities, thinks there were two, and the people of the second migration he calls the Brythons. Both Brython and Celt were of Aryan stock. It was probably to this branch of the Celtic race that the Britons of Strathclyde belonged. It was distinguished by the name of Cymri, and though of the same original stock as the older Celtic people it gradually diverged into a distinct family, whose descendants are now found in Wales and Cornwall.

The language spoken by this people, differing only slightly from the Gaelic, is still traceable in Eskdale. It was they who named the rivers Esk and Ewes, and gave names to some of our higher hills and to many of our glens, a strong and virile race, able to perpetuate its qualities down through many centuries and to impress itself profoundly upon the history of the world.

THE ROMAN

130 A.D. Next in order was the occupation by the Romans who left singularly little mark on Eskdale. North of Hadrian's Wall their occupation was wholly military, intermittent and separate from the more intimate life of the people. The Roman influence, in its effect on the language, was not appreciable, but it helped to emphasise the gradual separation of the Strathclyde Celts from the other branches. On the departure of the Romans about 410 A.D., the Celtic tribes were left in a chaos, many reverting to their former pagan customs

THE ANGLIC OR SAXON

670 A. D. Perhaps the most influential factor in the evolution of the people of Eskdale has been the Saxon invasion. The coming of the Saxon affected not only the appearance of the race, but completely altered the structure of the language. The ancient Gaelic or Cymric language of the people of Strathclyde had begun to lose its hold when Malcolm succeeded to the throne of Cumbria in 1056. Then the Scots element soon became the dominating factor in the speech and life of the people. But the Saxon invasion, slowly but surely, brought about the complete Saxonisation of the whole of Eskdale and the lowlands generally, and the Celtic tongue once general in Strathclyde gave way to the language of the colonists.

With the coming of the Saxons we may conveniently group the earlier invasions by the Frisians and the contemporary invasion by the

Angles. All these were Teutonic in race and speech. The Saxons brought to Eskdale the fair complexion and the blue eyes. The conjunction of these features with the darker hues of the Celt produced a type that is still characteristic of the lowlands.

The language was also profoundly affected, not in Eskdale or the lowlands alone, but throughout the east of Scotland and the north of England. This effect has lived longest in the lowlands, and many of the words, phrases, and idioms which are accounted as of the Scots tongue, were contributed by the Angles and the Saxons over 1000 years ago.

The union of Saxon and Celt, and later of Celt and Norseman, is interestingly shown in the occasional conjunction of terms in the placenames of Eskdale, this word itself indeed is a conjunction of the British *Isca* and the Norse *dale*. The welding of place-names is an indication of the gradual decay of racial feeling which would at first be acute between the old and the new settlers.

Through the marriage of Malcolm with Margaret, the disintegrating forces at work on the Celtic language were reinforced, so that by the accession of Alexander III, in 1249, the spoken language of the Celts had entirely disappeared from Eskdale and a Teutonic speech had taken its place.

THE NORSE

800 A.D. In the ninth century the Danes and Norwegians poured down upon the coasts of Scotland, and after much warfare and struggle, established themselves in the country. From their base on the Solway they would speedily spread themselves over both Annandale and Eskdale, an event which can be traced today in the many place names in Dumfriesshire of Norse origin.

Their coming introduced another factor into the progression and development of the people of Eskdale. A tall, fair complexioned, sandy-haired race, pagan in religion but brave and strong in physical powers. The Norse people contributed many of the qualities which are characteristic of the present population of Eskdale, and also some which were perhaps more observable in the grim old days of the Border raiders. Between these raids and the piratical voyages of the Norsemen there is a strong affinity.

Perhaps quite as much as the Saxons, the Norsemen influenced and altered the language. They introduced the word *holm*, for instance, and the word *Langholm* itself is Norse in form. Not a few of the families who afterwards became conspicuous in Eskdale and the Borders, came originally with the Norsemen. Many of our family names are of Norse origin, those ending in *son,* the Andersons, Hotsons, and others, being either Norse or adopted from Norse custom.

THE NORMAN

1150 A.D. The last great migration of an alien people into Eskdale was that which took place when the Norman barons, who had come over with the William the Conqueror in 1066, came into Scotland. This was during the reign of David, whose residence at the English court had familiarised him with the Norman manners, customs and speech. On his accession to the throne he made grants of land on a feudal tenure to many of his Norman friends.

Nowhere was this influx greater or its results more pronounced than in Eskdale and Ewesdale. The old communal or tribal lands were divided amongst the Norman barons. These brought with them into Eskdale servants of Saxon descent, whose intermarriage with the natives helped still further to obliterate the characteristics of the ancient peoples.

This Saxon intermixture was intensified by a further migration which occurred when Malcolm made his notorious raid into Northumberland and Durham in 1070. He then burned and pillaged the country, either putting its people to the sword or taking them as his serfs to Scotland so that, says Simeon of Durham, there was "scarce a Scottish home but had its Anglic slave".

The effect of all these migrations is evident in modern customs and speech and in the system of land tenure. The feudal system was of Norman planting, but so complete was David's policy that the new tenure quickly settled throughout the lowlands.

The Normans exerted also a considerable influence upon the written and spoken language of the people and many words and phrases, which are regarded as Scots, were brought into the language at that time. Some of the customs introduced by the Normans still prevail in village life.

The ringing of the bell in Langholm every evening at eight o'clock was a survival of the old Norman curfew bell. This custom continued well into the twentieth century but presumably ceased at the outbreak of war in 1939. All bell ringing was then forbidden as it was to be used as a warning of invasion.

No trace of Norman architecture is left to us, except stray portions, such as the old sedilia in Canonby kirkyard. There is also the Hasp found some years ago at Wauchope Castle, a rare and beautiful specimen of French enamel work of the School of Limoges of the thirteenth century, no doubt brought over by the De Lindesays

These then are the constituent elements which, during many centuries, have gone to the moulding of the people of Eskdale. Each migration has left an impress, which can be traced in the features of the people, in their mental characteristics, in their customs and beliefs, in their laws and in their language.

Eskdale itself has remained the same throughout all these ages. The rivers run a little deeper in their channels. These channels have changed. The gullies on the hillsides have been eaten deeper by the frosts and storms of many centuries. Forests have given place to fields. The climate has been modified by these physical changes and the wild life of Eskdale has been completely altered. Yet in its main features Eskdale is today what it was to the primitive race who erected the Girdle Stanes or built the great cairns. Through all these ages, however, the people have been changing. Their physical attributes, their colour, their stature, their customs and speech have been slowly modified, and those who now people the valley of the Esk are but the long result of time, the amalgam composed of all these various elements.

CHAPTER 12

THE PLACE-NAMES OF ESKDALE

The various races, left behind them many evidences of their residence in Eskdale. It is especially by the evidences in the language or dialect of a district that their successive occupation can be traced. Words, now regarded by literary purists as provincial, are present in the lowland Scots tongue by an ancient lineage, and have been used in centuries past, not only as the means of expressing the thought and emotion of the people, but as the language of culture and of learning.

The speech in which Burns and other lowland poets wrote was not the patois of an ignorant peasantry, it was a language capable of conveying the thoughts, hopes, loves and sorrows of an intelligent and virile race. Alas, that tongue is fast becoming obsolete, even in Eskdale.

The speech of Eskdale, as of the entire lowlands, is a mixed language containing words and idioms from the Celtic, Saxon, Norse and Norman, with the additions of recent centuries. The words *Celtic and Norse* are used throughout this chapter as sufficiently accurate to indicate all the different branches of these languages

The fact has been already noted that no word, even in local placenames, can now be identified as coming from the Iberian race, which is supposed to have preceded the Celtic in the occupation of our Islands. But with the Celtic era there seems to have begun the naming of places and natural features which continued down the days of the Normans and then proceeded by way of corruption or modification of the original, a process which is still going on.

It is this modification which makes all efforts definitely to fix the origin of the placenames difficult and uncertain. Because a place to-day, for example, is known by a Celtic, Saxon, or Norse appellation, it does not of necessity follow that it actually received its name from the Celts, or the Saxons, or the Norsemen, or that it even existed, say, 1000 years ago. The name may belong to one of these languages, but it may possibly have been given to a particular place long after the people speaking that tongue had disappeared from Eskdale, or, as will be seen, a name attaching to a place now may be compounded of two or even three different root-words.

But whilst this is admitted, it may be assumed that the terms used to denote certain physical features, such as rivers or mountains or homesteads, were brought into the district by the race speaking the language to which the nomenclature belongs. And not unnaturally, it follows that as places are fixed and not liable to changing influences, they will generally retain those early names with possibly some modification.

Arguing back then, we shall not be seriously wrong if we take it that most of the names of natural objects, and of the main physical features of Eskdale, were really bestowed by the people who spoke these languages, and likewise that those placenames which have remained virtually the same for several centuries, date approximately to the periods indicated.

The oldest placenames in Eskdale belong naturally to fixed and permanent objects, such as the rivers, hills and glens, and the various aspects which they present. Consequently we find a large number of the names are Celtic. Some have become united to Saxon or Norse suffixes, as in *Corsholm, Lyneholm, Eskdale, Wauchope*. Others have undergone a change of form as well as conjunction with other root-words. An instance is *Wud*-Carrick, now pronounced and spelt *Wat*-Carrick. In such cases the more modern denomination has probably displaced an original Celtic suffix. But in many cases the entire Celtic name remains. Some of these are here indicated:—

ESK or EWES. Celtic root *uisge,* meaning water or a current. From this root came the early British *Isca*. Variants of the words are *Ouse, Usk, Exe, Axe, Ux* and others.

WAUCHOPE. Probably from the Celtic *wagh,* a den, (or perhaps *wau*, indicating the source of a stream), and the Norse *hope,* a valley. One of the old forms of spelling quoted by R.B. Armstrong is W*alghope.*

ALLANGILL. Is probably compounded of the Celtic (*alwen* or *all,* white, and the Norse *gil,* a ravine.

GARWALD. From the Celtic *garw,* rough, and *alt,* a brook, or possibly the word is a combination of the Celtic *garw* and the Teutonic *wald*, a wood.

In the case of GARWALD WATER the *wald* probably refers to the ravine, but in St. THORWALD'S it is more likely that the meaning is that of a wood, as in the English place-name *wold*. The LONGWOOD referred to in the verses prefacing the Proclamation of the Fair at the Langholm Common-Riding, stretched along the side of Whita, where the remains of it may still be seen in the old oaks near the Round House.

From the same Celtic root *garw,* the river names *Yarrow and Garry* are also derived.

In LYNEHOLM we have *linn,* a pool, and Norse *holm*.

DUMLINNS. In Wauchope Water, possibly from Celtic *dun,* a fortress or hill, and *linn,* giving the pool at the hill.

LYNE. A tributary of the Esk ; also from *linn*.

Curiously enough the Celtic roots do not appear so prominently in the names of the Eskdale hills. *Pen,* meaning a head, or a hill, appears in TIMPEN, PENTON. What has of late years been called the TIMPEN is designated GALASIDE HILL in Blaeu's map of 1654 and in PENANGUS, the ancient name of Mosspaul, (meaning a hill named after Angus, who, perhaps, was the King of this name occupying the Pictish throne about 730), and in the PEN OF ESKDALEMUIR, often called ETTRICK PEN. The word is the equivalent of the Gaelic *ben, as* applied to mountains.

Tor, Celtic for a towering rock, may be the root of TERRONA, spelt by Blaeu *Torronna*. Probably it also enters into TARRAS, though this may be a corruption of the Latin *turrus,* a tower. In either case the reference implied would probably be to Tinnis Hill rather than Whita.

Craig or *carraig* is a Celtic root indicating a rock. We have it in THE CRAIG, and in the Celtic-Norse compound CRAIGCLEUCH, and in WUD-CARRICK, that is *wudu,* Anglo-Saxon a wood, and Celtic *carraig,* a rock, the name being a literal description of the place.

Glen is a Celtic root which has come down to us with its original meaning. Its form in the Gaelic is *gleann,* a valley. In Eskdale it is of frequent occurrence:—

GLENDEARG. *Glen, and dearg, red, i.e.,* the red glen.

DOWGLEN. *Dubh,* black, and *glen:* the black glen.

GLENCORF. *Glen,* and *garw, rough*: the rough glen.

GLENVOREN. *Glen,* and *mhoran,* plenty, or *mhor,* big: the glen of plenty, or the big glen.

GLENFIRRA. *Glen,* and *firean,* an eagle: the eagles' glen.

GLENDIVEN. *Glen,* and probably *dubh,* black.

FINGLAND. Originally Finglen in Blaeu's map, *finn,* white, and *glen:* the white glen.

GLENTENMONT. The higher reach of the Wauchope. There is also the Celtic *cnoc,* meaning a hill. It appears in Eskdale in THE KNOCK and in the pleonasm KNOCKHILL, and in GILNOCKIE, where it is joined to the Norse *gil,* a ravine. THE KNOCK itself is on the farm of Tanlawhill. In Westerkirk parish there are MID-KNOCK and NETHER-KNOCK.

In NEASEHILL we have a pleonasm of Celtic *neas,* a hill, and the Saxon *hill.*

In AUCHENRIVOCK, we have a distinctively Gaelic name. It comes from *auchen, or achadh,* a field, a very common prefix in Scotland; *rivock* is probably a corruption of the Gaelic *riabach,* meaning grey: thus the grey field.

In GALASIDE we get the Celtic *gal,* an open plain, the reference being no doubt to the Castleholm, or possibly from *gala,* clear water, referring to the Esk.

CORSHOLM is the union of the Celtic *cors,* a marsh, and the Anglo-Saxon or Norse *holm.* The word really means the boggy island.

Dun, a fort, is Celtic. It appears in DUNABY, in DUMFEDLING and in DUMLINNS. If the residence of the Celt was on low-lying ground instead of on a hill, it was called *logan* instead of *dun.* This may be the origin of the name of LOGAN WATER, given to one of the sources of the Wauchope.

In BONESE, or BOONIES as it was spelt 200 years ago, and still is so spelt in the Estate papers (and in BONSHAW) the *bon* is probably *ban,* meaning fair or beautiful.

The Celtic *caer or car* also occurs. As already mentioned, it means a stronghold or fort, and in this signification left its name in the farm of KERR, between Wauchopedale and Canonby, and also in the patronymic KER or KERR, a well-known Border name, which has probably descended from the days of the Strathclyde Britons, though certain writers have suggested a Norman origin. It is also found in CARWOODRIG in Ewesdale, originally Carrotrig or Kerriotrig.

In the place-name of Cooms we have the Celtic *cwm,* meaning a hollow or shelter between hills. This, we believe, is the only instance of its survival in the Eskdale district.

In RASHIEL the root may be the Celtic *rhos,* a moor, or perhaps *rasach,* in either of its meanings, the ridge of a hill, or a place covered with shrubwood.

In BAILEY HILL we have the Celtic *bane,* a village. The same word is very common in Ireland as *bail.* In some charters granted after the coming of the Norman barons it is spelt *La Baly.*

The *tan* in TANLAWHILL is probably the Celtic *ton,* the back of a hill or knoll, the *law* and *hill* being one of those duplications already referred to as so frequently found in districts in which there has been a succession of different races. Thus the same root idea is expressed in each of the three syllables.

The race succeeding the Celtic in Eskdale was the Saxon who effected a complete change in the language, substituting the Anglo-Saxon for the old British tongue. They, too have left their traces in the placenames in Eskdale. Not infrequently a Saxon name is conjoined to a Celtic root. Nearly all the distinctive Saxon names for natural objects and features are found in Eskdale. These, so far as they were given to permanent objects, such as hills and streams and burns, very probably date back to the Saxon invasion, but naturally the names given to dwelling places, either singly or in groups, though Saxon or Norse in form, may be of recent date.

Many of the original placenames have, of course, been modified or corrupted by that inevitable transmutation which occurs in a language spoken in various dialects, but many of the original words still remain.

One of the most frequent affixes in Eskdale is *ton* or *toun.* This is the Anglo-Saxon *tun,* meaning an enclosure, and in this sense it has been applied, not only to towns and villages in the lowlands, but even to separate farms. It is still the custom in Eskdale and the lowlands generally to speak of a farm as a *farm-toun.* The *ton* is seen in:—

STAPELGORTOUN. This name is composed of three Anglo-Saxon roots : *Stapel* refers to an authorised market town, and is found in Whitstable, Barnstaple, Dunstable, and others. Trades are now described as *staple*, but in the days of the Anglo-Saxons it was the place that was so styled. *Gor* is a muddy or marshy place, and *toun* is town. So that the name may be construed as the market town on the marsh. What trade

STAPELGORTOUN was staple for can only be conjectured, probably it was wool. In this connection we have the word wool-stapler.

ARKLETON. From Scandinavian *ark*, a temple, and *ton*, or from the Celtic *ar*, a hill, *kil,* a church or cell (e.g. UNTHANK), and *ton*.

ARKIN is from the same root, with possibly the Celtic suffix *kin*, which is also seen in BOYKIN or BYKEN. This suffix seems to be used as a variant of *pen*.

FIDDLETON. Possibly from Celtic *fidd*, a wood, or *fich*, a castle, and *ton*.

KIRKTON, i.e. *kirk* and *ton*, the village grouped around a kirk.

MILNTOWN or MILTON. From Anglo-Saxon *miln*, a mill, and *ton*, the village near the mill; or in some cases the *middle* town. The prefix is frequently met with in Canonby: SARKMILNTOWN, MILNSTEADS, HARELAWMILN, &c.

DAVINGTON. Evidently from the name *David*, i.e. David I., and *ton*.

We have already mentioned that in Eskdale there are placenames made up partly of Celtic and partly of Anglo-Saxon or Norse roots. Some have been given and others are:—

ABERTOWN or EVERTOWN. The Celtic *aber*, indicates the mouth of a river, but it seems doubtful whether in this case it is not a corrupted form of some other prefix. The place not so long ago was called OVERTOWN, and half a mile from it there is still a NETHERTOWN, so possibly there would also be a *Middletown,* a group corresponding to OVERBY, NETHERBY, and MIDDLEBY.

BROCKETLINNS. From Anglo-Saxon *brocc,* a badger, and Celtic *linn*, a pool. Compare with BROCKWOODLEES.

BOGLE-GILL. From the Celtic *bwg*, a spirit, and the Norse *gil,* a ravine.

CARLESGILL. The *car* may be from the Celtic *caer, a* fort, or from *carle,* a man of low social class or a husbandman, but more probably from *Carl,* the name of a Scandinavian hero, and *gil*, a ravine.

The Celtic *root kil,* the synonym of the Welsh *llan*, meaning a cell, the residence of a hermit or a saintly personage, is very seldom found in Eskdale.

One instance, linked to an Anglo-Saxon suffix, is KILNCLEUCH, and of course it is also in KILNGREEN, in which instance the *kil* referred to was possibly the old kirk of Stapelgortoun, although on

Blaeu's map of 1654 there is noted a place called KILHILL near to Stapelgortoun kirk.

In KILNCLEUCH the cell might be that of Thor the Long. The *n* added to *kil is* probably recent.

The word water as applied to a stream is a well known term throughout the south of Scotland. In Eskdale we have WESTWATER, STENNIESWATER, GARWALDWATER, WAUCHOPEWATER, TARRAS WATER, and others. *Water* in the Anglo-Saxon is *waeter,* a pronunciation still used in Teviotdale.

STENNIESWATER is the stony stream, from Anglo-Saxon *stan,* a stone. The same word comes into STANEHOLM SCAR, often wrongly spelt STEENOM, where one time there was a farm.

Burn, so common in Eskdale, is Anglo-Saxon. *Cleuch* is from the Anglo-Saxon *claugh,* a cleft in the rock. It occurs in CRAIGCLEUCH, CLEUCHFOOT, HOGILLCLEUCH, and others.

Haugh is from the Norse *hagi,* pasture ground, and occurs in CRAIGHAUGH and WHITHAUGH.

The Anglo-Saxon *hall,* a safe place, or a stone house, is found in HA'CROFTS, the double L being dropped in conformity with the Scottish custom, CALLISTER HA', and WESTERHALL, the pronunciation of which was formerly Westerha', a name dating only from the seventeenth century. The name given in Blaeu's map of 1654 to Westerhall is DARDERRENN, but in the oldest charters it is DALDORAN or DALDURIANE. The *dor* is probably Anglo-Saxon *deor,* a deer. The *Gal,* which also occurs in DALBETH, an old place on the opposite bank of the Esk below Lyneholm, may be the Norse, but more likely still the Celtic, for dale. *Croft* is a piece of land that has been cropped.

Cote or cot is Anglo-Saxon for a cottage, generally a mud hut, the only instance in Eskdale being the farm of COTE.

Feld, a field, occurs in CALFIELD and GEORGEFIELD. In HAGG-ON-ESK we have the Anglo-Saxon *hagg,* a small estate.

WHITA is from the Anglo-Saxon *hwit* meaning white.

WARBLA, pronounced *Wurbla* and so spelt on Blaeu's map, is probably a modified form *of Wardlaw,* a name given to hills on which the watchers were posted in times of danger. On the first Ordnance Map of 1859 the spelling was Warb Law. *Law is* Anglo-Saxon *hlaw,* a small hill. *Ward* is used in the same sense as in *Warden* of the Marches. We also get the Anglo-Saxon *watch* in the WATCH KNOWE. We thus have precisely the same idea in different forms in WARBLA and WATCH KNOWE, the two hills of observation for the valley.

In MOODLAW, the *law* also refers to a hill. *Mood* is probably a corruption of *mid*, or *middle,* and the word is locally pronounced *midlaw*. The term MOODLAWPOINT referring to a district in the new town of Langholm, is said by old inhabitants to have been given through the farmer of Moodlaw pasturing his sheep at this particular point of the old Meikleholm farm.

BRECKONWRAY, which is now spelt BRACKENWRAE, is a union of the Anglo-Saxon *braccan,* the plural of *bracce,* a tern, and the Norse *wran* or *ra,* a corner. The latter may also be the root of the WRAE in Ewes, though possibly this may be from the Danish *rath*, a fort.

The name *shaw* applied to a wood is fairly frequent in Eskdale, e.g., EARSHAW, SHAW RIG, THE SHAWS, &c. It is from the Anglo-Saxon *scaga,* a little wood.

In that patch of hazel wood on the east side of Castle Hill, known as THE SCROGGS, the happy hunting ground for hazel nuts, beloved of every Langholm boy, we have the Anglo-Saxon *scrob,* meaning brushwood.

DORNIEGILL is doubtless from Anglo-Saxon *deor*, a deer or a wild animal, and the Norse *gil*. Nothing now remains of the steading of Dorniegill. It stood on the right bank of Megget Water, about two miles from its junction with the Esk.

A noticeable omission from the place-names of Saxon origin in Eskdale is that of the suffix *wick,* as in HAWICK.

The ending *ham,* Anglo-Saxon for a home or dwelling place, is seldom found in Eskdale, perhaps the only instance being the farm of MIDDLEHAMS, sometimes wrongly called *Middleholms.*

Reference has been made to the possibility of the placename RIDDINGS being derived from Rhydderch Hael. Or it may be from the Celtic *rhyd,* a ford. The syllable *ing* is usually an indication of a hamlet or village in Anglo-Saxon, therefore it may be the dwelling at the ford.

The Anglo-Saxon *ley,* a pasture land, is found in Eskdale in WOODHOUSELEE, WOODSLEES, EWESLEES, and BROCKWOODLEES.

The Norse appellations in Eskdale are equally common with the

Saxon, to which they are frequently conjoined. The best known is of course *holm*, which is so predominant a suffix in the placenames of the Eskdale valley. The word is also Saxon. Originally it meant an island in a river or bay, hence a meadow near the sea or a river. The instances in which the word is used in Eskdale are numerous and the following may be quoted:—

Langholm, Broomholm, Meikleholm, Castleholm, Arkinholm, Eldingholm, Bowholm, Glencartholm, Nittyholm, Knottyholm, Potholm, Staneholm, Corsholm, Lyneholm, Enzieholm, Flaskholm, The Holm, Murtholm, Stubholm, Bigholms, Billholm, Holmhead.

The name of LANGHOLM is sometimes attributed to Scandinavian origin, but both parts of the name are also Saxon words, and the same may be said of MEIKLEHOLM, which is doubtless from the Saxon *micel,* meaning much.

The suffix *by* or *bye,* which in Eskdale has so often been corrupted into *bie,* is a Norse term meaning a habitation or dwelling place. It appears in NETHERBY, CANONBY, MUMBY, BOMBY, OVERBY, SORBY. The derivation of CANONBY is traced by some to the old ecclesiastical foundation, the Priory at Hallgreen, and in this connection it would mean the residence of the canons. Others connect it with the Latin *Caenobium* from the Greek *Kolvos Blós*, common life, indicating the communal life of the monastery. Near Maryport, in Cumberland, there is a parish called Cross-Canonby.

Another Norse word almost identical with this suffix is byre, a dwelling. It comes into BYREBURN, DINLYBYRE, and YETBYRE. The last is the old name of CASTLE O'ER, or CASTLE OWYRN. The late Mr.Richard Bell gives the meaning as, the chief's stronghold, but a more accurate rendering would probably be the house by the gate.

The Scandinavian term *rig or ryg,* a hill, is often found along the watershed of the Esk, e.g., SHAW RIG, WESTERKER RIG, CALFIELD RIG, THE RIG, HOPSRIG, OVER RIG, PARSON'S RIG, BLACKRIG.

Fell, from the Norse *fjall,* is less frequently met with among the hills of Eskdale, but it appears in COOMSFELL in Tarras, EWENSHOPE FELL at the head of Ewes, and a few others.

The Norse *beck,* a burn, is seldom found, perhaps the only instances being THE BECKS in Wauchopedale and ARCHERBECK in Canonby.

The suffix *gil* is of common occurrence: BOGLEGILL, EFFGILL, CARLESGILL, KERNIEGILL, GABERGILL, and others. In all of these it indicates a ravine.

Grains, as in THE GRAINS, an old farm which once stood behind Wauchope Schoolhouse, and in CHAPEL GRAINS, further up the same valley, and the GRAINS WELL, also in Wauchopedale, and CLERKHILL GRAINS, in Eskdalemuir, is from the Norse *greni,* meaning a branch, as applied to a valley where it divides into other smaller glens, or to the fork of a stream. These seem to be the only instances of the word occurring in the Eskdale district.

Shields, as in BROOMHOLMSHIELDS, ARKLETONSHIELDS, WHITSHIELDS and others, is from the Norse *skali,* a shepherd's hut.

Hope, a small valley between hills, may be either Celtic or Norse. Probably in Eskdale it was the Scandinavians who brought it into use. It appears in WAUCHOPE, TUDHOPE, HOPSRIG, MARTINHOPE, WOLFHOPE, and many others.

Hass, a hill pass, is seldom found, but we get it in SORBY HASS, the wild hill-road leading from Ewesdale into Eskdale, in WRAE HASS close to it, and in GUILE HASS at the head of Carrotrig Burn. The word *hass,* as applied to the throat, once current in Eskdale, is now obsolete.

The word *thwaite,* a clearing, is not so common as in Cumberland, indeed it is hardly found at all in Eskdale. It is present in HARPERWHAT and THORNIEWHAT.

In COPELAWGAIR the first syllable may be the Anglo-Saxon *cop,* a hill or mound, as in Copshaw. If so, then there is a duplication in adding *law.* Or the root may be the Danish *copen,* as in Copenhagen, i.e. a place for traders. *Gair* is also found in RAWGAIR, the name of the hillside between Warbla and Earshaw.

In ELDINGHOLM, the name given to the holm on which the present Established Kirk of Langholm stands, we have the old north-country word *elding,* meaning fuel, doubtless derived from the Norse *eld,* fire. In this case the name suggests that once the holm was thickly covered with brushwood, instead of the stately oaks and beeches of recent years.

The word *dale,* which is found so abundantly in the lowlands, and in Cumberland and Yorkshire, is a Norse appellation. It is said that in England there are no fewer than one hundred and fifty-two valleys known as dales. This suggests the wide extent of the Norse settlements.

Both in the south of Scotland and north of England the Norse influence in place-names and in the general dialect of the people has been most marked.

In the places named after wild animals we get a glimpse into that far-past age when Eskdale was the habitat of species now completely extinct in the district. These placenames are suggestive of their having been the special resorts of these animals, e.g., BROCKETLINNS and BROCKWOODLEES would be the resorts of the *badger,* TODSHAWHILL of the *fox*, WOLFHOPE, and WOLFCLEUCH of the *wolf,* CATGILL of the *wild cat,* DORNIEGILL of the *deer,* and so on.

Some discussion has taken place anent the derivation of CASSOCK in Eskdalemuir. The local pronunciation is *Cassa,* and this has suggested the theory that it might indicate the locality of an old Roman causeway, which in Eskdale is also pronounced *cassa,* and not *causey* as in some parts of Scotland. It appears much more probable, however, that the name is derived from the Latin *casa,* a cottage. Compare with *Candida Casa* in Galloway.

The place-name WOODHOUSE, occurring so frequently throughout the Borders, either in this form or in conjunction with a suffix, relates to that period in local history when the chief house in the hamlet was built of wood and not of mud, as those of the vassals were. It is, therefore, almost synonymous with TOWER.

For lists of words derived from the Celtic and Norse, now or recently in regular use in the speech of Eskdale, see Appendix 1.

CHAPTER 13

THE NORMAN BARONS

David the First came to the throne of Scotland in 1124 on the death of Alexander his brother. The new king, in whom there met the Celtic and Saxon lines of kings, had already ruled, as Earl, over Cumbria, in which territory Eskdale was situated. With his accession another epoch in the history of Scotland dawned. David had spent some of his earlier years at the English court, where, as the Earl of Northampton, he had an acknowledged position.

During this impressionable period of his life he had been brought into close touch with the Norman Barons who had settled in England after the Conquest. He was considerably influenced by them and conceived an admiration for many of their customs, their language, and especially for that theory of the social basis of society on which they erected their feudal system. On his accession to the Crown of Scotland, David set about the entire reorganisation of its system of land tenure. To carry out this purpose quickly and efficiently, he granted to his Norman acquaintances the superiority of lands on a strictly feudal tenure, that of vassalage and obedience to himself as the chief feudal lord.

Throughout the Celtic and Saxon periods the tenure of land in Scotland had been, more or less, on a feudal basis. The feudal idea, indeed, lay at the root of the tribal system and also entered into the social and economic life of the clans. But *their* feudal tenure was indigenous and had a communal purpose, whereas that now introduced by David was a foreign importation and was personal and regal. Consequently it entirely shifted the fulcrum of government. At its base lay the theory that "every man should find a lord", and on this axiom David now proceeded to set up a system which profoundly altered both the political and social history of the country. David had inbibed this feudal theory from his Norman associates, but in essence it was only a modification of the system of fiefage which had long prevailed in the Germanic states.

The introduction of the Norman nobles into the lowlands produced an effect out of all proportion to their numbers. At the most, only a few thousands of them settled in the country. Their disproportionate influence arose through the power which, by virtue of the feudal laws, they were enabled to wield over their vassals and bondmen.

As the superior under the feudal system of tenure, the Baron was a person of very great authority. It was largely by virtue of his power over these Barons and their Anglic vassals that, during his Earldom, David had exercised his sovereignty over Cumbria. Both then and during his reign, all the grants of land in Scotland were made upon the feudal condition of vassalage and military service.

This vassalage was fundamental to feudalism and it provides the explanation of the many changes in the ownership of the lands in Eskdale during the centuries which followed the reign of David. Baron succeeded baron as the lord of these territories, and the changes were nearly always due to some violation of this basic feudal principle. Failure to provide military help or to give due service and homage was at once visited by forfeiture.

Grants of land were made by Royal charter, but were subject to repeated confirmation, or as frequent revocation, if the feudal conditions were not fulfilled. Their possession of those estates did not render the Barons themselves immune from service. They had to hold courts and dispense justice on behalf of the King, but as his representatives, liable to be called upon for an account of their stewardship.

The essential dogma of the feudal system was that the King was the embodiment of the State, and was also the fount and origin of wealth and of every other good. As well as these civil duties, military service was being continually demanded of the Barons, who were likewise responsible for the good conduct and obedience of their dependants.

Another feature of the policy of David I speedily made itself felt in Eskdale. The personal character of that King is said to have been one comprising attractive qualities. Fond of gardening and tree culture and of gentle habits, he was devoted also to religious exercises. One of his successors, with dry humour, styled him "ane sair sanct to the Croon".

His inclination to serious things doubtless came from his mother,

Queen Margaret, for his father, Malcolm Canmore, was not by nature either gentle in habit or religious in practice. David showed his sympathy with the church by gifts of land to religious communities and of these benefactions Eskdale received a fair share.

Along with the feudal system there came into being the practice and recognition of chivalry as an obligation upon those placed in high positions and in touch with the throne itself. A trace of this practice of chivalry survives in Eskdale in the name, *Turnerholm*, given to that strip of land, divided by the Ewes road, immediately south of the Whitshields Burn. The name is a corruption of, *Tourney-holm*, the place where were decided those tournaments, combats and tests of military skill or courage which were such prominent features of the romantic days of chivalry.

In its main effects the Norman invasion was nowhere more complete than in Eskdale and the neighbouring dales. These were portioned out amongst David's Norman friends. Amongst those thus introduced into Eskdale were the De Kunyburgs, Avenels, De Rossedals, De Lindsays, Lovels, Frasers, Moffats and later the Douglases. Annandale was awarded to Robertus de Brus, a Norman name which, modified into Robert the Bruce, was afterwards to become dear to the heart of every Scot.

Teviotdale was divided among the families of Ridel, Corbet, Percie, and others. Lands in Clydesdale and the Lothians were given to Walterus de Lindesaya, whose family was afterwards to play a very influential part in the history of Eskdale and Wauchopedale. Other Norman names appearing in Dumfriesshire at this time were Comyn, Jardine, Sinclair, Johnstone, Balliol, Grant, and Fleming.

It will be seen from this list that the Bruce was of Norman blood, as was the father of Sir William Wallace, the greatest and most unselfish of all our Scottish patriots. The elder Wallace is said to have come from Wales with the Norman Walter Fitz-Allan, who founded the Scottish Royal House of Stewart. Margaret Crawford, the mother of the patriot, is said to have traced her descent back to Thor the Long.

The name of Maxwell which was destined to wield so great a power throughout Dumfriesshire, and especially in Eskdale, was, in ancient documents, written in the Norman form of Maccusville[1.] But the original form of the name seems to have been Maccus-well, from a Saxon lord one Maccus who lived about 950 near Kelso, and there became possessed of a famous salmon pool.

The name of Moffat, with its synonym Mowatt, is said to have come from the Norman De Montealt. Frequent reference will be made in the following pages to the Maxwells, but something should be here noted of the connection with Eskdale of the family of Moffat.

R. B. Armstrong mentions[2] that there are records of four charters from Robert I (the Bruce) of lands in the Barony of Westerker to persons of the name of Moffat. Two of these were grants to Adam Moffat of the lands of Knocis and Crokis, (the Knock and Crooks), and two to Thomas Moffat of the lands of Glen-crofts and Suegill, and another of the lands of Suegill only. These latter places cannot now be identified. The Moffats continued, as owners, to occupy the Knock, in Eskdale, until it was purchased by the Buccleuch family, probably by Anne, Duchess of Buccleuch and Monmouth.

When the Duchess came to reside at Branxholme, at the beginning of the eighteenth century, she made it her policy to buy all the lands in the district she could possibly obtain. Thereafter the Moffats remained in the Knock, or Mid-knock, as tenants of the Duke of Buccleuch until 1905. The last tenant of the name was Mr. Robert Moffat, J.P., of Gowanlea, Canonby, who entered into the tenancy in succession to his father, the late James Moffat. The termination of so long an occupancy, dating as we have seen from about 1300, and probably without parallel in Eskdale, was a matter of keen regret to his Grace the Duke of Buceleuch.

Some of the Moffats of the Knock, it is said, accompanied Robert the Bruce to Bannockburn. From the Privy Council Records it appears that on August 12th, 1504, King James V held a Court at Dumfries, and amongst other business despatched was the trial of John Litill for the cruel slaughter of the King's liege man Thomas Moffet, of Knock, and "being at the King's horn for the same slaughter, and for art and part for supplying and assisting the rebels of Eskdale". Of this crime Litill was found guilty and was hanged.[3]

In this manner, then, began Eskdale to take on some of those characteristics which it still retains, not a few of which were acquired from the Norman Barons who had so summarily dispossessed the Saxon settlers, even as they themselves had dispossessed the ancient British chieftains.

CHAPTER 14

THE BARONIES

With the settlement in Scotland of the Norman and English Barons, the entire political administration of the country underwent a change. The government by the King, with the advice and consent of the Seven Earls, which had been the constitutional rule, now gave place to a system imported from abroad. In the place of the Earls, David set those Barons of Norman or English race whom he had brought into Scotland on his accession and amongst them he divided the land.

The areas over which the Barons were placed were appropriately termed Baronies and these corresponded roughly to the Manors of England. These territories were granted, usually by charter, to the favourites of the King, to be enjoyed by them at His royal will and pleasure, or during such time as the Barons might remain loyal to His person and throne. The latter stipulation was essential to the feudal system, especially in Scotland, because many of the Barons introduced by David were already vassals of Edward of England, and the feudal obligations to the two thrones were often difficult to adjust.

A further consideration for the due enjoyment of these possessions was obedience and military service. Occasionally the Barons were seriously distracted by their being under the same rule of service to the two different Kings. The vacillation of some of the Scottish Barons during the War of Independence was induced by these irreconcilable obligations, which afford the key to what is otherwise very puzzling.

By remembering this, the seemingly arbitrary actions of Edward I may perhaps appear in a different perspective, and also the apparent lack of patriotism of many of the Scoto-Norman Barons during those days of trial and testing. The same military service and the same obedience which the Barons gave to the sovereign, they exacted from their vassals and from all their feudal inferiors. The system certainly had the recommendations of simplicity and ordered arrangement.

One of the immediate results of this more settled order was that the people were enabled to attend more zealously and continuously to the cultivation of their land, which had not been possible during the frequent wars which previously harassed the country. The pious habit of the King of making settlements of the religious orders also helped this civilising process.

The monks of the conventual houses were skilled in agriculture and other useful crafts and thus they were enabled to instil habits of industry into the surrounding population. This movement, however, was arrested, however, by the war which followed the attempted usurpation by Edward I of England. In like manner, the commercial intercourse which had been steadily developing between Scotland and England received a severe check, which, so far as Eskdale and the Borders were concerned, was not to be completely overcome for several centuries.

The Barons who had settled on lowland soil soon accommodated themselves to the requirements of their new allegiance, and throughout the troublous years which were to follow most of them remained loyal to the Scottish cause, although there were some exceptions.

A Barony, then, was the feudal possession and the sphere of influence of the Baron. Within its limits he had almost unlimited power over tenants and vassals, being subject only to the overlordship of the King, from whom directly he held his rights and privileges. These powers were not only political and administrative, but also judicial. Within his Barony the Baron possessed not only all the subordinate powers of fine and imprisonment, but also held the right of dismemberment and wielded absolute powers of life and death.

It must be admitted, however, that though the vassals and inferiors were often arbitrarily treated by their Barons or immediate superiors, they were, nevertheless, recognised as occupying a definite position in the State, and in Scotland this position was respected more than in any other feudal country. When a change of ownership occurred it was marked by some ceremony which took place, sometimes in the church, sometimes in the churchyard. Such a ceremony would doubtless serve as a proof of title in the absence of a charter or a bond.

From the time of David to that of Robert the Bruce, Annandale and Eskdale were both under this baronial jurisdiction, which was separate from, and practically independent of, that of the sheriff. In Annandale such jurisdiction was exercised by the ancestors of the Bruce, but in Eskdale, it was exercised by the different land owning Barons. The county of Dumfries, as then constituted, consisted of the Sheriffdom of Nithsdale, the Stewartry of Annandale, and the Regality of Eskdale, jurisdictions approximating roughly to the three main river systems.

The Regality of Eskdale consisted of the different Baronies enumerated below. The Lord of the Regality held the same powers over the larger area that the Baron himself held over the smaller. Should the Lord of Regality fail to perform his judicial functions, these reverted theoretically to the Sheriff, but, in actual practice all the powers and privileges were again assumed by the King himself.

In 1610, by Royal charter Langholm was created a free Barony, with an area carved out of several of the other Baronies of Eskdale. Such a burgh was inferior in status and privileges to a Royal burgh, but there were assigned to it some of the prerogatives of the Baron or the Lord of Regality, though to him many rights were still reserved.

Gradually most of these special prerogatives, exercised by the Baron within his Barony, fell into disuse, notably his capital jurisdiction, and his right of dismemberment and imprisonment in civil cases, but it was not until 1747 that most of his judicial functions, and certain other privileges, were formally resumed by the Crown.

The Eskdale Baronies, which, in a rough and indefinite way, comprised the entire dale, were:—

STAPELGORTOUN

WESTERKER

DUMFEDLING

WAUCHOPE

LANGHOLM

BRYNTALLONE, BRETTALACH or CANONBY

TARRAS

It does not appear from the records that Ewesdale was ever constituted into a separate Barony, though in some of the documents allusion is made to the Lordship of Ewes. Probably it was apportioned between Stapelgortoun and Westerker and in its northern parts it was held by smaller owners.

In estimating the effect of this Baronial settlement and jurisdiction, regard must also be paid to the rise into positions of power of the conventual foundations, to which, not only the King himself, but the Barons as well, made frequent and considerable grants of land or teinds and other privileges.

In Eskdale there was a considerable number of these foundations, not all of them being under the same diocesan authority. The growing influence of these religious houses afterwards created a factor often distinct from the power of the Barons. Thus the monasteries became in effect Barons and exercised all their feudal functions. This was legally the case with the higher dignitaries of the church, both in Scotland and England.

The Bishops of the Palatinate counties of Durham and Lancaster, especially, held their lands on the ordinary feudal tenure. They were not infrequently called upon to marshal their vassals and lead them into the fight. The Regality of Eskdale corresponded to these Palatinate counties, whose rights and duties were akin to those attached to the lordship of the Regality. In the Regality of Hexham, the Bishops of the early church also exercised Palatinate rights.

It is worthy of note, too, that the monks were as eager as the barons to use and enjoy the sports of the field. They preserved their forest and fishing rights as tenaciously as they held their dogmas.

Attached to each Barony there was, what might be called, a municipal or baronial corn mill, at which the holders of land were required, as a condition of their tenure, to have all their grinding done. The tenancy of the mill, with all its concurrent privileges, was commonly given with the grants of land, and, as a result of this custom, the religious foundations often possessed this, even as they acquired other, industrial privileges. To the vassals or feuars there was no option given of selecting any other mill for the grinding of their corn. They were feudally bound to go to the mill within the Barony, and the miller, or his superior, had grounds of action against any one who failed to perform this condition of tenure.

This law continued to a comparatively recent date. As in the case mentioned below, grants were sometimes made which carried with them the privilege of grinding at the Barony mill *without multure*. According to the old Scots law, multure was the quantity of grain payable to the miller for grinding the corn for the tenant.

From the frequent mention of freedom from multure, it would appear that the feudal superior was, on the principle of to him that hath shall be given, generally exempt from the dues, but that his vassals and inferiors were always required to pay the tribute. The monks, however, had all their goods and merchandise admitted duty free.

The mill of Stapelgortoun would be a very important centre of activity in the "toun". It probably stood on that side of the river opposite to the feudal castle, which is still called the Milnholm. Near to the present Milnholm House there are evidences of a mill lade once having existed.

The mill belonging to the Barony of Westerker was on the Shiel Burn. From a rent roll of the Buccleuch Estates supplied to the Commission of 1679, we find that "the milne of Shiel and Holm with the pertinents were sett in tack to the Laird of Westerhall for 21 years". In later years there was another mill at the Knock.

Wauchope mill was at the Earshaw, a little to the west of the Big Dowie Stane. On Blaeu's map it is marked on the left bank of the Wauchope, but we hazard the suggestion that the mill was not there, but on the right bank of the river. An examination of the ground in the recess formed by the curve of the hill, about a hundred yards west of the Big Dowie Stane, suggests that a dam had once run in this place. The bed of gravel can be traced almost into Wauchope. If this was not the actual site of the mill, it must at some date have been used for a similar purpose.

Langholm mill was of course where it still stands to-day, but has not been a mill for a long time. It was, for a number of years, a small farm belonging to the Buccleugh Estates. Around the mill was clustered the mill-town, a name attaching until quite recently to the dwelling house at the end of Ewes Bridge. Today, the Rugby ground is situated there.

To the tenancy of the "corn and walk-milne of Langholm", was sometimes attached the right to farm "the pettie customs of Langholm and salmon fisheries of Esk and Ewes". We read of one such tenancy held by Robert Elliot and Jannet Maxwell, his spouse, at a rental of £466 13s. 4d. Scots, or about £39 sterling.

The mill of Bryntallone Barony, or Canonby, as it afterwards came to be called, was at the Hollows. Where the Tarras mill stood does not appear to be known, unless the old mill which stood near to Sorby served for Ewes and Tarras jointly, an arrangement not unlikely, seeing

seeing that farms both in Ewes and Tarras were comprised in the Barony of Stapelgortoun. There was also a mill attached to Arkleton, and it doubtless served for the higher parts of Ewesdale. That at the Holm of Eskdalemuir no doubt belonged to the Barony of Dumfedling.

STAPELGORTOUN

Of all the Baronies created in Eskdale that of Stapelgortoun was the most compact and preserved for the longest time its ancient Baronial boundaries. Perhaps owing to its geographical position it came to be the most considerable and powerful of them all, developing into a town of some importance. Afterwards, in 1628, it was merged into the Burgh of Barony of Langholm under the charter of the Earl of Nithsdale.

Stapelgortoun appears to have had some claim to the dignity of a burgh. Until a comparatively recent date there was within the Barony a tract of some twentysix acres of land known as the burgh-roods of Stapelgortoun. This portion remained distinct from the rest of the Barony. At one time it was in the possession of the Earl of Annandale, the only land he owned in Eskdale, and it ran as a wedge into the Duke of Buccleuch's land.

The explanation given concerning these twentysix acres is that, originally, they were church lands, granted to the Knights of St. John of Jerusalem as a reward or thank-offering for the defeat of the Saracens in the Crusades. They were, consequently, held as inalienable until, at the Reformation, they reverted to the Crown and were afterwards granted to the Earl of Annandale.

When first mentioned, the Barony of Stapelgortoun, which extended southwards from Westerker on both banks of the Esk, was in the possession of one William de Kunyburg, to whom, evidently, the Barony had been granted by David I in the twelfth century.

The boundaries of the Barony are difficult to demarcate exactly. Probably it lay between the neighbouring Baronies of Westerker and Langholm, and extended, as a fourteenth century rent-roll would show, into Ewesdale, and included Arkin, Tarrisholm, Rashiel, and Whitshields. Westward it would march with the Barony of Wauchope. The so-called Roman road along the flank of the hill, known as the Timpen, was probably the main line of communication between the two Baronies and also between Stapelgortoun and Canonby.

During the reign of Alexander III a son of the above named Sir William de Kunyburg was in possession of the lands and he granted to Herbert Maxwell one carucate of land in Langholme in feu-farm. A carucate, or ploughland, was the extent of land that a team of oxen could plough in one season.

Some of the boundaries of this grant were defined as: "Beginning at the end of Langholme, as the fountain of St. Patrick runs down into the Eske and ascends in the same direction as far as the Blakesike which descends into the Eske . . ."[1] The grant also included part of the Langfauld, and half a carucate of land in Brakanwra, and there was added to the grant the right "that the said Herbert and his heirs shall grind at the mill of Stabilgortoun freely without multure".

There appears to be little further trace in Eskdale of the Kunyburg family. A daughter of the second Sir William married Sir John Fraser of Ewes, to whom there was given, evidently as a marriage portion with his wife, a grant of the lands of Rig, in Westerkirk, on payment of a nominal acknowledgement. This mention of Herbert Maxwell is the first occurrence of the name in Eskdale, where, in later centuries, it was to be so intimately associated with the varying fortunes of the valley.

In 1281, however, Herbert Maxwell, or de Makiswell, resigned these lands of Langholm and Brakanwra. Possibly they reverted to the Crown on the decease of Sir William de Kunyburg.

Alexander III then conferred the lands of Stapelgortoun on Sir John of Lyndesay, his chamberlain. Four years later the King made Lyndesay another gift of lands in Stapelgortoun and Wauchope. It is as feudal Barons of Wauchope that the Lindsays principally figure in the history of Eskdale, but even at this period, about 1290, they must have wielded a paramount influence throughout the district of which the town of Langholm is now the centre.

Sir Philip Lindsay, son of Sir John, had a son, also named John, who seems to have adopted a religious life and become canon of Glasgow. At Newbattle, in 1315, he resigned into the hands of King Robert the Bruce, the Barony of Stapilgortoun[2] This was possibly, because being a monk, he could not hold property on his own behalf and separate from his community.

His father, Sir Philip, was an English as well as a Scottish Baron, and held lands in Cumberland, Northumberland, and Lincolnshire under Edward I, with whom he sided in the wars of succession. Bannockburn had only recently been fought, and Bruce was now sifting the wheat from the chaff of the Scottish Baronage so it could have been as a part of this process that the resignation of John Lindsay occurred.

The lands thus reverting to the King were granted by him in 1319 to James Douglas, surnamed The Good. Other grants, also within the Barony of Stapelgortoun, were made from time to time to Sir James for his homage and service. On his death they all passed to his heir, Sir Hugh Douglas.

The annual value of the Barony of Stapelgortoun was (*circa* 1376) returned at this time as under:—

PROPRIETORS

Stapilgortoun	£10 0s 0d
Langholme	£6 0s 0d
Brakanwra	£6 13s 4d
Dalblane, with Rig	£6 13s 4d

TENANDRIA

Carlowsgyl	£0 4s 4d
Bondby	£4 0s 0d
Cowchargland	£6 0s 0d
Cragg	£6 13s 4d
Douglenn	£5 0s 0d
Ardkane and Tarrisholme	£20 0s 0d
Rischelbusk	£2 0s 0d
Tenetschel	£1 4s 0d
Quitschel	-----------

Near to Stapelgortoun kirk stood the Castle of Barntalloch, its site now, alas, only a grassy mound. It was doubtless originally a Baronial house of considerable strength, encircled as it was by the river Esk. That William de Kunyburg built or occupied this castle is now largely a matter of conjecture. But it became the centre of a hamlet, which served as the market town for an extensive area.

WESTERKER

The Barony of Westerker was situated between the Barony of Stapelgortoun and Dumfedling, or upper Eskdale. The Rev. James Green, writer of the Statistical Account of 1841, says "This name is derived from the British *caer,* a fortlet, which stood near the hamlet of Westerker upon the Megget Water a little above its confluence with the Esk. In Scoto-Saxon times this was named Wester Caer, or Ker, to distinguish it from the Eastern Caer, which is still visible on the farm at Effgill. There is another supposition that Westerkirk derived its name from being the most westerly of the Five Kirks of Eskdale".

The Statist of 1793 refers to Westerkirk as being in the Barony of Hawick. The first Baron of whom we have knowledge was Sir William de Soulis. But mention is made of Westerker some years earlier than the appearance of Soulis.

During the wars of succession the valley of the Esk was claimed by Edward I, King of England, as within the territories of his kingdom. In 1298 he issued an Order dated from Newcastle upon Tyne to "his people of Westerkere in the valley of the Esk", appointing "our faithful and beloved Simon de Lindsay" chief keeper of the district, and commanding the attention and obedience of the people. Simon was the second son of Sir John Lindsay previously mentioned.

It ought to be said concerning this Order that people of Eskdale never, apart from some of the Barons such as the Lindsays, recognised the right of the English King to their obedience. Soon afterwards Edward formally acknowledged that all the lands of the monks of Melrose, which included the Barony of Westerker, belonged to the kingdom of Scotland.

Soulis had received the charter of these lands, described as being "in the Barony of Watistirkir in the valley of the Esk and shire of Roxburgh", from John of Grahame. He came into possession through descent from the daughter of Robert Avenel, who had held lands both in the Barony of upper Eskdale and in that of Westerker. Soulis forfeited these lands to the Crown during the war of succession and Robert I, who had the previous year at Berwick confirmed the Graham charter, now granted one moiety of the Barony to the conventual house of Melrose, and the other he gave to Sir James Douglas.

From another charter quoted by Mr. A. Bruce Armstrong, it would appear as if Sir James had been given the enjoyment of the entire Barony, but the term *whole Barony* must be construed as meaning only this moiety, seeing that Robert I had already granted charters of lands in Westerker to the Moffats.

Certain lands in Westerker were bestowed on one Sir James Lovel who also held lands in Ewes were forfeited by the treason of Lovel in the reign of David II, who then granted them to Sir William Douglas. After the battle of Neville's Cross in 1346, however, the half Barony of Westerker was again settled, by Edward II of England, on Richard Lovel. In 1354 David II restored them to William, Lord of Douglas.

The rent-roll of Westerker is interesting because of the names of lands there given, some of which are now impossible to identify, and also because of the Norman-French style in which some of them are set forth. Thus:—

PROPRIETORS

Wodkoclandis	£1 0s. 0d.
Dalbech	£4 0s. 0d.
Le Irahw	£0 4s. 4d.
Crimyanetoun	£5 6s. 8d.
La Schilde	£2 13s. 4d.
La Wdhond	£2 0s. 0d.
Watirstirkertoun	£4 13s. 4d.
Albraisterland	£3 6s. 4d.
Terre dominice	£2 0s. 0d.
Le Howis (in manu domini)	£2 0s. 0d.
Lyneholme	£1 4s. 0d.

TENANDRIA

Eskdalemur	{ c. s. tenente Domino }
La Baly	Ade de Glendenwyne
Le Howis et the Harperswate	£3 0s. 0d.
Le Knock	£6 13s. 4d.
Botkane	£3 6s. 8d.
Dalduran	£8 0s. 0d.
Ivegill	£2 0s. 0d.
Pegdale	£8 0s. 0d.
Megdale	£5 0s. 0d.
Glenscharne	
Glenchroichon	
Le Wetbothinis	
Glendow	£4 0s. 0d.

The above roll, and also that of Stapelgortoun, was taken by Mr. A. Bruce Armstrong from the *Morton Registers*.

Several of these places still retain the names here given or are easily recognisable, but others are impossible of exact identification.

DUMFEDLING

Concerning the early history of the part of Eskdale now comprised in the parish of Eskdalemuir, there is little information on record. It is generally accepted that most of the lands of upper Eskdale were in the Barony of Westerker. Support is given to this idea by the record of Sir Adam Glendonwyn being a tenant in 1376 of the lands of "Eskdale mur and La Baly" within the Barony of Westerker, but whether Eskdale mur was anything more than a vassal's holding is very doubtful.

Other evidences point to there having been a separate unit in the feudal division of Eskdale with Dumfedling as its centre. Justice was dispensed and business transacted at Stapelgortoun and Dumfedling[3] which seem to have been the administrative centres of Eskdale, though curiously enough the gallows, then an instrument very freely employed in the administration of the law, was situated in Westerker. Mr. A. Bruce Armstrong mentions that David I, in return for certain services rendered, granted a charter to Robert Avenel of the lands of "Tumloher and Weidkerroc in Upper Eskdale".

There was generally a church attached to a Barony, and that at Wat-Carrick served the district comprised in these grants. At Wat-Carrick, only the old kirkyard remains to identify the spot where the kirk once stood. From an entry in the Taxt Roll of Melrose, it would appear that the terms Dumfedling and Eskdalemuir designated the same place and were interchangeable. This Barony may therefore be conveniently distinguished as that of Dumfedling.

In his later years, Robert Avenel entered the monastery of Melrose. He had previously invested the monks with the teinds of the Barony. He died in 1186 and was buried at Melrose, as was also his son Gervase, who had succeeded him.

His grandson, Roger Avenel, confirmed the various grants, but disputed with the monks as to the forest rights which his grandfather had expressly reserved in his gift of the teinds. Incidentally, in the award made by the King and his Barons in this dispute, an interesting glimpse is given of the wild life of Eskdale at this date. The monks, we observe, were prohibited from snaring any animals except wolves.

Roger Avenel's only child married Henry de Graham, who by her became possessed of all the lands. Henry Graham's grandson, Sir John, conferred additional privileges to those already given by the Avenels to the conventual house of Melrose. He yielded to the monks all the rights of hunting, fishing, and hawking, which the Avenels had so jealously reserved. He also added the right of adjudging to death anyone who robbed the property. A somewhat doubtful compliment to a religious foundation!

From Graham the lands passed to Sir William Soulis and then, on his forfeiture, to Sir James Douglas The obscurity concerning the bestowal of the whole Barony of Westerker on Douglas may be cleared by considering the Barony of Dumfedling to have been included in the grant. On this assumption, the Douglas would, in 1321 be possessed of virtually all the lands within the Baronies of Westerker and Dumfedling, except those in the former, which Robert the Bruce had given to the Moffats, viz., the Knock and Crooks.

The Avenels were Barons of considerable importance. Robert, the Baron, had a daughter by whom William the Lion had a natural daughter Isabel, who, in 1183, married Robert Bruce, the third Lord of Annandale. Both his son Gervase, and his grandson Roger, were in turn hostages for the Scots King.

The ownership of considerable portions of the lands comprised within the Barony or *Tennendrie* of Dumfedling underwent frequent changes. A considerable number of new proprietors were created after the battle of Arkinholm in 1455, and some of the smaller lairdships, then formed, continued into the twentieth century, whilst others existed separately until only the middle of the eighteenth century.

An estate plan of the parish of Eskdalemuir, dated 1718, shows the subjoined lairdships then independent of the Duke of Buccleuch but which later belonged to him:—

Nether Cassock; Aberlosk, later part of Langshawburn; Grassyards, later part of Dumfedling; Johnstone; Clerkhill; Rennaldburn and Cot.

The lairdships still in existance at the beginning of the twentieth century were Davington; Over Cassock; Raeburn; Moodlaw and Castle O'er or Yetbyre. The lands of Burncleuch belonged to the laird of Crurie, who exchanged them with the Duke of Buccleuch for those of Castlehill, which adjoined his property of Yetbyre.

WAUCHOPE

In 1281 Sir John Lindsay, great chamberlain to Alexander III, was in possession of the lands of Langholm. In 1285 he received lands in Stapelgortoun and Wauchope. His son, Sir Philip, died in 1317 and was succeeded by his son John, canon of Glasgow.

Sir John Lindsays second son, Sir Simon, was made guardian of Hermitage Castle by Edward. He was taken prisoner by the Scots at Bannockburn, but was afterwards released. Robert the Bruce restored his son, Sir John, to the Barony of Wauchope. This knight, who was forfeited by Edward Balliol in 1340 fought on the side of David II at Neville's Cross in 1346, and there lost his life, David himself being made a prisoner.

The Lindsays continued in possession of Wauchopedale until 1505. They also held Fiddleton, Blakhaw, Glenvorane, Glenvachane, Hardway, Mosspaw, Unthank and Mosspeble in Ewes. At that date John Lindsay was sentenced to forfeit his life and his estates for the slaying of Bartholomew Glendonwin, the sheriff or bailie of Eskdale. Justice was apparently satisfied with the sentence only, for it was never carried out. All these lands in Wauchopedale and Ewesdale were indeed forfeited, but John Lindsay soon afterwards received grants of lands in other places to compensate him.

The lands in Wauchope were restored in 1593. Mr. A. Bruce Armstrong says[4] they remained in the possession of the Lindsays until 1707, when they passed to the House of Buccleuch, but this statement is scarcely accurate. As early as 1679 the Duke and Duchess of Buccleuch were in possession of virtually the whole of Wauchopedale. In the information given to the Commission of this date, consisting of Walter, Earl of Tarras, Alexander, Master of Melvile, Sir William Scott of Harden, elder, and Sir William Scott, younger, the following farms are returned as then belonging to them:—Irving, Coldstoune, Middleholm, Mirtholme, Stubholme, Ersha, Hole, Neishill, Cross-Mungo, Blochburnfoot, Bigholms, Glentinmont, Whitchope Knowe, Hallishaw, Racknows, Wallholm, Dewiscore, Kinglandfoot, Currieholm, Westwater, Puttingstaneholm, St. Bride Hill, Brigstand, Waterholm, Glencorve, Tanabie, Water Grains, Cleuchfoot, Calfield, "and the milne together with the Rownie Hole sett to Hugh Scott minister".

This list is quoted in full partly to show that there could have been very little left for the Lindsays to possess, and partly to give some idea of the population of Wauchope at that date. This list comprises no fewer than thirty farms and a corn mill. Included are Irving, Coldstoune, &c., which one would have expected to find in Canonby.

LANGHOLM

The Barony of Langholm was one of less importance than either Stapelgortoun or Wauchope and like that of Tarras seems to have been of later creation. It was situated partly where the Old Town of Langholm now stands. The first notice of the lands of Langholm is the grant made by Sir William de Kunyburg of Stapelgortoun to Herbert de Maxwell in1268 of one carucate of land in Langholme, which, from the boundaries defined, appears to have been virtually what are now known as the Castle Holm and Kilngreen. As already indicated this land was resigned in 1281 to Sir John of Lyndsay.

The occasional mention in contemporary records of the lands of Arkin (or Ardkyne) may relate to what in some of them is called Langholm During the fourteenth and fifteenth centuries the site of the Old Town of Langholm was known as Arkinholm, so it is possible that the references in these ancient documents to Arkin and Langholm may indicate the same territory. In common with those of the neighbouring Baronies, the lands of Langholm came into the possession of the Douglases. In 1451 James II gave to the eighth Earl of Douglas a charter of the whole lands in the Regality of Eskdale.

After the battle of Arkinholm in 1455, when the power of the House of Douglas in Eskdale was broken, there was a re-arrangement of territories, whereby Langholm, together with the possessions and privileges belonging to the Lordship of Eskdale, was awarded to the Earl of Angus "on account of his faithful service". Later all these lands passed to the House of Maxwell.

BRYNTALLONE OR BRETALLACH

There is considerable doubt as to whether the Barony of Bryntallone was within the Regality of Eskdale. It was one of a group of three comprising what was afterwards known as the Debateable Land. These were Bryntallone, Morton, and Kirkandrews-on-Esk. In 1528, Lord

Dacre declined to admit that the Hollows was in the Lordship of Eskdale, but claimed it as "a parcell of the Debatable grounde".

The first mention of Bryntallone is in the reign of David I   A Norman baron, one Turgot de Rossedal, was then in possession of the lands.   In the succeeding reign, that of Malcolm, Turgot de Rossedal bestowed them upon the monks of Jedburgh, then a religious house of great influence. From this date the lands of the Barony seem to have been administered as church property, the grants having been confirmed by William the Lion, the control of the ecclesiastical foundation was substituted for that of the feudal baron.

It was in 1220, following the arbitration between the Bishop of Glasgow and the Abbot of Jedburgh, that the religious foundation received a separate and definite position with the customary rights and privileges of such establishments.   The Barony of Bryntallone, thereafter, became known as Canonby, the residence of the canons, and from this date the history of Canonby is principally a record of the religious house.

TARRAS

The Barony of Tarras was one of late creation. As we have seen, the Barony of Stapelgortoun stretched through Ewes and into the Tarras valley. On the south, embracing most of the lands of lower Eskdale, was the Barony of Bryntallone. When the Barony of Tarras was created in 1606 it comprised the lands lying between those of Bryntallone and Langholm. These had previously been the property of the Priory of Canonby, but had been transferred to the Crown by the General Annexation Act of 29th July, 1587, which enabled the King to dispose of the vacant lands. The properties mentioned below he formed into the Barony of Tarras.

Others were granted to Alexander, Earl of Home, under dates 1606 and 1610. In 1619 these were purchased by Walter, the first Earl of Buccleuch, who, in 1629 by a bond, conferred on his son David "the cloister-houses, biggings and yards of Canonbie", which included Bowholm, the mains of Canonby, and also "the lands of Hoillhouse". Although Hoillhouse is thus assigned to David of Buccleuch, the Barony of Tarras in which it was included is expressly reserved by the bond. The occasion of he erection of the Barony was   a grant to James Maxwell and Robert Douglas.

The Act of the Scots Parliament recites the charter as follows:—
". . . . to his hienes domestick servitoris James Maxwell ane of the gentlemen ischearis (ushers) and Robert Douglas ane of the equyriers to his hienes derrest sone the Prince for guid trew and thankfull services and for other grave wechtie and proffitable catissi the land is under writtin of before callit the debetable landis viz. the landis of Tarresfute, monibyherst, broumshielhill, quhitliesyde, bankheid, menmeirburn, harlaw & harlaw wod, rowingburne, wodeheid, thorniequhattis, waberhillis, barresknowis, wodhousleyis, hoilhous, torcune, broumshielburne, auchinriffok lyand w'in the parochin of Cannabie and of the landis of glunzeart, mortoun, and barnegleis, lyand within the parochin of mortoun . . . . to be unite annexit erectit & Incorporat in ane haill and frie baronie to be callit in all tyme cuming the baronie of Tarres. To be haldin of oure said soverane lord and his successoures in frie blenshe for the payment of a pair of gilt spurs. . . . . Zierlie at the feist of witsonday beis askit allenarlie" (only).

It was from the Tarras Water that the title of Earl of Tarras was given, in 1660, to Walter Scott, of Highchester, the youthful husband of the even more youthful Countess Mary, daughter of the second Earl of Buccleuch. The marriage of this boy of fourteen and girl of eleven was of brief duration, for she died in about a year. Walter Scott was the first and only holder of this title.

EWES

The valley of the Ewes, though the river is a tributary of the Esk, was not regarded as an integral part of Eskdale. During the period of the Baronies, Ewesdale was under separate jurisdiction, and does not seem to have been ever ruled over by any one great feudal lord. As has been shown, the valley was cut across by the Barony of Stapelgortoun, and that portion of it south of Arkin belonged either to Stapelgortoun or Langholm.

The upper portion of the Ewes valley was in the possession of several feudal owners. It was probably its nearness to Roxburghshire which originally brought it, and Eskdale too, within the Sheriffdom of that county. Indeed, Ewes seems to have been more closely linked with Liddesdale than Eskdale.

In 1528, when the English Warden, Earl of Cumberland, enquired of Lord Maxwell, Warden of the West March, whether he should look to him to redress the injuries done by the Liddesdale raiders, Maxwell replied that not only Liddesdale, but Ewesdale also was "out of his commission, and he would not answer for them". At one time, Ewesdale was esteemed of greater importance than Eskdale itself. In Blaeu's map of 1654 the title given is "Eusdail and Eskdail".

The earliest owners of land in Ewesdale were the Lovels and Kunyburgs. Where precisely their lands were situated we have no means of knowing. The Lovels possessed lands in Eskdale, adjoining those granted to the Moffats, as well as in Ewesdale, but forfeited all their possessions in 1341. They were the first holders of the Barony of Hawick, which, with Branxholm, remained in their possession for about 250 years. It may therefore be presumed that the lands owned by them in Ewesdale, marched with, or, at least, were near to, those in Teviotdale. This would place them in the neighbourhood of Mosspaul.

The Lovels were English both by birth and sympathies, and consistently supported the claims of Edward. It was owing to this that their lands in Ewesdale and Eskdale were alienated. On the forfeiture of the Lovels, David I granted their possessions to Sir William Douglas. The name of Lovel does not again appear in the history of the district.

A daughter of Sir William de Kunyburg, about the year 1240, married Sir John Fraser, a feudal lord of Ewesdale, who, by the marriage, became possessed of certain lands at Rig, in the Barony of Stapelgortoun. The Frasers appear to have been, about this time, proprietors of Arkleton. They were a family of considerable repute, one of them being mentioned as holding the office of Sheriff of Aberdeen.

The charter granting these lands in Ewesdale to the Frasers was resigned by them in 1426 to the Duke of Albany, whom James I, his nephew, had made Governor of Scotland. James at once bestowed these lands upon "his beloved and faithful Simon Lytil", who in return agreed to "perform to the King and his heirs the services due and wont from the said lands".

The territory thus granted included "Mikkildale, Sourbie, and Kirktown". Probably it was at the last place that Simon Lytil then resided as in the printed inventory of the Maxwell Muniments he is given "as of Kirktown" in witnessing a document dated 29th December, 1469, though he seems afterwards to have gone to Meikledale, from which he took his territorial designation, "the Laird of Mikkildale".

It is of interest to note that when, in 1482, the Duke of Albany laid claim to the Scottish Crown, the price to be paid by him to the English for their help was the cession of Ewesdale to England, a promise that Albany was never able to fulfil.

In 1456 there were Armstrongs in Sorby, David and Archibald Armstrong appearing at that date as witnesses to a notarial document. In the sixteenth century grants of land in Ewesdale were made to certain of the Armstrongs. In 1528 Lord Home obtained from David Armstrong a bond of man-rent in consideration of certain lands in the "Uvyr parrochin of Ewisdale". In 1535 a charter was given by the King to Herbert Armstrong of the lands of Park, now called the Bush, in Ewesdale, and in 1537 Robert, Lord Maxwell, by charter, conferred the land of Arklitoun on Ninian Armstrong.

At this time the Douglases dominated the Esk valley and endeavoured to extend their sway to Ewesdale as well. There, however, they had a rival in their own kinsman the Earl of Angus, who held the Lordship of Liddesdale, to which Regality, Ewesdale was more closely attached than it was to Eskdale.

An instance of this interference of the Douglas with the prerogatives of Angus is on record, wherein the Countess of Angus, widow of the fourth Earl, sues one of the Douglases in respect of £100 damage caused by him in the "spoliacion" of her Ewesdale revenues. Most of the lands of Ewesdale, like those of Eskdale, fell into the hands of the Maxwells when that House rose to power.

CHAPTER 15

THREE ESKDALE FAMILIES

It was a saying of Thomas Carlyle that the history of a nation was the history of its great men. If this be true of a nation it is also true of a locality and it is undoubtedly true of Eskdale.

For a period covering some 500 years the valley of the Esk was dominated by three great families, in whose life-story its history is almost completely merged. During that long stretch of time one or other of these families exercised a controlling influence in Eskdale. As the story of its fortunes and misfortunes, its successes and defeats, rises or falls, so do the destinies and well-being of the entire people of Eskdale.

The narrative of these centuries is one of excitement, of struggle, and of tumult. The great barons quickly rose to power and influence and as quickly fell into disfavour and disaster. It may appear as if, in those intriguings for power, the ordinary undistinguished people of Eskdale had neither part nor lot. But that was not so.

By the rigidity of the feudal system, the people were tied tightly to the baron. His fortunes could not fall without theirs also declining. He could not go to war and they remain at home in peace and quiet. Should the paramount lord quarrel with his neighbour, the quarrel was not confined to him alone, the entire vassalage was in it. Individuality was disobedience while personal success was incipient treason.

Thus, for 500 years, the history of Eskdale was the history of its leading barons, their jealousies and quarrels were the people's politics, the supercession or defeat of their lord was a household and personal disaster.

From *circa* 1300 to 1800, then, the fame and fortunes of Eskdale were successively under :—

125

1. THE HOUSE OF DOUGLAS
2. THE HOUSE OF MAXWELL
3. THE HOUSE OF SCOTT OF BUCCLEUCH

It must not be concluded that at any time one of these families had sole possession of the lands in the watershed of the Esk. Proprietors were continually changing and, even in the days of undisputed supremacy on the part of a single family, there were other barons and owners of land. But the above division is definite enough to indicate the main lines of local history. The periods of these great divisions are approximately:—

DOUGLASES, 1319 to 1455
MAXWELLS, 1455 to 1643
SCOTTS OF BUCCLEUCH, from 1643

As indicated above there were other families who wielded some power in Eskdale during these periods. The Lindsays occupied Wauchopedale for some 300 years, but this family exercised a surprisingly small part in shaping the destinies of the district. There were other smaller and less powerful clans in upper Eskdale and Ewesdale, but their effect on the stream of Eskdale history was a ripple, not a wave.

THE HOUSE OF DOUGLAS

The first mention of the Douglases in Eskdale is about 1319. Bannockburn had been fought five years previously, and the adherence of some of the Eskdale barons to the standard of Edward had placed in the hands of Robert the Bruce a number of forfeited estates. It was in the allocation of these that the Douglases were introduced to Eskdale.

Like most of the other barons who had come into Scotland during the reigns of Alexander and David, they were English as well as Scottish barons and had sworn fealty to the English Edward. But when John Balliol, the vassal-king, summoned his first Parliament at Scone in 1293, the Douglas and the Bruce both failed to appear, and Balliol declared them defaulters. This seems to have been the first occasion on which these two barons were united by a common purpose.

The father of Sir James Douglas, the Good, had adhered to the cause of Wallace, when most of the Scottish barons had fallen away, and

Sir Alexander Lindsay of Wauchope had also remained true to the national cause. On the field of Bannockburn, Sir James Douglas was created a knight-banneret by King Robert the Bruce. And when the allocation of the vacant lands was made, in 1319, the King gave to the Douglas those in the Barony of Stapelgortoun, which had been resigned by canon John Lindsay of Glasgow.

It was here, at Stapelgortoun, that was signed, in the reign of David I, the charter, which first gave to the great-grandfather of the Bruce those lands in Annandale with which went the lordship of that dale.[1]

The faithful friendship between King Robert the Bruce and Sir James Douglas is known and cherished by every Scotsman, and that Eskdale should have provided one of the tangible tokens of that friendship is indeed pleasant to remember.

These grants were confirmed, in 1324, by the famous Emerald Charter, which was not so much a conveyance of lands, as a story from the olden days of chivalry. After giving to Sir James the criminal jurisdiction of all the Douglas possessions, and releasing him from the customary feudal services, excepting those required for the defence of the realm, the Charter proceeds:—

"And in order that this Charter may have perpetual effect, We, in our own person and with our own hand, have placed on the hand of the said James of Douglas a ring, with a certain stone called an Emeraude, in token of sasine and perpetual endurance to the said James and his heirs for ever".

Sir Herbert Maxwell laments[2] the loss of the emerald ring. The Charter remains, but the Ring is gone. Sir James had fought by the Bruce's side throughout the War of Independence. His patriotism was almost solitary amongst the Scottish Barons, in its undoubted sincerity.

Some four years after the Emerald Charter had been granted, Robert the Bruce died, and the Douglas accepted the solemn charge to bury the King's heart in Jerusalem. However, beset by the Moors in Spain, and seeing that death was imminent, Sir James took from round his neck the silver casket containing the heart of the Bruce, and, flinging it into the Moorish ranks, cried "Forward, gallant heart, as thou wert wont, the Douglas will follow thee or die".

Later, Sir James was found dead with the casket clasped in his arms which is somewhat contradictory! Was there on the finger of the knight at that moment the emerald ring which had been given him by the Bruce? Most likely there was. Who knows, then, but that this ring, for which today Scotland would give a king's ransom, now adorns the finger of someone ignorant of its history?

After his death, the body of Sir James was brought home and buried in the church at Douglas, in Lanarkshire, and his lands in Eskdale fell to his brother, Hugh, Lord of Jedworth Forest. Hugh Douglas granted one moiety of the lands of Westerker to William Douglas, Knight of Liddesdale, but he reserved to his own use the manor-place, with the church lands and mains. The reservation seems to indicate that Sir Hugh Douglas, occasionally at least, resided at the baron's house of Westerker, the situation of which cannot now be identified.

The Douglases did not usually reside in Eskdale. Their paternal estates were in Lanarkshire, but from the reservation of the manor-place, and also from the fact that Archibald, the Grim, the 3rd. Earl of Douglas, issued his summons to his vassals from "his castell in Eskdale", it would appear that at times he, at any rate, resided there, probably in the old baronial Castle of Barntalloch.

Further estates were given to this family, in 1341, when, on the Lovels being attainted as traitors, David II granted to Sir William Douglas part of their lands in Eskdale and also Ewesdale where the Earl of Angus already held the principal share. By early in the fourteenth century, the Douglases were virtually masters of Eskdale, excepting that the Lindsays had the lands of Wauchope, and the Red Douglas, Earl of Angus, had some part of Ewes.

In 1389 Archibald Douglas, who was the natural son of Sir James, registered his title to the Barony of Stapelgortoun before the Scots Parliament. Archibald was Warden of the Marches, and, in 1385, did useful work in amending and codifying the old Border laws, and was assisted by his factor, Sir Herbert Maxwell. The Douglases and Maxwells were, at that time, in close friendship, which, alas, was severed when the fateful day of the battle of Arkinholm had dawned.

The splendour of Archibald Douglas's station was scarcely inferior to that of the King himself. He and his family exercised almost unlimited power over half of the lowlands. Small wonder then that the Douglases excited the suspicion of the King and the Barons. Even their allies and friends grew resentful, not against their semi-regal state, but rather against their tyrannous and insolent bearing.

At the date of his succession to the lands of Eskdale, Archibald Douglas was probably the most powerful subject of the King of Scotland. His life, accordingly, was full of adventure. Raids into England, that unfailing resource of the Border baron, skirmishes with hostile clans, acting as umpire at duels, a lighter recreation thrown in to balance the more serious duties of his position, these filled up the days of Archibald, the Grim.

Not lacking in humour, either, was this Archibald. When the first Scottish dukes were created, in 1398, he was offered a dukedom, and the Herald addressed him as "Sir Duke", or as he would pronounce it, "Sir Duik", to which the jocular Archibald made answer: "Sir Drake! Sir Drake!"

Archibald, died in 1400, and at the time of his death the family possessed, not only the extensive lands in Eskdale and the paternal estates in Lanarkshire, but also territories in Stirlingshire, Moray, Selkirk Forest, Clydesdale, Annandale, and Lothian. He was succeeded by his son, known as Archibald, the Tineman, the loser of battles. With his accession the Douglas star began to wane. Factions, jealousies and conspiracies worked their inevitable result. The Red Douglas intrigued against the Black, and the House, being thus divided against itself, could not stand, and began to totter to its fall.

In 1451, the forces of disintegration were at work, but the cracks in the structure were plastered over by a charter, granted by James II., confirming to William, the 5th Earl, then a young man of 25, all the possessions his family had enjoyed, and amongst the lands enumerated were Eskdale, with Stapilgortoun, in the county of Roxburgh.

In the following year, the Douglas received a summons to attend the King at Stirling and, evidently without any suspicion, obeyed the mandate. Next day, as he sat at the King's table, after supper, the monarch beckoned him into an ante-chamber, and there, it is supposed, demanded of him a renunciation of an offensive and defensive alliance he had entered into with Lindsay, Earl of Crawford, a relative of the Lindsays of Wauchope and chief of their clan.

To this demand, the Douglas peremptorily refused to accede, whereupon, without further parley, the king stabbed him in the neck, and Sir Patrick Gray finished the treacherous deed. This incident tarnished the honour of the King, but his subservient Parliament passed a whitewashing Act to wipe away the stain of the murder.

William had married his cousin Margaret, the Fair Maid of Galloway, but by her had no children. After his murder she married his brother, James, who had succeeded, as 9th. Earl, to the family estates. In 1452, the new Earl of Douglas and his brother, the Earl of Ormond, refused to attend Parliament, but later the King effected a reconciliation with them and things went more smoothly. But only for a time.

The King harboured a suspicion, more or less well founded, that the Douglas was not sincere in his professions of homage and loyalty so, in 1455, without warning, he made war upon him. Douglas sought the aid of Henry VI. of England, but was refused, and the King's forces laid waste his lands in Douglasdale, Annandale and Ettrick Forest.

The battles went against Douglas, who fled to England, leaving his brothers, the Earl of Moray, the Earl of Ormond, and young John Douglas of Balveny, to defend the family cause. These three established themselves in the fastnesses of Ewesdale, whence they harried all the surrounding country arousing the anger and hostility of the other barons.

The man to strike the blow which was to reduce the fortunes of the House was another Douglas, George, the fourth Earl of Angus, known as the Red Douglas, who considered himself to be the rightful owner of the family titles and estates. Angus accepted the King's commission to meet the redoubtable trio of knights. In this he was assisted by a body of Border chiefs, to whom the supremacy of the Douglases had been distasteful, their arbitrary methods being a cause of ill-feeling and irritation.

This combination of chiefs included the Scotts of Buccleuch, the Johnstones, Beattisons, Carlyles, Glendinnings, and others. The hereditary friendship with the Maxwells had also been broken by the ill-advised policy of the Douglases, and they, too, were found amongst their enemies.

The united forces of the King and the Border chiefs joined battle with the forces of the three brothers on the 1st May, 1455 in the battle of Arkinholm. This battle was fought on the ground upon which the town of Langholm is built, and it was decisive. Angus won the day. Moray was slain. Ormond was wounded and taken prisoner. John of Balveny fled and joined his brother, the Earl, in England. A price of 1200 marks was set upon his head. For eight years he eluded his pursuers, but at last he was captured in Eskdale by John Scott and eight others[3], taken to Edinburgh and beheaded.

The estates of the Douglas were declared forfeited, as was his occupancy of the office of Warden of the Marches. The Douglas lands in Eskdale were apportioned amongst the chiefs who had borne a conspicuous part in the battle. The main share fell to Angus, but the Scotts and Beattisons (Beatties) and the Glendinnings were all rewarded with ample grants.

The lands attaching to the position of lord of Eskdale were given to Angus in 1458 "all and whole the lands of Stapilgortoun and Eskdaile". Jane Douglas, the Earl's sister, in 1472, married David Scott, heir-apparent of Buccleuch. One of the provisions of the marriage settlement was that the Scotts were to have the bailiaries of Eskdale and Ewesdale for a period of seventeen years.

The battle of Arkinholm was, an event of great importance in determining the future of Eskdale. By it, in addition to the establishment of the Beatties and Glendinnings, the Scotts were given a firm footing in the district, and the Maxwells came into immediate prominence.

THE HOUSE OF MAXWELL

The Maxwells, had been known in Dumfriesshire, and partly in Eskdale, for some 250 years. As early as 1093, one Ewen de Maccuswell accompanied Malcolm III to the siege of Alnwick. This Baron had married a daughter of the Lord of Galloway, with whom he received the castle of Caerlaverock.

The first mention of the Maxwells in Eskdale was in 1268, when Herbert, son of Sir Eymer Maxwell, Sheriff of Dumfries, received from Sir William de Kunyburg the grant of land in the barony of Stapelgortoun. Herbert Maxwell held these lands until the death of the grantor in 1281.

Sir Herbert adhered to the Bruce during the war of independence, and was killed at Bannockburn, as was his second son Sir Eustace. John, son of Sir Eustace, went with David II in 1346 to the Battle of Neville's Cross, and shared both in the defeat of the King and in his subsequent imprisonment in the Tower of London. The next Maxwell, like so many of the Scottish barons, made his submission to Edward III and received back from that monarch the castle of Caerlaverock.

When the Douglases rose to power in Dumfriesshire the Maxwells were on terms of friendship and alliance with them, and the friendship remained intact until the Douglas rebellion. It was on the joint summons of the Douglas and Maxwell that the Scottish barons were called to Lincluden in 1450 to codify the Border laws. These were then embodied as Acts of the Scottish Parliament. Amongst the provisions of these Acts was one restoring the system of bale-fires as signals of danger.

As early as 1425 a Maxwell was appointed Warden of the Marches. In 1488 John, the fourth Lord Maxwell, held this office, and was also Lord of the Regality of Eskdale. Maxwell was nominally on the side of the King in the second Douglas rebellion, but after the death of James III. at Sauchieburn he managed to get himself nominated to these positions, whilst Angus was made Warden of the East and Middle Marches. These two, therefore, practically ruled Dumfriesshire at this time. John was slain at the battle of Flodden in September, 1513.

It is to his son Robert, the fifth Lord Maxwell, that the interest of Eskdale people chiefly attaches. In 1505, the Lindsays had forfeited their lands in Wauchope and Ewesdale. In Ewesdale the ten pound lands of Mosspaul, Fiddleton, Blakhaw, Unthank and Mosspeble were bestowed upon Alexander, Lord Home. They reverted to the King, however, on the execution of Home in October 1516, and were given to Robert, Lord Maxwell, who was quickly rising to a position of influence and power on the Borders.

In 1510 Robert had received some of the lands of the Lindsays in Ewesdale. On Lindsay's forfeiture, his possessions in Wauchope had gone to the Crown, but Lord Home was in possession of some parts of that dale, for in 1523 he is enjoined "to put rewle in his landis of Wauchopdaill or ellis to discharge him of the same to the Lord Maxwelle", from which it would appear that Home was holding Wauchope with a somewhat slack rein.

However, in 1525, Maxwell was granted a tack for nine years of all the lands of Wauchope with the mills, fortalice, and fisheries. But in 1530, before the tack had expired, Maxwell received a charter putting him in full possession of the lands, one of the conditions being that he should build and repair the house, tower, and fortalice of Wauchope, and retain it for the King's service.

Two years later, in a charter dated July 27, 1532, Maxwell's possessions and power in Eskdale were further augmented by a grant from the King of some of the lands which had been given to the Beattisons for their services at the Battle of Arkinholm, viz., Enzieholm

[Eynze], Lyncholm, Shiel, and also Billholm, and other places

In 1540 Maxwell obtained from the Prior of Canonby a lease of the glebe land of Wauchope for a period of five years at five marks per annum. He thus had a position of great responsibility and power and his task was not made any easier by the distractions on the Borders.

To help to pacify the broken men, Maxwell, on 4th. August 1525, had granted to "my lovit frend" Johne Armstrong a charter of certain lands in Eskdale. On 2nd. November of the same year, Johne Armstrong gave to Maxwell a bond of man-rent[4] undertaking to yield him "in manrent and service first and before all others, myne allegiance to our soverane lord the King allanerly excepted and to be trewe, gude and lele servantis to my said Lord".

In return for this bond, and under the same date, Robert, Lord Maxwell, gifted to Johne Armstrong, and to his ayris, the lands of "Dalbeth, Schield, Dalblane, Stapilgortoun, Langholme, and Crwsnowte, (this is probably Crawsknowe, a lonely cottage far up the side of Whita), with the pertinentis". Armstrong accepted the bond with his hand at the pen, and by affixing his seal. In 1529 Armstrong resigned the lands of Langholm in favour of Lord Maxwell.

It seems fairly well agreed that if Maxwell did not actually instigate many of the raids made by the Armstrongs, he at any rate winked at them, and in the presence of Lord Dacre, the English Warden, he sometimes resisted, not always passively, the attempts to bring them to justice. Of course, he was bound, as their feudal superior, to defend them from unjust attacks and false accusations, but there is ground for the suspicion that his protection amounted to something beyond that.

In connection with Johnie Armstrong's death in 1530, when he was entrapped and murdered by the King at Carlenrig, in Teviotdale, some doubt has been expressed concerning Lord Maxwell's good faith. It seems to be based on the fact that, three days after Armstrong's murder, Maxwell received an absolute grant to himself of the lands Armstrong had held under the bond of man-rent. Probably, however, the grant was only a legal formality. It will be remembered that when James V contemplated the decoying of the Armstrongs he took the precaution of first inviting Maxwell, Buccleuch, and other Border chiefs to Edinburgh where he had them securely imprisoned before he set out for the Borders.

In after years the Armstrongs loyally served the heirs of Maxwell, which they would never have done had they suspected him of being privy to the contemplated treachery and guilty of breaking his word, a sin heinous above all others in the eyes of the Borderers.

In 1536 Maxwell was entrusted by the King with a mission of a very delicate nature. He was sent to France to arrange the marriage of the King to Madeleine, daughter of Francis I, King of France. On the successful completion of the mission, though the poor princess died soon after her arrival in Scotland, James is said to have given to Maxwell the patronage of the Five Kirks of Eskdale.

In 1542 Lord Maxwell, at the battle of Solwa Moss was taken prisoner, as were also his brothers John and Henry, and the son of his traditional enemy, the laird of Johnstone. Sir Thomas Wharton, in his report, describes Maxwell as Admiral of Scotland and Warden of the Marches, and his resources are given as "in lands per annum 1000 marks sterling (English) and in goods £500 which is £2000 Scotch". The resources of his brother Henry are given as nil. Whilst Maxwell was thus imprisoned the King "ordainit our lovit Johne Johnestone of that Ilk", to act as Warden of the West March.

Maxwell was liberated in the following year, but in 1544 his parole was cancelled and he was commanded to go to London, his son Robert being appointed in his stead as Warden of the West March. Soon after his son's appointment, he was waylaid by certain Armstrongs, at Yellowsike Head near the farm of Blough in Wauchopedale, and was sent to London where he was imprisoned.

In 1546 Maxwell was liberated, but died a few weeks after his reinstatement. He was succeeded by his son Robert, sixth Lord Maxwell, who is also recorded as succeeding to the patronage of the churches within the lordship of Eskdale.

In 1557, Cristofer Armstrong, son of Johnie, gave a bond of manrent to John, Lord Maxwell, and received from him a grant of the lands held by his father at the time of his murder in 1530. In 1562 another bond was executed by which Christie Armstrong of Barnegleis was made keeper of Langholm Castle, and factor of all Maxwell's property in Eskdale, until John, Lord Maxwell, should be of age.

At this time the Armstrongs appear to have held the lands of Broomholm in addition to other places in Eskdale. Their tenancy of Broomholm lasted probably until 1585, that is after Lord Maxwell's raid to Stirling. In 1572 Lord Maxwell was handfasted to a niece of the

Regent Morton. Whether this took place in Eskdale, at Handfasting Haugh, does not appear. More probably it was at Unthank, of which at this date Maxwell had the right of patronage.

In 1578 there happened an incident the effects of which were felt for many a long year in Eskdale, and throughout the Borders, viz., the appointment of the Laird of Johnstone as Warden of the West March. Lord Maxwell's tenure of the office of Warden was characterised by gross misgovernment. So evident was this that Lord Herries, another Maxwell, and uncle of the Warden, made a recommendation which can be best described in his own quaint language:—

"It is expedient that the Lord Maxwell quhais guidsire gat the maist part of the lands of Eskdale Ewisdale and Wauchopedale fra the said late Kingis heines of gude memory, gif he be Warden and remaine at Lochmaben, have ane honest man his depute and capitane in the Langholme and to dantoun that gret nowmer of mischevous thevis, spend upoun him and ane household thair, the haill proffeittis that may be gottin of they landis and kirkis of Watstreker, Stephen Gortoun, Wauchope and Natherkirk of Ewis (alwyse Goddis service the ministeris to be first sustenit), the haill advantage with the maillis, multuris manis and utheris detfull dewiteis to be spendit in the Langholme quhilk I think, may wele sustene twelf habil horsemen with thair capitane".

Maxwell replied that such a proposal was needless, as he was already bound to keep the peace. He had, however, so incurred the displeasure of the Regent Morton that the latter removed him from the office of Warden, which he gave to Johnstone. Scarcely anything could have occurred more likely to intensify the bitter feeling already existing between these two great Barons.

The Wardenry, a thankless office certainly, was nevertheless the symbol of power on the Borders, and was as eagerly coveted by the Johnstones, as it was jealously retained by the Maxwells. They had been rivals for the office ever since the defeat of the Douglases at Arkinholm.

The point now at issue seems to have been connected with the tenancy of the house or fortalice of Langholm. The Johnstones were in possession of it, and, possession counting as nine points of the law, they refused to give it up to the Maxwells to whom it really belonged. The Johnstones themselves were not living in the fortalice, (which, of course, was that situated on the Castle Holm), but clung to it on principle. No doubt Maxwell's complaint was that the Castle remained "unhabite be him or ony of his and the key thereof is cassin only in ane byre to the said Lordis awin servandis that duellis in the laich housis besyde the same; the want of the said house is hurtful to the haill country", and so on.[5]

The arrangement come to was that the Johnstones were to let the Maxwells have the fortalice when they themselves were not requiring it, but when, for the better government of the Border, the Johnstones might want it, then they must have it, though if, at any time, they left it, the Maxwells were to get it. On paper, this seemed quite an equitable and friendly arrangement, but for clans, at such bitter enmity, there were lurking in it possibilities of considerable friction

In the year 1581, after the execution of the Regent Morton, Maxwell was again restored to favour and granted the title of Earl of Morton. This so enraged the Earl of Angus, that he made a raid into Eskdale, ravaged the lands of Maxwell, and seized the Castle of Langholm. The hostilities continuing, Maxwell, as Warden, was summoned, in 1586, to answer before the Council for the disturbances.

Refusing to obey, an edict was issued again depriving him of his office and titles, but graciously permitting him to leave the country. This he did. He went to Spain where he assisted the King of Spain to prepare the famous Armada, and was able to offer him very valuable counsel.

He then returned to Scotland. When the King heard of this he resolved upon active measures, and, marching into Maxwell's lands, he burned some of his castles, Langholm and Lochmaben amongst others. Maxwell himself was seized, and lodged as a prisoner in Edinburgh Castle, but two years later he was set at liberty. The climax of the feud between the Johnstones and the Maxwells was reached in 1593.

The Johnstones had raided the lands of Lord Sanquhar, who appealed to Maxwell, as Warden, for redress. Despite the fact that he had only recently concluded an amicable agreement with his hereditary enemies, Maxwell marched against the Johnstones with 1500 men. He was heavily defeated on Dryfe Sands by Johnstone, who was supported by the Elliots, the Grahams and the Scotts of Eskdale and Teviotdale.

The Armstrongs, however, loyal to their bonds, rode with Lord Maxwell, who not only lost 700 men, but was himself killed, murdered really in a barbarous manner, after being sorely wounded in the fight.

His son, John, who succeeded him, was only a youth of sixteen, but, naturally desired to avenge his father's cruel death. Very soon he began to make himself felt, and, for the next few years, he managed to keep the whole of Annandale and Eskdale in a state of unrest and turmoil. Not only was he antagonistic to the Johnstones, but he and Angus came to a rupture over their respective jurisdictions in Eskdale.

Both Barons called out all their forces and Maxwell, who seems to have been of an impetuous and turbulent nature, challenged the Earl of Angus to a duel, to decide by single combat in the orthodox Norman way, what had failed to be determined by legal right and equity. For this he was thrown into prison, but escaped, with characteristic daring and resourcefulness.

He next endeavoured to heal his feud with the laird of Johnstone. Securing the good offices of a mutual acquaintance, he succeeded in arranging a meeting between himself and Johnstone, each accompanied by a friend. These friends quarrelled, and the chiefs, of course, were soon embroiled. In the commotion, Maxwell fatally shot Johnstone in the back. He fled the country and went to France, in connection with which the Border ballad entitled *Lord Maxwell's Good-night* was written. Naturally, this treachery exhausted the King's patience, never too abundant at any time, and he declared the fugitive's lands forfeited.

This was in 1609, when Maxwell was 32. Some years later, thinking the murder would be forgotten, he ventured to return to Scotland, and was arrested, and, finally, on 21st May, 1613, he was beheaded. As usual, the lands he had held were divided amongst those who, for the time being, were in the favour of King James.

In Glenriddel's MS, Maxwell of Broomholm is specially "mentioned as having attended his chieftain in his distress and as having received a grant of lands in reward of his manifestation of attachment". Whether these were the present lands of Broomholm, or whether the grant was made by Robert, tenth Lord Maxwell, when the family estates were restored, is not clear.

Following the flight of Lord Maxwell, his lands were apportioned at the King's pleasure. This fact has a most important bearing upon the history of the district, for it was then that Langholm was erected into "the free barony". Maxwell's lands in Eskdale remained alienated from the tenth Lord until the year 1618, when, by successive Acts in this and the two following years, they were restored.

Robert, Lord Maxwell, seems to have taken warning by his brother's wild and tragic career, for he speedily ingratiated himself into

BROOMHOLM HOUSE

the royal favour. In 1620 Lord Maxwell was advanced a step in the peerage, being made Earl of Nithsdale and given precedence as Earl from the date of his father's being made Earl of Morton in 1581. In the following year he received a grant of the teinds of Nether Ewes.

In 1628 Lord Nithsdale made the grants of land to the ten members of the Maxwell family, on the condition that each of them should erect a house of certain dimensions in the High Street of Langholm. This charter is dealt with more fully in a later chapter.

Lord Nithsdale about this time must have granted throughout Eskdale a considerable number of perpetual tenancies of lands. When the Commission of 1679 was appointed to make a return of the Buccleuch properties, claims were frequently made that such tenancies had been granted by the Earl of Nithsdale, evidently without any charter or other deed.

When the controversies between the Scottish Parliament and King Charles I became acute, Nithsdale adhered devotedly to the Stuart cause, with whose fortunes he and his successors rose or fell. He was commissioned by charter to summon the Convention of Estates, for the express purpose of annulling those Acts of the two preceding reigns which alienated the old church lands and settled them on the nobles.

During the Civil War in England Nithsdale safeguarded the

King's cause on the Borders. His castle of Caerlaverock was the rallying point of the Royalists, and was besieged by Colonel Home, the Parliamentary general. In the end it had to surrender, one of the conditions being that the Earl of Nithsdale should have a safe journey guaranteed to either Springkell or Langholm Castle.

The Earl came to neither place, but, crossing the Border joined the Royalist forces operating in the north of England. In condonation of what seems to have been Nithsdale's breach of good faith, it is urged that Colonel Home had given orders for both Springkell and Langholm to be closed against the Earl.

Meanwhile, in 1643, Nithsdale's estates had been declared forfeit by Parliament, and thus ended the predominance of the House of Maxwell in Eskdale. Thereafter, the Scotts of Buccleuch became the paramount feudal lords.

THE SCOTTS OF BUCCLEUCH

The Scotts did not come over with William the Conqueror. They were indigenous to the country and this assurance comes as a relief in the story of our noble families. Some writers trace the ancestry of the Scotts to Michael Scott, the wizard; others to Duns Scotus, the scholar. But the lineages back to saints or heroes are often mythical, so we prefer to date this sketch from, Richard Scott of Rankilburn, who, in 1296, signed the Ragman Rolls, rather than from Michael the enchanter and seer.

The Scotts had been mentioned earlier than 1296, as witnesses to the *Inquisition* of the See of Glasgow made by David I. But this action of Richard Scott of swearing allegiance to Edward I in 1296 simply brings the family into the main stream of the history of that period. In 1346, fifty years later, it is recorded that Sir Michael Scott fell at Neville's Cross fighting for his King. Thereafter the Scotts were among the foremost Scottish barons.

Walter Scott of Kirkurd is the ancestor of the Scotts of Buccleuch, with whom we are here concerned. This chief was knighted for the help he gave in defeating the Douglases at Arkinholm and he also received grants of various lands including Buccleuch and part of Branxholme.

W. Riddell Carre states[6] that Scott of Kirkurd obtained in 1458 certain lands as well as part of the barony of Langholm. It is doubtful whether Langholm was a barony at this date, or that Scott of Kirkurd then received any grants in Langholm.

There is a charter quoted in Fraser's *Scotts of Buccleuch,* dated 10th September, 1455, which sets forth that Sir Walter Scott, knight, and David Scott were given "the lands of Quhitchester in the barony of Hawick, for the faithful services rendered to us in the victory against our traitors Archibald Douglas called Earl of Moray and Hugh of Douglas his brother, Earl of Ormonde", but no mention is made of any grant of lands in Langholm.

Down to the middle of the seventeenth century Branxholme was the chief seat of the Scott clan, but Sir Walter was styled "of Buccleuch". This title is said to have originated in an incident which occurred one day whilst James III was hunting in the royal forest of Ettrick. The King had pursued a stag from Ettrick Heuch to the glen now called Buccleuch. There it stood at bay, when one of the Scotts seized it by the antlers and, it is said, carried it to his sovereign, who exclaimed:—

> "As for the buck thou stoutly brought
> To us, up that steep heuch
> Thy designation ever shall
> Be John Scott of Buckscleuch"[7]

Though this territorial designation was always given, Kirkurd and Branxholme were also used, but ultimately they were entirely superseded by Buccleuch. When Sir Walter Scott died in 1469 he possessed a considerable portion of the shires of Roxburgh and Selkirk. He was succeeded by his son David, who had also fought at the Battle of Arkinholm. From James III he received a charter erecting many of his lands into free baronies, for payment of a red rose as blenche-ferme.

In 1470 the Earl of Angus gave a charter of certain lands in Liddesdale to his kinsman Douglas of Cavers, failing whom they were to revert to David Scott of Buccleuch. Two years later his son, also called David, married Jane Douglas, sister of Angus. With this marriage David Scott received some territory in Liddesdale, and in the Lordship of Ewesdale, as part of the bride's dowry, as well as the appointment of himself and his father to the bailiaries of Eskdale and Ewesdale for a period of seventeen years.[8]

Some years later, in 1484, the monks of Melrose appointed David Scott of Branxholme, and Robert, his son, to the office of bailies of the abbey lands in Eskdale for a period of five years, and this office the lairds of Buccleuch held heritably until the passing of the Heritable Jurisdictions Act of 1747. This appointment marked an important stage in the connection of the Scotts of Buccleuch with Eskdale and their subsequent predominance there.

It is interesting to note that at this time there was a marriage relationship of the Scotts, not only with the Maxwells but also with the Johnstones, the historical antagonists of the Maxwells.

About the year 1488, Adam, laird of Johnstone, who was first cousin to the governing Maxwell of that day, married a Scott of Branxholme and Buccleuch, and by a precept of sasine in 1493 he was charged "to infeft Walter Scott of Buccleuch" with certain lands in the Stewartry of Annandale. Thus, gradually, four centuries ago, there was being built up the acreage of the Buccleuch territories in Dumfriesshire. In 1578 the rental from the Buccleuch estates in Dumfriesshire was not less than £79,000.[9]

David Scott, who had received the honour of knighthood from James III., died in 1492 and was succeeded by his son Walter. The inventory of David's will gives an interesting indication of the nature and extent of the wealth of the Border lairds of that day. The value of his oxen, sheep, cows, and growing crops amounted to £740 Scots, or some £61 13s. 4d. sterling.

This trifling valuation is explainable by the facts that most of the lands were waste, and that the value of farm produce and live stock was very small. One could buy an ox for six shillings and a horse for thirteen or fourteen. A boll of wheat brought two shillings and a boll of oats about sixpence. He left a sum to the kirks of Hawick, Rankilburn, and St. Mary of the Forest for a suitable priest to pray for his soul.

The Sir Walter Scott just mentioned was taken prisoner in the Battle of Flodden in 1513 and died in 1516. He was succeeded by his son Walter. Walter's mother was a Ker of Cessford, between which family and the Scotts, there sprang up one of those prolonged and bitter feuds which characterised the mediaeval life of the Borders. The feud arose out of an attempt of Sir Walter Scott to aid James V. to free himself from the irksome surveillance and domination of his powerful stepfather, the Earl of Angus.

At this time Buccleuch could easily raise 1000 horse from Eskdale, Ewesdale, Teviotdale, and Ettrickdale, and perhaps it was this power over his own clan, as well as his influence over the Armstrongs and Elliots, that caused Lord Dacre to describe him as "the chief maintainer of all misguided men on the Borders of Scotland". The Kers supported Angus, and it was supposed that Sir Andrew Ker had slain one of the Elliots, who were then allies of Buccleuch. This initiated the feud which reached its culmination in 1552, in the brutal murder of Sir Walter Scott in the streets of Edinburgh.

A further step in the consolidation of the power of Buccleuch in Eskdale was taken during the lifetime of this Sir Walter. In 1524 he received the heritable office of the bailiary of the lands of Eskdalemuir, i.e. in the Barony or Tennandry of Dumfedling. This office enabled him to hold courts, appoint officers, execute justice, and to levy rents for the behoof of the monks of Melrose with Dumfedling as the seat of authority.

On Angus being exiled in 1528, his lands were divided amongst some of the King's supporters, and Buccleuch again received a fair share. It was this laird of Buccleuch who, in 1530, was commanded by the King to Edinburgh, where, with Maxwell and others, he was quietly imprisoned, whilst the crafty King repaired to the Borders.

Sir Walter was succeeded in the title and estates in 1535 by yet another Walter, whose occupancy of the family lands was distinguished by a raid into England to further the interests of Mary, Queen of Scots, to whom both the Scotts and the Kers were devotedly attached.

Queen Elizabeth retaliated by sending an expedition to the Borders. Writing of this raid, Lord Hundson says, "My Lord Lieut. [i.e. Sussex] and I with sertan bands of horsemen only went to Branksum, Bukklews pryncypale howse which we found burnt to our hand by hymselfe as cruelly as ourselves cowld have burnt ytt".

There was an old tradition that when Maxwell came up into Eskdale to take effective possession of his lands, the Beattisons did not take kindly to the arrangement and forcibly resisted his action. Things were looking very threatening for the Lord Maxwell, when one of the Beattisons, Rolland of Wat-Carrick, urged him to escape, and offered him the loan of his white mare. Maxwell was wise enough to recognise the golden moment and sped with all haste to Branxholme. There he offered to sell his rights in Eskdale to Scott "for a cast of hawks and a purse of gold". Scott closed with the bargain and speedily mustering his retainers proceeded to Esk-dalemuir to take forcible possession of his purchase. He expelled the Beattisons but on Maxwell's appeal granted to Rolland Beattison the perpetual tenant-right of Wat-Carrick, for a consideration.

The Beattisons remained a fairly compact clan until the dawn of the seventeenth century. It was certainly not the Scotts who scattered the clan, but the steady application of repressive measures against the broken men of the Borders that finally destroyed the power of the Beattisons. There were, however, many feuds between the Scotts and the Beattisons, and we read of one reprisal by the latter when, in 1547, being then under assurance to Lord Wharton, they attacked Branxholme and did a certain amount of damage to his barmekyns and towers.

The Rev. Dr. Brown, minister of Eskdalemuir and author of the *Statistical Accounts* of 1793 and 1841, says that when Scott of Branxholme had cleared out the Beattisons he proceeded, according to the custom of the clans, to grant feu-rights to his vassals and dependants. He gives a list of these settlements without, however, vouching for its accuracy:—

The apportionment was:—Scott of Harden got Over Cassock. Scott of Davington got Upper and Nether Davington, Fingland, and Pentland, Upper and Nether Dumfedling, Nether Cassock, Wester Polclive, Wetwood Rig, and Burncleugh. Scott of Johnston got Johnston, Johnston Dinnings, Raeburnfoot, Craighaugh, and Saughill. Scott of Raeburn got Moodlaw, Raeburnhead, Harewoodhead, Yetbyre, and Yards. Scott of Rennelburn got Rennelburn, Aberlosh, Midraeburn, Clerkhill, Greystonelee, Cote, and Coathope. Scott of Bailielee got Moodlaw Knowe, Grassyards, Kimmingsyke, Langshawburn, and Crurie. Scott of Branxholme reserved to himself the upper part of Thickside, Easter Polclive, Garwald Holm, Castle Hill, and all Black Esk.

This list, more or less accurately represents the holdings of a clan of Scotts, in Eskdale, but Dr. Brown has wrongly assumed that they were the Scotts of Buccleuch. These lands belonged not to the Scotts of Buccleuch but to the Scotts of Howpaslet and Thirlestane, known in Border history by the somewhat misleading designation of *The Scotts of Ewisdaill*, who at that date recognise Buccleuch as head of the clan.

Most of these estates did ultimately come into the possession of Anne, Duchess of Buccleuch and Monmouth, by purchase or in some other way, but in no case until the end of the seventeenth century.

Further proof of the incorrectness of the above list is obtained from a charter, dated 7th June, 1568, by which James VI. confirmed a grant made by the Commendator of Melrose to Alexander Balfour, of Denemylne, of, amongst others, the lands of Cassock, Finglen, Raeburn, Dumfedling, Poweliff [Polclive], Cruikithaugh [Craighaugh], and Moodlawheid.

Sir Walter Scott of Buccleuch took an active part in resisting the deplorable raids into Scotland made by Hertford, afterwards Duke of Somerset, who, amongst other atrocities, burnt Jedburgh and Dryburgh Abbeys. Sir Walter accepted one of the commands in the army of the Earl of Arran, and was assigned the duty of driving the English out of Eskdale and Ewesdale. He besieged the Castle of Langholm, and reduced it after three days, carrying its captain prisoner to Edinburgh.

In 1551 Sir Walter was made Keeper of Liddesdale by Mary, Queen of Scots. Though owning devotion to the cause of the Queen, Buccleuch headed the Border Barons in 1569 in signing a Bond in support of the young King (James VI.). In this Bond "they professed themselves enemies of all persons named Armstrong, Elliot, Nickson, Little, Beattie, Thomson, Irving, Bell, Johnstone, Glendinning, Routledge, Henderson, and Scott of Ewisdale, in fact of those families who had fought on the side of the Queen at Langholm".[10] All such, the signatories declare, "we salt persew to the deid with fyre, sword, and all other kynd of hostilie".

Sir Walter died in 1574, whilst yet the task of rebuilding Branxholme was unfinished, and was succeeded by his son Walter. Whilst only about twenty years of age he was appointed Warden of the Middle Marches. He, perhaps, more than any of his predecessors, raised the fame and prestige of the House of Buccleuch. Fearless, brave, full of resource, he won the title of the *bold Buccleuch* and these qualities established the Scotts of Buccleuch in the undisputed position they have since occupied.

His mother married young Francis Stewart, Earl of Bothwell, who made over all his property to Walter Scott, his step-son, but who, afterwards had to restore the lands of Liddesdale to Bothwell's son. Later, however, the Scotts of Buccleuch again came into the possession of Liddesdale.

Probably the incident which appealed most of all to the order clans was the oft quoted rescue of Kinmont Willie. This William Armstrong, in 1596, had been arrested, or as some say caught, by the English Warden, Lord Scrope, and imprisoned in Carlisle Castle Now this was a breach of the truce then existing between the Wardens.

> "And have they ta'en him, Kinmont Willie,
> Against the truce of Border tide?
> And forgotten that the bauld Buccleuch
> Is keeper here on the Scottish side?"

Scott of Buccleuch did not hesitate long. After exhausting the usual diplomatic means of protests to the English Warden and representations to the Ambassador, and wearying of the delay, he resolved to take the settlement into his own hands.

The plan of campaign was settled at Langholm, where the principals met at a race meeting. Assembling his retainers from Teviotdale, Liddesdale, and Eskdale, he marched down Ewesdale and concentrated his forces at the Tower of Sark. Providing himself with ladders and masons' and smiths' tools he set off with 40 picked men.

(Lord Scrope declared there were 500; Tytler's *History of Scotland* says 80; the ballad of Kinmont *Willie* says 40, and a MS. *History of Scotland* preserved in the Advocates Library gives the number as under 70).

> "He has call'd him forty marchmen bauld
> Were kinsmen to the bauld Buccleuch,
> With spur on heel and splent on spauld,
> And gleuves of green and feathers blue.
>
> There were five and five before them a',
> Wi' hunting horns and bugles bright,
> And five and five came wi' Buccleuch
> Like Warden's men arrayed for fight."

The story of how he tried to scale the walls of Carlisle Castle, but failed and had to undermine a postern to obtain entrance, how in the face of the amazed garrison with Lord Scrope himself at their head, who discreetly kept within his chamber, and how he effected the release of Kinmont Willie and bore him over the Border, fording the Eden and the Esk both in flood, is it not in the records of the House of Buccleuch?

This brave deed has been accounted one of the finest achievements and it compelled the admiration of even Queen Elizabeth herself. As a Queen she was grievously offended at this daring raid into her kingdom, and demanded and obtained the arrest of Buccleuch, but as a woman, she admired the dash and gallantry he had shown.

It is said that she asked him how he dared to undertake so hazardous an enterprise, when he replied, "What is there, madam, that a man dare not do?" This answer so impressed the Queen that she exclaimed "This is a man indeed! with ten thousand such men our brother of Scotland might shake the firmest throne in Europe!"

The rescue created a profound sensation throughout the Border country. Amongst the forty rescuers were Roby of "ye Langhame", three Armstrongs of the Calfield, Jock o' the Bighames, young John o' the Hollows and one of his brethren, the Chingles, (Zingles on the map of 1590. The tower stood near Ewes kirk and the name survives in Swingle) and Christie of Barngleis.

A formidable list of charges was formulated against Buccleuch, one of them being that he had "bound himself with all the notorious riders in Liddesdale, Eskdale, and Ewesdale". Evidently to give moral support to this indictment, Lord Scrope, smarting, no doubt, under the chagrin of having been so outmanoeuvred by his fellow Warden, marched into Liddesdale with a large following, burned many homesteads and literally massacred many of the people.

However, Buccleuch came safely out of the difficulty, in which he had the sympathy, if not the help, of his King, who seems to have stood in mortal fear of offending Queen Elizabeth, whom he hoped to succeed on the English throne.

Sir Walter Scott of Buccleuch was, in 1606, raised to the Peerage of Scotland with the title of Lord Scott of Buccleuch, and the secondary titles of Lord Scott of Whitchester and Eskdale. He died in 1611, and was succeeded by his son Walter, who was made an Earl in 1619. He also received grants of land and obtained other territories by purchase.

In 1619 he bought the Lordship of Eskdalemuir and, from Sir John Ker of Jedburgh, he bought all the lands belonging to the old Cell of Canonby which had been under the Abbey of Jedburgh. This purchase put Buccleuch into possession, not of Canonby alone, but also of the extensive church lands of Wauchope, which were usually conjoined with those of Canonby.

A man of considerable learning was this Lord Scott, and a noble of almost princely hospitality. He had a library of about 1200 volumes in Latin, French, Italian, Spanish, and English. He died in London in 1633 aged 46 and was succeeded by his second son Francis, who was then only seven years of age. His eldest son had died in infancy.

Francis added considerably to the family estates, acquiring Dalkeith, by purchase, from the Earl of Morton, and on 7th April, 1643, also receiving a charter of the Barony of Langholm. The granting of this charter coincided with the forfeiture of the Earl of Nithsdale and it made the Earl of Buccleuch the principal baron in Eskdale, the greater part of which now fell into his possession. Francis warmly espoused the cause of Charles I against the Parliament, and when Cromwell assumed the government, he imposed upon the Earl of Buccleuch a fine, the largest ever inflicted it is said, equal to about £200,000 Scots.[11]

The second Earl died in 1651. The year before his death, having lost his only son in infancy, he had had the patent of his Peerage extended to heirs-female.

In 1653 the teind sheaves and other teinds of the kirk of Westerker, within the regality of Melrose, formed part of the property of Mary, Countess of Buccleuch, who had succeeded her father, Francis, at the age of five. She married Walter Scott of Highchester, afterwards Earl of Tarras, and died without issue in 1651.

Her sister Anne became the next Countess of Buccleuch and on her marriage to James, Duke of Monmouth, he was created Duke of Buccleuch and she became Duchess. Some time later she became Duchess in her own right.

CHAPTER 16

OTHER ESKDALE CLANS

According to some authorities there were eighteen recognised clans on the Scottish Border, besides a number of what were known as broken men. The latter were numerous groups, more or less closely bound by family ties to act in co-operation, though not necessarily recognising one head. The principal clans, such as the Maxwells, Scotts, and Johnstones, held their baronies from the Crown, and their chiefs exercised a firm control over their members and retainers. The chief of the clan was loyally obeyed by his followers and possessed more disciplinary power over them than did the most powerful baron outside the clan. This suggests that the clan system was really a survival of the old tribal laws of the Celts, modified by the altered conditions of tenure.

The head of the clan was looked to by the government to pledge the good behaviour of his followers, and was frequently required to give hostages as guarantees of this assurance. These hostages or pledges could be changed for others. The Privy Council Records of the period contain lists of the pledges and their substitutes, and also indicate the various castles where such are to be warded.

The clan system, to which much of the lawlessness of the Borders was, no doubt, attributable, was a corollary of the feudal system. The well regulated clan made for law and civil order; but with the broken-men things were different. Every man's hand was against them.

When the Border barons combined against the broken-men in 1569, the latter were not permitted "nor their wives, bairns, tenants, or servants to dwell, remain or abyde or to pasture their gudis upon any landis outwith Liddesdaile". Their raids, plunderings and feuds, were often the result of the weakness of the central government and the

148

political relationships existing between the two countries. Amongst these clans, or broken men, the Armstrongs, Elliots, Littles, Beattisons, and Irvings were the most numerous and powerful in Eskdale.

THE LINDSAYS

The Lindsays were amongst the earliest settlers in Eskdale. As early as 1285 they possessed lands in Langholm, Stapelgortoun and Wauchope and for several centuries they maintained a connection with Wauchopedale. Their sympathies, for the most part, were with the English King, and at Bannockburn, Lindsay of Wauchope fought against Robert the Bruce, and was taken prisoner.

At the Battle of Otterburn, however, the Lindsays fought bravely on the side of Douglas, one of the most conspicuous being Alexander Lindsay, lord of Wauchopedale. The head of the House of Lindsay at this time was Sir James of Crawford, and he, too, fought for Douglas at Otterburn.

Their stronghold was Wauchope Castle adjoining the present kirkyard. Here they kept state as lords of Wauchope and here many an exciting incident occurred. One such, indeed, resulted in the Lindsays losing, for a time at least, their possessions in Wauchope. The sheriff of Eskdale at this time was Bartholomew Glendinning, in whose family the office was hereditary. In 1505, in pursuance of his official duties, he had to proceed to Wauchope to distrain the lands of the Lindsays in respect of the third portion which formed the jointure of Margaret, widow of John Lindsay. His son John, who was in possession, resisted the distraint with the full muster of his feudal retainers, and in the skirmish which ensued, Glendinning and his brother Symon were both killed.

John Lindsay followed up this incident with several lawless raids and when summoned to appear before the King and his justices, he failed to answer. The proclamation summoning him to appear was made at the "merkat croce of drumfries", and he had to "compear personaly" at Edinburgh, "or quhar it sal happen thaim to be for the tyme". In his absence he was found guilty of high treason, and sentenced to lose his life and his goods. His lands in Ewes — Fiddleton, Unthank, Mosspaul and Mosspeeble— were given to Lord Hom, and those in Wauchope reverted to the Crown.

There seems, however, to have been an element of insincerity in this sentence because, in the April of the following year, Lindsay received grants of land in Galloway and Annandale. From *Pitcairn's Criminal Trials* we get a further glimpse into this fray at Wauchope Castle. One Patrick Dunwedy was convicted in 1508 of "art and part" in the killing of the Laird of Glendunwin, and "treacherously going forth of Scotland and treasonably remaining out of Scotland for common theft, and for the inputting and outputting of goods between England and Scotland". For his offences, which appear to have been sins of omission, as well as commission, Patrick was hanged, and his goods escheated.

THE GLENDINNINGS

This family, though it rose to considerable importance and social position in Eskdale, did not greatly influence local history. Its earlier representatives appear to have come from near Hawick and to have been introduced into Eskdale by the Douglases. Members of both families fought side by side at Otterburn, where Sir Simon Glendinning was killed. The Glendinnings maintained cordial relations with the Douglases until the Battle of Arkinholm, when they abandoned their old friends and helped in their disastrous defeat.

As early as 1376 Sir Adam Glendonwyn occupied, as a tenant, the farms of Eskdalemur and La Baly, now known as Bailey Hill. In 1380 Sir Adam was the receiver of the Douglas revenues for Eskdale. Later, he attained the high position of Ambassador to the English Court, and about this time received grants of the lands of Bretallow, i.e., Barntalloch or Stapelgortoun. In 1391 he mortified certain of his lands in the barony of Hawick for the establishment of a church or chapel in Westerker, which was that of Byken.

In 1407 Sir Simon Glendoning was appointed by Archibald, fourth Earl of Douglas, hereditary bailie or sheriff of Eskdale, an office which remained in the family for at least 100 years. It was in the exercise of the duties of this office that the conflict at Wauchope Castle occurred. Towards the end of the fifteenth century John of Glendonwin and Parton "was possessed of the 80 pound land of old extent of Glendoning, the lands and baronies of Bretallow, Wauchope, Langholm, Westerker". Amongst the last were those of Daldorane, the name then given to Westerhall.

In 1458 the Glendinnings received a charter of the lands of Parton, and possibly most of the family removed there, but a considerable remnant remained in Eskdale. Part of the lands of Daldorane belonged to his sister-in-law, but John seems to have appropriated the harvest, and now, by an Order of the Lords of Council, he was ordered to restore it, to wit:—"ij chalders and a half of mele and twenty four bolls of mele, price of the boll *xs*. takin up be the said John of the fermes pertening to the said Merjory of her third and terce of the lands of Skraisburgh and Daldorane". John of Glendoning did not seem sympathetic towards this arrangement, for when summoned by the Lords he failed to appear, whereupon they issued letters of distraint.

A similar Order was made in 1492 in respect of almost the same lands, in favour of Bartholomew, his son and apparent heir, and his wife Margaret, daughter of John Gordoun of Lochinwer. Later, in 1532, we find the Glendinnings occupying Billholm and claiming Harperwhat and Applewhat, which probably had been given to them as their portion of the spoils after Arkinholm.

In Monypeny's *Chronicle,* published in 1587, the name of "Glendyning of Portoun" appears in the list of the lairds of Dumfriesshire and Kirkcudbright. This laird was a descendant of the Glendonings of Eskdale. In 1606 Robert married Margaret Maxwell, daughter of Lord Herries By this marriage he obtained the enjoyment of Arkin and Broomholm, in addition to the lands above mentioned. After this date most of the Glendinnings seem to have left Eskdale, though representatives of the family are still found in the valley.

THE JOHNSTONES

The Norman name of which Johnstone is the Scots form was de Janville and sometimes de Jhoneville.[1] Like most of the Border barons, the Johnstones came into Scotland in the early part of the thirteenth century. When Edward I was trying to subdue Scotland, the Johnstones, like so many other barons swore the oath of fidelity to him, for Scotland was as yet only the land of their adoption, not the land of their fathers.

But by the date of Otterburn these Scoto-Norman barons had become more strongly imbued with Scottish aspirations, and so we find the Johnstones fighting on the side of Douglas.

The Johnstones were, of course, more intimately associated with Annandale than Eskdale. Their principal estates lay in the Stewartry.

Their nearness to the Maxwells and the consequent clash of ambitions, provided the opportunity for the long lasting family feuds. Personal rivalry between the Lords of Caerlaverock and the lairds of Johnstone excited much unrest and bitterness, aye, and much needless bloodshed on the Borders during the fifteenth and sixteenth centuries.

The Johnstones, who were the direct descendants of Johnstone of Westraw, do not come upon the scene in Eskdale until early in the seventeenth century. In 1608 Johnstone of Westraw was associated with his nephew, the laird of Johnstone, in a petition praying for vengeance to be taken on Lord Maxwell, for the slaying of the laird's father.

In 1624 he sold his Lanarkshire estates, which had been given to his ancestor for his services at Arkinholm, and bought lands in Eskdale from the Glendinnings. These lands were known as Daldoran but Johnstone changed the name to Westerhall after his old estate.

The connection of Johnstone of Westraw, afterwards of Westerhall, with the Annandale Johnstones, is indicated by his being made a party to the suit, begun in 1619, by the Earl of Buccleuch and other Border barons against the guardians of the young laird of Johnstone, for the recovery of the Annandale charter chest, which, after some litigation, was finally restored by Lady Wigtown, mother of the laird.

The son of the first laird of Westerhall was the Sir James Johnstone who became notorious in the days of the Covenanting persecution. At first a zealous supporter of the Presbyterian party, he changed sides and became a fierce enemy of the Covenant. In the Eskdale persecutions he was associated with John Graham of Claverhouse, but more relentless and more inflamed with fanatical passion, as renegades usually are, than even Claverhouse himself.

Concerning the house itself there is very little that is noteworthy. Its architecture is mixed and, of the old Scottish baronial style of the original building, only a small portion remains. Many weird stories concerning Westerhall have been handed down in Eskdale — stories of strange sights being seen, and strange sounds heard. Many of these no doubt owed their origin to ordinary and natural causes, but they came to be associated with the religious feeling of the dale and centred themselves in Johnstone, whose name was held in such evil repute by the generation following the Covenanting period.

Some of the "prophecies" of Alexander Peden, the Covenanter, related to the Johnstones of Westerhall, and not a few of these are believed by Eskdale people to have come to pass.

The laird of Westerhall was knighted by Charles II for the part he took in the suppression of the Covenanters. The baronetcy dates from 1700.

WESTERHALL

One of the grandsons of the first Sir James was Governor Johnstone, who acquired a considerable repute as an administrator of Britain's East India possessions, concerning which, in 1771, he published a work entitled *Thoughts on our Acquisitions in the East Indies*. In early life a naval commander, he was, in 1778, along with Lord Carlisle, sent out as one of the Commissioners to treat with the Americans and to offer them liberal terms of peace. Congress, however, declined to negotiate with the Commissioners, unless they acknowledged the independence of the United States, so they were compelled to return home without having accomplished their objective

Another member of the Westerhall family who rose to considerable distinction was Sir William Pulteney, lawyer and politician. He married the heiress of William Pulteney, Earl of Bath, the famous Parliamentarian of the reign of George II, and added her name to his own.

The Johnstone family owned the Westerhall estates for 287 years

153

but in 1911, during the life of the 8th Baronet, Sir Frederick John William Johnstone, the estates were broken up and sold in portions. The historic mansion house, the lands attaching, and the Hostelry at Bentpath and several farms, were purchased by Mr. F. Berkley Matthews, of Lartington Hall, near Barnard Castle.

THE ARMSTRONGS

Among the Border clans none was more powerful, none more famous, than the Armstrongs. During the sixteenth century the clan wielded an immense influence on both sides of the Border, an influence which had to be reckoned with by both the Scottish and English Governments. The Armstrongs occupied many of the well known Border towers, around which the different branches of the clan were grouped. Not only in Liddesdale, but in Ewesdale, Eskdale, Wauchopedale, and Annandale, they formed a considerable portion of the fighting men. It is said that no fewer than 3000 Armstrongs from the Border dales would answer the call of their chief.

Their raids and expeditions are matters of history. Wardens corresponded about them, as did Kings and Queens, but the Armstrongs persisted and succeeded, despite all the resources of civilisation which were requisitioned for their suppression.

The head of the clan was the Laird of Mangerton in Liddesdale. As early as 1376 there was an Armstrong in Mangerton and the connection between the family name and the place lasted until well into the seventeenth century.

Whithaugh was also a lairdship belonging to the Armstrongs, and its chieftain ranked in importance next to Mangerton. From Liddesdale they had spread into Eskdale and are also recorded as early as 1456 in Ewesdale, a David Armstrong occupying Sorby. The original charter of Whithaugh having been lost, Francis, Earl of Bothwell, re-granted the lands in 1586 to Lancilot Armstrong.[2]

In 1501 James IV ordered Bothwell, who was then Warden of the West March, to extirpate the Armstrongs, so evidently, even at that early date, the clan had become obnoxious to the ruling powers. When the King in person visited Eskdale in 1504 on his tour of repression, known in history as the Raid of Eskdale, he summoned the Armstrongs to his Court, but it does not appear that they obeyed. They had been put to the horn in the previous year. This state of outlawry was declared by an accompaniment of three blasts on a horn.

It must be admitted that during the times of unrest on the Borders the Armstrongs were not consistent upholders of the Scottish authority. They seem to have been swayed by motives of expediency and, occasionally, they even incur the suspicion of double dealing. Evidence is not altogether wanting that, whilst they were hunting with Lord Maxwell, they were also running with Lord Dacre. In one of the letters of Dacre to Wolsey dated 1517, whilst yet the English, flushed with their victory at Flodden, were devastating the Borders, Dacre tacitly admits that the Armstrongs are in his service in these raids.

The main interest in the Armstrong clan, so far as Eskdale is concerned, centres in the famous border reiver, Johnie Armstrong, brother of Thomas Armstrong 7th Laird of Mangerton. During the 19th century he became known as Johnie Armstrong of Gilnockie and the name continues to be used. However this title arose for the first time in the ballad, where it can be attributed to poetic licence rather than historical fact, and also in Pitscottie's *History* in which he has copied his wording from the ballad. In all documentation during the 16th century Johnie Armstrong is described as *John the Larde,* or *of Stubilgortoun,* or *of Langholm* or *of Hole-house.*

The Armstrongs were, under Lord Maxwell as superior, in possession of very considerable holdings in Eskdale. Johnie Armstrong held lands under a charter dated August 1525 in Stapelgortoun and Langholm, and at Shiel and Dalbeth. These lands were gifted to him by Lord Maxwell in November 1525 in exchange for Johnie's bond of manrent.

David and Ninian Armstrong were vassals of Lord Home in respect of lands in the Over-parish of Ewes. The clan formed almost a circle round Langholm, and Christopher Armstrong, Johnie's brother occupied Langholm Castle itself, a disposition of their forces which afforded the Armstrongs a great strategic advantage, both in attack and defence.

The repeated raids by the Armstrongs naturally evoked reprisals, and considerable confusion resulted from the fact that neither the English nor the Scottish Warden was quite sure that the other was not aiding and abetting them. Maxwell was suspected of complicity in their raids into England, and Dacre admitted employing them in his secret service.

At length the question became one of serious import to both countries, and to solve the problem it was proposed by the Scottish Council to lay waste the entire Debateable Land, and not only dispossess but slay its inhabitants. The Government thought to make a desert and doubtless they would have called it "Peace!"

The plan to be followed was to take from the people, notably the Armstrongs who had caused the commotion, "all ther gudis and possessiones, byrn and destroy ther housis, cornys hay and fewall and tak all thar wiffis and barnys and bring them to portis of the see and send them away in schippis, to be put on land in Irland or uther far partis quhar fra tha might nevir return haim agane". This root and branch policy required a like resolve on the part of the English Government as to the English raiders and the idea came to nought.

The Armstrongs paid small respect to the commands of either the Scottish or English Warden but, when occasion demanded, played off one against the other with much advantage to themselves. In 1526-7 the heads of the clan erected a number of strong towers on the Debateable Land contrary to the agreement between Lord Maxwell and the Earl of Cumberland.

The main stronghold of Johnie Armstrong was Holehouse which he may have built as early as 1518. Later the spelling became Hollas and then Hollows. During the 19th century, it became known as Gilnockie's and then Gilnockie Tower.

To destroy these towers Lord Dacre raised a force of 2000 men, and in February 1528 he marched into the Debateable Land. Armstrong and his followers had got intelligence of this proposed raid from, it was supposed, Richard Grame of Esk and were prepared to meet Dacre. In the fight the Armstrongs defeated the English; but Dacre, evidently with the aid of artillery supplied by the Earl of Northumberland, attacked and burned Holehouse. As a set-off, Armstrong went down the same day and burned Netherby.

These occurrences were followed by demands for redress from both Wardens. Dacre claimed from Maxwell in respect of the burning of Netherby, and Maxwell claimed from Dacre in respect of the raid on the Hollows. The bills given in by the two Wardens set forth the claims very clearly and picturesquely. Dacre recites the story of the attack on Netherby, and asks "redresse as the law of march will". Lord Maxwell's answer is:—

"As to the burnyng of the houses in Nederby, in Ingland, this is myn ansuer. The same day before none, com the Lord Dacre, Sir Cristofer Dacre, their complicis and servantis, to the nombr of ij thousand men, within the ground of Scotland and the landis of Cannonby; and there brynt ane place called the Holehouse, and houses and cornes, and draif and took away certain goodes; and desires the said lord that that may be redressed, for causs that all was done at ane tyme accordanly to the todes".

Maxwell at the same time sends in a bill in which "complenes John Armstrang of Stubilgorton, Scottisman", that Dacre came "to the Holehouse within the lordship of Eskdale and the grounde of Scotland, and ther took had and reft, of the said John, goodes, and his servantis, horse, nolt, shepe, gayt, and insight of houses, and brynt houses byggingis and cornes, again the vertue of the treux", &c. Lord Dacre replied that the Hollows was not in the Lordship of Eskdale, but was on "a parcell of the Debatable Grounde", and there the matter seems to have rested.

The great confederation of the Armstrong clan was broken up by the murder of Johnie Armstrong by King James V. But although the power of the clan was crippled, the Armstrongs continued in considerable strength in the various parishes of Eskdale well into the eighteenth century.

The story of the King's treachery has been often told. The massacre, for such it was, had been carefully planned by him and his councillors. In May 1530 those Border chiefs, such as the Maxwells and Scotts, who might have thwarted the King's purpose, were, by a trick, enticed from the Borders and put in ward in Edinburgh or other places.

When all the preliminaries had been thus completed James set out, at the end of June, for the Borders, arriving at Carlenrig in Teviotdale, on 5th July. It has been said that the King and Armstrong met near to the old toll bar at Fiddleton, and that the former had his camp on the hillside opposite, which thereby received the name of Camp Knowes. The King was accompanied by 8000 men, barons and lords amongst others, all well armed and provisioned for a month. His purpose was a double one: to hunt game, and to hunt those who were responsible for the unrest on the Scottish Border, or were suspected of raiding.

Very good sport of both descriptions had the King and his gentlemen, who had brought their deer hounds with them. Three hundred and sixty deer were killed[3], and "efter this hunting the King hanged Johnie Armstrong, laird of Kilnockie quhilk monie Scottis man heavilie lamented for he was ane doubtit man and als guid ane chieftane as ever was upon the borderis aither of Scotland or of England. And albeit he was ane lous lievand man and sustained the number of xxiiij weill-horsed able gentlemen with him yitt he never molested no Scottis man".

So says Pitscottie in his picturesque narrative of the King's hunting. According to the well-known ballad it seems that the King had invited Armstrong to meet him, the letter being couched in terms of peace and friendship. Trusting implicitly in the good faith of the King, they accepted the invitation.

Buchanan hints that Armstrong failed to obtain the King's pass for his security, but this mattered little, for the King was bent on the massacre. Tradition says that Armstrong's company consisted of 50 horse, and that they went unarmed. The failure to provide himself with a pass only shows the more clearly that he had accepted the King's letter in absolute good faith. Armstrong and most of his company were hanged, the trees at Carlenrig serving as the gallows. There is still a tradition in Ewesdale and Teviotdale that the trees on which the executions were carried out withered away.

Nothing in the history of that century created more consternation and indignation on the Borders than this. Much of the later bloodshed was owing to this judicial murder. The Borderers deeply resented the treachery and breach of faith.

King James himself seems, at length, to have seen the dishonour of it, for not a word is found in any of the State papers concerning the matter. The trial is not recorded and no mention is made of the hanging. The story lives still on the Borders, enshrined in the most famous of all the ballads.

One historian refers to Johnie Armstrong as him "who keipit the Castell of Langhame"[4]. This is incorrect as in February of 1529 Johnie had resigned the lands of Langholm to Lord Maxwell. Three days after the murder all Johnie's other lands were assigned, by order of the King, to Lord Maxwell. These lands were held by the Maxwell's until 1558 when Christopher Armstrong of Barngleis, also known as John's Christie, gave a bond of manrent to Maxwell in return for his father's lands.

On the date of the above bond Sir John Maxwell of Terregles grants a warrant to "my fameilar frend, Christie Armstrang callit Jhons Christie, to intromet with the haill teyndes of the perroche of Stabillgortoun . . . . the said Christie payand tharfoir yeirly ay and quhill he be dischargit, to me, my aris and assignais the sum of viij^{lb} good and usuale money of Scotland at Lames".

In 1562 Christie was appointed by a contract, dated at Lochmaben, keeper of "the hous and place of Langholme" until John, Lord Maxwell should be of "perfyct age, ... when he cumis to the handling of his levin". In consideration thereof, Christie was to have yearly "in tyme of peax the soum of xl pound", and in time of war a sum thought reasonable by "four honest gentlemen".

Christie himself resided at Barngleis, and delegated his duties at Langholm Castle to his sons, Archie and Robert, his third son John meanwhile occupying Hollows Tower.

With Lord Maxwell, when he went to Stirling in 1585, there were Christie Armstrong of Barngleis, Archie and Robert Armstrong of Langholm Castle, and also Armstrongs from Potholm and Milnholm.

After the murder of Johnie Armstrong in 1530 some Armstrongs sought refuge in England and served as mercenaries of the Crown, but many had remained in Eskdale.

There is a record of a trial in 1605 in which appears a number of Armstrongs "delaitit for taking airt and pairt for the treasonable burning of the House of Langholme, (the term treasonable was probably used as Langholm Castle had been taken over by the Government) and taking Herbert Maxwell of Cavense prisoner and for the thieftious stealing of certain nolt, horse, sheep, gait and burning certaine coirnis pertaining to the said Herbert, Alexander Bell in Eikeholme [i.e. Arkinholm], William Bell in Gallosyde and George Irving in Holmhead".

The Armstrongs concerned in these acts, which had occurred in 1581, were: "Ingrie Armstrang, Enzieholm; Archie Armstrang, the merchand in the Hoilhouse; Johnne Armstrang in the Hoilhouse; Ninian Armstrang called Roweis Niniane, in the Murtholme; Cristie Armstrang cosine to the Gudeman of Langholme (Johnne Armstrang)".

The demonstration against Herbert Maxwell of Cavense was due, possibly, to his having dispossessed the Armstrongs as keepers of Langholm Castle. Scrope, in a letter to Burghley, of date 30th Sept., 1581, refers to this incident as the "burning and spoiling about the

Langholme and taking prisoner Herbert Maxwell the captain.

The Earl of Morton, the Warden, demands delivery of certain English Borderers who were present and intends on Tuesday or Wednesday next to seek for the fugitives"[5.] Scrope adds that "James VI. and counsele are verie much offended with the burning of Langeum in Euesdale . . . and keeping the captain of the same prisoner, being the Lord Maxwell his lande, wherefore the said Lord Maxwell threateneth to revenge yt with burnings in the maner in England".

After this trial sureties were required that "the said Herbert Maxwell, his wife and bairnis, shall be harmless and skaythless in their bodies, landis, and gudes and geir, of the said John and Christie Armstrang, the said John under pane of ane thousand pundis and the said Christie under pane of five hundreth pundis".

By a special Act of the Scots Parliament, marriage with the daughters of the broken men of the English Border was forbidden to Scottish subjects, without the King's express licence given under the Great Seal. Thomas Musgrave, writing to Burghley in 1605, gives some interesting facts concerning the Armstrongs:—

"John Armstrong of the Caufield dwelleth on the Cawfeld, not marryed in England. Gorthe Armstrong of the Byganis dwelleth on the Bygams and marryed Will of Carl(i)lles daughter. All these are the Lord of Mangertons unckles or uncles sonnes at the furthest. The Armstrongs of Langholme, and their allys with England: Creste Armstrong, goodman of Langholm Castell marryed Robbye Grayme's sister called Robbe of the Field ; John Armstrong of the Hollous married Walter Grayme's sister of Netherby".

The Armstrongs of Enzieholm, and other places in upper Eskdale, first came there in 1525 and their occupation seems to have continued until 1605, but after this date no trace of them is found in upper Eskdale.

In Ewesdale the Armstrongs occupied Arkleton and Sorby. Arkleton was given, in 1537, to Ninian Armstrong by Robert, Lord Maxwell. In Ewes Kirkyard there is a stone recording the death of Thomas Armstrong of Sorby, who died 14th. May, 1761, aged 81 years, and also of William, his son, who died 31st. July 1782, aged 72. At the end of the eighteenth century Sorby was sold to the Duke of Buccleuch and the daughter of the laird of Sorby at that time was the grandmother of Mr. Simon Irving of Langholm mill.

In 1528 Lord Home had granted to Ninian and David Armstrong, in consideration of their bond of manrent, the lands of the "Uvyr [Over] parrochin of Ewisdale". Probably both of these grants relate to Arkleton. In 1535 David Armstrong received from the King a charter of the lands of Park, now called The Bush, in Ewesdale, which had previously belonged to Robert, Lord Maxwell. In 1607 Andrew Armstrong was in Kirktoun and Thomas Armstrong in Glendovane. Both were put to the horn and denounced as rebels for not restoring certain teinds to Lord Home.

Frequent reference has been made to the Armstrongs of Wauchopedale. Their stronghold was at Calfield, sometimes called Calfhill. In some of the documents Calfield, like Dumfedling, is entitled a *Tennendrie*. In the charter of Langholm given to the Earl of Nithsdale in 1621 Calfield with its mill is mentioned. The reference is probably to a mill on the Becks Burn. That there were more mills than one in Wauchope is seen from the Tack of Wauchopedale to Robert, Lord Maxwell, in 1526, in which occur the words "with the mylnis, fortalice, and fischeing of the samin". Calfield therefore was a place of some importance. Here they occupied a position dominating the Water of Wauchope.

In his *Minstrelsy of the Scottish Border,* Sir Walter Scott mentions Jock and Geordie of Calfield as well as Archie, the hero of a ballad entitled *Archie o' Ca'field,* which celebrates the forcible rescue of Archie from Dumfries jail.

There were other members of the clan in Wauchope besides those of Calfield, from whom they had probably descended. There were Armstrongs in Bloughburnfoot and in the Grains, a farm which, at the beginning of the nineteenth century, stood a little to the north-west of Wauchope Schoolhouse. It is from these Armstrong's the present writers are descended in the female line. An account has been orally handed down in the family that John Armstrong, shepherd, lived in the Grains at the date of the Gonial Blast in 1794, the disasters of which he experienced very severely. He was the father of James Armstrong, meal dealer and carrier, in New Langholm.[6]

One of the quaintest Armstrong characters is Archie Armstrong, Court fool in the reigns of James VI and Charles I. Archie is said to have been one of the Armstrongs of the Stubholm, probably a son of Richie, and to have been himself addicted to the fashionable pursuit of freebooting.

The story of the Sheep and the Cradle is possibly only a legend, but if true it may have established Archie's claim to be a humorist. When pursued on one of his sheep stealing expeditions, Archie managed to get home to Stubholm, where he quietly dropped the sheep into the child's cradle. He was sitting composedly at the ingle-nook, apparently rocking the baby to sleep. when the Warden's men arrived. When accused of the theft, Archie is said to have answered:—

"If ere I did sae fause a feat
As thin my neighbour's faulds,
May I be doomed the flesh to eat
This very cradle haulds!"

Search, however, revealed Archie's clever deceit, and he was marched off to Jedburgh where King James was then holding a Court. Sentence of death was passed, but even then Archie's wit did not desert him. He asked to be permitted to read the Bible through before he suffered the penalty of his misdeeds. The King granted this, whereupon Archie exclaimed, "Then deil tak me gin I read a word o't as lang as my een are open!" The King was struck with the originality of the youth, and at once took him into his service as jester.

The Court fool was, of course, a prominent figure at the royal banquets. "The guests", we read, "made him their butt, and he repaid their ridicule in his own fashion, with impunity and applause. To the Sovereign his society was almost indispensable".

In the British Museum there is a scarce and curious pamphlet entitled *Archie's Dream,* which contains some account of the antagonism between Archbishop Laud and Archie Armstrong. The jester lost his position at the Court of Charles I. through having incurred the anger of the Archbishop. This quarrel provoked much amusement at Court, though Laud himself does not seem to have enjoyed it. The story goes that on one occasion Archie asked permission to say grace at a dinner at which Laud was present, and the request was granted. "Great praise be to God", he said, "and little *laud* to the devil!"

On another occasion, during the commotion caused by the attempts of Charles and Laud to introduce Episcopacy into Scotland, Archie, who sympathised strongly with the Presbyterians, encountering the Archbishop on his way to the Council chamber, remarked: "Ah, who's fool now?" This sneer is said to have so enraged Laud that he made formal complaint to the King, and Archie Armstrong of the Stubholm was dismissed from his post as Court Jester.

The order is dated Whitehall, 11th March, 1637, and is to the effect "that Archibald Armstrong, the King's fool, for certain scandalous words of a high nature, spoken by him against the Lord Archbishop of Canterbury . . . . shall have his coat (the coat and cap were the symbols of the jester's office) pulled over his head and be discharged of the King's service and banished the Court . . "

Whilst Archie was in the King's service he received the freedom of the city of Aberdeen. He lived to hear not only of the death of Laud but also of the beheading of King Charles. He returned to Eskdale and died in 1672 and was buried at Arthuret.

THE ELLIOTS

The Elliots, like their allies, the Armstrongs, were a Liddesdale clan having moved there from Angus in the time of Robert the Bruce.[7] They did not at any time rival the Armstrongs in numerical strength, but they were generally found acting in co-operation with them, and also with other smaller clans.

In the list of assurances taken in 1544 by Lord Wharton, after he had so completely subdued Annandale, Eskdale, and Nithsdale, the Elliots, to the number of 74, are grouped with the Armstrongs and Nixons. But in a subsequent list of "Scotesmen bound and sworne to serve the Kinges majestie", the Elliots are grouped with the Simpsons of Liddesdale to the number of 80.

The intimate association of the Elliots and the Armstrongs is humorously illustrated by a story of Armstrong of Sorby. When on circuit, the Lords of Justiciary passed down Ewesdale, and Sorby was accustomed to show them hospitality. On the occasion when Lord Kames went on circuit for the first time as Advocate Depute, Sorby noticed him and enquired of Sir Gilbert Elliot, "Whae that lang black dour-looking chiel was they had wi'them?" "That", jocosely replied Sir Gilbert, "is a man come to hang a' the Armstrongs". "Then", observed Sorby, drily and significantly, "it's high time the Elliots were riding!"

The general alliance between the Elliots and the Armstrongs, however, did not always bind the entire clan, for in 1579 a feud arose between them and the Armstrongs of Ewesdale. These would probably be the Arkleton Armstrongs, and possibly those of Park. But the feud was not deadly, nor of long duration, and was confined to the sections of the two clans in Ewesdale.

The name Elliot, which in Eskdale is still pronounced as it was frequently spelt in the fifteenth and sixteenth centuries, *Ellot*, was found in the north of England at an early date, but it was the early part of the fifteenth century before it was common in Liddesdale. In 1549 one Robert Elliot was captain of the Hermitage.

The chief of the clan was the laird of Redheugh, and in 1573 Robin Elliot of Redheugh is mentioned as chief. Braidlie and Larriston were also Elliot strongholds, and towards the end of the sixteenth century the clan numbered 800 to 1000 men. In 1563 Robert Ellot of Reidhoucht, and Martene Ellot of Braidlie, signed a bond to enter one of their clan, Gawin Ellot of Ramsygell, a prisoner to Sir Thomas Ker of Ferniehirst. It was in honour of Jock Elliot of Larriston that James Hogg wrote *Lock the door, Larriston, Lion of Liddesdale*.

By reference to the Rent-roll of Crown lands of 1541, some idea can be obtained of the great extent of the lands tenanted in Liddesdale by the Elliots. It was probably from one of these Liddesdale branches that the Elliots came into Ewesdale. The members of the clan who went with Johnie Armstrong to Carlenrig would be those from Arkleton in upper Ewesdale. The clan does not seem to have established itself at any time in the lower part of Eskdale.

An interesting bond of connection between Eskdale and the Liddesdale Elliots comes through the Elliots of Midlem Mill, from whom the Elliots of Minto are descended. The last of the name to hold Midlem Mill was Robert Elliot, who became Chamberlain to the Duke of Buccleuch at Branxholme. In 1726 his daughter Magdalen was married at Langholm Castle to James Paisley of Craig in Westerkirk, and they had eleven children all of whom reached maturity.

The Elliots of Ewesdale and the Scotts (probably of Howpaslet) were at feud in the year 1565. In pursuance of this feud it seems that the Elliots had attacked the Scotts and carried off a great quantity of plunder. The Scotts quickly retaliated. They mustered all their forces and set off in pursuit of the Elliots, who enticed them into Ewesdale. They had reached Ewes-doors, the narrow pass which, skirting the Wisp, branches off in a north-westerly direction from the foot of Mosspaul Burn into

Teviotdale, when some 400 Elliots and supporters, who had been lying in ambush, suddenly appeared. The pass, which shows traces of ancient earth fortifications, is narrow and easily defended.

In the sharp encounter which ensued the Scotts were taken by surprise, and being considerably inferior in numbers they were heavily defeated. A number of them was slain and sixty were taken prisoners. It is said that not only were the Elliots highly delighted with this success, and by the gratification of their feelings of revenge, but that they were highly commended and rewarded by the Government for their defeat of the powerful Scotts.

The Elliot clan branched off into several families of repute, the principal being those of Stobbs and Minto. Members of the clan settled in Eskdale after the cessation of the Border raids, and in some instances they have occupied as tenants, for several generations, lands held from the Duke of Buccleuch.

In 1679 Walter Elliot, was tenant of Calfield, and also had sett to him the farms of Glencorf, Tanabie, Water Grains, and Cleuchfoot. In 1793 there was an Elliot in Yetbyre, the ancestor, we believe, of the Elliots of Westwater. It is from the Redheugh stock that the Elliots of Arkleton are descended. In Unthank churchyard are the graves of the Elliots of Millburnholm, the Dandie Dinmont family of Sir Walter Scott's *Guy Mannering*.

THE LITTLES

The Littles formed one of the small clans of Eskdale, and inhabited part of Ewesdale and part of Westerkirk, easy access being obtained from the one to the other through Sorby Hass, and they were also found in Wauchopedale. The earliest mention of the name in Ewesdale is Edward Little of Meikledale[8] who was a nephew of William Wallace and accompanied him during his exploits in the Wars of Independence. A Nicol Litil is mentioned in 1398 as one of the sureties for the Earl of Douglas, who at that date was Warden of the West March.

In 1426 James I confirmed a grant which had been made by Robert, Duke of Albany, of the lands of "Mikkledale of Kirktoun" in favour of "his beloved and faithful Simon Lytil". The grant comprised not only Meikledale and Kirktoun, but also Sorby, and there were also included certain lands which had belonged to the Frasers of Arkleton, viz.:— Senbigil, Malnarlande, Pullis, "lyand in the barony of Mallarknok within the Sheriffdom of Drumfres"[9], but they do not appear to have been places in Ewesdale, which at that date was within the Sheriffdom of Roxburgh.

Simon Lytil of Meikledale was the head of the clan and his descendants continued in possession of the estates for more than two hundred years. The last Laird of Meikledale was David Little who, in1665, sold the land to Adam Elliot.

The clan was never a large one. Their name is not mentioned in the list of headsmen under English assurance in 1547, though, curiously enough in the summary of dales, Ewesdale is included with 364 men, whilst it does not once appear in the detailed list. In the list of clans in 1553 who were under oath to the English King, the Lytles are grouped with the Batysonnes, Thompsons, and Glendonynges, and the total number of men is returned as 304. The Beatties, Thomsons and Littles appear to have had a working alliance and were frequently associated in committing raids on both sides of the Border.

After the lands of Meikledale were sold in 1665 the Littles continued in Ewesdale and several names are to be found in Ewes kirkyard. One of the earliest gravestones there records that Thomas Little, son of David, Laird of Meikledale, died on 27th April 1675 aged 67 years. Thomas was married to Maisie Batie. They had a son Simon Little in Wrae, also recorded on the same stone, who married Isabel Dickson. Thomas Little in Carlesgill, born circa 1645, may also be a son of Thomas Little and Masie Batie.

Simon in Wrae and Isabel Dickson and had four sons:—

David, vintner in Langholm, who was the father of Simon Little in Nittyholm.

Simon in Terrona, married Margaret Little, who was probably the daughter of James Little in Sorby and his wife Margaret Gibson. They had ten daughters and three sons, two of the sons dying in infancy and the line from his third son, as far as we can tell, has died out.

William in Wrae

George in Stenniswater

The Littles of Eskdale and Wauchopedale were probably branches of the Ewesdale family, and acknowledged the headship of the laird of Meikledale. When, in 1532, James V granted to Robert, Lord Maxwell, the superiority of the lands in Eskdale, claims were lodged by the Beatties, Thomsons, and Littles, in respect of certain lands, such as

Yetbyre, Enzieholm, Lyneholm, and Shiel. The Littles seem then to have been located in the lower part of Westerkirk parish.

In 1679 William, Thomas, and John Little were joint tenants under the Duke of Buccleuch, with Walter Thompson and William Rewe, of Shiel and Bankhead, and at the same date one Matthew Little was a tenant in Bombie. Also in the same year the farm of Neishill, near to Calfield, was let jointly to Andrew Little and John Hislop, brother of Andrew Hislop the Martyr.

In Wauchopedale, the seat of the Littles was at Bigholms, but the number of this branch of the clan must have been small. One of the few references relating to this family is in a document of which the following is a translation:—"At Holyroodhouse, 19 Nov. 1628. The King, with the consent of John, Earl of Mar, Lord Erskine and Gareock, Treasurer, Enroller (and) Collector of Accounts, and Treasurer of the new augmentations, granted letters of pardon to Thomas Grahame in Bigholms, styled *of Shaw*, and to Robert Little of the same, for the. slaughter of John Grahame in the lands of Grains, in the month of June or thereabouts".

This association of the Littles and Grahame in Wauchope is interesting when noticed in relation to a record in the Books of Adjournal of the Justiciary Office, of date Dumfries, 13 August, 1504 "John Litill convicted of art and part of the cruel slaughter of the late Thomas Moffet and being at the King's horn for the same slaughter and for art and part for supplying and assisting the rebels of Eskdale and for the theft and concealing the sheep of Robert Grahame of Gillisbe, hanged".

During the seventeenth and eighteenth centuries the Littles were one of the most prominent families in Langholm. John Little, writer, merchant and banker in Langholm was, according to a Little pedigree produced by Bluemantle in 1811, another son of Thomas Little in Meikledale and Masie Batie.

John married, in 1685, Grizel Wylie of Canonbie. Grizel died in 1703 and was the first person to be buried in the new kirkyard (now known as the Auld Kirkyard) at the head of the Kirkwynd in Langholm. After his wife's death John married, in 1713, Helen Little of Westerkirk.

In 1730 John Little was granted an Honorary Burgess Ticket or Freedom of the Burgh of the City of Glasgow. This grant can be for special services or in recognition of distinguished visitors and is donated at the discretion of the Lord Provost. John died in 1741 and is buried with his wife in Langholm Kirkyard.

It is interesting to note that an antique desk, which at one time belonged to this John Little, came into the possession of the Littles of Old Carlesgill, and from them passed to the Bells of the Walk-mill of Langholm, and thence to Mr. Arthur Bell of Hillside.

John and Grizel had four sons, Thomas, of unknown occupation, and John, Archibald and James all merchants in Langholm, and one daughter, Blanche, who was twin to Archibald. This Archibald married Helen Hotson and died in 1778 without surviving male issue. He is buried with his parents in Langholm Kirkyard.

John Little, son of John and Grizel, married, in 1721, Elizabeth Aitchison and died in 1733.

Their son John, born 1729, also a merchant in Langholm, became known in Langholm and district as Laird Little. He married Miss Mary Maxwell of Broomholm, daughter of William Maxwell and Agnes Scott. Their residence was at Rosevale House. It was from Laird Little that *The Laird's Entry* received its name.

When, by the order of Court, the Commonty of Langholm was divided in 1759, this Laird John Little, together with Simon Little in Nittyholm, and Archibald Little, feuar in Langholm, was in possession of three of the ten merklands of Langholm, having the year before conveyed one other merkland to John Maxwell of Broomholm, presumably his brother-in-law.

Laird Little met with an untimely death in 1794. He had been riding and took his horse down to the river Esk. The night being very dark he was unable to see that it was in flood, and both horse and rider were swept away at the place now known as St. Mary's Stream.

Laird Little's eldest son, John, died without surviving issue. His second son, William, was a doctor in Ecclefechan and his descendants are now in Australia.[10] They appear to be the only surviving direct male line from Thomas Little and Maisie Batie. Other lines exist but all are through the female side.

John Little and Grizel Wylie's daughter Blanche, 1694-1761, married, in 1716, Matthew Little in Turnerscleugh and Whitshiels, who was the son of Matthew Little, previously mentioned, in Bombie. They had two sons, Matthew and Archibald, their father dying soon after his younger son's birth.

RELATIONSHIP OF LAIRD LITTLE AND BAILIE LITTLE

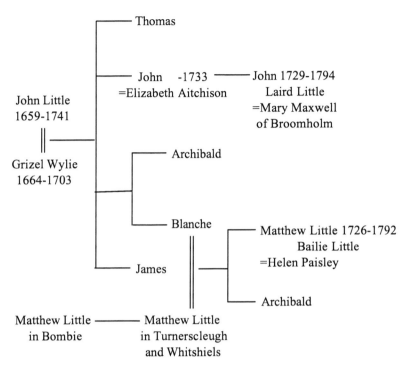

His uncle Archibald made Archibald junior heir to his merkland in Langholm and a tenement of houses and yards in the Kirkwynd and a seat in the kirk. Archibald, junior, married Jean Beattie and he and his family are known as the Brae Littles. They and their eldest son, Matthew, are recorded on John and Grizel's gravestone.

Matthew Little, the elder son of Blanche and Matthew Little in Whitshiels, married Helen Paisley. In 1768 he was appointed by William Ogilvie, Chamberlain to Henry, Duke of Buccleuch, to be his Chamberlain-depute and baron-bailie for the parishes of Canonby, Langholm, Castleton, Ewes, Westerkirk, and Eskdalemuir. His surety and cautioner on this appointment was George Malcolm in Douglen, who was his wife's brother-in-law, George Malcolm being married to Margaret Paisley sister of Helen, and both being daughters of James Paisley of Craig and Magdalen Elliot.

Twelve years later Matthew Little received a factorship from the Duke himself, authorising him to collect the revenues of Westerkirk, which had accrued to the Duke as patron of the parish in the vacancy between the translation of the minister, the Rev. Mr. John Scotland, late minister of that parish, to the parish of Linlithgow, and the induction of his successor, the Rev. Mr. William Little.

Matthew Little, holding the important office of baron-bailie, was one of the most influential men in Eskdale. He became known, and is still spoken of, as Bailie Little. For a long period he exercised, both wisely and well, his great influence in Langholm, and was regarded by the townsfolk with pride and affection.

In addition to the administration and accounting of the Buccleuch estates, there was laid upon him by this instrument of factory, the duty of holding baron's courts, a feudal custom and right which had survived to the Duke, even after the passing of the Heritable jurisdictions Act of 1747.

THE BEATTISONS

That the Beattison clan, and its various spellings of Batison, Baty, Batie and Batysonne, was one of some importance in Eskdale, even before the Battle of Arkinholm in 1455, is evidenced by the fact that they are grouped with the Scotts, Glendinnings, Maxwells, and Carlyles, as taking a considerable share in the overthrow of the Black Douglas.

In 1458 three Beattison brothers were given grants of land as a suitable acknowledgement of their services at Arkinholm and as compensation for the slaughter of their brother by the Douglases, which occurred the night before the battle.

John Beattison was given, by James II, a grant of two and a half of the merk-lands of Daweth or Dalbeth. Nicholas Beattison was given, two days later, a similar grant. This charter professes to be signed and witnessed on the same day as the charter given to John, yet, though they are numbered consecutively in the *Great Seal Register,* the first is dated October 20, and the second October 22. In the first, the lands are described as in the barony of Westir Ker; in the second, as in that of Westerker. The third brother, Robert Beattison, was given a grant of two Merk-lands in Whitshiels.

The Beattisons seem to have been given, or to have acquired, during the second half of the fifteenth century, a much larger stretch of territory in Eskdalemuir than the charters of 1458 conveyed.

The chief of the clan is said to have lived at the Score, or Skoire, situated on the left bank of the Esk just to the north of Rennelburn. In 1584 there were members of the clan in Black Esk, in Whisgills, and in Corse, and in 1605 there were Beattisons in Byken. This summary conveys only a small idea of the strength of the clan in Eskdale in the sixteenth century.

In 1544, like the rest of the Border clans, the Beattisons came under English assurance as the result of Lord Wharton's raids. In his list they are included with the Thomsons, and the total number returned is 166, and an additional number of 116 is given as under the headship of Sander Batie, making a total of 282. In 1553 the Beattisons appear with the Glendinnings, Lytles and Thomsons under a similar assurance, and the total number is 304.

In 1504 James IV organised his famous Raid of Eskdale, and on his way there he visited Dumfries to hold an ayre, or criminal court. At this court Nicholas Beattison was called for his lands of Dalbeth, and, not compearing, he was fined £10, as was also the laird of Lymin [Lyneholm], who was also a Beattison.

During the days of raiding and reiving, the Beattisons appear as bold, venturesome and, it must be added, somewhat unscrupulous riders. Like the Armstrongs they were not greatly troubled by considerations, either of patriotism or sentiment, and raided the Scottish Border, on Lord Wharton's instructions, with a zest which was not less than that which they displayed when harrying the subjects of England.

Perhaps the most active period of raiding by the Beattisons was from 1540 to 1550 when the Borders were in a state of great tumult and unrest. Large companies of the different clans made incursions into England, the Beattisons being generally well to the front in these forays. Here is a short list, compiled with the care of an accountant by Lord Wharton himself, of those in which the Beattisons took an active part:—

"The Batysons and Thomsons of Eskdaill have burnt a town called Grange, with all the corn there and brought away nolt and other goods amounting to eche of them in their dividing 8s".

"The Batysons, Thomsons and Lytles of Esshdayle, Ewesdaill, and Wacopdale burnt a town on the Water of Dryff called Blendallbush and brought away 16 oxen and keyne, some naggs with all the insight of the town".

"The Batysonnes, Thomsons and Litles, Scottishmen, burnt a town upon the Water of Lyne and brought away as muche boutie as was to eche of them 10s".

After the notorious invasion by Lord Wharton in 1544, the clans were brought to terms and received under English assurance, the Beattisons, on Wharton's orders, turned upon their own countrymen, and burnt and raided in Scotland with as much dash and daring as they had exhibited at the Water of Lyne.

Writing to the Earl of Shrewsbury, Wharton says:—"Advertising also your Lordship that by my command one hundrethe of the Batysons of Eskdaill who with the rest of their surname and the Thomsons entered in bond and delyvered thare pledge unto me in fourme, as I write to your Lordship therein, the same night afore that meeting with Bukcleughe, brent a town called Fastheughe of George Carr landes taking away all the insight certaine naggs and fiftie nowte".

In one expedition initiated by Wharton, they attacked Branxholme and Mosshouse, and "smoked very sore the towers". In another they "burned Old Melrose and overrun Buckleugh". Moreover, they did not confine themselves to the Borders in their ravages and forays, but ventured even into Edinburgh itself. We read that the "Beatisons and Scottishmen of Eskdaile wanne a tower of the captains of Edinburgh Castle, called Burdlands, burnt all the roofs within the walls and coming home took many oxen and shepe besides 1 Scott slayn".

In 1569 many of the Border barons, landed men and gentlemen of the shires, combined against the broken men. Whether their ardent professions of loyalty to the King, and their desire for peace on the Borders, were quite sincere, may be doubted. Some of the barons were not in their secret hearts such "inymeis to all thevis inhabitants of the cuntreis of Liddisdail, Eskdaill, Ewesdaill, and Annandaill" as they "professit". But their declaration sounded well, though there is not much evidence of steps being taken for the restoration of order.

When the Regent went to Hawick, in October, 1569, "Hew Beattie callit Johnne the Braid enterit plegeis to my Lord Regentis Grace for thame selffis, thair sonnis, men, tenentis, servandis and haill surname of Batesonis and als in name and on behalf of the surnames of Thomson and Glendonyng, thair men tenentis and servandis; that they sall redresse all attemptattis agains England for tymes bigane and to cum, and all Scottismen offendit to sen the Kingis coronation at thair uttir power".[11]

The above pledges could be relieved by "David Batie, brother to Hew Batie, Mungois Arthour Batie, Nicholl Batie of the Schield, Nickoll Batie of Carnisgill, Johnne Batie in the Yardis, Johnne Batie, son to Wat in the Corse". In accordance with this arrangement, we find, in November, 1569, that David Batie was "placeit" in the Castle of St. Andrew's and Johnne Batie of Yards in the Castle of Glasgow.

In 1584 many of the clans gave assurances of good conduct at Hermitage Castle, and among these occurs the name of David Batie of the Black Esk. But this assurance on his part did not bind other members of the clan, for, only three years later, John Beattison, called John of the Score, John Armstrong, called the Laird's Jock, and four other Armstrongs with 500 men ran a day foray, which was an aggravated offence against the Laws of the Marches, and "carried off 600 kye, 600 sheep, 35 prisoners and insight worth £40 sterling".

About the year 1590 a complaint was entered by Sir Walter Scott of Branxholme "that Johnne Batison in the Scoir, Nickie Batisonn his son, David and Archibald Baitiesonnis his brothers, all dwelling in Eskdale, reft from Somerville furth of the lands of Meineinchald, 26 cows and oxen, 2 horses and one staig; and from Mowbray 10 cows and oxen and 1 mare with the plenishment of his house worth 100 merks". Being called as bailie of Melrois to answer for the Batisonns he (i.e. Sir Walter Scott) declares that not he but Lord Maxwell is answerable.

Moreover, that though he, the complainer, is bailie of the Abbey of Melrose yet the inhabitants of Eskdale never have acknowledged him in the said office, but on the contrary have committed "divers herships and oppressions upon him and his servants for which there is deadly feud now standing more especially between the said Sir Walter and the Batiesons of whome the said persons viz. John Batieson of the Scoir, etc. are principalls".[12]

This extract, the latter part of which is taken from the *Privy Council Registers,* is interesting as showing not only the state of tension between the two clans, but also as an indication of how there arose that conflict of title as to lands in Eskdale.

In 1598 special proclamation was made by the King, with the advice of his Council, concerning the broken men of the Borders. A commission of eight honest gentlemen was set up to try the offences committed by the Armstrongs, Beattisons, Irvings, and Johnstones. To these clans the King offered his clemency "giff they sall make full redress for their evil deeds", but if they should resort to deceit and trickery, then no mercy would be shown them, "they sall be hangit without mercy or favour".

The Beattisons did not rush to accept these terms, and very soon afterwards a charge was made against certain of the clan, to wit, John Batie of Tanlaw Hill, David Batie his brother, Alic Batie of Black Esk, Rowie Batie, Andro Batie *alias Steenie Home*, Adam Batie of the Yards, Johnne Batie of Rennelburn, Cristie Batie of Bankhead, John Batie of the Score, and Archie Batie his brother, that they had refused to pay to Lord Maxwell "his mailles, fermes, and duties owing to him by them furth of the Lordships of Eskdaill, Ewisdaill, &c". For this refusal they were denounced as rebels. Several were hanged, including John of the Score, their reputed chief, and the clan generally was broken up.

Nevertheless, the Beattisons were not yet wholly driven out of Eskdale. The clan was broken, but many of its individual members remained. Even the King seems to have partially relented of his severity towards them, for in 1605 he granted to Hugo Batye de Boykyne certain lands in the parish of Westerker, which lands Hugo sold in 1610 to Walter Scott of Tushielaw.

This possession of the lands of Byken by Hugo Beattison is the subject of a ballad by William Park,[13] the Eskdale poet, entitled *Burn and Byken*. The poet himself was a descendant of the Beatties of Burn. His grandmother, Grizel Beattie was the daughter of William Beattie of Airswood, the third son of William Beattie of the Lyneholm,who died in 1693 aged 80 years and who was a son of Beattie of Burn, one of the reputed combatants in the duel. William Beattie of Lyneholm, also known as Will o' Burn, married Grizel Porteous of Hackshaw.

The ballad recites the story of a duel which, tradition says, was fought between the lairds of Burn and Byken, both of which places are in the parish of Westerkirk. The author says the former belonged to the Beattison clan, and that a great number of that name then (in 1833) resided in Eskdale. He says further that "A large stone, at a pass in the range of hills which separates Eskdale from Wauchopedale, and just at the point where the farm of Craig and those of Calfield and Cleuchfoot meet, is supposed to mark the spot where the rivals fought and fell". The dual, it is said, was followed by a lawsuit between the families which terminated in the ruin of both and the alienation of their estates. This tradition, however, is not corroborated by historical research.

Some of the Gravestones in Westerkirk, Canonby, and Ewes churchyard bear the arms of the Beattison clan, and these sculptured arms are similar to those of the different families of Beattie, or its synonyms, found in most of the churchyards of the Borders.

In virtually all of the arms, the cross keys and the draughtboard design are found, but it does not necessarily follow that both or either of these indicates an armorial bearing. The cross keys are found in many ecclesiastical coats, and are the emblems of St. Peter. In mediaeval times they were a common sign of inns attached to religious houses. A local illustration of this is the Cross Keys hostelry in Canonby, a name which doubtless came down from the days of the old Priory.

On the break up of the Beattison clan in 1599 many of its name migrated into Kirkcudbright, while others went to different parts of Scotland and England. With these migrations there came modifications of the name Beattison. In Eskdale it changed to *Beattie,* in other places to *Bateson, Baty,* and other forms.

Early in the 20th century there were still residing in Eskdale several descendants of the Beattisons of Dalbeth. One was Thomas Beattie, Esq., laird of Davington. The lordship of Davington was in the possession of the Scotts of the Howpaslet branch. About the year 1784, through some dispute about the succession of the Davington estate, it was sold by order of the Court of Session and was purchased by James Beattie, son of John Beattie of Dalbeth, of whom the above Thomas Beattie is a lineal descendant.

One of a list of "plegeis" of 28th October, 1578, is "Johnne Batie of Daventoun, in the custody and keeping of David Boiswall of Balmuto". So that this purchase of 1784 brought about a return of the Beatties to Davington after a lapse of 200 years.

Another link with the Beattison clan, though with the section of it that migrated into Northumberland when the final dispersion occurred, is the ownership of the estates of Meikledale, in Ewes, by Miss Beattie of Crieve. Her ancestor, Mr. Beattie, laird of Meikledale, is said to have supplied Sir Walter Scott with information concerning Eskdale given in his *Antiquities of the Scottish Border,* and also with many of the tales and traditions introduced into his *Minstrelsy and Lay of the Last Minstrel.* It is a matter of historic interest to note that Wat-Carrick was also in the possession of a descendant of the Beatties at the beginning of the 20th century.

THE THOMSONS

The Thomsons were a small clan occupying lands in upper Eskdale. Where their lands were or who was chief of the clan is not definitely known. The clan seems to have obeyed the call of the Beattisons of the Score and generally acted with them, sharing the fruits of their many raids and apparently, too, their reverses and punishments.

THE IRVINGS

The Irvings, who claim descent from a line of Scottish Kings, were a large and powerful clan on the Borders. At one time, probably in the early days of the Saxon period, the Irvings are said by the historian of the clan to have possessed all the lands between the Esk and the Nith.

They were originally an Ayrshire sept and came to the Borders with Duncan when, as Earl of Cumbria, he assumed the government of the lowlands. It is interesting to note that their placenames in Ayrshire are the same as those which afterwards came to be associated with the clan in Dumfriesshire, viz., Bonshaw, Bridekirk, Corsehill, Langshaw, and Balgray. The principal seat of the chief of the clan was Bonshaw Tower on the Kirtle.

The last chief of Clan Irving to reside there was Captain Sir Robert Beaufin Irving, K.B., O.B.E., R.D., D.L. who had a long and distinguished career at sea. He died in 1955 leaving no issue. His heir, Commander Snow-Irving, R.N., sold Bonshaw to Mrs. Eileen Keys Irving Stratton-Ferrier.[14] In 1975 she established the Bonshaw Tower Preservation Trust to ensure that Bonshaw would remain in Irving hands as it has been since the year 1020.

In the days of Robert the Bruce the Irvings were a clan of power and influence and support to the King. An ancestor of the Drum branch was his armour-bearer.[15] Bruce was a guest at Bonshaw in 1298 and again in 1306 when he was fleeing from Edward I. The room he occupied is still called "King Robert the Bruce's room".

When he came to the throne, the Bruce conferred upon one branch of the clan the lands of Drum in Aberdeenshire, and assigned to them the armorial device of three holly leaves, which now appears on the Irving coat of arms. This branch continued to hold these lands until 1976 when the late Mr. H. Q. Forbes Irvine of Drum bequeathed them along with an endowment to the National Trust for Scotland.

The Irvines of Ireland are another branch of the clan. Christopher Irvine was granted lands in Fermanagh by James VI and there he built Castle Irvine. The Irish and Drum branches of the clan adopted the spelling of "Irvine" but the Bonshaw stock retain the terminal "g".

The Irvings were mostly horse soldiers and as such they fought at Flodden, and on many another Border battlefield. The muster of the clan when strongest is given as 500 by Mr. A. Bruce Armstrong, who formed his estimate from the number of Irvings under English assurance in 1547, but Col. Irving of Bonshaw gives their strength as 742 men.

The position occupied by the clan in the councils of the Border chiefs may be inferred from the fact that, in 1547, when Lord Wharton had devastated virtually the whole county of Dumfries, it was the Irvings who were deputed to negotiate the terms upon which the clans would come under English assurance. The numbers of Irvings, or Yrwen as it is written in the documents relating to this matter, who then yielded to Wharton were Bonshaw 102, Robgill 34, Dyk's Ritchie 142, and various other branches 153, or a total following of 431.

The Irvings of Eskdale were the earliest of the Irving cadets[15] and occupied the peel tower of Stakeheuch, or Auchenrivock, on the higher ground on the south side of Irvine Burn a short distance from the road between Langholm and Canonby. It is around this tower that most of the history of the clan in Eskdale is circled. It need scarcely be said that the Irvings took their full share in the raids and tumults of the sixteenth and seventeenth centuries.

Dyk Irwen was one of the most famous and daring of the freebooters of the sixteenth century. On one occasion Lord Dacre complained that Dyk respected neither true pilgrims of the church nor the King's letters of safe conduct. In the list of ravages committed by the Scots in the West March of England in 1528, it is complained that:—

"The Irwens of Staikhugh to the number of vj did enter Englond ground and lyght upon Sir John Aruthureth and Jame Grayme, called Jame Fern, Englyshmen, and chasyd them to the howsez of Long Will Grayme of Stuble and brent the said Long Will best howse, with xxx other howsez standyng next to the same and toke and had away the said Inglyshmen and their horsses".

This incident occurred on the 9th of May, and on the 17th the Irvings, accompanied by Sande Armstrong, went to Brakanhill, slew

BONSHAW TOWER

William Waugh and Thomas Stavert, and "hed away certain goodis and cattlis".

On the 30th of the same month, the Irvings of Hoddom, and the Armstrongs with whom they co-operated in many raids and forays, paid a visit to the ground between the Esk and the Lyne and burnt 41 houses and 12 barns, and bethinking themselves that in their raid of the 9th to Stuble they had left a few houses standing, they repaired thither and burnt them also.

More than once, Stakeheuch suffered a like fate to Bonshaw, but it was all part of the game, and probably either side would have held the other in slight respect had there been no such reprisals. In 1547, the Irvings made their submission to Lord Wharton.

There existed for several generations an informal alliance between the Irvings and the Johnstones of Annandale, although the former were on terms of friendship with the Armstrongs, who were at feud with the Johnstones. The families had also intermarried, and probably through this relationship some branches of the Irvings had been "kindlie tenants" of the laird of Johnstone. Another tie between the two clans was their mutual enmity towards the Maxwells.

When John, Lord Maxwell, was slain at the Battle of Dryfe Sands in 1593, the Irvings were found fighting on the side of the Johnstones. *The Book of Caerlaverock* makes mention of the respite granted by James VI to Sir James Johnstone, and eight score others, for the slaughter of Maxwell, and the list of Irvings includes "John of Lus, Habbie of Turnschaw, Richie in Staikheugh and Ekkie his brother, William callet Kange, Edward of Bonshaw and his sons".

The fact of the names being individually mentioned, in this and in similar lists of assurances, indicates that the authority of the head of the clan was not invariably accepted as sufficient. Clearly recognised is the individual responsibility of each man.

The Irvings are not very often mentioned in Border song or story, but in the popular ballad of *Fair Helen of Kirkconnell*, the clan claims the heroine as one of its members. Helen was loved by two suitors, one was Adam Fleming and the other was said to have been a Belof Blacket House.

Adam's was the favoured suit, and the jealousy of the other being aroused, he waited for a favourable moment to slay his rival. This came as the lovers were strolling along the beautiful banks of the Kirtle Water.

Seeing the danger her lover was in, Fair Helen stepped between him and his opponent. Receiving in her own bosom the bullet meant for her lover, she died in his arms.

Accounts differ as to what ensued. One tradition is that there and then the rivals fought and the murderer was slain. Another says that he fled to Spain, pursued by Fleming, who slew him in the streets of Madrid. Returning to Kirkconnell, the distracted lover cast himself upon Fair Helen's grave and died. Their graves may be seen in Kirkconnell churchyard and on his tombstone are inscribed the words "HIC JACET ADAMUS FLEMING".

Such is the story of Fair Helen of Kirkconnell. But the family of the heroine is a matter of dispute. She is claimed confidently by the Irvings, who possessed Kirkconnell until the year 1600, when Robert, Lord Maxwell, deprived them of it. But she is also claimed by the Bells of Blacket House, and it is now impossible to ascertain to which family Helen really belonged.

THE SCOTTS OF EWESDALE

The last Eskdale clan to which reference need be made is that formerly known as the *Scotts of Ewesdale*. This title has been the cause of some confusion respecting the identity of the clan. Not unnaturally, it has been sought for in Ewesdale, as a place distinct from Eskdale. But the Scotts were one of the Upper Eskdale clans, and do not appear to have had any connection with the valley now known as Ewesdale.

The explanation of the use of *Ewesdale* lies in the fact that, in the latter part of the seventeenth century, the whole of Eskdale, with its tributary valleys, was included in the county of Roxburgh. Ewesdale, being adjacent thereto, assumed therefore a much greater importance than Eskdale itself. In some of the old maps the entire district is called Eusdale, and Eskdale is only brought in as a subtitle.

This clan of Scotts, distinct from the Scotts of Buccleuch, sprang from Scott of Howpaslet, now called Howpasley, on the Borthwick Water, a valley stretching roughly east and west between Eskdalemuir and Teviotdale. Scott of Howpasley's son became Scott of Thirlestane, and the family was known by either designation.

Robert I gave to the conventual house of Melrose certain lands in Upper Eskdale, and that the Avenels and Grahams also gave to the monks certain proprietary rights in Eskdalemuir. From 1504 to 1517, the Abbot of Melrose was William Scott, eldest son of Sir William Scott of Howpasley, and in 1564 Michael Scott, of the same family, was Commendator of Melrose.

There is a tradition that the Abbot granted Davington to his relatives of Howpasley, and in 1568 the Commendator granted a charter of the lands of Thirlestane, Ettrick, and other lands to Robert Scott of Thirlestane. When the monasteries were annexed to the state in 1587, the possessions of the Abbey of Melrose were forfeited to the Crown. By a charter, dated 24th. March, 1613 at Newmarket, England, the King granted certain specified lands "all formerly incorporated into one tenandry of Dumfedling in the Regality of Melros", to William, Earl of Morton, who, having resigned these lands, the King, by a charter dated Edinburgh, 7th. April, 1613 , granted them to "Walter, Lord Scott of Bukgleugh".

Robert Scott of Thirlestane married Lady Margaret Scott, sister of Buccleuch. Their grandson Patrick Scott of Tanlawhill, was great-grandfather to Lord Napier of Magdala. Robert Scott of Thirlestane's great-great-grandson was Robert Scott of Davington, who, on the death of his brother John, became heir-male of line to the ancient family of Scott of Howpasley and Thirlestane.[16]

The grandfather of Robert Scott of Davington had borrowed on wadset, an arrangement akin to a mortgage, a sum of £120,000 Scots from Sir James Douglas of Kelhead, with Thirlestane and Davington as security. On 21st January, 1688, Sir James raised a summons against the heir, requiring him to assign over to him in satisfaction of the wadset, the lands of Davington, Fingland, Pentland, Dumfedling, Nether Cassock, Wester Polclive, Westwoodrig, and Burncleuch. He succeeded in his action, and having obtained these lands, assigned them, in 1702, to Anne, Duchess of Buccleuch and Monmouth, who at that time was eagerly acquiring whatever properties in Eskdale she could obtain.

Exempt from this action-at-law were Thirlestane and Davington Mains, both of which had been previously disposed of. In 1786 another lawsuit arose over these lands, which, by order of the Court, were sold and, as already stated, were purchased by James Beattie of Dalbeth.

Anne, Duchess of Buccleuch, soon acquired other properties which had formerly belonged to the various families of the Scotts of Ewesdale. From John Scott she bought Rennelburn He was the last laird of Rennelburn and in 1679 was a tenant of the Duke of Buccleuch in the farms of Langholm Mains and Balgray. He became factor to the Duchess, and it is doubtless in this capacity that he appears in the rent-roll for the farms of Arkinholm, Turnerholm and the Ten-Merk-Land. From Scott of Tushielaw she bought Moodlaw Knowe, Grassyards, Kimmingsyke, and Lairshawburn, from Scott of Raeburn, Raeburnhead, Yetbyre and Yards and from Francis Scott, Tanlawhill.

Whilst dealing with these changes in the ownership of lands in Upper Eskdale, originally belonging to this large clan of Scotts, we may mention the following:—

Robert Scott, the last of Davington, had sold Burncleuch to George Bell of Woodhouselees, whose descendants exchanged it with the Duke of Buccleuch for Castlehill. The Bells also acquired Crurie, Yards and Yetbyre. The father of the late Mr. Richard Bell, not liking the last name, changed it to Castle O'er.

The rest of the properties in Eskdalemuir which are now owned by the Duke of Buccleuch, but were formerly in the possession of other persons, mostly Scotts of the Howpasley or Thirlestane branch, are Causivay, now part of Nether Cassock, Aberlosk, now part of Langshawburn, Johnstone, Clerkhill, and Cot.

Considerable doubt seems to have existed as to who was entitled to style himself chief of the whole clan of Scotts. One writer on heraldry, quoted by the late Mr. T.J. Carlyle of Templehill, gave it as his opinion that whilst a male-heir of Thirlestane was alive, neither Harden, placed by Burke as chieftain, nor any other branch of the Scotts could succeed to the chieftainship of the Scotts.

At an Assize Court held at Peebles in November, 1587, Scott of Buccleuch appeared before the King at Neidpath Castle, when he and his friends expressly disclaimed all responsibility for, or connection with, the Scotts of Ewesdale.[17]

When, in 1590, certain chieftains were required to give cautionary bonds for the good conduct of their followers, the Scotts of Thirlestane, Tushielaw, and Harden were amongst those enumerated. But, in practice, Scott of Buccleuch had been recognised as, at least, first amongst equals, though the Scotts of Ewesdale did not obey his call.

The Scotts both of Howpasley and Thirlestane and also of Harden acted independently of Buccleuch until the year 1596, when Sir Walter Scott of Buccleuch enrolled them in his clan and guaranteed that their actions should not be obnoxious to the Government.

There were marriage connections between the Scotts of Howpasley and the Johnstones of Annandale. Auld Wat of Harden's wife was Mary Scott who, for her grace and beauty, was called *The Flower of Yarrow*, and her grandmother was a Johnstone of that Ilk. When the feuds between the Johnstones and Maxwells reached their culmination on Dryfe Sands in 1593, Johnstone was supported by the Scotts of Eskdale, that is of Howpasley and Thirlestane

When James V. contemplated an invasion of England in 1542, John Scott of Thirlestane was the only baron who responded to the summons of the King. He brought with him 70 lances, and the King, in gratitude, created him a baronet, and granted him an augmentation to his arms, a double tressure of *fleurs-de-lis* on his shield, a bundle of lances for crest, and "Ready, aye ready" for a motto.

We have dealt at this considerable length on the identity and history of these various clans, because all through the sixteenth century their raids and forays affected so intimately the history of Eskdale, and at the present time afford an interesting study of Border life.

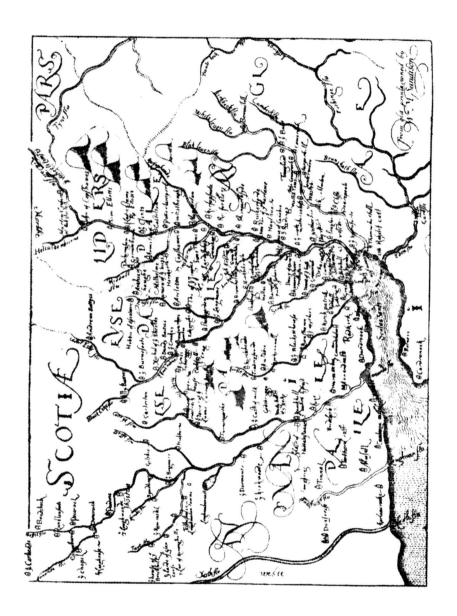

TOWERS ON THE DEBATEABLE LAND
From an old print owned by Wm. M. Sandison

CHAPTER 17

THE DEBATEABLE LAND

DETAIL TO SHOW HOLLAS TOWER

The ancient kingdom of Strathclyde, or Cumbria, extended from the Clyde in the north to the river Derwent in the south. But the tract lying between the Solway and the Derwent, with Carlisle as its chief town, was wrested from Malcolm, King of Scotland, by William the Conqueror. When David I came to the throne the boundaries of the kingdoms were settled virtually as they are to-day.

However this did not prevent the Kings of both countries from casting envious eyes upon the lands adjacent to the Borders, and whilst the Edwards were seeking to subjugate Scotland, they repeatedly made claims to land which the Scottish King and nation did not admit. In 1298 Edward I. seems to have claimed Eskdale as belonging to England and appointed Simon Lindsay chief keeper of the district. But this claim was soon withdrawn. Probably, from motives of care for the safety of the Priory, the monks of Canonby, during the incursions both by Scots and English, obtained for themselves a writ of protection from the English King, whilst at the same time they possessed charters from the King of Scotland.

In 1403, after the Battle of Homildon Hill, Henry IV gave the lands of Eskdale to the renowned Henry Percy, who, however, only saw his promised land from a far distance, and did not venture to take possession of it. Henry's gift was, therefore, a paper compliment only.

In 1528 the people of Canonby, evidently from motives of precaution, had been paying a certain tribute to England. Dacre, writing to Wolsey, mentions that when he had set a day for the people of Canonby "to bring in their protection", they replied "denyeing that they lived under any protection of this realme but claimed to be of Scotlaunde", and saying that the tribute they paid was an acknowledgement of their access to Carlisle market, and they quoted in support of their contention the "Indentur of Canabe".

In 1532, the English King requested Lord Dacre to combine with Maxwell in measures for completely destroying the inhabitants. The English Government, however, continued at intervals to press its claims as to Canonby. In 1543, when it was first proposed to divide the Debateable Land, the Scottish Ambassadors were instructed to agree to the division, "providing alwayis that Canoybe fall hale to Scotland".

When, at length, the division of the Debateable Land was determined upon, the Privy Council forbade the Scottish representatives to treat Canonby as debateable. The conference between the representatives of the two kingdoms in 1552 resulted in peace between the realms, and hopes were also entertained that the division of the Debateable Land would put a stop to the Border raiding. This hope, however, was not realised.

The Debateable Land included the baronies of Bryntallone, Kirkandrews and Morton, and all of these seem at one time to have been recognised as within the kingdom of Scotland, though it was afterwards claimed on behalf of England that this district was left undivided when the frontier was settled in the reign of Robert I. Early in the fifteenth century the district was held to be Debateable, and was so named in 1449, though we believe that on no occasion was this admitted by Scotland. Lord Maxwell, in 1528, claimed Hollows Tower as within the Lordship of Eskdale, though Lord Dacre denied this, and included it in the Debateable Land, the boundaries of which were as follow:—

From the Solway Firth to near the head of Tarras Water. On the east the boundary was the river Esk as far as the Mote of Liddel and then along Liddel as far as Greena Tower. On the west the boundaries were the Water of Sark and the Pingle Burn. The line then ran eastward by the Irvine Burn until the latter joined the Esk at Irvine House. The river Tarras formed the northern boundary. The district was over ten miles in length and six at its greatest breadth. On its eastern side stood the Towers of Hollows and Stakeheuch, or Auchenrivock. On its southern it was bounded by the famous Solway Moss and the Tower of Plump. On the north was Tarras Moss and in the centre were the Towers of Barngleis and Sark.

By the division of 1552 Canonby was given to Scotland, whose ancient claim to it was thus upheld, and Kirkandrews was given to England. The line of division was the stone and earthen wall known as Scots Dyke, part of which can be seen in the plantation opposite Scots Dyke Station, on the North British Railway from Carlisle to Edinburgh. This railway line was closed in the 1960's. The Dyke ran from this point on the river Esk over the hill to the Water of Sark, a distance of about five miles.

CHAPTER 18

CASTLES AND TOWERS.

The maps showing the strongholds in Annandale, Eskdale, Ewesdale, and Liddesdale in the year 1590 makes no distinction between castles and towers, or between towers and those little stone houses which existed in considerable numbers on both the Scottish and English Borders during the sixteenth and seventeenth centuries. Many of the places shown as towers or keeps must certainly have been houses of very moderate dimensions and strength. This was a necessity of the times because the residences of the less wealthy or powerful chiefs were liable to sudden raids and destruction. Houses were burnt one day and re-built the next. There was, therefore, no inducement to spend either time or means upon them. But dotted here and there were strongholds of a superior order. Towers like Hollows and Stakeheuch were meant to serve as refuges in times of more serious warfare, and upon them, therefore, both skill and labour were spent.

Of greater superiority still were the castles of the feudal barons, such as Wauchope, Barntalloch, or Meikledale, whilst military depots such as Langholm Castle, Thrieve, and especially Hermitage, were not only strongly built, but were well garrisoned and adapted to withstand a siege of considerable duration.

BARNTALLOCH.

Probably the oldest of the feudal castles in Eskdale was that of Barntalloch at Stapelgortoun. It stood on an eminence overlooking the Esk towards the south-east. On the north-east was the burn, into which there was a precipitous descent from the Castle, and on the west there

188

was a constructed fosse. No record has been left of its erection and only a fragment of the outlines can now be traced, though the site itself is distinguishable. Little doubt exists that the Castle of Barntalloch was of a strength and massiveness in keeping with the size of the barony of Stapelgortoun. This town was the centre of a large agricultural trade, and the baron's castle would be its principal residence, well built, strongly fortified by nature.

Barntalloch also served as the seat of justice for the district. There the baron's out-door court, perhaps held on the grassy slopes of the Castle grounds, would form one of the picturesque phases of a slowly advancing civilisation. The Castle would be occupied by the barons as they quickly followed each other in those days of rapid change:— Sir William de Kunyburg; possibly at times Sir John Lindsay or one of his sons; then the succession of the Douglases, or their factors, for it does not appear that they themselves habitually resided in Eskdale. No relic of those days remains. References in the contemporary records are few, so we can only to conjecture as to what manner of place it was.

WAUCHOPE

More historical data exist respecting Wauchope Castle. It was built by the Lindsays and continued in their hands, with little intermission, until their final forfeiture. It stood at the confluence of the Wauchope Water and the Becks Burn, on a plateau some 34 feet above the river, and occupied a site admirably adapted for defensive purposes. The plateau extends from north to south about 103 yards, and from east to west about 30 yards. The Wauchope runs the entire length of the buildings on the east; the Becks Burn forms a natural fosse on the north-west, whilst from north-west to south-west there ran an artificial fosse from the Becks Burn to Wauchope Water, which it joined at the Auld Stane Brig.

The Lindsays probably placed more value upon military strength than natural beauty, but the situation they selected for their Scottish castle offered both of these inducements, and herein it may be ranked with Barntalloch. When Lord Dacre made his notorious raid into Dumfriesshire after the Battle of Flodden, he boasted that he had laid waste almost the whole of Ewesdale and Eskdale, and that "all these these ploughs and townships are now clearly wasted, and no man

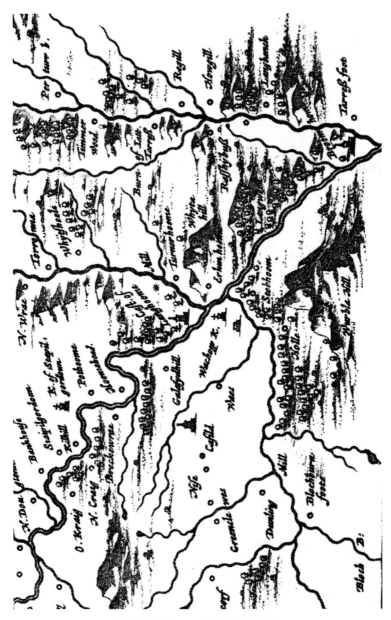

EUSDAIL AND ESKDAIL

Detail from Timothy Pont's map, circa 1590, published by Blaeu in 1654

dwelleth in any of them at this day, save only in the touns of Annan, Stepel, and Wauchope". The term "toun" meant the retainer's huts surrounding the baron's castle. Stepel may refer to Stapelgortoun. The fact that it and Wauchope remained unreduced is evidence of Dacre's inability rather than of his unwillingness to take these strongholds.

Wauchope Castle would be erected soon after 1285, when Sir John Lindsay received from King Alexander III the lands of Wauchope and Stapelgortoun. The Lindsays held the Castle almost continuously until 1505, possibly the only break being after the Battle of Bannockburn in 1314 when they forfeited their estates, until 1319 when the Bruce restored the property of Wauchopedale to the grandson of the original holder. When, in 1505, the lands were again forfeited after the killing of the brothers Glendinning, the Castle seems to have been left to decay.

During the unsettled days of 1518 the Wardens of the different Scottish Marches took counsel as to how peace and order could best be restored. One of their proposals was that Maxwell, Warden of the West March, should take up his residence in Wauchope, in which event they trusted "he with thaire help and with the help of other cuntremen nixt adjacent, mycht put reule to the cuntreis of Ewisdale and Eskdale, to the quhilk thai sulde be redy quhen the said Lord Maxwell walde require thaim".[1]

Eight years later in 1526, Maxwell obtained a tack of Wauchopedale "with the mylnis fortalice and fishing of the samin and thar pertinentis quhilkis pertenit to Johnne Lindesay of Wauchop". The consideration set forth in the tack, or lease, is Maxwell's service "in stancheing of thift and uther misrewle in the cuntre and for the bigging and reparatioun of the hous, tour and fortalice of Wauchop".

This charge implies that the Castle of Wauchope had fallen into a state of disrepair if not into actual ruin. By the year 1547, when Wharton and his coadjutors were over-running Eskdale and the adjoining dales, the Castle seems to have become a complete ruin, probably owing, in some measure, to Lord Maxwell being a prisoner of the English King. It is recorded of Sir Thomas Carleton that on one night of their march he and his party "lay in the old walls of Wauchope Tower".

In 1549 on his return from London, where he had been held as hostage, Robert, Lord Maxwell, appears to have set himself to restore his Wauchopedale properties. He appointed Patrick Bell as Sergeant of Wauchope.[2]

The Bells seem to have settled in Wauchope, as in 1679 we find there a Patrick Bell, no doubt a descendant of the sergeant, tenant of the Duke of Buccleuch. The following entry taken from the Stapelgortoun Registers relates to the same family:—"January 6, 1679. The sd. dy. Besse Bell d. to Patrick Bell in the Parish of Wauchope bapt. Wit. John Bell in Galaside and Adam Bettie, yr". May not this entry explain the origin of the name "Besse Bell's Brae", that picturesque corner in Wauchopedale, concerning which there has been much speculation?

On Blaeu's map of 1654, reproduced from maps by Timothy Pont, who carried out his survey of Scotland sometime between 1583 and 1596, Wauchope Castle is marked *Waes,* meaning a ruin.

Portions of the walls remained standing until well into the 19th century. A considerable piece of the eastern wall, fronting Wauchope Water, stood until about the year 1886 when, loosened by frost and rain, most of it fell into the river bed. This piece of wall, had been long undermined and there was a local tradition that it was the entrance to a cave. On the north side, another portion of wall stood until about the same date, when it fell into the Burn, probably dislodged by the roots of the great beech under which it stood. This piece of masonry was known as The Auld Wa's.

Excavations on a slight scale had been made before 1912 by some local antiquaries and the foundation walls were uncovered and an idea of the ground plan was obtained. These discoveries revealed a place of considerable strength, but were too partial to admit of a definite idea being formed as to the dimensions of the fortalice itself.

In the year 1726 some of the pipes supplying the moat of the Castle were dug up, and from their position it would appear that the moat was filled from Wauchope.[3] When the new road into Wauchopedale was made, about the year 1794, the workmen cut through a leaden pipe laid towards the higher ground to the west, and it was surmised that it had brought the water from a cistern on the adjoining hill-side.

Occasional relics have been discovered on the site of the Castle, but the most important is the hasp of a coffer, found in 1895 by James Reid, Langholm, and now in The Museum of Scotland, Edinburgh. In the *Proceedings* of the Society of Antiquaries of Scotland it is described as the "Enamelled Hasp of a Coffer found in the bank of Becks Burn, between the graveyard of the old church of Wauchope and Wauchope Castle, near Langholm. This beautiful example of thirteenth century

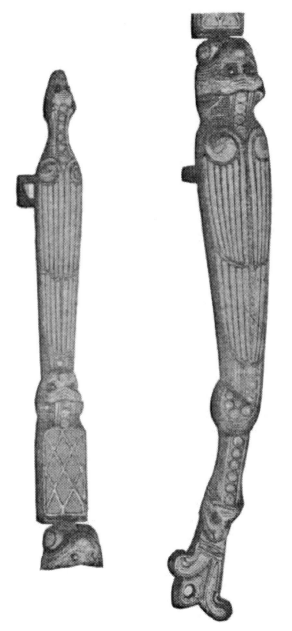

HASP OF COFFER, WAUCHOPE CASTLE

enamelled metal-work, of the school of Limoges, consists of two parts, each made in solid copper, and united by a hinge. The larger part, which was fastened across the top of the coffer, is modelled in the form of a dragonesque creature, with folded wings and a twist in its tail, which terminates in another head, from the mouth of which issues a floral scroll.

The other part, united to this by a hinge, which allowed it to fall down on the front of the coffer, carries on the under side a loop for the bolt of the lock. It is also modelled as a dragonesque form of slender proportions, issuing from the mouth of another. The enamel is *champlevé* in three colours, a pale blue, a light green, and a glistening greyish white. The ridges of metal between the enamelled surfaces have been highly gilt but have become corroded.

Coffers with such enamelled hinges, and other decorations of Limoges work, were largely used both in France and Britain in the thirteenth and fourteenth centuries, although this is the only example hitherto known in Scotland. There is in the Museum, however, a crucifix of similar work, in *champlevé* enamel, which was found in the churchyard of Ceres, Fife."

Further excavation in 1966 located the foundation of the castle wall. A fragment of pottery dating from the 13th century was also found.[4]

LANGHOLM CASTLE.

The Castle of Langholm belonged neither to the order of baronial residences such as Barntalloch and Wauchope, nor to the ordinary type of Border peel-tower such as the Hollows. It was obviously built for purposes which were military rather than residential, and conformed to a type common all along the Borders, ranking with such castles as Thrieve, Lochmaben, and Norham. It may, therefore, be regarded as occupying a middle position, of greater strength and importance than the Hollows Tower, but yet much inferior to Hermitage Castle, which was the military situation on the western Borders.

The site of Langholm Castle is one of charming natural beauty. Built on that fine alluvial tract known as the Castle Holm, it stands almost at the confluence of the Esk and the Ewes. At the date of its building both rivers probably flowed much nearer the Castle than they now do. This is according to evidence given before the Court of Session

LANGHOLM CASTLE
Photograph May 2000

in 1759, when the question of the division of the Kilngreen, in association with the Commonty, was being argued. Thus on two sides it was well protected. The position was chosen with judgement, commanding as it did the passes into Eskdale, Ewesdale, and Wauchopedale The castle is said to have been built by Christopher Armstrong, brother of Johnie of Holehouse, and son of Alexander, 6th Laird of Mangertoun.[5]

The photograph shows all that remains of the Castle. Most of the material, it is said, was afterwards quarried to build other houses in Langholm. Probably, what is now left was but part of the central tower. Judging by the wall still standing, and by the part of the foundation visible, this tower would appear to have measured from north to south about 56 feet, and from east to west about 30 feet. The walls were about five feet three inches in thickness.

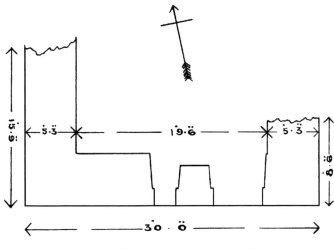

LANGHOLM CASTLE GROUND PLAN

In 1557, when Mary, the Queen-Regent, introduced the Gascoigne soldiers into Scotland, 600 of them were apportioned to Langholm Castle and to Annan for the defence of the Borders. It seems scarcely likely, however, that the Castle itself was capable of holding such a company. Its regulation garrison was a captain and 24 men. Possibly for the temporary accommodation of these troops, tents were requisitioned, and the laich houses about the Castle also brought into use.

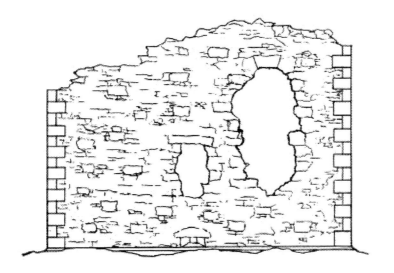

ELEVATION OF LANGHOLM CASTLE

Some confusion has been caused by the Castle of Langholm being referred to under other titles. In addition to Castle it is named the Place of Langholm, Langholm Tower, the Fortalice of Langholm, the House of Langholm, and sometimes as the House and Place of Langholm. Allowing for the lack of definiteness which characterised the wording in documents of that period, it would appear that all these designations attached to one and the same building.

In 1525 Johnie Armstrong received the gift of various lands in Eskdale from Robert, Lord Maxwell, in exchange for a bond of man-rent. Langholm Castle was then built by his kinsman, Christopher. However, in 1529 the Castle would pass absolutely into Maxwell's hands, when, to him, Armstrong resigned the lands of Langholm.[6]

Langholm Castle is first brought into prominent notice in 1544 when Lord Wharton made his notorious raid into Dumfriesshire. Towards the end of that year Langholm Castle came into his possession. Various writers have said that he obtained possession of it through the treachery of those Armstrongs, who had given bonds of man-rent to Lord Maxwell. So far as we are aware the only, or at least the most definite, statement on the point occurs in a letter dated 1546, from the Scottish Estates to the French King and his Ambassador in London.

In this letter they state that "Ane tour callit Langhope had been thiftuouslie taken by a Scottis tratour" and they pray the French King to "caus the King of ingland to leiss the said hous free to our Soverane Lady". It will be observed that the name of the "Scottis tratour" is not given. In a letter from Lord Wharton dated 27 October 1544 we get some further information. He says "certen of the Armstrangs of Lyddesdaill wan and spoyled the tower of Langhope, brought away all the goods in the same and 4 prisoners".

On this statement it has been taken for granted that the Armstrongs handed over the Castle to the English. It is not improbable. Like most of the other Border clans the Armstrongs were at this date *at the horn*, outlawed by the Scottish Government and were under English assurance.

In the early autumn of 1544 they committed five raids in Scotland whilst the Beattisons and Thomsons had but three to their debit. But the Armstrongs can scarcely be blamed for this transference of their allegiance. They were undoubtedly actuated at this time more by motives of expediency than by patriotism. But so were the nobles and barons. Opportunism was not then, and is not now, confined to the broken men and is readily adopted in the field of high politics.

We are not concerned to defend the Armstrongs but it seems necessary to state clearly the facts concerning the cession of Langholm Castle, and it does not seem to us that the treachery of the Armstrongs has been established. Admittedly the presumption may be against them, but presumption is not proof. And there are other factors in the case.

It will be remembered that after the Battle of Solway Moss in 1542, John, Lord Maxwell, had been a prisoner in London. But in 1543 he had been permitted by the English King to return to the Borders, on the clear understanding that he was to assist that monarch to achieve his designs in Scotland. Bound in this way by the conditions of his parole, Maxwell could not honourably do anything against Henry VIII.

However, by a delicate piece of casuistry, he conveyed to the Regent Arran a hint to the effect that though he himself was thus precluded from defending Scotland, his sons and all his means were at the Regent's service. Maxwell was then re-appointed Warden of the Marches, whereupon the English King immediately cancelled his parole and summoned him to London.

The petition to Queen Mary for the restoration of Langholm Castle did not meet with a favourable response from the English King. The Scottish Government thereupon determined to try to take it by force of arms. An army was assembled at Peebles on the 20th July, 1547, and marching to Langholm, it besieged the Castle for three or four days. The garrison, consisting then of 16 men with their captain, destroyed the lower portion of the tower, and from the highest floor stubbornly defended the place, until the besiegers, bringing artillery into action, fired seven shots, on which the garrison capitulated and Langholm Castle was once again in Scottish hands.

Concerning Langholm Castle after the siege, several writers say it was demolished, but the precise condition in which it was left does not appear. In 1562 we find Christie Armstrong of Barngleis, also known as John's Christie, son of Johnie Armstrong, appointed keeper "of the hous and place of Langholm" for John, Lord Maxwell, at a salary of forty pounds a year in time of peace. Other matters, such as the outlay for the upkeep of the house, and Christie's payments during time of war, were to be referred to the arbitration of two Maxwells and two Armstrongs. Christie deputed these various duties to his sons Robert and Archie.

They seem also to have been constables of the peace, under Lord Maxwell, as they were allowed a force of 24 men to police the Borders. It may be surmised that this appointment of Christie Armstrong was part of a scheme of reorganisation and repair of Langholm Castle which probably, since the siege of 1547, had stood in a dismantled condition

The stewardship of Langholm Castle held by Robert and Archie Armstrong appears to have ceased after Maxwell's raid to Stirling in 1585. In the list of those who, on that occasion, assisted Maxwell, are mentioned, "archie and ro[t.] armestrangis, sonis to christie in langholme". These are the only names given in the Act of Amnesty as from Langholm.

We have already mentioned the appointment of the laird of Johnstone as Warden in 1578, and the dispute between him and Maxwell about the key of Langholm Castle. Lord Maxwell's government as Warden had been so lax, that even his kinsman, Lord Herries, recommended that Maxwell should have "ane honest man his depute and capitane in the Langholme", and further that there might be placed at his service "twelf habil horsemen". It was possibly in conformity with this suggestion that Herbert Maxwell of Cavense was appointed captain, thus superseding the Armstrongs. However, in 1581 Scrope mentions "Creste

Armstrong, goodman of Langholm Castell", so evidently the Armstrongs remained there notwithstanding the appointment of Herbert Maxwell.

During the period 1578-1590 Langholm Castle was the object of more than one military expedition. When Lord Maxwell was restored to favour and made Earl of Morton, on the execution of the Regent Morton in 1581, Angus was so jealous of his privileged and powerful position that he made an inroad into Eskdale, burned and ravaged Maxwell's lands and also captured the Castle. By an order of the Secret Council dated 17 Sep., 1583, Johnstone and Christie Armstrong were ordered to deliver the place and fortalice of Langholm to John, Earl of Morton, within 48 hours, on pain of rebellion.

Maxwell, however, appears to have re-taken the Castle, for in June, 1585, we find Scrope writing to Wolsingham as follows:— ". . . . I am advertysed that the Lord Maxwell upon Tuesday last, himself being present, took the House of Langholme which was in the keeping of one of the Armstrongs called John's Christie, but of the Lord Maxwell's own inheritance, and had placed therein gunners and men of his own".

But the star of Lord Maxwell set once more in 1586. By the attainder against the family of Morton being cancelled, the title of Earl of Morton which Maxwell had obtained, reverted to the Earl's son, and Maxwell found himself under suspicion for his leanings towards Romanism.

He was permitted to leave the country, but, venturing on the advice of some friends to return, he again incurred the displeasure of King James, who was so outraged by Maxwell's insolence and by reports of his having promised assistance to the King of Spain in the equipment of his great Armada, that he was forced to take action against him. As Angus had done five years before, so now did King James. He marched into Eskdale, destroyed Maxwell's property and burned his strongholds, including Langholm Castle.

In 1597 a Commission of the Wardenship of the West March was granted to Andrew, Lord Ochiltree, in which the Castles of Annan, Lochmaben, Langholm and Thrieve are referred to as His Majesty's "oun houses". From this and other references it may be inferred that, though Langholm Castle was Maxwell property, yet when occasion demanded, it was considered as at the command of the Government.

No exact date can be given of the final abandonment of the Castle as a garrisoned fort, or a place of residence. The year 1725 has been named by some writers, but evidence to the contrary exists. At the Castle in 1726 James Paisley of Craig was married to Miss Magdalen Elliot, of Midlem Mill. Her father had come from Branxholme to reside there about the year 1724, as Chamberlain to the Duke of Buccleuch. In this capacity he succeeded a Mr. Melville who had occupied the Castle for many years. In the records of the Kirk Session Mr. Melville is mentioned in 1721, so probably he continued to reside there until 1724.

From the Registers of Stapelgortoun, (see Appendix 6), it will be seen that near the end of the sixteenth century there must have been a considerable number of persons living in the Castle, and in what Lord Maxwell called "the laich housis besyde the same".

But whatever power or glory clung around it in the brave days of old, lives there no longer. Not as a fortress does it now exist, but as a historic relic set in a frame of hill and wood, embowered in beauty, a reminder of the Langholm that once was but is no more. However at the end of the 20th century and due to the efforts of Clan Armstrong Trust, Langholm Castle has now been declared a site of National Historic Importance.

HOLLOWS TOWER

There was a third kind of strong house scattered throughout the Borders, built and inhabited by chiefs of clans and by landed men. In Liddesdale alone, there were about 50 such houses and towers. Round these towers the mean huts and other dwellings of the vassals and retainers were grouped, the whole forming the touns so often mentioned in the records of the period.

These peel-towers owed their existence to the unrest on the Borders during the sixteenth and seventeenth centuries, and they were the cause of much concern to the Governments of the two countries. The Armstrongs built a number of them about the year 1525. Later in the century, on the English Border, the Grahams did the same, the report of which is given by Lord Herries to James VI in 1578, their location being "foranent your Majesties Kingdom".

Many of these places, even those of chieftains and lairds, were very mean dwellings, for it was not until the middle of the eighteenth century that the average dwelling house on the Scottish Border offered any degree of comfort or even adequate shelter. Some towers on the map of 1590 were probably not peel-towers at all, but merely houses built of stone, or by their being the abode of the chief of a section of a clan, or of a laird.

These houses were the rendezvous of the raiders and broken men of the Borders and they thus obtained a certain distinction. It was on this account that the Wardens agreed, about the year 1525, to prohibit the erection of such places, but when many of the clans ignored this prohibition complaint was made by the Earl of Northumberland that such action was a violation of the truce.

However, in the year 1535, the Scottish Parliament passed an Act requiring every landed man having one hundred pound land of new extent, to build a barmkyn for the protection of his vassals. He might also build within the barmkyn a tower for himself. Men of smaller means were to build smaller places. All the buildings erected under the Act were to be completed in two years.

Of all the peel-towers and houses the only one still remaining into the twentieth century in a state of preservation, sufficient to show its original construction, is the Hollows Tower. Of the date of the building of the Tower it is not possible to speak with certainty but a tower on this site is mentioned as early as 1518. Its original name was Hole-house. Later spelling refers to it as Hollas which then became Hollows. Due to its connection with Johnie Armstrong of Gilnockie it has, during the nineteenth century come to be called, by many local people, Gilnockie's Tower which later became Gilnockie Tower.

In 1976 the Tower came into the ownership of Major T. C. R. Armstrong-Wilson who undertook its restoration. Its situation, on the western banks of the Esk, is a level platform with superb all round field of vision for hundreds of yards.[7] The Esk protects it on three sides and is indeed its strongest outer fortification.

Scotland's leading historical architect, Mr. Murray Jack, has demonstrated that Hollows was a "two-stage" tower, the lower half being built in the early sixteenth century and the top half in about 1600.[7] The stone built Tower, is oblong in form and is 60 feet in length by 46 feet at the ends and in general features corresponds with similar erections on both sides of the Border. The walls are about nine feet in thickness and about 70 feet in height. The entrance was secured by two doors, the outer of oak studded with large nails, the inner of grated iron. The walls were of such strength that when the Tower was set on fire, either by the enemy or in self-defence, little damage was done to the main structure.

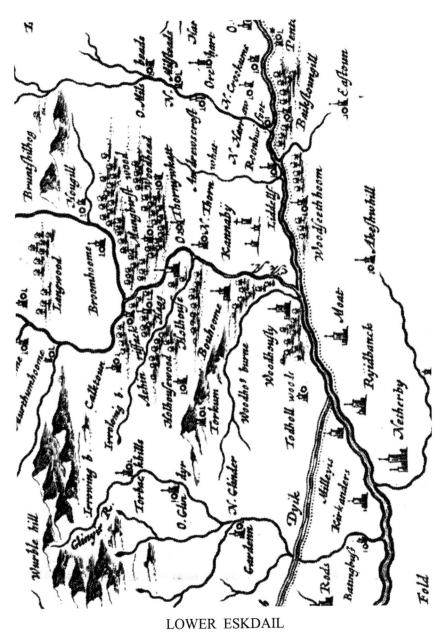

LOWER ESKDAIL

Detail from Timothy Pont's map of Liddesdail circa 1590, published by Blaeu in 1654

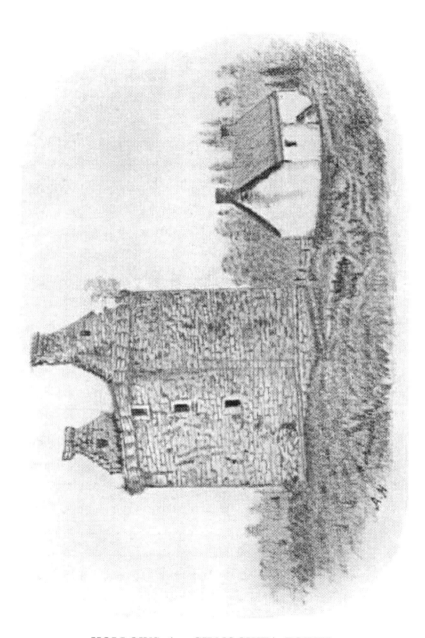

HOLLOWS (or GILNOCKIE) TOWER
Drawing by Ann Hyslop

INSCRIBED STONE IN HOLLOW TOWER

Inscribed stone which formed the door-sill of the vault in Hollows Tower. It is
not known from whence it came or the origin of these markings.

A noticeable feature of the Hollows Tower, which to this day
attracts the eye of the spectator, was the beacon-turret. The Laws of the
Marches required the owner of every castle or tower to give a warning
signal of any night-fray by means of "fire in the topps of the castle or
towre". Failure to give this signal incurred a penalty of three shillings
and four-pence.

Some historians hold the opinion that the tower still standing at
the Hollows was not the one in which Johnie Armstrong himself lived,
and that his Tower stood at the eastern end of Gilnockie Bridge where
there is an earth mound which is thought to have been an early
fortification. The present Hollows Tower, they say, was not built for
many years after his death. This opinion is based on a remark supposed
to have been made by Lord Herries in a report, dated 1578, to the effect
that certain of these houses or peel-towers had been recently erected. But
in the text of Lord Herries' report given in the *Privy Council Records,*
the words *recently erected* do not occur.

Again, if Hollows Tower was not built until many years after
Johnie Armstrong's death, where was the "Hole-house" which Dacre

argues was on "a parcell of the Debatable grounde", and which he admitted belonged to "John Armstrang of Stubilgorton"?

The second argument urged in favour of the alternative site at Gilnockie Bridge is that some old people in Canonby, spoke of hearing persons tell of stones being quarried from the old Tower for the building of the Gilnockie Bridge. Hear-say reports are not scientific evidence. They may also be confusing this with the story that stones for Canonby bridge, older than Gilnockie, were brought from the Priory at Hall-green.

Against this argument there is the report on his parish written by the Rev. John Russell, minister of Canonbie, for *Sinclair's Statistical Account* in 1793, which mentions that "the bridge was only finished last summer" yet he makes no allusion to any such quarrying. He too discusses this question of the sites, and says "The spot of ground to which the east end of the [Gilnockie] Bridge is joined, is indeed called *Gill-knocky,* but it does not exhibit the smallest vestige of mason work, and, therefore, could not have been the site of the chieftain's Castle, which, from the name, has been commonly supposed".

Dr. Russell then describes the invulnerable position of Hollows Tower as follows:— "a promontory giving a curve to the river Esk which washes its three unequal sides, and being steep and rocky is scarce-accessible but on the land side, which has been fenced by a deep fosse, over which very probably a drawbridge had been thrown".

Apart from Dr. Russell's individual opinion, had there been such a use made of the stone as tradition affirms, he would have been cognisant of it, and it is unthinkable that he should have omitted all mention of it.

Thomas Pennant, on his Tour of Scotland in the years 1771-75 was the guest of Mr. John Maxwell of Broomholm, who was himself an antiquary and writer of very considerable distinction. It was from Mr. Maxwell that he obtained his archaeological data about lower Eskdale and, though he refers to the mound at the east end of the Bridge, he makes no mention of Armstrong's Tower having stood there. Yet he describes Holehouse as being one of the seats of Johnie Armstrong.[8]

Sir Walter Scott, writing in the late 18th century, states that the Hollows Tower was Johnie Armstrong's residence.[9] "His place of residence (now a roofless tower), was at the Hollows, a few miles from Langholm, where its ruins still serve to adorn a scene which, in natural beauty, has few equals in Scotland". In 1812 Scott published *Border Antiquities* in which two illustrations of Hollows Tower are described as the home of Johnie Armstrong.

It is also significant that the Rev. James Donaldson, in February 1836, when writing the Canonbie parish notes for the *New Statistical Account* of 1845, gives no hint to any such tradition. Indeed, he does not even name the Gilnockie Bridge site, though he, too, ought to have been familiar with the report.

He writes as follows:— "Among the men of former times noted for their border exploits, we may mention as a native of this parish the celebrated Johnie Armstrong of Gilnockie whose place of residence was at the Hollows". He then goes on to describe the ruins of Hollows Tower but made one mistake by saying it was near the east end of the bridge. This remark has been seized upon by those who would have us believe that Johnie had another tower or castle there. However, in another section of his *Account* he describes some mineral deposits as being "on the **west** side of the Esk **near Hollows House Tower**".

In 1915 the Eskdale Archaeological Society initiated an excavation of the Mound at the east end of the Bridge. The trenches were cut transversely through the Mound and were inspected by Mr. W.M. McKenzie, secretary, and Mr. G.H. Watson, principal architect, of the Royal Commission on Ancient Monuments (Scotland), who visited the site on Saturday, 27th March 1915.

They reported that there is not the slightest evidence of a Border Tower having ever been on the site. Secondly, that there do not appear to be any **old** stones in Gilnockie Bridge and thirdly that the stones in the wall of the reputed site of Gilnockie stables are not mediaeval stones, the tooling being of comparative recent date, and they have no manner of connection with the remains at the Bridge.

The report of the Archaeological Sites and Monuments of Ewesdale and Lower Eskdale, dated May 1981,[4] referred to the Mound, situated at the east end of Gilnockie Bridge, "as medieval earthwork fortifications which have been extensively quarried".

But the argument continues amongst different Armstrong factions. Hollows, or Gilnockie, Tower is still owned by an Armstrong who has leased it to the Armstrong Clan Association. Meanwhile in 1998, not to be outdone, Clan Armstrong Trust erected a monument, near the eastern end of the Bridge, proclaiming it to be the site of

Gilnockie Castle! But this claim has not gone unchallenged.

On examination of the earliest maps we find Hollows is marked but no Gilnockie Castle. Timothy Pont surveyed Scotland between 1583 and 1596 and his maps were published by Blaeu in 1654. Castles, towers and churches are clearly shown on his map of Liddesdail. Hollows, marked as Holhouse, is shown on the west side of the Esk. On the eastern side only Thornywhatt and Broomholme are marked.

For Timothy Pont, so meticulous in marking the ruins of Wauchope Castle as *waes,* not to have noticed a castle, or the ruins of one, is beyond belief. Obviously no such castle existed.

On the map dated 1590 and entitled *Towers on the Debateable Land,* Hollas and Stakeheugh are marked on the west side of the Esk, Thorniewhatt and Broomholme on the east. Again no sign of Gilnockie Castle.

Taylor and Skinner's survey of the roads of North Britain published in 1776 shows *Gilnock Hall ruins* at the eastern end of the bridge. The road being surveyed ran along the west bank of the Esk and the surveyors, who may never have crossed the river, saw only the mounds and ditches and made an incorrect assumption.[10]

Around 1804 surveys were carried out by Crawford and Son for the Atlas of Scotland and published in 1828 by John Thomson of Edinburgh. Their map of Dumfriesshire shows Holehouse Tower on the west side of the Esk and only Thorniewhats and Broomholm on the east side.

The controversy will probably never be resolved but we believe that Timothy Pont's survey in the sixteenth century is more reliable than Taylor and Skinner's survey nearly two hundred years later.

STAKEHEUCH or AUCHENRIVOCK

As already mentioned, this Tower stood on the Irvine Burn and was the stronghold of the clan Irving.[11] The name of Auchenrivock seems also to have been applied to it. Its position was one excellently fortified by nature. The deep gill of the burn was on its northern side and on the east there was a steep declivity towards the Esk, which the Tower, set picturesquely on the top of the knowe, overlooked.

These Border peels were frequently set in couples so that the line

STAKEHEUCH
photograph by Alan J. Booth in 1993

of fire from the one was crossed at right angles by the fire from the other. Thus Stakeheuch and Hollows seem to have been complementary, and communications by signals could be easily picked up.

But Stakeheuch is undoubtedly of earlier date than Hollows, for in a letter of Dacre, dated 29th October, 1513, i.e., just after Flodden, he describes how his brother, Sir Christopher, made a raid into Scotland, and "on Thursday he burned the Stakehugh, the manor-place of Irewyn and the hamlets down Irewyn Burn".

Only a very small fragment remains of this ancient stronghold and the photograph gives a very inadequate idea of the original size of the the Tower. However, from pieces of wall standing here and there about the knowe, we may conjecture that at one time it was a place of considerable strength, certainly not inferior to the Hollows itself. There is a ventilation hole near the ground on the west wall which is clearly seen in the photograph.

OTHER ESKDALE TOWERS

Throughout Eskdale and the neighbouring dales, towers of varying dimensions and degrees of importance were to be found. These are indicated on the map at the beginning of chapter 17. The majority of them were simply houses, probably of stone, larger than the ordinary houses, and constructed, more or less, with the view of their having at any moment to be defended from a sudden attack. Naturally, the Debateable Land contained a large proportion of them. Wherever the Armstrongs exercised an influence, towers sprang up, and their occupation of so many on the Debateable Land gave them a very tangible advantage in their own raids, and in the reprisals against them.

Amongst other places where such towers were erected, mention may be made of:— WOODHOUSE-LEES. This placename implies that here stood one of the *wood houses* of the Border, built of wood so that the damage inflicted upon them during the Border raids might be the sooner repaired.

Kinmont's Tower of SARK was a famous place, known also as the Tower of MORTON. Buccleuch made this his base when he made his final plans the night before his rescue of Kinmont.

There was a tower at YE RYDINGS, and another at YE MOTE. The map shows one marked FFRANCIE OF CANOBIE, and another marked to DAIVY OF CANOBIE

To the west stood the Tower of BARNGLEIS but no remains can be seen. It was probably built by Christie Armstrong, (John's Christie).

There were also Towers at ARCHERBECK, THORNIEWHATS, and MUMBYHIRST.

BROOMHOLM would probably be built by the Armstrongs, who, we read, occupied it in 1569, and some writers give even an earlier date. It stood until about 1740 when it was taken down by the owner, who soon repented of his action.[12]

The Tower of YE LANGHAME. is obviously Langholm Castle, and it is of interest to note that no other building of this nature is shown. The Castle being the place indicated on the map, then the "Rob o' ye Langhame", who helped in the rescue of Kinmont Willie, would be Robert Armstrong, son of Christie of Barngleis, keeper of Langholm Castle. Apparently as late as 1596, the Armstrongs were still acting as deputies for Lord Maxwell.

STABLEGORDEN, mentioned on the map, may be the remains of Barntalloch Castle.

There appears, also, to have been a Tower at BIG-HAMES, and another is mentioned by the Statist of 1793 as being at NEIS-HILL.

Proceeding up the valley of the Esk we find Towers marked at CRAIG and CARLESGILL. The tower of Craig cannot be identified but it may have stood near the present farmhouse of Craig. Carlesgill maybe

210

FIDDLETON BANK END

Carnisgill, the residence of Nicholl Batie.

Amongst the possessions of the Beattisons we have the following Towers:— CORSE, called CROSS on the map. This name is usually associated with dyke-rygg, hence the modern name Croosdykes; DANDY BAITIE'S; NICHOL OF YE SHEELD'S, mentioned on page 173, who was probably a son of John of the Score and ANDREWE BATTYE'S on the White Esk, probably the SCORE.

Towers are also indicated at BOMBIE, WATSTERKER, and BURNEFOOTE now called Bankburnfoot.

There is also a Tower marked at YE CROOKES, traces of which were clearly discernible until the early years of the twentieth century.

The Rev. James Green, the Statist of Westerkirk parish in 1841, mentions that there were then visible the remains of an old Castle at GLENDINNING and another at WESTERHALL.

Coming now to the Ewes valley, we find that here, also, there was an abundance of Towers. Probably, the most important was that of ARKLETON, on the site of which the present mansion house stands. Moulded stones from this old Tower have been built into the walls of the house.

The illustration is of the house in Ewes, at one time known as the

211

Waterhead, and now as Fiddleton Bank End. Almost on the site of this little farm, tenanted by McVitties from 1812 for 110 years, stood the strong Tower of Glenvoren, marked on the map as that of HOBBIE O' GLENVORE.

A few years ago, whilst digging in the stack-yard a little to the west of his house, Mr. Walter McVittie, an antiquary well versed in all the ancient lore of Ewesdale, came upon a piece of very substantial masonry which he believes to have been part of Hobbie's Tower. This Hobbie was of the clan of Elliot, among whom Hobbie was a common Christian name. Musgrave, writing to Burghley in 1583, refers to "Hobbe Eliot called Scotes Hobbe - - - - Gowan Eliot called the Clarke; Hobbe Eliot his brother".[13]

On the same side of Ewes as Glenvoren, there was a Tower which belonged to RUNION OF YE BUSS, who also was an Armstrong. The tower may have been near the present farm of Bush. In the charter of 1535 to Ninian Armstrong this place is called PARK. At BURNFOOT (of Ewes) there was a Tower marked as belonging to one, ARCHIE OF WHITHAUGHE, and it too was probably an Armstrong stronghold.

In the neighbourhood of the present kirk of Ewes, stood the Tower of ECHY or EKKE GINGLES, and on the east bank of the river, near to Glendiven, that of THO. OF YE ZINGLES. The proprietors of the Chingles were Armstrongs.

Other peel-towers doubtless existed at one time in Eskdale, but those here enumerated are the most noteworthy. Many of them saw stirring scenes and deadly encounters between raiders or clans at feud. Now the grass grows green over their foundations and the men who built them have passed into the shadows. Few of their names are even engraven upon the rude stones of the Eskdale kirkyards.

CHAPTER 19

BATTLES AND RAIDS

Few districts in the country have been the scene of more tumult and fighting than the Scottish Border. From the earliest times until the end of the sixteenth century the land had scarcely rest or peace. The early inhabitants opposed the Romans. In the centuries which followed the abandonment of the Roman ambition to subdue Scotland, the lowlands were the scene of internecine strife and many a fierce conflict.

The Saxon invasion changed the parties but continued the strife. The Danish pirates followed and swarmed over Annandale and Eskdale. Scarcely had the Cumbrian kingdom been merged into that of Scotland when the Wars of Independence began. England was fighting for supremacy and Scotland for national existence.

When the forces mustered for the Armageddon of ARTHURET, the Christian Cumbrians from Eskdale, not only bore their part under Rhydderch Hael, but the valley itself heard the shouting and the tumult.

When David I, ambitious to recover the lost territories of the northern English counties, invaded England and suffered so grievous a defeat in 1138 at the BATTLE OF THE STANDARD, which finally settled the map of Great Britain, Eskdale would send its quota to aid its King. A contingent of Cumbrians with men from Teviotdale formed one of the wings of the Scots army, and it is not difficult to picture the men, en route, recruiting their ranks from Ewesdale and Eskdale.

At BANNOCKBURN, too, Eskdale was represented, but, alas, its men fought against the Bruce and Scotland. The Lindsays were in possession of Wauchope and Stapelgortoun and Langholm and they fought for Edward. Ewes was under the domination of Robert de Clifford, Edward's vassal, or of the Lovels who, possessed of large tracts

213

of territory on the Borders, yet devotedly adhered to the English cause.

However, by 1388 at the Battle of OTTERBURN the divided allegiance of the early barons had given place to a definite national sentiment, and the Eskdale barons fought bravely for the Douglas, and took their followers with them to the memorable fight.

So did they in 1513 on that woeful day of FLODDEN. On this dire and stricken field, Eskdale men fought and died by the side of their defeated Sovereign, and in many a home in Eskdale, Wauchopedale, and Ewesdale, there was "dool and wae" when the men returned not. Inexpressible dismay settled like a pall upon the Border dales:—

> "Dool and wae for the order, sent our lads to the Border!
> The English for ance, by guile wan the day:
> The flowers of the forest, that fought aye the foremost,
> The prime of our land, are cauld in the clay.
> We'll hear nae mair lilting at the ewe-milking;
> Women and bairns are heartless and wae:
> Sighing and moaning in ilka green loaning —
> The flowers of the forest are a' wede awae."

Buccleuch was one of the few Border lords who returned from the field. The Maxwells were there; the Armstrongs fought by their side; the Irvings fell, as did the Johnstones and the Lindsays.

> "Scotia felt thine ire, O Odin,
> On the bloody field of Flodden;
> There our fathers fell with honour
> Round their king and country's banner."[1]

And again, at SOLWAY MOSS, in 1542, Eskdale men did their part. The Battle of Solway Moss was a part of the perplexing game which Scotland and England played during the sixteenth century, intriguing, openly or secretly, against each other, and the whole Borderland became the theatre of lawlessness and disorder.

It has long been believed by superficial readers, and by that mysterious personage, the man in the street, that the Raids of the sixteenth century were wicked and unprovoked incursions by Scottish robbers into the peaceful cattle sheds of their English neighbours. The word mosstrooper is tacitly understood to be synonymous with "Scottish Borderer". Needless to say, such an idea is both untrue and unhistorical.

The Border Raids arose, not from a feeble grasp of the Ten Commandments by the men of the Scottish dales, not from sheer wantonness or ill-temper, nor yet from a preference for English beef or mutton. Nor had the Raids their origin in a dislike of their English neighbours, though dislike there most assuredly was, and it was mutual. They arose, rather, from the frequent wars between the two countries and the consequent impoverishment of the Borders.

Those who assume that the Raids were always committed by the Scots err greatly. Some of the most cruel forays were carried out by English leaders, men like Dacre, Hertford, and Wharton. Probably no raid by the Armstrongs, Elliots, Scotts, or Beattisons equalled in callous cruelty Hertford's progress through Roxburghshire, or Wharton's through Dumfriesshire. Raiding was a game of beggar-my-neighbour, in which the winners were not always Scotsmen.

The continual wars produced a state of economic stagnation. In the dales there was no industry save that of agriculture. It was useless to spend time or labour sowing a crop when there was no certainty of ever reaping it. As a result, the entire Borderland was in a condition of the most hopeless poverty. The Borderer nevertheless, was faced with the necessity of living. And all these forces co-operating, produced the conditions which made mosstrooping almost a lawful trade.

Concerning the morality of mosstrooping or freebooting, a lot of pious nonsense has been written. The mosstrooper did not consider for one moment that his raiding was theft. Johnie Armstrong prided himself on his honesty. Raiding was not vulgar stealing, it was an act of war. The Border clans went into a foray, often in broad daylight, with banners flying. An act, which in times of peace is piracy, is regarded as lawful in times of war. And for the most part Border raiding was war.

Added to all these facts were the conditions of tenure and vassalage clinging round a rigid system of feudalism. The tenants were at the mercy of the barons and landed men, who, whilst openly frowning at raiding, secretly encouraged it for their own personal ends.

Even the Kings were not oblivious to what was going on, and if they did not actually promote the disorders they were content to reap some benefit from them. Indeed, the English Wardens frequently reported to their sovereign that the Scottish King was fully aware of what was being done, and many of the incursions of Wharton and others were made with the approval of the English sovereign.

So it came to pass, that, to deal with this exceptional state of affairs, an exceptional code of laws was slowly compiled. The Borders became a state within a state, subject to the common law, it is true, but a state whose inter-relationships were regulated by customs and statutes which did not obtain elsewhere. These laws were enacted by the national Parliament, or might be the recommendations of special commissioners, or minutes of agreement between the Wardens, or even customs observed by the dalesmen. Gradually, they formed a compact, though intricate, system of jurisprudence. These many laws and usages were codified by Bishop Nicholson of Carlisle in 1705 under the title of *Leges Marchiarum,* which soon became the recognised authority on all Border laws and customs.

The enactments related to stealing, trials and the course of procedure thereat, harbouring and tracing fugitives, conditions relating to days of truce, Warden's meetings, fines, murders, fire-raising, perjury, receiving stolen goods, lawful and unlawful prisoners, (the people of Eskdale and Ewesdale, it is said, had a practice of taking their own countrymen prisoners, and holding them to ransom or letting them to surety. This was legislated against by an Act of 1567), hunting, sowing, reaping, and felling timber in the opposite realm, wounding, the valuing of stolen cattle, (the lawful value for an ox was 13s. 4d., a cow 10s. and a sheep 2s.), feuds, and the more serious deadly feuds.

There was much scope for very serious disagreement, and raids and disorders arose through an interpretation of the law which the other side would not accept. To assist the Warden's officers bloodhounds were kept at certain specified places. On the English side of the Border there was established a line of communications with setters, watchers, and sleuthhounds, ready by day and night to track freebooters, whilst fords and hill-passes were watched and guarded. Signals were given by bonfires on selected hills. In Eskdale, we have the names Warbla and Watch Knowe, on both of which, the signal fires have burned during many an exciting night. In Liddesdale, Tinnis Hill was the beacon hill.

The cases arising out of these Border Laws were tried at the Wardens' Courts. These Courts were generally held on the Scottish side, and the day of the Court was a day of truce. The Borders were divided into three sections called the East, Middle, and West Marches, and a

Warden, at £100 a year, was set over each. The West March included Eskdale, Ewesdale, and Wauchopedale, though Ewesdale was sometimes included in the Middle March.

As early as 1504 the condition of affairs on the Borders was engaging the attention of James IV who determined to investigate them in his own august person. In this wise originated his famous Raid of Eskdale. The people of Eskdale were then outlawed and at the horn. James made elaborate preparations for the visit, even writing to the English King towards "keping of the bordowris agane the Raid of Eskdale". The King's pavilions were repaired for the occasion, and he got a new scarlet cloak, the cost of which is duly set forth in the Lord Treasurer's accounts:—

"Item, the vj day of August, for iiij elne scarlet, to be ane cloak to the King agane the Raid of Eskdale, ilkelne iij *li.*; summa xij *li.*"
"Item, for iij ½ elne wellus to bordour the samyn, ilke elne xls. summa vij li." "Item, for sewing silk to the samyn, xvjd".
"Item, for v quartaris taffeti to the collair of the samyn, vijs".

From these items it would appear that the garment cost a grateful country the moderate sum of £19 8s. 4d. Scots., but the one-and-fourpence for sewing silk was perhaps for "ane jacat". In his zeal against the Eskdale "thevis" James was not unmindful of other interests. We read of his having with him a silver chalice, ecclesiastical vestments, altar cloths, and splints, bucklers, cross-bows, and arrows. The pavilions were sent off from Edinburgh in two carts, which performed the journey in 33 days. This item was an expensive one, costing £19 4s. 0d.

Being fond of music, the King brought "organis" with him into Eskdale, probably the first which had as yet been in the valley. As well as the "organis" there came Italian minstrels and "tua Inglis wemen that sang in the Kingis pailyoun", and pipers, local men they seem to have been, who were paid at Dumfries, "and whilst numbers of the unfortunate marauders were seized and brought in irons to the encampment, executions and entertainments appear to have succeeded each other with extraordinary rapidity".[2]

Perhaps of equal importance for the King's pleasure and comfort, was "a maister cuke", who received the sum of eighteen shillings and fourpence "for ane litill barrell witli grene gynzear, (green ginger), quhilk he tuke with the King in Eskdale". A retinue of considerable size must have followed the King, for in it were musicians, cooks, courtiers, judges, ministers of law, huntsman and falconers, and morris-dancers. According to The Lord Treasurer's accounts, James Hog was paid fourteen shillings for carrying the King's armour to Eskdale. A donation of fiftysix shillings was given to Sir Richard Camply's minstrels. "Tua Inglis wemen" came to the royal pavilion and sang to the Court. To them the King gave 28s. To the Priory of Canonby, the King gave 14s.

Of course, there was serious business to be done amidst all the gaiety and hunting. The King does not appear to have gone further into Eskdale than Canonby, and within two days of holding his Court there, he was at Lochmaben. Possibly, the transportation of so much baggage farther into the valley, was not easy even for the King of Scotland. Whilst in Canonby the King dwelt in his own pavilions, but he seems to have transacted some judicial business at the Priory, but the most important part of the work was afterwards done at Dumfries. Some of the principal Eskdale lairds were fined for non-appearance, and thieves were hanged.

To James V the Borders presented an attraction greater even than that of the restoration of law and Order. The forests of Eskdalemuir and Ettrick provided him with sport, to which the pursuit and execution of thieves and raiders formed only an interlude. In 1534 James came to the Borders to hunt, after having made proclamation that "na man hunt in Megotland, Askdalemure or Tweedmure unto the King is coming".

The Battle of Flodden brought in its train many misfortunes to the Borders. Dacre, by order of the English King, and aided by the Armstrongs, who had been outlawed by the Scottish Government, made his notorious incursion into the Border dales. This occurred one month after Flodden, when he and his troops, three thousand cavalry and three hundred infantry, marched through the Border villages, burning every house and putting to the sword all the men they could seize. Dacre exultingly reported his successes to the Council. Places laid waste included Broomholme, Waighopp, Baggraye, Murtholme, Langham, and the Water of Esk from Stabulgortoun down to Canonby.

His brother, Sir Christopher Dacre, "roode all night into Scotland and on Thursday in the morninge they began upon the said middle merches and brynt Stakeheugh with the hamletts belonging to them down Irewyn bwrne, being the chambrelain of Scotland oune lands and undre his reule, continewally birnyng, from the Breke of day to oone of the clok after noon, and there wan tooke and brought away cccc hede of cattell, ccc shepe, certaine horses and very much insight, and slew two men, hurte and wounded diverse other personnes and horses and then entered Ingland ground again at vij of the clok that night."[3]

These dangers from invasions by the English had the effect of drawing together the various Border clans, who, for mutual protection, placed themselves under Lord Maxwell, many of the lairds giving him bonds of manrent.

During the year following Dacre's raid, the unrest on the Borders grew more pronounced, and from Eskdale, Ewesdale, and Wauchope, and other dales along the Borders, cattle-lifting and fire-raising were rampant. No security existed either for life or property. In 1524 apprehensions were again aroused that the English contemplated a dash over the Marches and the headsmen of the clans were commanded by the Government to repair to the Borders to be in readiness against the advance of the English, which, however, did not take place.

Attempts were made by the Scottish and English Governments to come to some agreement recording these Border tumults. Commissioners met in 1528 at Lochmaben Stone on the farm of Old Graitney and arranged terms of peace between the two countries, each side agreeing to use all means to stop the raiding.

As a result of this conference the Wardens sent out intimation to the men of Eskdale, Ewesdale, Wauchopedale, and Annandale, that all Englishmen unlawfully taken prisoners must be set at liberty. A most unwise concession however, was also made at this conference, viz., that the English King should be at liberty to invade Liddesdale to obtain redress "at his grace's pleasure" for the hurt done to his own subjects by the freebooters of that dale. This had the effect of loosening the allegiance of the Borderers to the Scottish Crown, whom it also placed at the mercy of the English King and his agents. Instead of putting out, it added fuel to the flames which were now, enwrapping the long harassed Borderland.

During all these events Eskdale, as will be readily understood, was in a condition of disorder approaching chaos. Despite the suspicion that he secretly encouraged the raiding by the clans under his jurisdiction as Warden, Maxwell was granted new powers and bound himself to keep the broken men in order.

The Acts of the Council relating to his Wardenry recount:—"As anent the inhabitantis of Ewisdale and Eskdail, quhilk makis dalie refis, heresschippes, slaughteris and inconvenientis, alswele apone the leigis of this realme as apone the legis of Inglande, the Lordis understandis that the saide Lord Maxswell, be reasonne of his office of Wardenrie may call the inhabitants of the said countre or ony of thaim for thair treasonable deidis and proceed againis thaim as it war in Parliament and convict thaim of treasonne, quhilkis thai command him to do and the saidis personnis so beand convict of treasonne the said Lord Maxwell to have thair esehetis both of thair landis and gudis and for his gude service, and signatorris to be maid to him tharapo."

Remembering these tempting inducements for the maintaining of order, and the sequel to the murder of Johnie Armstrong, when within a short time thereof Maxwell received a grant of all his lands and personal belongings, doubtless in compliance with this order of Council, one can easily understand how there arose a suspicion that he had connived at the King's treachery.

One of the most disastrous raids of the sixteenth century was that made by the Earl of Hertford in 1544 whilst the Border Scots were still smarting under the defeat of Solway Moss. In retaliation for the Scots people opposing his project to marry the Prince of Wales to the infant Princess Mary of Scotland, Henry VIII sent Hertford to reduce the Border counties to ashes, and he carried out his commission with brutal zeal and industry.

To Hertford belongs the discredit of destroying the sacred shrines of the Borders. Melrose, Dryburgh, Kelso, and Jedburgh Abbeys were reduced almost to ruins. The victorious Hertford penetrated to Edinburgh, burning and ravaging as he went. For these operations he was made Duke of Somerset. In the following year Latour and Evers were sent to conclude the dire work Hertford had so far carried on, and they again attacked the Border abbeys, destroying the Douglas tombs in Melrose.

There can be no doubt that it was the bitter memories left by these cruel raids, and the inheritance of hate thus brought into being, which afterwards produced much of the passion and tumult amongst the Borderers. When, in 1547, Lord Wharton with 5000 troops overran the Border dales, he left the greater part of Dumfriesshire a smouldering waste, a wilderness of despoiled towns and homesteads. Those who resisted Wharton's advance were massacred, and after a devastating whirl through the dales he starved the clans into submission and then received them under English "assurance".

During these Border raids many deeds of conspicuous bravery were performed. Heroic events were not chronicled so much in written history as in the folk-songs, embodying the traditions and poetry of the people. Such ballads as *Kinmont Willie; Archie o' Ca'field; Jock o' the Syde; the Lads o' Wamphray; Christie's Will;* and *Jamie Telfer of the Fair Dodhead,* recount deeds of personal prowess and the story of these stirring exploits is set forth in this ballad-poetry in a way which no modern writer can emulate.

One of the circumstances which helped to make Eskdale and Liddesdale the scene of so many gallant and exciting events was the existence of the famous Tarras Moss, stretching between the two dales in miles of desolate moss-hags and morasses. To this safe retreat the moss-trooper betook himself when pressed by the emissaries of the law. The nearness of Tarras rendered it less necessary for the broken men to build peel-towers or other strongholds. They were safer there than in stone houses, for the dangers associated with any attempt on the part of strangers to penetrate its morasses were a surer protection than iron yettis or masonry.

Through the midst of this sea of moss and peat-bog ran the angry Tarras, a red, rocky and turbulent stream, which runs into the Esk at Irvine. Following up the stream from Esk, one passes first through a densely wooded linn, which gradually widens into a broad, open moor, the upper part of which is Tarras Moss proper. Then, some four miles up, the country narrows into a rocky glen shut in by low, steep hills, and so for another four miles, when suddenly there is a great basin three miles long by a mile across, all thick with birken scrub below, and on all sides shut in by mighty hills. Here, among the forests and treacherous bogs, the Armstrongs boasted that they could live for a year or more and snap their fingers at all the royal troops of Scotland.

We need give but one illustration of the splendid use to which the moss-troopers put this great weapon which Nature had so thoughtfully placed at their hands. Hearing that the Armstrongs contemplated an incursion into England in 1598, Sir Robert Cary resolved to penetrate into their own country, and await a favourable opportunity of taking the chief outlaws. He accordingly marched to Carebhill in Liddesdale with

200 horse, and there built himself a camp, in which he remained from the middle of June to the end of August.

But the Armstrongs had betaken themselves to their mountain-fastness in Tarras. "Believing themselves to be perfectly secure, they sent me word", says Cary in his *Memoirs*, "that I was like the first puff of a haggis, hottest at the first, and bade me stay there as long as the weather gave me leave; they would stay in Tarras wood till I was weary of lying in the waste, and when I had my time, and they no whit the worse, they would play their part which should keep me waking the next winter".

Whilst this waiting game was being played out, the Armstrongs, sent a party into England where they harried Sir Robert Cary's folds. On their return to Tarras, they sent him one of his own cows, and a message to the effect that fearing he would be short of provisions, they were sending him some English beef!

Sir Robert, however, kept quietly to his plan. He sent 150 horsemen round by along detour to the Ewesdale side of Tarras and blocked up this and other passes. He then attacked the Armstrongs from the English side and compelled them to flee. Five of the chief outlaws were taken, and "such a quantity of sheep and cattle as were sufficient to satisfy most part of the country they were stolen from". This was the only successful attempt, to remove the outlaws from Tarras Moss.

There is one feature in the efforts to suppress the moss-troopers which must not be overlooked. The political efforts having failed, and the whole machinery of law and order having broken down, it seems to have occurred to some one that another agency might be invoked, that of the Church.

As we have shown, the raiding was frequently connived at by Wardens on both sides, and even by the Kings of the two countries, and it would appear that even the Church was not perfectly clear of suspicion. Priests were known to have entered into the game with zest and some success. Surtees, in his *History of Durham*, says that "the priest and curate of Bewcastle are both included in the list of Border thieves in 1552".

The assistance now sought was the hierarchy of the Church in the person of the Lord Archbishop of Glasgow. He sought to overawe the turbulent Borderers by excommunication. His Monition of Cursing is mentioned briefly, but no history of the Borders during the sixteenth century would be complete without giving some outline of it:—

"GUDE FOLKS, heir at my Lord Archbishop of Glasgwis letters under his round sele", he begins, and at once comes to the point at issue. It has been reported to him that "our souverane lordis trew leigis, men, wiffis and barnys" have been "part murdrist, part slayne, brynt, heryit, spulzeit and reft . . . . be commoun tratouris, revaris, theiffis, duelland in the south part of this realme, sic as Tevidale, Eskdale, Liddisdale, Ewisdale, Nedisdale, and Annerdaill . . . . And thairfar my said Lord Archbishop of Glasgw hes thocht expedient to strike thame with the terribill swerd of halykirk, quhilk thai may nocht lang endur and resist". The Monition then recites the archbishop's authorities:—

The Holy Trinity, the Virgin, archangels, patriarchs, prophets, apostles, martyrs, the Pope, the cardinals, archbishops, bishops, abbots, priors, prelates, and ministers, and DENOUNCES, PROCLAIMIS, and DECLARIS, all the works of the freebooters to be accursed. The archbishop then descends to particulars :—

"I CURSE thair heid and all the haris of thair heid, I CURSE thair face, thair ene, thair mouth, thair neise, thair toung, their teith, their crag, thair schulderis fra the top of thair heid to the soile of thair feit, befoir and behind, within and without. I CURSE thaim gangand, I CURSE thaim rydand, I CURSE thaim standand."— sitting, eating, drinking, walking, sleeping, rising, lying. "I CURSE thaim at hame, I CURSE thaim fra hame . . . .

I CURSE thair wiffis, thair barnis and thair servandis". The curse then falls upon their barns, their corn, and everything else a dalesman could possibly be possessed of, ploughs, harrows, all were swept within this terrible curse.

Not content with the authorities already named, the archbishop somewhat irrelevantly drags in Adam; Cain and Abel; Noah and the Ark, Sodom and Gomorrah; Babylon and Egypt, Moses, Aaron, David and Absolom.

The angry prelate then quotes Nebuchadnezzar, Judas, Pilate, Herod and the Jews, Jerusalem, Simon Magus, and Nero, and works up his Monition to a long conclusion wherein he DISSEVERS and PAIRTIS the Borderers from the Kirk, INTERDITES them from divine service, FORBIDS "all cristin man or woman till have ony cumpany with thaim".

CONDEMNS "thaim perpetualie to the deip pit of hell to remain with Lucifer and all his fallowis, and thair bodeis to the gallowis of the burghmoor, first to be hangit, syne revin and ruggit with doggis, swine, and utheris wyld beists", until they "ryse frae this terribill cursing and mak satisfaction and and pennance".

The Archbishop's fulmination produced on the Borderers absolutely no effect that can now be detected. The raiders rode, and enjoyed the riding as keenly as before.

Although the visits paid to Eskdale by the insurgents of 1715 and

1745 were not exactly Border raids, yet it may not be inappropriate to include them. The incidents of the '45 marked the end of the fighting days on the Borders

It was on 13th October, 1715, that, in sympathy with Mar's rebellion, Lord Kenmure, at the Market Cross, Lochmaben, proclaimed James Stuart as King. This was the beginning of the Rebellion on the Borders. Next day Kenmure was at Ecclefechan, where Sir Patrick Maxwell of Springkell joined him. On Saturday, 15th October, they reached Langholm. At each town the insurgent army proclaimed King James and at each they received recruits to their cause. Kenmure hoped to take Dumfries, believing that if he could do so the Borders would be won. But Annandale rose in defence of the Crown, and he had to abandon the project.

The Jacobite army intended to march into England to join the forces of the Earl of Derwentwater. The Highlanders, however, were reluctant to enter England and had to be bribed with extra pay before they would cross the Esk.

The decisive fight took place at Preston where the Royalist troops heavily defeated the insurgents and took many prisoners, amongst whom was the Earl of Nithsdale, head of the Maxwell family. He was condemned to death for his treason. The Countess of Nithsdale, being rebuffed in her pleading with the King on her husband's behalf, romantically and bravely effected his escape from the Tower. They then escaped to the Continent and settled in Rome. His estates were confiscated, and on his death in 1744 were purchased by a syndicate who sold them again to members of the Maxwell family.

In the Rebellion of 1745 Langholm took no sympathetic share, but again witnessed the march of the Jacobite troops on their way into England. One division of the army came by way of Hawick and Mosspaul and passed through Langholm, where the townspeople regarded the movement only as a lawless raid. The rebels, as might be expected, levied contributions of victuals from the townsfolk. The attitude of the Langholm people, it is said, was largely due to the moderating influence of Mr. Archibald Little, brother of Bailie Little.

Prince Charles Edward Stuart, with another division of his army, went down Liddesdale and stayed a night at Riddings. The mother of Mr. Robert Smellie was wont to relate that she was acquainted with a woman who waited on the Chevalier on this occasion. As she was going out to church on the Sunday morning, he remarked to her that no doubt she would pray that he might be unsuccessful in his attempt on the Throne. To which she replied that it was not whom he willed, nor whom she willed, but whom the Lord willed, that would be King. A most diplomatic reply.

An interesting tradition has been handed down of a visit paid by the Chevalier's troopers to William Hounam, a farmer in Langholm The original authors had the story from Mr. John Hounam, of Gilnockie School, and great-great-grandson of the farmer, but the name William is incorrect.

We have received information from Mrs. Doreen Thomson, née Hounam, who has been meticulous in her research of the Hounam family, and she can find no trace of a William Hounam. She is convinced that the above farmer was named John and he is her great-great-great-great grandfather.

This John Hounam occupied the farm house on the old Drove Road, on the site of which the house known as Mount Hooly was built. His father, also named John, had died there in 1742. In 1743 John married Jean Elliot. He and his brothers and uncles, also living at the farm, had no sympathy with the Stuart cause. On hearing of the approach of the rebel troops, they betook themselves with their horses and cattle to the wilds of Tarras for safety, but leaving his wife at home.

When the army arrived in Langholm, an officer, with a company of soldiers, was despatched to Hounam's farm to enlist the men and commandeer the horses. Not finding the men, the officer demanded to be informed of their whereabouts but Jean Elliot resolutely declined to do so. The officer then threatened to cut down the beam supporting the roof of her humble abode, but still she declined. He was as good as his word, and drawing his sword he slashed at the beam, which being of good stout oak withstood the attack. It was afterwards built as a lintel into one of the windows of a later house.

The last of the Hounam family to occupy Mount Hooly Farm as a shared house were brothers Christopher and David. Christopher Hounam called his half Mount Pleasant while David Hounam's half was Mount Hooly which was the southern half of the original house. Mount Hooly was in the possession of the Hounam family until 16th May, 1921 when it was sold, by Joseph Edward Hounam, brother of John Hounam of Gilnockie School, to Thomas Morrison, for £250.

It is doubtful whether Charles Edward Stuart was ever in Langholm, but we know that he crossed the Esk on the retreat from Derby. Baroness Nairne's famous song, *A Hundred Pipers,* celebrates the crossing of the flooded Esk by the army of the Chevalier. She represents them as swimming "o'er to fell English ground", and the Englishmen as being dumfounded. But it was actually on the return journey that this incident occurred. Chevalier Johnstone in his Memoirs of the Rebellion writes as follows:—

"The Scottish army left Carlisle, and retreated into Scotland by crossing the Esk at Langtoun . . . . The Esk, which is usually shallow, had been swelled by an incessant rain of four days to a depth of four feet. Our cavalry formed in the river to break the force of the current about twenty-five paces above the part of the ford where the infantry were to pass; the Highlanders formed themselves into ranks of ten or twelve abreast, with their arms locked in such a manner as to support one another against the rapidity of the river's current . . . . Cavalry were likewise stationed in the river below the ford to pick up and save those who might be carried away by the violence of the current. . . . By this means our army passed the Esk in an hour's time without losing a single man. Fires were kindled to dry our people as soon as they quitted the water, and the bagpipes having commenced playing, the Highlanders began to dance, expressing the utmost joy on seeing their country again."

The defeat of the Jacobites at Culloden produced a feeling of relief. In Langholm Kirk the victory was duly announced and a Day of Thanksgiving observed.

CHAPTER 20

THE TOWN OF LANGHOLM

Following Chalmers's Caledonia, virtually all the writers of local history have stated that Langholm was erected into a Burgh of Barony by Maxwell in 1610.   Such a statement is wrong.   Langholm was not erected into a Burgh of Barony until 19th September, 1621; and the grant of 1610 was not made by Maxwell who possessed no power or right to make such a grant, nor was it made to him. At that date Maxwell was an exile in France because of his murder of the laird of Johnstone in 1609. He was executed in 1613 and his brother, who afterwards became Earl of Nithsdale, was not restored to the estates until 1618.

CRANSTOUN'S CHARTER OF 1610

It was whilst Maxwell was outlawed that King James VI, by a charter, (see Appendix 2), dated at Royston, 15th January, 1610, granted to Lord William Cranstoun the free barony of Langholm. The *narratio* recites that the grant was made because of the services rendered by Cranstoun in pacifying the inhabitants of the Borders.

It will be recalled that in the early years of the seventeenth century strenuous efforts were being put forth to reduce the Borders to a condition of tranquillity and from 1605 to 1607 Cranstoun had played a prominent part. The Cranstouns seem to have been a Border family of some note. The name appears in the bond signed in 1569 by the barons and landit men promising support to James VI and his Regent, against Queen Mary and Bothwell.   Lord William is doubtless the Captain Cranstoun who in 1586 was sent into Annandale from Edinburgh to support Johnstone, Warden of the West March, in his efforts to arrest

Maxwell.   Perhaps it was the service he then rendered which commended him to King James.

Lord William's name also appears in a list of the Justices of the Peace for Dumfriesshire in 1610.   In the Border ballads the name Cranstoun frequently occurs and is therein often associated with the Gledstanes of Cocklaw, the ancestors of the late W. E. Gladstone.

Briefly, by the charter of 1610, Lord William Cranstoun was granted "the lands of Langholm, with its fortress, manor, mills and fisheries, the lands of Broomholm, Arkinholm", and others specified, "which the King has incorporated into the free barony of Langholm, appointing the fortress of Langholm to be its principal messuage".   The rent covenanted for is "one silver penny in name of blench-ferme".

The lands granted to Cranstoun were in the baronies of Stapelgortoun and Westerker, but no grant was made to him in Wauchopedale, nor in Ewesdale excepting Arkin, Balgray, and Whitshields.

Most of the Ewesdale lands formerly possessed by Lord Maxwell, — Flaskholm, Howgill, Glendiven, Burngranes, Park or Bush, and Wolfhope — and also Murtholm, Gallosyde, Watergrains, Bigholms, and Glencorf in Wauchopedale had, on Maxwell's forfeiture, been given to Sir Gideon Murray, treasurer-depute.

It must not be concluded that this charter conferred any dignity upon the town of Langholm.   As a matter of fact Langholm as a "town" did not exist.

The term free barony related not so much to the subject matter of the grant, as to the tenure upon which the lands were to be held by Cranstoun.   In the language of feudal conveyancing a barony was an estate created or confirmed by the Crown direct, erecting the lands embraced by the grant IN LIBERAM BARONIAM, that is, into a Free Barony.

This tenure carried with it important privileges, but none of these necessarily pertained to the barony but were the legal rights of the baron himself.

Presumably, Lord William Cranstoun remained superior of the lands of Langholm until 1621, for in the charter of this date to the Earl of Nithsdale, Cranstoun and his son John, his heir-apparent, are stated to have resigned them, and the same remark is applied to Sir Gideon Murray in respect of the lands in Ewesdale and Wauchope.

NITHSDALE CHARTER OF 1621

The Conveyance by the Earl of Nithsdale, dated 1628, has been held by some writers to be the legal instrument by which Langholm was erected into a Burgh of Barony, and considerable confusion of mind has resulted in the efforts to collate it and the charter of 1610.

In a most interesting review of the history of the town, on the occasion of the last meeting of the Police Commissioners, on the 15th May, 1893, Mr. Robert McGeorge, acting chief magistrate, very properly pointed out that this could not be, seeing that such a charter was a gift of the Crown alone and, therefore, could not be conferred by a subject.

In 1618, and at subsequent dates, the Maxwell lands, which had been declared forfeit in 1609, were restored to Robert, Lord Maxwell. In 1620, he was advanced a step in the peerage by being created Earl of Nithsdale. On the resignation of the lands of Langholm by the Cranstouns, and of Ewesdale and Wauchopedale by Sir Gideon Murray of Elibank, the King conferred them anew on the Earl of Nithsdale, by a charter dated 19th September, 1621, and by the same charter, (see Appendix 3), he erected Langholm into a BURGH OF BARONY.

It is therefore definitely from this document that Langholm dates its existence as a Burgh. By the charter, Lord Nithsdale was, *inter alia,* granted the right of having a public hall, of erecting a market cross and of holding annually two free fairs with a right to the tolls. He could also choose bailiffs and burgesses.

The first burgesses were his kinsmen, to whom, in 1628, he conveyed the Ten-Merk Lands. He appointed as his bailie, John Maxwell of Broomholm.

NITHSDALE'S CONTRACT OF 1628

It was not until, 1628, however, that the Earl of Nithsdale took steps to carry out the provisions of his charter of 1621. This he did by a feu-contract, (Appendix 4), conveying to ten members of the Maxwell family what afterwards became, and are still known as, the Ten-Merk Lands of Langholm. The consideration was that each of the Maxwells named in the contract should build "ilka ane of them ane sufficient stone house on the fore street of the said town of Langholm builded with stone and lyme of two houses height at least". These Maxwells were:—

James Maxwell of Kirkconnell, Master of Maxwell
James Maxwell of Tinwald
Archibald Maxwell of Cowhill
George Maxwell of Carnsalurth
Robert Maxwell of Dinwoodie
John Maxwell of Midleby
Herbert Maxwell of Templand
Robert Maxwell, brother of the said James Maxwell of Tinwald
John Maxwell of Holms
John Maxwell of Broomholm, brother of the said Archibald Maxwell of Cowhill

However, according to the Statist of 1793 only four of the houses had been built. It is said that one of these houses, at the foot of the Kirkwynd, was that once occupied by the late Archibald Glendinning. With the erection of these houses the town of Langholm may be said to have come into existence. But the superiority of the Earl of Nithsdale was of short duration. Owing to his espousal of the cause of Charles I his estates were declared forfeit by Parliament in 1643.

BUCCLEUCH CHARTER OF 1643

The Barony of Langholm then passed to the Earl of Buccleuch by a charter dated 7th April, 1643. By this grant the House of Buccleuch became the lords-superior of virtually the whole of Eskdale. They had obtained the lands in the barony or tennandrie of Dumfedling in 1613. In 1619 they purchased the Lordship of Eskdalemuir and, in the same year, from Sir John Ker of Jedburgh, they purchased all the lands, including Wauchopedale, belonging to the old Cell of Canonby. Certain lairdships in Eskdalemuir were still outside their holdings, but most of these were purchased in 1702, or afterwards, by Anne, Duchess of Buccleuch and Monmouth.

The charter is of much the same tenor as that to the Earl of Nithsdale, but includes other territories. By it the King "concessit et de novo dedit Francisco Comiti Buccleugh domino Scott of Quhitchester, et Eskdaill, in terris et Baronia de Langholm, terras . . . . terras de Dewscoir, Quhytscheles, Ovir et Nather Mylneholmes, Stapilgortoun,

Enzieholmes, Dalbeth, Scheill, cum molendino, Litill Megdaill, Meikil Megdaill, Trochoip cum pendiculo vocato Mairtfauld, terras de Braidheed, Boykin," &c. These last named lands, it will be observed, were amongst those given to Maxwell in 1532. The charter shows that the Scotts of Buccleuch obtained them by this grant and not by purchase, as tradition asserts.

The power placed in the hands of the House of Buccleuch by these charters and purchases was enormous. Tenure by barony was the highest and most privileged tenure of land known to the Scottish feudal system. It carried with it a number of rights and advantages, the principal being the right of jurisdiction, which Lord Neaves[1] declared to be the proper, characteristic, and original meaning of a barony.

This jurisdiction, which was expressly conferred by the charter, usually comprehended all crimes except the four pleas of the Crown, murder, robbery, fire-raising, and rape, but even these were sometimes included. Jurisdiction in capital crimes, however, required infeftment *cum fossa et furca*, with powers of pit and gallows. In civil matters, the baron was the judge in all disputes as to debts, rents, or maills among his tenants or vassals, who were required to give attendance at his Court. These great powers were generally exercised through a baron-bailie, to whom they gave a position of almost autocratic authority within the barony.

The charter of April, 1643, was granted to Francis, second Earl of Buccleuch. He died in 1651, and was succeeded by his daughter Mary, then only three years of age. She succeeded by virtue of the Patent granted to her grandfather Walter, the first Earl. Her marriage to the Earl of Tarras has been already mentioned. Some anxiety arose concerning its legality. The minister of Wemyss married them by licence, without banns. Three Sundays are required by law for the proclamation of banns, but by custom the three can be reduced to one and in the Countess Mary's case steps were at once taken to have the legality of the marriage established beyond all question.

ANNE, DUCHESS OF BUCCLEUCH

Countess Mary died in 1661 and was succeeded by her sister, Countess Anne, and from her succession the development of Langholm went steadily forward. In 1663, at the age of twelve, the Countess married James, Duke of Monmouth, who was himself only fourteen. Monmouth was the son of Charles II and Lucy Walters, the beautiful Welsh girl. On their marriage, the King created Monmouth, who had assumed the name of Scott, first Duke of Buccleuch, with the additional titles of Earl Dalkeith and Lord Scott. A few years after their marriage the King made a separate grant to the Duchess, by which she became Duchess in her own right, rather than just a courtesy title as the wife of the Duke, in the same way as she had inherited her title as Countess before her marriage.[2]

Little reference need be made here to Monmouth's rebellion and subsequent beheading in 1685. At one time his hopes of securing the throne were high, but his plans all proved abortive. On his knees he pleaded with James VII and II for mercy, but the King's hold upon the loyalty and affection of his subjects was too slender to permit of so popular a noble as Monmouth again exciting them to rebellion. So he paid the penalty of his ambition. Lord Tarras was also implicated with Monmouth and thereby lost his title and estates.

Monmouth himself does not appear ever to have visited the Borders, where, however, he was extremely popular. As Duke of Buccleuch, he exerted himself to further the material and social progress of his vassals. So far as the Town of Langholm is concerned, the Duke and Duchess obtained the sanction of Parliament in 1672 for the holding of two fairs, additional to those already granted, to be held on 5th April and 15th July respectively.

And in 1701 the Duchess and her son James, Earl of Dalkeith, received Parliamentary sanction for two more fairs to be held in May and September of each year. These fairs will form the subject of a separate chapter, and it is sufficient to note here that they, especially the Wool and Lamb Fair, held "on the 15th day o' July auld style", did more perhaps than any other means to benefit and increase the trade of Langholm and the surrounding district.

The Duke and Duchess, probably for the more convenient handling of their vast estates, petitioned Parliament for the transfer of the Eskdale parishes from the administrative county of Dumfries to that of Roxburgh. As we have previously observed, Eskdale had once before been included in Roxburghshire. It is so described in some charters of the fourteenth century. It was probably so included when Robert the Bruce re-arranged the territorial divisions, but, in the following centuries it is described in the charters as within the county of Dumfries. But now, in 1672, Parliament passed an "Act in favors of James and Anna, Duke and Dutches of Buccleugh and Monmouth for uniting the fyve paroches in Eskdale, namely Stapelgortoun, Ewes, Westerkirk, Wauchope and Canonby, to the Sheriffdome of Roxburgh".

After the execution of Monmouth, Parliament, under date 1686, passed a "Ratification in favors of Anna Dutches of Buccleugh disjoyning the five paroches of Eskdaill from the shyre of Dumfries and annexing the same to the shyre of Roxburgh".

One of the notable services rendered by Monmouth was the re-stocking of his Border estates after the great storm of March, 1674, known as *The Thirteen Drifty Days*.

After it had at length abated there were left in Eskdalemuir, which was capable of sustaining 20,000 sheep, only forty young wedders on one farm, and five old ewes on another. The storm entirely devastated the Border country, and so for the relief of the consequent distress Monmouth obtained licence to import from Ireland 4,800 nolt (cattle) of a year old, and 200 horses, and these helped materially to re-stock the farms of his tenants.

The Duchess of Buccleuch bore the loss of her husband with great fortitude, though her youngest daughter, a child of ten, felt her father's death so acutely that she pined and died a few weeks after her father. The Duchess was a woman of pronounced individuality and force of character. After the execution of her husband, the King, being assured that she had neither art nor part in the Rebellion, made a gift to her of all the real and personal estate left by her husband, which, of course, had been forfeited.

The Duchess seems then to have resolved upon a more intimate association with her Eskdale tenantry, and she also set herself to increase her properties in the district. We have seen how, in 1702 and afterwards, she purchased estates in Eskdalemuir which had not been included in the Melrose Abbey lands acquired by her ancestors in the early years of the seventeenth century.

She married Lord Cornwallis, but after ten years of married life was again left a widow. She died in 1732 at the advanced age of 80. On the people of her Border estates the Duchess left a lasting impression. Admiration for the splendid management of her estates was widespread and her name was always mentioned with respect.

A SOCIAL IMPRESSION

There is not much information to be gleaned showing what the social life of Langholm was in the early years of its existence as a burgh. In the Reprint of the MS. collection of the Earl of Lonsdale, issued by the Historical Manuscripts Commission in 1898, an account is preserved of a journey by three English tourists through Scotland in the year 1629. On their way to Edinburgh they passed through Langholm and they do not present a very entrancing picture of the place. Allowance must be made, of course, for their different standpoint, and for the fact that the Borders had scarcely yet recovered from the ravages of the raiders, and from the long continued poverty of the people. We learn from their notes that the ground along the Esk was good, but the ground on the heights was waste.

"Langholm" they say "is my Lord Maxfield's [Maxwell], but my Lord Buckpleugh hath it and all his land there mortgaged and is thought will have it. My Lord Maxfield hath gotten it to be a market within this five years, and hath given them of Langholm and Erkenholm land to them with condition to build good guest houses within a year. We lodged at John a Foordes at my Lord Maxfield's gate, (Langholm Castle), where the fire is in the midst of the house".

The fare provided by John for his English guests was liberal, consisting of mutton, fowls, girdle cakes, wheat bread, ale, and spirits. The narrative proceeds:— "We lay in a poor thatched house, the walls of it being one course of stones, another of sods of earth. It had a door of wicker rods and the spider webs hung over our heads as thick as might be in our bed. . . . All the churches we see are poor thatched and in some of them the doors sodded up and no windows in". Passing by Ewesdale they note between "Langholm and Ewes church, the place where Lord Buckpleugh did wapp the outlaws into the dubb". No clear indication is given of the exact location of this place so epigrammatically described.

ACT OF 1747

Undoubtedly, the next important epoch in the development of Langholm and Eskdale was the passing, by the united Parliament, of the Heritable Jurisdictions Act of 1747. The enormous power of the House of Buccleuch was abolished or considerably modified by this Act which limited it to the smaller crimes, and to actions for debt or damages not exceeding forty shillings sterling. But there was reserved to the baron the recovery of all rents, maills, and duties, and all multures payable to his mills. A reservation, which intimately affected Langholm, was that made in favour of existing jurisdictions of fairs and markets and other rights. Amongst the privileges usually conferred with the grant of a barony was the right of the fishings, but it has been legally held that this right did not necessarily include salmon-fishing, an interpretation which may have had some effect upon subsequent legislation concerning fishing rights, nor did it include the right of fishing by means of fixed nets.

On the passing of the Act of 1747 the heritable bailieries of Eskdalemuir, possessed at first by the Glendinnings, and afterwards by the Scotts of Buccleuch, were abolished, and the Duke of Buccleuch received the sum of £1,400 as compensation for the loss of his baronial rights. The general effect of the Act was formally to put an end to the greater part of the judicial and executive power of the barons and lords of regality which, through harsh and arbitrary exercise, had caused great irritation and resentment.

In addition to abolishing the heritable jurisdictions of the barons, this enactment also re-adjusted the boundaries of certain of the Scottish shires. The parishes of Langholm, Ewes, Westerkirk, Eskdalemuir, and Canonby, which, in 1672, had been transferred to the county of Roxburgh, were now restored to the county of Dumfries.

A charter erecting a Burgh of Barony usually reserved to the Baron the right to appoint magistrates, whereas, in the case of a Royal Burgh, the right was given direct to the Burgh. Owing to this provision, the Duke of Buccleuch, as lord-superior of the Barony of Langholm, retained the power, until the coming into operation of the Burgh Police Act of 1892. In the report of the Commissioners appointed in 1833, to enquire into the state of municipal corporations in Scotland, Langholm is stated to belong to the class of Burgh, "where the dependence upon the superior subsists unqualified and where the magistrates are appointed by him".

BARON-BAILIES

It was the practice of the Duke of Buccleuch who, for this purpose, obtained a Commission of Chamberlainry and Bailliary in

1767, to appoint his chamberlain as baron-bailie and chief magistrate, and the chamberlain in turn appointed a deputy baron-bailie and acting chief magistrate. There had of course, been barons-bailie earlier than this date, but probably their powers were more circumscribed than those now conferred. Some holders of this earlier office were Mr. Melville, who either died or relinquished the office in 1724; Mr. Elliot of Midlem Mill; Mr. Boston, son of the Rev. Thomas Boston of Ettrick and a Mr. Craigie.

The first baron-bailie appointed under this Commission of whom we have any record, was William Ogilvie of Hartwoodmyres, chamberlain for the counties of Dumfries, Roxburgh, Selkirk, and Peebles. By a Deed of Deputation, he appointed in 1768 Matthew Little, merchant in Langholm, to be his deputy baron-bailie and acting-chief magistrate. In 1793 the office was held by William Armstrong, writer in Langholm. How long he continued to hold the office we do not know, but in 1845, when the residents adopted the cleaning, lighting, and water clauses of the Act of 1833, Alexander Stevenson, writer, had the appointment, which he held until 1862, when it fell to Hugh Dobie, who held it until 1873. On his death, in that year, he was succeeded by his son-in-law, Mr. Robert McGeorge, who retained the office until May, 1893, when the Burgh Police Act of 1892 came into force.

On the death of Anne, Duchess of Buccleuch, in 1732 she was succeeded by her grandson Francis, eldest son of her son James, Earl of Dalkeith, who had died in 1705 at the age of 31.

In 1751 he was succeeded by his grandson Henry, son of Francis, Earl of Dalkeith, by his marriage with Lady Caroline Campbell, eldest daughter of John, Duke of Argyle and Greenwich.

Henry, third Duke of Buccleuch was the farmer-duke. His interest in, and knowledge of, agriculture were deep and extensive. Under his direction the estates in Eskdale and Liddesdale were enormously improved. Born in 1746, he was only six years of age at the date of his succession. His mother had married Charles Townsend, who greatly interested himself in the boy's education, but kept him away from his Scottish estates lest he should become too fond of Scotland.

After finishing his education the Duke travelled with Adam Smith, the famous philosopher and political economist, for whom he came to have a great admiration and regard. At the age 21 he married Lady Elizabeth Montague, and soon afterwards the Duke and Duchess visited their vast estates in Scotland. This visit was made the occasion of a great popular welcome.

Duke Henry succeeded just at the time of a great revival of agriculture in Scotland. The old methods, or lack of method, the old carelessness and slovenliness, were quickly giving place to more intelligent ways and to greater industry.

HENRY, THIRD DUKE OF BUCCLEUCH

The money received by the barons in consideration of the abolition of their heritable jurisdictions was being largely spent on the development of their estates, and on every hand country life was obtaining a new attraction from the growing prosperity and more humane conditions being brought into existence.

In bringing about this better condition of things *Good Duke Henry*, as he afterwards came to be affectionately called, took a principal part. He was a sympathetic and helpful friend to the poor, who had easy access to him, and always took a leading part in every movement likely to benefit his tenants. In all his purposes and plans for the benefit of Langholm and Eskdale generally, he was ably seconded by his servant

Bailie Little. Perhaps to no other two men was Langholm more indebted during the latter half of the eighteenth century, than to the Duke and his baron-bailie. When Pennant made his famous Tour in Scotland in 1776, it was from Bailie Little and John Maxwell, Esquire, of Broomholm, that he received his information respecting Langholm

NEW-LANGHOLM

One of the most noteworthy and beneficent of their actions was the breaking up of the farm of Meikleholm and the laying out thereon of the New-Town of Langholm. Prior to this date, the term Langholm applied only to the part on the eastern side of the Esk. The river-banks were unconnected by any bridge, the only means of communication being the boat-ford.

The site of New-Langholm was then a large farm called the Meikleholm, with which was generally associated the farm of Waas or Walls, which was really part of the glebe land. In 1679 these united farms were sett to Robert Allan, minister of Stapelgortoun and son of the minister of Wauchope.

The last tenant of Meikleholm was James Beattie, farmer, of Bailie Hill, Airswood, and Downahill, a descendant of the Beattisons of Eskdale and a relative of Bailie Little. James Beattie did not live at Meikleholm but continued to reside in Eskdale. His brother, John Beattie, was a generous subscriber to the fund for building Langholm Bridge and was a humane and generous man of piety and considerable learning. His library, consisting mostly of philosophical, astronomical and scientific works, was a notable one for the period.

The leases for the new houses, of which there were about 140 built, were for a term of 99 years. The work of building them began in the year 1778 and went on for a period of about 20 years. The feu-rent, or quit-rent, for house and garden was two shillings and eight-pence per annum, that is, at the rate of about twenty-one shillings an acre, and the houses were of either one or two storeys in height.

Each house of one storey had a field allotted to it of two acres in extent, whilst those of two storeys had fields of four acres, on leases of about 14 years, at rents ranging from three to fourteen shillings an acre. Each cottage carried also a right of grazing for a cow, at eighteen shillings a year, on one of the three hills, Warbla, or Stubholm Hill, as it was often called, Castle Hill, and Meikleholm Hill. The fields referred to were on the slopes of those hills, and a great boon they proved to the cottars of New-Langholm. In addition to these concessions the Duke allowed the tenants to cast peats on Warbla Moss; and the Peat Road, which was cut for the tenants' convenience, in this way received its name.

The laying out of the New-Town was virtually completed in 1800, but naturally, through the expansion of trade and the increase in population, other building schemes were subsequently entered into. As the leases of the cottages matured, others were granted, and in place of the cottages two storey houses of freestone, quarried from the Common Moss, were erected. However, some of the original one-story cottages still remained on one side of Manse Street, now named Caroline Street.

In the diary of a tour in Scotland in the year 1803 undertaken by Wordsworth and his sister, the latter gives a pleasing glimpse of Langholm at that time:—

"Arrived at Langholm at about five o'clock. The town, as we approached, from a hill, looked very pretty, the houses being roofed with blue slates, and standing close to the river Esk, here a large river, that scattered its waters wide over a stony channel. The inn neat and comfortable — exceedingly clean. I could hardly believe we were still in Scotland".

From an old MS. account of Langholm[3] we learn that in 1726 there were in the parish of Stapelgortoun only two gentlemen's houses, one of which belonged to the Earl of Dalkeith, and mention is made of a fine *bow*, in which the Duke's chamberlain dwelt, in the middle of Langholm, built of stones taken from the Castle walls. It is stated to be "about a mile from the church on the north side of the Esk". We may take it that these notes have been written by a stranger and are somewhat confused. In 1726, as we have remarked, the chamberlain dwelt *in* the castle, which is the only place answering to such a description. Where the Earl of Dalkeith's house stood, is not known, indeed its existence apart from the Castle may very well be doubted.

The MS also mentions that in 1631 the Langholm district was visited by an influx of sturdy Irish beggars, who extorted alms where not freely given. In 1644 there was a visitation of plague, and in 1651 a great dearth occurred, when barley was sold at £20 Scots per boll and grain had to be imported from England.

CAROLINE STREET COTTAGES

Reproduced from Robert Hyslop's original glass plate. Photograph taken about 1897. He was born in number 15, the second house from the left. The family later moved to number 21. Standing at the door are Robert, his wife, and his daughter Hilda. At the door of number 19 are Janet Hyslop, wife of Robert's brother William, and son Walter.

We read further, that in 1723-4 the churchyard had been walled round with a stone and lime dyke, and set round with young timber. There had also been built a Town-house, a prison, and a Cross. The Town-house and prison were built in 1812 on the site of the old Tolbooth, and are still standing, serving the purpose only of a Town Hall.

THE CROSS

The Cross, of which a drawing is here given, was removed about the year 1840 to make room for the statue of Sir Pulteney Malcolm. In olden days the Cross was the focus of all important events. Proclamations, royal and otherwise, were there made, and at it were held all important meetings. It stood in the Market-place and well within the nineteenth century what is now called the Market-place was then called The Cross.

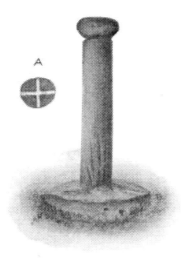

LANGHOLM MERCAT CROSS
Drawing by Ann Hyslop

After the removal of the Cross its existence seems to have been entirely forgotten. About the year 1867, when road works were being carried out in the Market-place, the shaft of the Cross was discovered. It had, evidently, been carefully buried for preservation, doubtless on the spot where it had originally stood, in front of which there was also a cruciform design in the pavement, for Langholm High Street was then paved with cobble-stones. It is a plain shaft of Whita sandstone set into a roughly hewn plinth of the same stone. It would appear from the socket holes, which can be seen in the illustration, that some other stone had been clamped to it. The shaft of the Cross was surmounted by a red granite stone of oval shape, into which had been roughly cut the *cross*, as shown in the inset "A". The top-stone was afterwards found in the Blacksyke, which once ran near by, but was long ago covered in.

The old Cross, thus recovered, was given to Mr. Hugh Dobie, then acting-chief magistrate, who had it erected within his grounds at Greenbank, where it remained for many years. A hundred years later, in 1967, when Greenbank became an Eventide Home, the Cross was relocated in the Library Gardens but unfortunately its plinth has been either lost or buried in the re-siting.

LANGHOLM MARKET PLACE

The MS. proceeds to record that the town was then furnished with all kinds of tradesmen; a weekly market and six yearly fairs, from which accrued a considerable revenue in customs. In addition to the Town-house and prison, there was an excise office, and, of course, an exciseman, who was then even more indispensable than the policeman.

In 1726 a wool-combing business had been established and the writer laments:— "What a pity it is, it wants a wool manufactory, being a great wool country!" He also suggested that, to this end, a few farmers should send their sons, as apprentices, to Huddersfield and other Yorkshire towns, there to learn the manufacture of woollen goods, presumably with the idea that they should afterwards commence business in Langholm. Could the writer of the MS. have foreseen the development which since then has taken place in the woollen trade of Langholm, his prophetic hopes would have been fully satisfied.

Such a woollen factory was, however, in existence in the town at a later date, and it is curious to note that it was an object of some concern to the Kirk-Session, whose oversight of the religion and morals of the town did not exhaust their activities. On 28th February, 1750, there is the following minute in the Session records :—

"The Session appoint the Treasurer with the other members of Session, to intimate to such women able to spin to get any money in charity, that they employ their labour and spin for the WOOLLEN FACTORY in town preferably to any other that shall employ them with certification."

It was during the lifetime of the Good Duke Henry that Langholm Lodge was built, but burned to the ground before it was ever occupied. It was rebuilt in 1790 of white freestone of remarkable durability from Whita Hill.

"This handsome mansion", says the Statist of 1793, "much admired by travellers for its elegant simplicity and fine situation, stands in the middle of a delightful valley about half a mile north from Langholm". The family of Buccleuch continued to reside there for a certain period each year. During the war years of 1939-45 the Lodge was used by the Army and was demolished in 1950 due to dry rot.

It is interesting to note that at this time Langholm ranked, in regard to population, as the second town in the county, a position from which it has since fallen, owing to the lamentable emigration from the town. Houses in Langholm were then rented at from fifteen shillings to £12 a year.

In New-Langholm, about the year 1789, there was established a cotton manufactory. The cotton yarn made was known as "No. 30", and found a market in Carlisle and Glasgow. The factory was in the Meikleholm Mill and gave employment to nearly 100 people. But in

LANGHOLM LODGE

in 1793 difficulties arose through the great financial panic when, from unsound methods of finance and troubles abroad, so many banking houses were forced to suspend payment. Public credit was entirely undermined and Langholm suffered equally with other places all over the country.

However, in 1794, work was resumed in the cotton industry at Meikleholm Mill by one James Carruthers. The machinery contained 3,552 mule spindles and, by 1841, there were stated to be over 90 persons engaged in the mill. In later years the cotton weaving was abandoned and the mill was converted into a flour mill.

In 1797 High Mill, near Ewes Bridge, was built. It was run by Irvine & Co. and employed about 50 workers. Their hours of labour were from 6 a.m. to 8 p.m., with an hour off for dinner. Numerous styles of textile manufacture were carried out here and also on other sites in the town.

Up to about the same year a paper mill, situated near the Skipper's Bridge, where later the distillery was built, was in operation employing 20 workpeople, with an output of 80 reams weekly. It was about the same date that the manufacture of checks and thread developed in Langholm. In 1792 some 20,000 yards of cotton checks and other coarse linens were sold. The manufacture of stockings also sprang up and for many years remained one of the staple trades of the town.

Woollen manufacture developed early in the nineteenth century and, as the tweed industry developed, the working conditions of the weavers improved. Instrumental in the development of the industry was Alexander Reid who had been a small handloom manufacturer. He carried his own patterns to London and, by the excellence of his goods, very soon established a large connection. He later went into partnership with Joseph Taylor.

The Shepherd's Plaid design was manufactured by Reid and Taylor although family tradition maintains that the original weave was produced by Marion McVittie, wife of Archibald Grieve, clogger. Marion's father, James, son of Robert McVittie in Murtholm and Marion Little, was a weaver to trade. Marion's great-great-grandson was James Grieve, the last Provost of Langholm.

A considerable trade was done in other branches of merchandise. An Act passed in 1808 amended certain Acts of the Scottish Parliament relating to trade between the Royal Burghs and the Burghs of Regality

ALEXANDER REID

and Barony. The object of the Act was to impose upon places other than Royal Burghs, certain of the duties which, by Scottish legislation, had been exacted solely from them, and for which in return they had been granted certain privileges of trading amongst themselves and with foreign parts.

The privileges had been gradually appropriated by Burghs of Regality and Barony, and the Act was to re-adjust the burdens. Any quota of the duties which a Burgh of Barony might thereby contribute could be recovered from persons trading, but not actually residing, within the Burgh. Langholm was scheduled in the Act as a Burgh of Barony which did not contribute in any way whatever to the relief of Royal Burghs, and by the Act it was made liable to a tax of 10 per cent. on its tax-roll.

The Statist of 1793 gives us a very interesting glimpse into the occupations of the Langholm people. In the town, he notes, there were two surgeons, two writers (lawyers), 14 shopkeepers, six manufacturers in checks, thread, or stockings, one tanner, one skinner, one clockmaker, one saddler, two dyers, five bakers, two butchers, three bleachers, and two barbers. There were 30 masons, 20 joiners, eight blacksmiths, 43 weavers, 11 shoemakers, three cloggers, four gardeners, and 15 tailors. There were also 15 innkeepers and publicans, "exclusive of some who keep private tippling-houses and dram-shops".

It is also recorded that masons' and joiners' wages were from 1/6 and 2/- a day; day labourers 10d. a day in winter and 1/2 or 1/4 in summer; women 8d. to 10d. a day; male servants, resident in the family, were paid from six to eight pounds a year, and female servants three to five pounds.

Beef then sold at about 4d. a pound; mutton about 3d.; fowls were 8d. to 10d.; geese, eighteen pence or two shillings; butter was 6d. to 7½d. per English pound ; eggs were 3d. to 4d. a dozen; and meal was two shillings a stone.

(For those readers unfamiliar with pre-decimal coinage 12 pence = 1 shilling, 20 shillings = £1. 1/6 means 1 shilling and 6 pence. The sign for pence was d. from the Roman, or Latin, word denarius e.g 8d. means 8 pence, 7½d is sevenpence ha'penny. When decimalisation took place 1 shilling = 5 new pence.)

A detailed account is also given, by the Statist, of a Friendly Society, with 150 members, which then existed in Langholm, and he optimistically looked to such Societies to abolish poor's rates. "But the dawn of that day has not even touched the brow of Whita", wrote Robert Hyslop in 1911. It was not until 1947 that the Poor Law system was abolished.[4]

ACT OF 1833

The meeting of the occupiers to consider the adoption of the Act of 1833 was held on 26th September, 1845 and was convened by intimation affixed to the doors of the Town-house and the parish church, and by "tuck of drum" by Peter Graham, the town drummer. In addition to the adoption of certain clauses of the Act, the meeting determined the limits of the Burgh, "within a distance not exceeding 1,000 yards from the bounds", to be as follows:- "on the east of Langholm by a place called the March-gill, later called Jenny Noble's Gill, on the north by Whitshields Cleuch; on the south by Stubholm Hill; and on the west by Meikleholm Hill".

When the arrangements for constituting the Burgh boundaries were submitted for the approval of the Sheriff, a difficulty arose owing to the local authorities being unaware of the charter to the Earl of Nithsdale of 1621. According to the Act of 1833, the boundaries of the Burgh had to be fixed, not exceeding 1,000 yards from those defined by the Royal charter. But as there did not appear to be any charter, the local authorities could not conform to the requirements of the Act. It evidently did not occur, either to them or the Sheriff, to consult the *Great Seal Register*. However, the difficulty seems ultimately to have been overcome.

WATER-WORKS

At first the Act of 1833 was only adopted in respect of the cleaning and lighting. The water supply of the town was in the hands of the subscribers to Langholm Water Works, who in 1856 handed over the control to the Commissioners of Police. In the same year it was resolved to place an inscription on the lintel of the cistern at Mount Hooley, and the following, prepared by Dr. Brown of Milntown, was adopted:—

"Langholm Water-Works were commenced in the year 1853 and finished during the following year. Funds were raised by the voluntary subscriptions of the inhabitants of Langholm and the adjoining districts, aided by a munificent donation from the Duke of Buccleuch, by liberal contributions from natives and friends of Eskdale in the United Kingdom and abroad, and by a most successful Bazaar which took place in July, 1854."

The supply of water which then provided for the wants of a population of over 3,000, soon proved inadequate, and has been on several occasions augmented.

POLICE COMMISSIONERS

The number of Police Commissioners was fixed at 15, besides the acting-chief magistrate, and the maximum rate of assessment for the ensuing three years at 4d. in the £. The Poor's Fund of Langholm had been obtained, since the year 1775, by a voluntary assessment, but in 1845 an Act was passed "for the amendment and better administration of the Laws relating to the relief of the poor in Scotland".

Parochial Boards were then constituted, and the first meeting of the Langholm Board was held within the Town-house on 16th September, 1845. Those present were A. Harley Maxwell, preses,

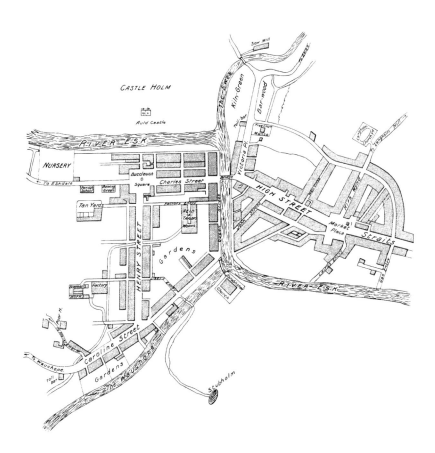

MAP OF LANGHOLM CIRCA 1850

chamberlain to the Duke of Buccleuch, the Rev. William Berry Shaw, minister of Langholm parish church, and Messrs. George Maxwell of Broomholm, Alexander Stevenson, writer, Matthew Jamieson, sawyer, George J. Todd, parish schoolmaster, and John Fenwick, stationer, elders. Mr. Todd was appointed Clerk and Inspector of the Poor.

The Board consisted of all owners and occupiers of property of an assessable value of £20 and upwards, some members of the Kirk Session, and four members chosen by the ratepayers. These annually appointed a sub-committee of four to manage the affairs of the Board, whose principal duty was the administration of parochial relief.

The Parochial Board was superseded by the Parish Council on 15th May, 1895. It consisted of eight members for the Burgh and five for the Landward part of the parish. The first Council was composed of the following:—

The Revs. James Buchanan and J. Wallace Mann, and Messrs. Arthur Bell, James Cunningham, John Hotson, John Hyslop, Charles Paisley, and Thomas Telfer, representing the Burgh; and Messrs. James Burnet, Thomas Gaskell, Frederick W. Medhurst, James Scott, and Morden Carthew-Yorstoun of East Tinwald, chamberlain to His Grace the Duke of Buccleuch, representing the Landward portion of the parish.

The first chairman of the Parish Council was Mr. John Hyslop, who for nearly 12 years had occupied the same position on the Parochial Board, of which he became an elected member in 1872, and who continued to occupy the post until his death in November 1911.

The first clerk was Mr. Henry Erskine, on whose death, in 1896, Mr. James Morrison succeeded to the position.

COMMISSIONERS' CLERKS

The following are the names of those who, from 1845 to 1893, filled the office of Clerk to the Police Commissioners:—

Mr. Robert Wallace, bank agent, 1845-8; Mr. George Henderson, from 1848 until his death in 1859, Mr. Hugh Dobie, writer, from 1859 until 1862 when he was appointed acting-chief magistrate; Mr. William Grieve from 1862 until 1864 when he resigned. Mr. Robert Scott, postmaster, was then appointed and held the position for over 28 years until the new Act came into force in 1893.

BURGH POLICE ACT

The Burgh Police Act of 1892 came into force in Langholm on 15th May, 1893. The first Provost elected under the new Act was Mr. J.J. Thomson, merchant. He held the office until November, 1908, when he was succeeded by Mr. Thomas R. Easton.

The Town Clerk first appointed was the late Mr. Andrew Johnstone, who held office until his death in 1906, when Mr. Samuel McKune, Town Clerk, was appointed to succeed him.

The first Town Council elected under the Act consisted, with the Provost, of 9 members, viz.:— Bailies: John Goodfellow, painter; and James Rutherford, engineer; Councillors: John Baird Balfour, merchant; John Hotson, builder; Robert B. Milligan, joiner; John Dalgleish, tweed merchant; Matthew Knox, joiner; and Adam Watt, hotel keeper.

On the incorporation of the Burgh an official seal was prepared, of which, by the courtesy of Provost Easton, and the Town Clerk, Mr. S. McKune, we are permitted to give this illustration:—

THE OFFICIAL SEAL OF LANGHOLM BURGH

The Town Arms are : Azure, a saltire argent; between — in chief, a thistle slipped proper, imperially crowned or; on the dexter, a spade

251

in pale, blade upwards, wreathed with heather proper On the sinister, a wooden platter surmounted of a barley-meal bannock, surmounted in turn of a salt-herring paleways, and marked with the letter B on each side of the herring; and in base a toison or. (i.e.golden fleece).

The main shield is simply the national flag of Scotland and is so scored upon the seal. The three top most devices represent the following articles which are carried in the Common Riding Procession :— (i.) A large Scots thistle with a floral crown on its top; (ii.) a barley-meal bannock with a salt herring fastened with a large nail to a wooden dish, with the letter B on the bannock on each side of the herring; (iii.) a spade decked with heather, which is used for cutting and turning over the sods along the boundaries of the Commonty. The fourth device on the Seal is the golden fleece, which represents the trade of the town — woollen manufacture.

Only one further development in the corporate life of Langholm need now be recorded. In 1872, the Education Act for Scotland became law, and, in pursuance of its requirements, a School Board was first elected on 8th April, 1873. This Board consisted of the following:— Dr. Eneas Macaulay, surgeon; Rev. J. W. Macturk, AB., parish minister; James Burnet, architect; George Maxwell of Broomholm; Walter Scott, skinner; Robert Smellie, merchant; John Connell, distiller. Mr. Maxwell of Broomholm was appointed to be chairman, and Mr. Hugh Dobie, clerk and treasurer. Owing to the death of Mr. Dobie, Mr. Maxwell took over the duties of clerk also, and acted in that capacity, without salary, until 1886, when he resigned his posts and seat on the Board.

The new Board took over the control of all the schools in Langholm. The old Parish School was enlarged for the reception of the scholars of the Free Church School and others, and Mr. John Howie, of Airdrie Academy, was appointed head master over the united institution. During Mr. Howie's occupancy of the position the School developed greatly, both in the number of scholars and scholastic distinction, and its name was changed to Langholm Academy, with Mr. Howie as its first Rector. On his death in 1908 the Rectorship was given to Mr. R. Hamilton, MA., BSc.

CHAPTER 21

THE BRIDGES OF ESK

During the latter half of the eighteenth century a great advance was made in the social and industrial condition of the south of Scotland. The money which the barons had received, in 1747, as compensation for the abolition of their heritable jurisdiction, became available for the improvement of their estates, and to the credit of the barons, it must be admitted, the money was spent to the advantage of the country.

Another factor making for the better development of the great landed estates was the freer sale of land, which was induced partly by the confiscations following the Rebellion of '45, when large portions of land were placed on the market, and partly by the eagerness of pensioned servants of the East India Company to acquire estates on which they could settle after their return to this country.

Money, too, came into freer circulation by about the middle of the eighteenth century. Up to this period very little coin had been in use in the south of Scotland, landlords received only about one fourth of their rents in actual cash, the rest in kind. This entailed an enormous waste, for the grain often stood rotting in the granaries waiting for a market. But now banks were rapidly springing into being and landlords were being paid in cash.

Farmers, too, by the Act of 1747, were released from the tyranny of thirlage, a compulsion which placed them at the mercy of the miller, and greatly hampered the natural evolution of agriculture. They were also relieved from their obligation to give so much free labour to their landlords, and from his levy upon their produce. For the last a quicker and readier market was being found, and the great Fairs, such as Langholm Summer Fair, served as excellent markets for sheep and wool.

253

Added to these agencies was the beneficent operation of the Turnpike Acts leading up to that of 1831. By these Acts farmers and proprietors were assessed in equal proportions for the maintenance of efficient public roads, thus improving the means of communication between the farms and the markets instead of the old cart-tracks which previously had to answer the purpose.

Virtually all the roads, excepting perhaps the road to Westerkirk and Eskdalemuir, in Eskdale had been constructed by statute labour according to the Act of 1669, whereby each resident was required by law to contribute his share of labour, or its equivalent in money, to the making of the highway.

The Act of 1751 and various other supplementary Acts, not only provided for a legal assessment upon proprietors and occupiers, but also enabled those responsible for the upkeep of the roads, that is, parish authorities or Road Trustees, to convert certain of the main roads into turnpikes, and to levy tolls on the traffic, the revenue helping to maintain the roads. The turnpikes in Langholm district were the roads from Langholm to Carlisle, Langholm to Hawick, and Langholm to Annan. The tolls on the turnpike roads continued in force until they were abolished when the Roads and Bridges Act of 1878 came into operation.

The three Langholm toll bars were the last ones in Scotland to close their gates in 1883. Many of the old toll-bar cottages still exist, such as at Scotch Dyke, Langholm Townfoot, Langholm Townhead, and at Fiddleton on the Carlisle to Edinburgh turnpike.

The result of all these factors was a great revival in agriculture. Newer methods were welcomed. Land was drained and brought under cultivation and hedges were planted. Houses were greatly improved, both in furnishings and in food and soon there was seen a striking improvement throughout the entire lowlands.

The land had rest after the centuries of Border strife, and lairds, farmers and cottars could attend to the less exciting, but more praiseworthy avocations of the country-side, in assurance and peace of mind. One of the immediate consequences of the revival of agriculture was the improvement in the ways of communication. The latter half of the eighteenth century saw the construction of many of the main roads and the building of bridges, without which social and economic intercourse could not thrive.

In Eskdale this improvement was due to the enlightened policy of the great lairds. Henry, Duke of Buccleuch, set himself with to improve his estates in Eskdale. Sir William Pulteney planned the coach road of the Ewes valley, and in 1763 obtained an Act of Parliament for carrying out the work[1]. Sir William was a brother of Sir James Johnstone and succeeded to the baronetcy. He married the heiress of William Pulteney, Earl of Bath, and took her name.

The Eskdale parishes were now connected by the building of those Bridges over the Esk, which were not only to be an ornament to the landscape, but a potent force in the development of the dale.

SKIPPER'S BRIDGE
Reproduced from Robert Hyslop's original glass plate

Probably the oldest of the Esk Bridges is that at Skipper's, a mile south of Langholm, where it forms a picturesque object in a scene of magnificent natural beauty. The Bridge, founded strongly on an outcrop of rock, consists of two separate erections. The earlier, the south-ward, section was built about 1693-1700. It was a narrow bridge, similar to many others in the lowlands, and its erection was necessary to link up the main route from Carlisle to Edinburgh. In 1807 it was widened by the addition of that part nearer Langholm. The two sections are easily distinguishable. The Bridge is designed in two semi-circular arches with a third and smaller one at the western approach, and it is interesting to note that the flat, square stones built into the west end of the Bridge were obtained from the old Roman way between Skipper's and Murtholm.

Concerning the origin of the name, *Skipper's* there is a tradition that before the Bridge was built a ferryboat plied across the river at that part, and the ferryman was popularly called the skipper

LANGHOLM BRIDGE

The Bridge which spans the Esk at Langholm is a massive stone structure of three arches. It was built by Robert, or as he was called, Robin Hotson, the great grandfather of John Hyslop. Work started in 1775 and the bridge was completed in 1778. On one of the piers the date 1794 is carved, but this has evidently been done when some alterations or repairs were being carried out.

The cost was met by public subscription, liberally supported by the farmers of Westerkirk and Eskdalemuir, who were quick to see the great business advantage it would give them. Both Buccleuch and Westerhall interested themselves conspicuously in the movement.

A noteworthy circumstance connected with the building of the Bridge is that Thomas Telford, the famous engineer and bridge builder, having finished his apprenticeship, worked on it as a young journeyman and there received his first instruction in bridge building. His mason's mark can still be seen.

The story of the great flood in the Esk, which made the new bridge quiver, has often been told, and, to quote John Hyslop "people have laughed at the tale of my great-grandmother, Tibbie Donald, Robin's wife, setting herself against the bridge to stop it tumbling into the water." The originator of the story is Samuel Smiles when writing, almost 100 years later, on the life of Telford, but Smiles does not even have Tibbie married to the right person! He erroneously implies that she was the wife of Andrew Thomson, with whom Telford had finished his apprenticeship. Unfortunately subsequent writers have blindly quoted Smiles thereby perpetuating this inaccuracy.

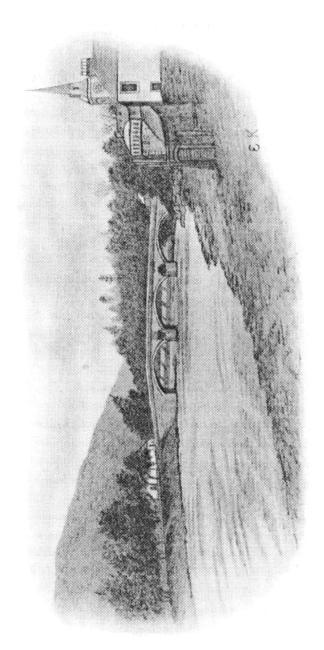

LANGHOLM BRIDGE

The true story, as recounted by Agnes Hotson, Robin and Tibbie's eldest child and a teenager at the time of the storm, to her grandson, John Hyslop, is as follows. Tibbie had placed all the savings of herself and her deceased first husband, William Aitken, to the amount of £100 sterling, in the hands of her second husband, Robin Hotson, for this venture of the bridge. When she saw the river coming down in flood she feared that this considerable sum was to be carried down the Esk. Robin being away on other business at the time, she went bemoaning her ill-luck, wringing her hands and saying, "Oh, ma puir hunner pun'! Oh, ma puir hunner pun'!" Telford tried to reassure her saying that the bridge was in no danger.

THOMAS TELFORD'S MARK
Photograph by Alan J. Booth in 1993

When finished, the Bridge was of a somewhat narrow gauge with stone parapets. In 1880 it was widened at a cost of £1,188 4s. 9½d. The contract for this work was given to John Hyslop who wrote as follows:—

"I was highly gratified when to me was given the contract, in 1880, for widening and restoring Langholm Bridge. My father, who of course could well remember his grandfather Robin Hotson, was greatly interested in the work, and I remember one day the present Duke of Buccleuch, then the Earl of Dalkeith, coming to see what was being done. I happened to be away from the job at the time, but my father told the above facts to "the Yirl", as he called him, who expressed his personal pleasure that the extension of the bridge should have been

been entrusted to the great-grandson of Robin Hotson, its original builder."[2] Further work of strengthening the bridge had to be carried out in 1995 to cope with the weight of modern traffic.

GILNOCKIE BRIDGE

In the original edition of this book there is a printing error and the date of building Gilnockie Bridge is given as 1799. However, in Robert Hyslop's own copy, he has scored out that date and written in the margin "begun 1789, finished in 1792". The Bridge consists of a large arch and a smaller dry one and its length is 244 feet and height 46 feet. The keystone of this bridge was placed in position by the grandfather of Mr. Thomas Beattie, chemist in Langholm.

The scenery here is magnificent. Precipices, fifty or sixty feet in height, crowned with overhanging trees, rising sheer from the water's edge. The high road is diverted here from the west to the east side of the river, at the instance, and also at the expense, of the then Duke of Buccleuch, who desired a readier access to his coal mines at Byreburn.

CANONBY BRIDGE

The last Bridge across the Esk in Scotland is at Canonby. After the drowning accident of 1696, (see page 270) the idea of building a bridge was suggested. Dr. Russell in his Statistical Account of 1793 indicates that there had been other similar accidents. Eventually the bridge was built about 1745 and was of a very primitive construction and without parapets

The present structure was built between 1780 and 1790. It is said that many of the stones used for its construction were brought from the old Priory of Hallgreen. Originally the parapets were of stone, and it was widened to its present dimensions in 1899 at a cost of over £800.

The other Bridges over the Esk are in its upper reaches. The one nearest the source of the river is a short distance below Glendearg and Upper Cassock.

The next is near to Clerkhill and is a Bridge of two arches built in 1878 to replace an older structure. The cost, £1,061, was provided by the Road Trustees.

At Enzieholm there is a Bridge of a high single span.

The oldest bridge in Upper Eskdale is a narrow two span bridge at Bentpath. No date was inscribed upon it or any indication as to the builder. However, due to extensive research by Neil R. Paisley, we now know that the bridge was built in 1734 by Robert Paisley, Wright in Burn, in partnership with Andrew Coats, mason in Langholm[3]. The bridge is renamed the Westerkirk Bridge and a commemorative plaque records the Paisley connection. Robert, who died in 1737, was a younger brother of James Paisley of Craig.

WESTERKIRK BRIDGE
Reproduced from the photograph by John Gerrard, owner of the copyright. The original photograph is held by the RCAHMS.

Of more recent bridges mention may be made of those at Burnfoot and Potholm.

Ewes Bridge, a little above where that river flows into the Esk, is the old coach-road Bridge on the highway from Carlisle to Edinburgh. It was built some time before 1775, probably in 1763. The Bridge at the High Mill, on the new coach road, was built in 1822.

The Auld Stane Brig, at the site of Wauchope Castle was built in the spring of 1794 when the new road from Langholm to Annan was made by the statute labour trustees. The small Bridge over the Becks Burn at Wauchope Kirkyard was made in 1815. Previously the traffic crossed by a ford.

CHAPTER 22

THE KIRKS OF ESKDALE

The territory of Strathclyde, or Cumbria, had from an early date been the scene of much activity on the part of the Christian Church. St. Bride's Chapel is, undoubtedly, the earliest Christian settlement in Eskdale.

BYKEN

In December 1391 a church dedicated, like the Priory of Canonby, to St. Martin, was founded at Byken, sometimes spelled Boyken, in Westerkirk by Adam de Glendonyng, who set apart certain of his lands in the barony of Hawick for its support. Where the chapel was situated is not known, nor have we any clear record of its incumbents. Mr. R. Bruce Armstrong enumerates in his *History of Liddesdale, &c.* the following:—

BARTHOLOMEW GLENDONING *ante* 1459
    Grandson of the founder. He was deprived of the charge by the Bishop of Glasgow, for non-residence, in 1459.

CLEMENT CURROR *ante* 1501
SIR JOHN LAMB 1501
SIR WALTER KERSANE 1509

WATCARRICK

The chapel of Watcarrick, the location of which is determined by the postion of the old kirkyard, served the district of Upper Eskdale until the Reformation. In 1703 the parish of Eskdalemuir was formed, the new church being built upon the site of the present building. Vestiges of the ancient chapel at Watcarrick could be seen until near the close of the eighteenth century. A reference to the chapel in 1592, shows "teind schaves" of £6 13s. 4d. were returned.

UNTHANK

Here was situated the Over-kirk of Ewes, dedicated to St. Mark, but only the lonely kirkyard marks the site of the ancient chapel. Chalmers, in his *Caledonia,* states that the Over-kirk of Ewes was at Ewes-doors, and that Unthank was one of two chapels attached to it, the other being at Mosspaul.

This is accepted by the Statist of 1841, but undoubtedly Unthank was the Over-kirk itself, rather than a mere chapel-of-ease. So far as we are aware no evidence has been discovered pointing to Ewes-doors as its location.

John Lindsay of Wauchope had the right of patronage of Unthank, but on his forfeiture in 1505 through the slaying of the Glendinnings, it fell to Lord Home. On his decease it reverted to the Crown, by whom it was bestowed on Lord Maxwell in 1516.

One of the incumbents, Robert, was a witness to a charter in the reign of Alexander III. The Over-kirk of Ewes was deserted at the Reformation, after which the Nether-kirk alone supplied spiritual ordinances.

Sir Walter Scott has a note that it was to Unthank that the secular priests known as "Book-a-Bosoms" came to confirm the "hand-fasting", which had been only a mutual contract, unaccompanied by any religious ceremonial. But Unthank would be only one of many such churches, for hand-fasting was not exclusively confined to Eskdale.

MOSSPAUL

The name Mosspaul, suggests the existence of an ecclesiastical foundation and Chalmers places here a chapel of the Over-kirk of Ewes. Concerning it we have little information. Writing in 1835 for the *Statistical Account* published in 1841, the Rev. Robert Shaw mentions that the ruins of the church of Mosspaul could then be identified, but all trace of them has been long removed.

CANONBY

The most important church in Eskdale was that of Canonby. The Priory was founded for Canons Regular of the Augustinian Order by Turgot de Rossedal, during the reign of David I, 1124 to 1153. It was to be held as a cell attached to the monastery of Jedburgh, which had received various grants of land from the Rossedals and others. During the twelfth century it was known as the Church of Liddel.

In 1179 Pope Alexander III confirmed to Jocelin, Bishop of Glasgow and the biographer of St. Kentigern, or St. Mungo, the churches of Eskdale, Ewesdale and Liddesdale. The monks of Jedburgh disputed the ecclesiastical jurisdiction of the See of Glasgow and the questions in dispute were submitted to arbitration. The award placed the church of St. Martin of Liddel under the episcopal authority of the Bishop of Glasgow and attached, as dependencies of the Priory, were the churches of Castletown, Sibbaldbie, and Wauchope.

In 1540 Dean George Graym granted a lease for five years of the glebe lands of Wauchope to Lord Maxwell. In the document Graym's name is given as John but the signature is George Graym. Mr. R. Bruce Armstrong mentions that this document is still extant and that it is probably the only one remaining which was executed by a Prior of Canonby.

Canonby was in the deanery of Annandale, though Mr. Armstrong suggests that there was also a deanery of Eskdale and it may have been this fact which originated the name *Dean Banks* the beautiful stretch of woodland between Skipper's Bridge and the Irvine Burn.

During the Wars of Succession the Prior of Canonby swore fealty to Edward I, but neither the monks nor the people of Canonby renounced their claim to be regarded as Scottish subjects.

The Priory, naturally, was the place of most consequence in the whole district, judicial and other business being transacted there. According to a letter, dated 30th November 1544, from the Council to the Earl of Shrewsbury, the Bishop of Durham and Sir R. Sadler, it would appear that the Priory and the church were destroyed by Lord Wharton in his notorious raid after the battle of Solway Moss.

The Priory lands had long been the object of desire on the part of the English King, but the Scottish Government adhered to their declaration that they would not even discuss whether the lands were debateable. They indicated that they were even prepared to go to war to uphold their claim, which finally was recognised by the division of 1552.

By the General Annexation Act of 1587 the Priory and church lands became the property of the Crown. In 1606 they passed by charter to Lord Home who, in 1610, received also a grant of the churches, parsonages and teinds, and in consideration of these grants Lord Home undertook to pay the stipend of the minister and provide the Communion elements.

From Lord Home they passed to Sir John Ker and from him to Walter, first Earl of Buccleuch; but in 1621 the preceding grants to Lord Home of "the teynd schevis and utheris teyndis, parsonage and vicarage of the Kirkis of Wauchope and Cannabie belonging to the cell or pryorie of Cannabie" were ratified to his successor. In 1653 all the teinds were the property of the Countess of Buccleuch, and they have since remained in the possession of the ducal House.

We have already mentioned the generally accepted tradition that the stones for the erection of Canonby Bridge were obtained from the ruined buildings of the Priory. There was a right of way from the present church to Hallgreen, the site of the ancient Priory, and the path is still in existence. Very few pieces of the building are now extant, but, fortunately, the sedilia, which is a very beautiful piece of Norman work and perhaps the only specimen of its style extant in Eskdale, has been preserved.

It was transferred during the ministry of the Rev. James Donaldson and erected in the present churchyard. Rev. Donaldson performed an estimable service in securing the safety of this artistic and sacred relic and after his death a tablet to his memory was inserted. The inscription is as follows:—

"Sacred to the memory of the Revd. James Donaldson, Minister in Canonbie, who died August 20 1884 in the seventy-fifth year of his age and the fortieth of his ministry."

It was not until the year 1609 that a regular supply of ministers became available for Canonby. The definite settlement was no doubt due to a commission sent down by the General Assembly in 1608. The members were empowered to visit the kirks in these southern dales and, where necessary, settle ministers and perform other presbyterial functions, such as building and uniting churches and, in certain eventualities, to deprive ministers of their offices.

SEDILIA IN CANONBY KIRKYARD

THE KIRKS OF ESKDALE

The following is a list of the ministers of Canonby[5] since 1609:—

JOHN DOUGLAS, AM.   1609
    Translated from Longformacus. Presented to Wauchope and Canonby 1st Sept. 1609, by James VI. On 20th following, the Presbytery of Jedburgh proposed "to remember his planting" to the Synod, "to the great sclander of the Kirk". In 1615 he had also Morton Kirk, to which he was presented by Charles I, on 2nd April 1635. In 1639 he was served heir to his brother James. He died January 1653.

JOHN BELL, A.M.   1644
DAVID LAYNGE   1649
    One of the four ministers in the bounds of the Presbytery of Middleby who "conformed" to the Act of 1662. He seems to have lost, or otherwise disposed of, the Session book, for in 1694 there is a minute that "enquiries should be made at Mr. John Laing son to Mr. David Laing sometime minister at Cannabee for the Session Book and Kirk Utensils". The enquiry elicited "no notice".

DAVID HEDDERWICK, AM   168-
    Deprived 1689. Removed to Edinburgh in 1701. Died, 1723.

GEORGE MURRAY, AM.   1689
JAMES ARMSTRONG   1694
WILLIAM ARMSTRONG   1719
    Son of above. He was termed a new light or legal preacher and in 1730 gave much offence by his sermon at the opening of Synod. He was also one of a club who did not favour Confessions of Faith. Translated to Castleton in 1733.

ROBERT PETRIE, AM.   1734
    On the back of the sedilia just referred to, there is the following inscription:— "Sacred to the memory of the Rev. Robert Petrie, A.M., who was 30 Years Minister of this Parish. The tears of all his Parishioners, which were shed over his Tomb in great abundance, were the strongest testimonial of his worth and their affection for [the] loss they had sustained in his Death, which happened the — July, 1764, in the 61st Year of his age. He lived beloved, esteemed and respected, and he died lamented by all who were friends to Religion, Virtue and polite Learning". One of Mr. Petrie's sons was Dr. Robert Petrie, an eminent physician in Lincoln, and another, William, distinguished himself in India.

ANDREW WALKER   1765
    Translated from Ettrick. Presented by Henry, third Duke of Buccleuch.

JOHN DOWE   1773
JOHN RUSSELL, DD.   1784
    Translated from Eskdalemuir. His daughter, Margaret Helen married John Elliot of Cooms.

JAMES DONALDSON   1815
    Died 20th August 1854, aged 74 and in the 40th year of ministry.

GEORGE COLVILLE   1854
JAMES BARCLAY, AM.   1875
      Translated to Montreal, Canada.

WILLIAM SNODGRASS, DD.   1878
ROBERT HOGG KERR, MA.   1896
      Assistant at Shettleston Parish Church. Inducted to Canonby 1896. Died 1930.

ANDREW WELSH FARMS, MA. BD   1930
      Translated from Glenlivet to Canonbie 21ˢᵗ November 1930. Inducted to the
linked charge with Longtown on 18ᵗʰ March 1955. Retired June 1969.
JOHN WILLIAM MOULE, BSc.   1970
      Inducted to the linked charge with Longtown 18ᵗʰ March 1970. Retired 31ˢᵗ
August 1979 and died 29ᵗʰ April 1981.

Canonbie was linked with Langholm, Ewes and Westerkirk on 9ᵗʰ October 1980 and this arrangement terminated on 1ˢᵗ December 1998. The congregation then, with the agreement of the other three parishes, opted to be independent once more and the Presbytery gave permission for the appointment of a minister. On 28ᵗʰ May 1999 the Rev. Linda Williams was inducted to the vacancy.

The present church, which was built in 1822 at a cost of £3,000, has accommodation for nearly 1,000 worshippers. The church records date from 1694, and consist of five volumes, but in the session book there is, unfortunately, a break from 1715 to 1734.

On the commencement of the volume in 1694 the Session consisted of: the Rev. James Armstrong, minister; and Messrs. William Johnston in Barngleis, John Armstrong in Holehouse, James Irvin in Linsdubs, William Brown in Rowanburn, Adam Almas in Albaridge, (now Albierig or the white ridge). William Armstrong in Crookholm, William Armstrong of Grestail, John Waugh in Turcoon, Thomas Twedal in Sark, William Armstrong in Glenzier, and Thomas Armstrong in Milnsteads; elders.

The first entry in the records relates to Mr. James Armstrong who, "having been declared transportable by ane Act of the Synod of Mers and Teviotdale", had been admitted minister in Canonby. Some of the entries are characteristic of the ecclesiastical spirit of that day:—

"Cannabee Kirk Ap. 24, 1698. The Session being informed that Morise Dikie was at work in Franc Calverts ground upon the last fast day, orders ym both to be summon'd to ye next diet".

"Cannabee Kirk May 29, 1698. Fran. Calvert being lawfully summoned and called, compeared and sufficiently purged himself of the charge laid against him. Qrupon he was dismissed with ane admonition to prohibit and hinder the like in tyme coming. John Morise being lawfully summoned and being interrogate upon the lyb. laid against him confessed the same. Qrupon the Sess. dismissed him with a rebuke, in regard he is no parishener here".

"Can. Kirk Mar. 8, 1699. The Act of ye Assemblie Janr 26, 1699 and ye Act of ye Counsell enjoining a nationals fast qch is to be kept upon Thursday first. As also ye Act of Parliat. for a collection for repairing the bridge of Ancrum were read and the sd. collection to be upon Sabbath first and 2nd".

"Can. Kirk March 12, 1699. This day ye collection for ye bridge of Ancrum is six shill: starline: and qrof two shill: and four bodies are kept for ye poor and four shill: to be kept for ye bridge of Ancrum till it be so demanded".

In 1710 action is taken against a parishioner who confessed to having attended Quaker meetings, and in the following week, the Session reprove a man who confessed to their questioning anent his penny wedding. Strict superintendence over incomers was kept and the credentials of a domestic servant were rejected as insufficient and she was directed to go to Tundergarth and get satisfactory testimonials. The following are typical minutes:—

"Can. K. July 19, 1713. The Session being informed that William Jackson in Bowholm was carrying a chest and a trunk Sabbath last order him to be sumd". "Can. K. July 26, 1713. Holehouse and John Elliot are appointed to speak to James and Charles Russell anent their children 'playing upon the Sabbath day'".

In 1741 reference is made to the bridge question:—

"Can. Kirk Aug. 9, 1741. It being judged convenient at this time that ye Sacrament should be administered without the church, it was done accordingly but the Session unanimously resolve that as soon as a bridge is built over Esk it shall be administered only within the church and in the winter season."

In 1744, according to a minute of Presbytery, a collection was made in Canonby Kirk on behalf of Archibald Thomson of Westerkirk, "who had suffered a great loss by fire".

In the kirkyard of Canonby there are three gravestones set into the wall to the right of the entrance gate. The lettering is in relief and, in common with many 17th century memorials in all parts of the country, the letters are frequently united. The first stone is thought to be the oldest in Canonby kirkyard with a date of 1593 but this is now almost impossible to see.

The other two stones refer to the boat disaster mentioned on page 260 and we are fortunate that the lettering is so clear in the following illustration.   In the intervening years the stones have suffered greatly from the weather and very few words can now be deciphered.

There is another stone, situated a little to the south-west of the mausoleum, which also refers to the disaster. It is a small stone, almost hidden by vegetation, which has protected it, and the lettering has remained legible. The inscription is as follows:—

"Here Lyes Frances Armstrang son to William Armstrang in Glinyeir who died in the water on the Lords day Nov. 1, 1696 as he went from the Kirk after sermon. Aged 20."

STONES IN CANONBY KIRKYARD

Unfortunately the records of Canonby Church at this date are missing, but in those of the parish of Kirkandrews-on-Esk there are some details given of the occurrence. The following is the text of a note by the rector of the parish:—

"Upon Nov. 1, 1696 y^{r} happened a very sad accident 28 people were drowned at Canabie Boat as y^{ey} were passing y^{t} water from Church. Six persons come to years of discretion went from y^{r} own Church to Canaby. Every sone of y^{em} was drownded. These six lived in my parish. There happened in y^{ir} company two boys of 9 and 11 years old. They were in y^{e} midst of y^{e} pool over head and ears in water $w^{th}y^{e}$ rest of y^{e} peple y^{t} were drownded. And yet by a distinguishing privilege y^{ese} two only got out of y^{e} water safe. Surely god almighty thereby showed his displeasure to these persons who being of age passed by y^{r} own parish Church to Canaby but showed his mercy to y^{e} boys, who knew not wt y^{ey} did but went for company sake. In suffering persons of age that were of my parish to be drowned and in preserving ye two lads, safe even in as

270

great danger in all human probability as ye rest. This is so distinguishing a evidence y^t every one ought to take notice of it and take heed how y^y run from y^{eir} own parish Church. But y̌ thing is certain as witness my hand.

(Signed) EDW. WILTSHIRE, Rector."

It further appears from the parish Registers that two at least of the sufferers were interred at Kirkandrews, viz., Wm. Attchison and Adam Little, both of Millrighs, who were buried on the day following the accident. There is a tradition that the boat was over-loaded, a source of danger greatly increased by the Esk having come down in flood during the service. It is said that 28 out of the 35 passengers were drowned.

The fact that only three of the unfortunate people are buried in Canonby kirkyard and two at Kirkandrews, rather supports the suggestion that the remainder were carried to the sea by the swift current of the flooded river.

There are two Communion Tokens of Canonby extant:—

1. Octagonal, borders, and undated.

Obverse: CANONBY/KIRK, round the edge.

Reverse: I COR / XI., 23.

See No. 1 on Plate at the end of this chapter.

2. Canonbie, 1816. Round. Incuse around edge.

STAPELGORTOUN

The Kirk of Stapelgortoun was under the jurisdiction of the Abbey of Kelso, to which it was granted by William de Kunyburg in 1127.

In 1342 Sir William Douglas received the advocation of the church. In the rent-roll of the Abbey of Kelso the value of the carucate of land at Douglen, held by the monks, was five merks and the value of the rectory was £13 6s 8d.

In 1493 John of Glendonwyn was ordered by the Lords of the Council to pay to the Abbey of Kelso the sum of £8 yearly for the last seven years, "for the hale teynds, froits, proffits, and dewities of the kirk of Stabilgortoun".[1] But, as he did not attend to answer the summons, the Council ordered his goods to be distrained.

In 1550 Robert, Lord Maxwell, succeeded his father in the

advocation of the churches in the lordship of Eskdale. He granted to Christie Armstrong the teinds of the parish in consideration of the annual sum of £8 (Scots) paid by him.

In 1574 the valuation of the teinds is given as:— Stapelgortoun £8, and Douglen £5. By the General Annexation Act of 1587 the church and lands of Stapelgortoun became the property of the Crown.

In 1637 the kirk and teinds appear to have belonged to the Earl of Roxburgh, and on his resignation of them they reverted to the Crown, but later they, again, came into the possession of the Earl of Roxburgh. In 1689 on the abolition of Episcopacy, the patronage fell again to the Crown.

In the early years of the Reformation there was no fixed minister. Up to about 1612 the spiritual needs of the parish were ministered to by occasional preachers, but in that year the first Presbyterian minister was appointed.

The following are some of the ministers of this ancient parish :—

ARCHIBALD GIBSONE, AM.   1612
    In 1615 he received from the Abbey of Kelso a stipend of 200 merks and had, in addition, the vicarage, manse and glebe.

    In 1626 the Earl of Nithsdale, who, in 1621, had been granted the lands of Stapelgortoun and the barony of Langholm, paid the minister 320 marks. Gibsone was formerly of Dunscore and was presented to Stapelgortoun by James VI. He died in 1657, aged 78.

ROBERT LAW, AM.   1657
    Attained his degree at Glasgow, 1646, and became assistant to foregoing. Deprived by Act of Parliament 11th June, and Act of Privy Council 1st October, 1662. Law was one of the 350 Presbyterian ministers ejected at the Restoration. Law returned to the parish in 1687 and remained minister of Stapelgortoun until his death in 1702. He was buried in the churchyard, as was also his wife, who died 1694.

    Local antiquaries had observed the existance of his tombstone, but it was left to Mr. Clement Armstrong and his brother-in-law, Mr Carlyle, of Milnholm to have it rescued from obscurity and neglect. Through the Kirk-Session of Langholm they had the stone restored and erected against the west wall of the mortuary chapel of the Maxwells. The inscription is as follows:—

    "This Monument is erected in Memory of the Revd. Mr. Robert Law, descended from the Ancient Family of Laws Bridge, in the County of Air, minister of this parish. He was Pious, Learned, Wise, Judicious, Moderate and a Cheerful Surrerer for Religion, and his Memory is Dear to all who knew him.

    He died April 8, 1702, in the 72 year of his Age, and was Interred in Staple Gordon Church as was also Mary his wife who Died Jan. 9, 1694. She was Devout, Zealous, Meek, and of great Charity, and spent her time in doing good. Many daughters have done Virtuously, but thou excellest them all. This is put up by the

Order of their Son, Robt. Law, Doctr. of Physick, Deceased, and Performed by his daughter, Dame ELIZ. HALIBURTON, Relict of Sr. John HALIBURTON, Knight".

MATTHEW REID, A.M.   1663

Probably son of the Rev. Matthew Reid, minister of Kirkinner. Degree at University of Edinburgh, 14th July, 1659. Licensed 1664. Translated to Hoddam, 1669. The epitaph on his tobmstone at Hoddam is as follows:—

> "His name, he from St. Matthew took,
> His skill in physic from St. Luke.
> A *reed* of John the Baptist's kind
> Not blown about by every wind."

> "Ever a true Nathaniel,
> He preached, lived, and dyed well."

ROBERT ALLAN, AM. See Appendix 6.   1670

Son of Rev. Thomas Allan, minister of Wauchope. Graduated at Edinburgh, 1665. Deprived by the Act of Parliament, 1690. Went to England and died in 1720, aged 75 years.

ROBERT LAW, AM.   1688

After suffering imprisonment in Glasgow, in 1674, and being outlawed (and, according to some accounts, going to Ireland), he returned to Eskdale in 1687. He kept a Meeting House at Burnfoot, and entered Kirk of Stapelgortoun in 1688. After deprivation of above Robert Allan, in 1690, Law was formally restored to the parish. Member of Assembly in May, 1690 and 1692.

The foundations of the pre-Reformation Church are easily distinguishable in the churchyard, which was still in use early in the 20th century after nearly 800 years. There are many tombstones of local interest to be found. Stapelgortoun was the burial place of Bailie Little, who died in 1792 and his wife, Helen Pasley, who died in 1782.

Stapelgortoun is also the burial place of the Maxwells of Broomholm, and stones have been placed in the mausoleum in memory of many of the family who died in India and other places abroad.

In 1703 the parish was divided, part being assigned to Westerkirk and the remainder, together with Wauchope, and half of the parish of Morton, being united in the new parish of Langholm.

WAUCHOPE

The church of Wauchope was attached to the cell of Canonby and, like it, was under the jurisdiction of the Abbey of Jedburgh, though not assessed to its support.

Robert, Lord Maxwell, was possessed of the churches and chaplainries of Wauchope in 1530, and in 1539 he received from the Prior of Canonby a lease for five years of the vicarage and glebe-lands.

It was, doubtless, owing to its association with Canonby, as well as to the fact that the Irvine Burn was the boundary between the parishes, that the parish of Wauchope embraced such farms as Irvine and Cauldtown. In 1606 the Priory lands of Canonby and the teinds of Wauchope were granted to Lord Home, who seems to have experienced difficulty in collecting the teinds, both in Wauchope and Ewesdale.

In 1610 nine Armstrongs, seven Irvings, seven Littles, seven Grahams, and thirteen persons of other surnames in Wauchope were ordered to be denounced as rebels and put to the horn for not restoring and delivering again, each of them his own part, respectively, of the following teinds:——"Lambis teind, stirkis teind, butter teind, cheis teind, hay and utheris fruitis". These persons had been summoned before the Lords of Council but failed to appear, and this denunciation was the outcome.

In 1621 Wauchope passed to the Earl of Nithsdale by the charter erecting Langholm into a Burgh of Barony. The stipend was then fixed at 500 merks. Ultimately, about 1653, both lands and patronage passed to the House of Buccleuch who, by virtue of this, acquired part of the right of patronage of the newly formed parish of Langholm.

In 1703 one-half of the parish of Morton was annexed to Wauchope, and both were added to the portion of Stapelgortoun to form the new parish of Langholm.

Like the other kirks of Eskdale, Wauchope had no stated minister from 1576 to 1585. In 1587, by the General Annexation Act, its patronage was vested in the Crown. In 1609, when it was reached by the wave of interest set in motion by the Reformed Church, Wauchope obtained a resident minister.

The following are the incumbents from that date:——

JOHN DOUGLAS, AM.   1609
    Translated from Longformacus. Presented to Wauchope and Canonby by James VI. In 1615 he also had Morton.

JAMES MOWBRAY (or Moubrey), AM.   1635
    Formerly of Carmunock. Presented by Charles I. Died about 1642, aged 49.

THOMAS ALLAN (or Allane), AM.   1644

Had his degree at St.Andrews in 1635. Ordained 1644. Died 1684, (The Session Records give the date as 1689), aged 69 years. On the passing of the notorious Act of 1662, Mr. Allan conformed to the decree of the Privy Council, and obtained nomination by a Bishop, and was re-ordained. He was thus enabled to retain his church and manse, whilst his fellow presbyters in Staplegortoun, Ewes and Westerkirk "went out into the wilderness". During his incumbency Mr. Allan was the victim of a serious outrage by some Armstrongs of the Kinmont branch. They broke into his house, and after beating both him and his wife "verie pitifullie", they stole two horses. Hearing that the minister charged them with the outrage, and standing in wholesome awe of Buccleuch, in whose jurisdiction they were, they persuaded a fellow from the English side, as notorious a thief and outlaw as they themselves, to take the blame. This he did, and told the minister that he would never see a hair of his horses' tails unless he gave him five pounds, a sum Mr. Allan was obliged to pay to recover his own horses.

Mr. Allan had a daughter and two sons, one of them being a minister at Stapelgortoun. The other became an apothecary in Edinburgh.

SIMON WYLD (or WOOL in the Session Records). 1685

Ordained in 1685. After about three years in Wauchope he then went to Ireland, his native country. Died abroad before 1715.

JOHN LAURIE, AM. 1691

Graduated at the University of Edinbirgh in 1671. Ordained 10th September, 1691. Was a member of Assembly in 1692. Translated to Eskdalemuir in July, 1703.

The church of Wauchope stood within the present kirkyard. A wall was built, by voluntary subscription, (see Appendix 7), to enclose the burial ground. Until early in the 20th century a considerable number of moulded and carved stones were scattered about. Some of the stones have been built into the walls while others have been used as tombstones. The most noteworthy of these relics are shown in the illustration.

The ancient cross was fixed into the ground a few yards southwest of the foundation walls. We submitted the impression of it to the Bishop of Bristol (Dr. G.F. Browne), probably the greatest authority in Britain on early Christian symbolism, and he very courteously replied:—

"Dear Mr. Hyslop, I am glad to have your letter and the very interesting engraving from the three stones. They do not, I think, call for any special remark, but if you like to say something speculative about the cross, something of this kind might do:—

It seems probable that crosses of this type are meant to represent the cross upon the Orb. The super-position of the ordinary cross upon the St. Andrew's Cross within a circle probably arose in this way, —

the earliest symbols of the kind that we have in this Island are in Galloway.

They represent the Chi Rho* enclosed in a circle; the curve of the Rho, like the top of a capital P opened out, soon disappeared and left a St. Andrew's Cross with a vertical bar through the middle, all enclosed in a circle. To insert the horizontal bar and thus make two crosses was a very natural step in advance.

Yours very truly,

(Signed)   G. F. BRISTOI.

*The Chi Rho is an ancient religious symbol, a monogram of (1) the Greek X = ch, and (2) the Greek R. These make the first three letters *of Christos,* which has been shortened into *Christ.* The monogram is frequently seen on Roman coins of the fourth century. The symbol is graphically represented thus:—

In answer to other enquiries the Bishop said:—

"The first sepulchral crosses stood upright; the dated example we have now remaining is at Bewcastle in Cumberland. It was set up in the first year of King Ecgfrith, that is A. D. 670, and when set up it was about 17 feet high. A great many portions of sepulchral crosses beautifully sculptured are in existence in the north of England and the Midlands, usually of no great height. The cost of such ornaments must have been considerable, and I suppose that it would naturally become a practice to have the cross cut on the surface of the horizontal body stone, instead of placing a standing cross at the head of the stone."

The incised swords, which were built into the kirkyard wall on the Wauchope Road, one on each side of the gateway, are of English design of the thirteenth century. It will be recalled that in the late thirteenth and early fourteenth centuries, Wauchope was in the possession of the Lindsays, an English family who actively sympathised with Edward in the Wars of Independence. These swords may have been placed in memory of some of the chiefs of the Lindsays who fell fighting against Scotland at Bannockburn. Some years ago the cross and the stones with the swords were removed from the kirkyard and were missing for some

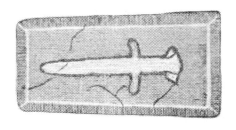

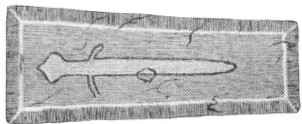

CROSS AND SWORDS IN WAUCHOPE KIRKYARD

time. They have now been recovered and are in the Erskine Aisle of Langholm Parish Kirk.

Some mediaeval tombstones still exist in the churchyard, most of them bearing the conventional symbols of mortality, whilst one or two are carved with grotesque figures. What is perhaps the oldest lettered stone in Wauchope stands near the middle of the northern wall. There are two inscriptions as follows:—

"Here lyes Andrew McVeti N. Murthm who died 16 day of Agest 1713, his age 66".

"Here lies John McVeti his son who died 25 April 1714 his age 29"

It has long been current in Eskdale that the family of McVittie settled in Eskdale as stragglers from the Old Pretender's army after its defeat at Preston in 1715. This is obviously incorrect as this inscription shows. In 1669 there were McVitties in Langholm, Wauchope and Stubholm. In that year John McVittie in Stubholm was one of the witnesses to the marriage of John Hyslop in the parish of Wauchope, and Bessie Little, in Hole, in the parish of Stapelgortoun.

There is no lovelier spot in Eskdale than the old kirkyard of Wauchope. The soft eternal sound of the river; still, after many millenia, cutting its way deeper into the hard rock; the song of the birds in the spring and summer days, the flowers and greenery of the opposite glade; the encircling hills, green in the spring, deep purple in the summer, russet brown in autumn; all these combine to make the frame which encloses the mortal ashes of our sacred dead, sleeping amidst the beauties of Wauchope.

LANGHOLM

The parish of Langholm dates from the year 1703 when the Eskdale parishes were re-arranged. The ancient parish of Stapelgortoun was divided, one part being conjoined with Westerkirk and the other with Wauchope, to form the new parish of Langholm, which town had now become, both as regards trade and population, the capital of Eskdale.

In 1703 a chapel was built at Half-Morton and was supplied every fourth Sunday by the minister of Langholm until 1825. The Session of Langholm had to pay 10s. on the annual occasion of each Sacrament, to Half-Morton in lieu of poor's rate. The chapel having fallen into disrepair, and the circumstances having been before several Assemblies, disjunction was resolved upon, and Half-Morton was erected into a separate parish by the Court of Teinds, 6th March, 1839.

The Eskdale parishes had been since the Reformation in the Presbytery of Middleby but, in 1743, they were disjoined by the General Assembly and, with Castleton from the Presbytery of Jedburgh, formed into the Presbytery of Langholm.

LANGHOLM PARISH KIRK
From Robert Hyslop's original glass plate

Since the formation of the parish of Langholm there have been four parish churches. The first was built in 1703, the second in 1747, the third in 1779, and the fourth, the present handsome structure in the Early Gothic style, on the Eldingholm, in 1845. The remaining portion of the third church is shown in the illustration on page 281.

The bell continued to hang in the belfry but, owing to the insecure condition of the gable, was never rung. It measures 18 inches in depth by two feet across the mouth and is inscribed "Armstrong, &c., Founderers. Edin. 1795". However, during a storm in February 1948 the belfry was blown down along with part of the gable. The bell was then kept in store by the Town Council but eventually in 1961 it was transferred to the custody of the Old Parish Kirk.

The following are the names of the ministers of Langholm[5]:—

DAVID GRAHAM   1706
 Licensed by the Presbytery of Jedburgh in 1700. Called 12th December, 1705, and ordained 24th March, 1706. Translated to Kirkmahoe 11th April, 1716.

ALEXANDER MEIKLE, AM.   1717
 Graduated at Edinburgh University 29th April, 1701. Licensed by five ministers at London 27th July, 1704 and was for some time assistant to Dr Isaac Watts, the well-known divine and hymnologist. Resided for a while in Kirkcaldy and had a testimonial from its Presbytery. On an almost unanimous petition, the Presbytery proceeded with a call 15th Nov., 1716, and Mr. Meikle was also presented by George I., and ordained 9th May, 1717. On account of bodily infirmity, he demitted in Dec., 1746, and reserved £40 yearly for his support. He died 17th July, 1757, aged about 76 years, and in the 41st of his ministry. Mr. Meikle had married 1st Nov., 1726, Julia, daughter of Thomas Henderson, of Ploughlands, in the parish of Dalmeny, and had four sons. His third son William Julius, born 28th Sept., 1835, was famed for his poetic genius. Mrs. Meikle mortified the sum of £3 sterling "for the beginning of a free school in that part of the parish of Langholm called Wauchope allenarly for teaching English.

JOHN DICKIE   1748
 Translated from Dunscore. Called 17[tn] September, 1747; admitted 21st January, 1748. Demitted 12th October, 1790, and went to reside in Edinburgh. Died 9th February, 1800, aged 91 years. He was deeply versed in the history of the Covenanting period and possessed many relics of the martyrs.

THOMAS MARTIN, AM.   1791
 Translated from Castleton. Presented by George III, and admitted 11th August, 1791. Died at Edinburgh, whither he had gone to attend the General Assembly, 29th May, 1812, in the 59th year of his age and 22nd of his ministry. Mr. Martin wrote the history of the parish for Sir John Sinclair's *Statistical Account,* in 1793. Shortly after his admission the new manse was built, and he had the so-called Roman bridge over Wauchope at the Auld Caul taken down, a deed which aroused considerable resentment.

WILLIAM BERRY SHAW   1812
 Translated from Roberton. Presented by Charles William, fourth Duke of Buccleuch, and admitted 6th Nov., 1812. Died 17th June, 1856, in his 81st year and the 55th of his ministry. Mr. Shaw wrote the *Statistical Account* of 1841.

JAMES WILSON MACTURK, BA.   1854
 On the recommendation of Venerable Principal Macfarlane of Glasgow appointed, on presentation by the Queen, assistant and successor to foregoing. Succeeded 1856. Died 26th Dec., 1878.

JAMES BUCHANAN   1879
 Educated, Glasgow University. Licensed by Presbytery of Glasgow 12th June, 1872. Assistant to Rev. Dr. Paul, St. Cuthbert's, and afterwards to Rev. Dr. Nicholson,

LANGHOLM KIRKYARD

St. Stephen's, Edinburgh. Ordained to parish of Rathven, Banff 11th February, 1875. Inducted to Langholm, 5th June, 1879. He died 23rd October 1921.

WILLIAL LINSEY   1922

JAMES LOGAN COTTER   1943-59

THOMAS CALVERT   1960
     Retired 31st August 1973

JOHN BALLANTYNE CAIRNS, LLB., LTh.   1975
     Ordained in 1974. Inducted to the United Ewes and Westerkirk linked with Langholm 16th April, 1975. Translated to Duntocher 1985. In 1999 he was Moderator of the Church of Scotland.

JAMES BROWNLEE WATSON, BSc., BD.   1986
     Inducted 26th February. Translated 7th January, 1990.

IAIN MACKENZIE, MA., BD.   1990
     Ordained 1st October, 1967. Inducted to Langholm 18th September, 1990. Translated July 1998.

ROBERT MILNE   1999
     Ordained and Inducted 20th December, 1999.

The parish Registers date as follows:— Baptisms from 1706; Marriages from 1719; and Deaths from 1704.

There are extant at least two specimens of the Communion Tokens of Langholm Kirk, each measuring 15 sixteenths of an inch. Number 2 on the Plate at the end of this Chapter is a round token. *Obverse:* LANGHOLM, around edge of upper segment. K in centre. With borders. *Reverse:* I Cor. / XI., 23.

That numbered 3 on the Plate is octagonal, with borders. *Obverse:* LANGHOLM, in semi-circle over KIRK. *Reverse:* plain.

There is another Token not mentioned by Mr. A.J.S. Brook, F.S.A. (Scot.), in his great work on the Communion Tokens of the Established Church of Scotland, nor by the Rev. H.A. Whitelaw, Dumfries, in his valuable book on the Tokens of Dumfriesshire, but which, nevertheless, we think is one of the earliest issue of Langholm Tokens. *The Obverse* is here shewn. The *Reverse* is plain.

$$\boxed{\begin{array}{c} \text{L.K.} \\ \text{1709} \end{array}}$$

We have submitted this to Mr. Whitelaw, who agrees with us that the Token is probably one of Langholm Kirk and was probably the first token to be issued after Langholm became a separate parish, although it is not mentioned in the Session records.

In 1712 there is a minute in the Session records about borrowing from Canonby, Ewes, and Westerkirk the utensils for the administration of the Sacrament, but no mention is made of Tokens. In 1716, however, there is given an inventory of these utensils and one of the items is "a bag with 400 or 500 communion tokens". So that, presumably, in 1712, and, assuredly, in 1716, Langholm Kirk, originating in 1703 had its own Tokens. When were they cast? The evidences point to a date *near* 1709. In 1749 there is a minute recording the casting of 8/900 new Tokens.

The Session Records contain some very interesting items, and deal with a range of subjects for which Kirk Sessions of the present day assume no responsibility. The following extracts are typical[2]:—

"July 20, 1695. Intimation was made from the pulpit of a general collection throughout the kingdom for redeeming some of our countrymen taken captive by the Turks."

"July 27, 1697. Four men had gone to Carlisle for victuals, and on their return found the Esk not passable at Canonby. They lay down by the river side and crossed early on Sunday morning. The Session held they should have left their burdens at the water side, come home on Saturday night, and returned for them on Monday morning. They were rebuked for their infringement of the Sabbath."

"May 31st, 1706. The Session fixed the fees for the Proclamation of marriage at 5 groats, whereof a shilling was to go to the precentor and eight pence to the church officer. The fee for baptism was fixed at 9d., 6d. to the precentor and 3d. to the church officer."

"August 4, 1706. Church officer's salary fixed at 10s. a year and a pair of shoes."

"Oct. 27, 1706. J.R. having lately come home from England married was ordered to produce a testimonial of his marriage."

"May 12, 1717. No Session this day because of the confusion caused by a troop of dragoons coming into the town during the time of forenoon sermon."

"Aug. 18, 1717. The Sabbath being badly observed, the Session renewed the patrol of the streets on that day by two of their number."

"Sep. 8, 1717. The elders reported that they saw no abuse of the Sabbath, but that they found two men sitting together at the fireside of another during divine service. They were instructed to speak to them privately and warn them of the consequences if it was repeated."

"June 3, 1720. The Session borrowed table linen for the Communion Tables from Ewes as a supply, for which a collection had been made in the parish, was not obtainable at the Fair."

"April 9, 1721. No sermon, the minister being "barred" by the waters. This occurred for 2 Sundays and application was made to Mr. Melville to have the bridge over Wauchope put right."

"May 6, 1722. The minister was appointed to apply to Mr. Melville for a warrant to the constables to put a vagrant boy, who resides commonly in this town, out of the parish."

"Sep. 23, 1722. The minister reported that he had received a letter from the Earl of Dalkeith wherein his Lordship promised to grant a warrant for £12 sterling towards the building of a dyke about the churchyard of Langholm. The Session considering that more money is required to build the dyke . . . . thought fit to ask a collection throughout the parish, and the question being moved what time was most fit for such a collection, the elders thought it most probable that money would be in the people's hands about the Winter Fair, and appoint the minister to make intimation of collection . . . .

"Oct. 13, 1723. There being complaint that several people walk by the water side after divine service is over, advertisement will be made from the pulpit that they will be take notice of according to the Act of Assembly if they continue in that practice."

"April 25, 1725. The minister reported that the mason work of the kirkyard dykes was finished about November last, together with the gates and styles, and that he had spoken to Middle-Milne, (probably Mr. Elliot of Midlem-Mill, the Duke's chamberlain, who had recently come to reside in Langholm Castle), for young timber to plant the churchyard with, which he granted."

"March 6, 1726. The Session allow J.L. and J.B., two of the poor scholars, a quarter to learn to sing the common tunes at threepence per month. The minister reported that he had tried who of the poor scholars had ears and none of them were capable but these two."

"Nov., 8, 1730. The minister reports that he had received a handsome compliment of books sent by the Society for propagating Christian Knowledge in Scotland, for the use of poor scholars at the Society's school at Half-Morton, consisting of "syllabing" Catechisms, Single Catechisms, Proverbs, Psalm Books, New Testaments and Bibles, with several of Guthrie's Saving Interests, Confession of Faith, some copies of Vincent on the Catechism, some arithmetic books, music and copperplate copy books with two quires of clean paper, for which the minister had returned thanks."

"Jan. 20, 1740. The Session, considering the rigorous season and straits of the poor at present, agreed to make frequent distribution to them and one is to be made on Tuesday next and every Tuesday while the storm lasts and they have money to distribute." In 1767 a similar minute is recorded to the effect that through "The present excessive storm of snow" there was no meal in the town and the Duke's chamberlain was to be approached on the matter.

"Jan. 4, 1789. The Session, taking into consideration the present inclemency of the weather, made it proper that some of the poor should be provided by the Session in fuel, resolved therefore that £1 1s. sterling should be laid out by the kirk treasurer for peat accordingly to be given to the poor by a list put into the hands of Robert Hotson,* at 1 cart full of peats each."

* Robert Hyslop thought that this referred to the builder of Langholm Bridge, but, listed under Rentals (Duke of Buccleuch's Muniments) there is, in 1783, a Robert Huttson, Carter, who, we think, was probably the person referred to, the spelling of surnames being very variable at that time.

There are frequent minutes anent the taking of collections for building bridges in different parts of the country, at Ancrum, Berwick, Bridge of Dee; for a new harbour at Banff; for a new meeting house in Carlisle. Naturally, many cases of moral discipline are reported and reference is made to rebukes from the Session, and by the minister before the whole congregation and, occasionally, by the Presbytery.

EWES

The Nether-Kirk of Ewes was dedicated to St. Cuthbert and stood near the site of the present church. The hamlet clustered round the church was named Kirkton or Kirk-town, a name which survives in Kirkton BurnNether-Ewes is first mentioned in 1296, when Robert, the parson, swore fealty to the English King Edward, and had his privileges restored by him, so far as he was in a position so to do.

The Douglases came into the possession of the advowson of St. Cuthbert's about 1342 on the forfeiture of the Lovels. In 1506, on the resignation by the Master of Angus of his lands in Ewesdale, the Crown granted the donation of all these churches to Alexander, Lord Home to whom also were granted the church lands of Wauchopedale on the forfeiture of the Lindsays. In 1516, on the forfeiture of Lord Home, all these donations were bestowed upon Robert, Lord Maxwell.

In 1621 the Earl of Nithsdale received the teinds of Ewes and, in 1623, he received from Sir John Ker of Jedburgh the patronage of Nether-Ewes. In 1643 the Earl's son, William Maxwell of Kirkhouse, succeeded his father in the church lands of Ewes, and as late as 1696 they were in possession of the family, but afterwards came into the hands of the Earls of Buccleuch.

In common with the rest of the Eskdale kirks both Over and Nether-Ewes were without a settled minister from 1576 to 1585, and in 1586 the minister was non-resident.

The following are the names of the of the ministers since the early part of the seventeenth century[5] :—

WILLIAM GRAHAM, AM.	1617
—— CHISHOLM	——
JOHN LITHGOW	1646

    Deprived in 1664 by the "drunken Act" of the Privy Council. Retired to Reidpath on the Tweed and preached at conventicles throughout Merse and Teviotdale. Condemned by Privy Council to imprisoned on the Bass Rock, and fined 5,000 merks.

JOHN HOME, A.M.	16—
JOHN MELVILL, AM.	168—
JOHN LITHGOW	1689

    After his imprisonment and persecution, he was restored to Ewes at the Revolution. Member of Assembly in 1694, when he demitted his charge and retired to Reidpath.

ROBERT DARLING, AM.   1694
Said to have been the only Episcopal minister who served the parish of Ewes, but of this there is considerable doubt, since, between the expulsion of John Lithgow in 1664 and the Revolution in 1688, two ministers are named as holding the living, and in 1694 when Darling was presented, the Presbyterian form had been restored. He is interred in Ewes kirkyard.

ROBERT MALCOLM, AM.   1717
Of Lochore, Fife. Presented by the Earl of Dalkeith, who also gave him the sheep-farm of Burnfoot (formerly called Cannel Shiels) at a very nominal rent to help with the stipend at Ewes, which was then very small. Mr. Malcolm's son, George, managed the farm. George Malcolm married Margaret, daughter of James Pasley of Craig. Four of their sons received the honour of knighthood and became known as the "Four Knights of Eskdale" In 1761 Mr. Malcolm founded the Poor-houses of Ewes for the support of four families.

RICHARD SCOTT   1761
JOHN CLUNIE   1790
JOHN LAWRIE   1791
ROBERT SHAW   1816
Brother of the Rev. W. B. Shaw, of Langholm. Writer of the *Statistical Account* of 1841. The two brothers were ministers of adjoining parishes for a continuous period of 36 years.

THOMAS SMITH   1852
DAVID PRESTON, BD.   1901
Graduated M.A. at the University of Glasgow 1896; BD. in 1899. Licensed by Presbytery of Hamilton, April 1899. Assistant in Greyfriars, Dumfries, 1899-1901. Assistant in Alloa, 1901. Ordained and inducted to Ewes, 18 July 1901.

JOHN ALEXANDER KERR, M A.   1918
Ordained and inducted to Tundergarth 20th April, 1917. Translated to Ewes 22nd November, 1918. Retired 1955.

The present church was erected in 1867 and replaced the pre-Reformation building, which had been extensively repaired. It is said that at one time the old church was thatched, and that young people who brought themselves under the discipline of the Session, were, as a penance, sent to the hills to pull heather for the repair of the roof.

When the old building was dismantled the bell was hung on one of the trees in the kirkyard where it has remained. The original tree became dangerous and had to be cut down but the bell was resited in another tree.

The kirkyard contains many interesting memorial stones, on which are found the clan names of the Ewes valley and of the neighbouring

EWES KIRK
Photograph November 2000

districts: Littles, Elliots, Armstrongs, Scotts, Jacksons, Rutherfords, Borthwicks, and Aitchisons. On the family stone of the Malcolms, appear the names of three of the Knights of Eskdale, though the mortal remains of Sir John lie buried in Westminster Abbey.

Two of the oldest memorial stones record the Littles of Meikledale and the Armstrong of Sorby. The inscriptions are as follows:—

"Here lyes Thomas Little son to the Laird of Meikledale. An honest gentleman and well beloved by all the country, who dyed in April 27th 1675. His age 67".

"Here lie John Armstrong of Sorbie, who died 17 March, 1685, aged 53, Margaret Murray, his spouse, who died May 17th, 1716, aged 76, and John Armstrong their son, who died November 1698 aged 14 years. Whither thou be old or young, think upon the time to come".

The Session Records date from 1646, and the Baptismal Register from the same date, whilst the Register of Deaths dates only from 1717. From 1680 to 1694 the records are not continuous. Like those of other Eskdale parishes they contain much interesting and curious information regarding the early discipline of the church.

Only one Token of Ewes is now extant. A round Token with borders 15 sixteenths of an inch in size. Obverse: EWES / KIRK Reverse: I Cor. / XI., 23.

EWES KIRK BELL
Photograph November 2000

On 21st November 1955 Ewes became linked with Westerkirk.

WESTERKIRK.

Westerkirk parish, or Westerker as in ancient documents, is one of the oldest and was one of the most extensive in Eskdale, comprising both the present parish and that of Eskdalemuir, and also a chapel at Byken. The church was under the Abbey of Melrose to which the lands and teinds of Upper Eskdale had been granted by Robert Avenel.

Sir William Soulis had received from John of Graham the advocation of Westerkirk and, in 1321, on the death of Soulis, Robert I granted it to the monks of Melrose to be held in "free forest", the grant being confirmed as occasion required.

Disputes not infrequently occurred between the conventual houses and the incumbents of their churches and chapels, regarding the allocation of the teinds. Such a dispute arose about the year 1360 between the rector of Westerkirk and the monks, as to the appropriation of the teinds of the seculars, who lived on the Abbey's lands of Watcarrick. By the award of the Bishop of Glasgow an equitable division was made.[3]

The church lands or mains, that is, the fields attached to a mansion house in the occupation of the owner, were afterwards held by the Douglases. In 1484 David Scott of Branxholm received a grant of the bailiary of the lands of Eskdale. This grant, which was made hereditary in 1524, was renewed to his successors, who also obtained extended powers in the administration of the Abbey lands. In 1550 Lord Maxwell held the advocation of the kirks of Eskdale.

From 1576 to 1585 Westerkirk was without a minister, and in 1586 the minister was non-resident. The lands were appropriated to the Crown by the Annexation Act of 1587.

In 1609 William, Earl of Morton, received a grant of the church, vicarage, and the teinds of the parish, out of which he had to pay the minister a stipend of 500 merks and provide him with a manse and glebe.[4] In 1653 the teinds were the property of Countess Mary of Buccleuch, whose successors retained the patronage.

The following is the list of ministers[5] :—

ROBERT DE MERLEYE	ca. 1296
ADAM BLITHMAN	ca. 1360
WILLIAM SCOT	ca. 1447
JAMES JOHNSTOUNE	1611
JOHN FORKE	1623
GEORGE JOHNSTOUNE	1625
JOHN HAMMILTOUNE, AM.	1634
JAMES PRINGLE, AM.	16—
ARCHIBALD INGLIS, AM.	166—
WALTER DALGLEISH, AM.	1668
JAMES PRINGLE, AM.	1679

JOHN BROWNE, AM.	1683
JOHN MEIN, AM.	1693
DAVID BALMAIN, AM.	1722
JOHN SCOTLAND	1768

> Translated from Eskdalemuir where he had been minister for five years. In 1779 presented to Linlithgow.

WILLIAM LITTLE   1779

> Married Isabella Borthwick in 1807. Died 1820 in 42nd year of his ministry.

JAMES GREEN   1820

> Writer of the *Statistical Account* for 1841.

WILLIAM BURNSIDE DUNBAR	1842
ALEXANDER YOUNG, BA.	1855
	1910

JOHN GILLIES, MA.

> Native of Gateside, Ayrshire. Educated there and at Beith, where he was Dux of School in 1895. Graduated Glasgow University in 1899, receiving prizes in Senior Greek and Philosophy, and Honours in Latin and English Literature. Theological training at Glasgow Divinity Hall, prizes in Divinity, Hebrew and Church History. Licensed by the Presbytery of Irvinein 1902. Assistant to Rev. A. W. Ferguson, BD. (a native of Langholm), in Maxwell Parish Church, Glasgow. Ordained and inducted to *quoad sacra* charge of Whiting Bay, Isle of Arran, April 1908. Translated to Westerkirk 1910. Demitted 18th November, 1948.

ANDREW ROY ALEXANDER, MA.   1949-55

JAMES JAMIESON GLOVER   1956-73

> Inducted 1956. Died August 1973.

JOHN BALLANTYNE CAIRNS, LLB., LTh.   1975

> Inducted to the United Ewes and Westerkirk, linked with Langholm, 16th April 1975.

The parochial Registers of Baptisms and Marriages date from 1693, but the Register of Deaths dates from 1804 only. Since these years all three registers have been regularly kept.

The present church was built in 1880, and stands probably on the site of the ancient churches of the parish. The previous church, shown in the illustration, was built in 1788 and was seated for 700 worshippers. The bell of the church dates from 1641, and bears the following inscription:—

> "Jacobus Monteith me fecit,
> Edinburgh, Anno Domini 1641."

WESTERKIRK

The bell had to be repaired in 1901 owing to a crack in the rim, and it was then found to weigh nine stones nine pounds. Installed in the belfry of the present kirk it has been summoning people to worship for more than three and a half centuries. It was one of the most interesting relics of the seventeenth century remaining in Eskdale, if not in Scotland itself.

The Manse was built in 1783, and in 1821 extensive repairs and enlargements were carried out. The glebe consisted of about 20 acres.

Only one Token of Westerkirk extant and is undated. It is of a type frequently found in the parish churches in the south of Scotland being round and measuring 15 sixteenths of an inch.

Obverse: WESTERKIRK around the edge. K in centre.

Reverse: I Cor. / XI., 23.

Westerkirk was linked with Ewes on 21st November 1955. There was a further linking with Langholm Erskine on 1st October 1970. This triple linking ended on 30th October 1974 to allow for the Union of Ewes and Westerkirk and of Langholm Erskine with Langholm Old under the name of Langholm. Also on the same date the linking of the United charges of Ewes and Westerkirk with Langholm.[5]

A few years ago the church building was bought from the Church of Scotland by a local benefactress, Daisy Douglas, who then presented it to the Westerkirk Parish Trust which had been formed by John Packer, Peter Buckley and Tommy Wood.

The building has undergone extensive restoration and was re-dedicated on Sunday, 6th October, 2001. Once a month a Church of Scotland service will be taken by the minister from Langholm but any orthodox Christian congregation may use the building. Twelve new windows depict the flora and fauna of the area, the twelfth window being dedicated to the Queen's golden jubilee. A new organ has been installed and choral concerts will also be held there.

ESKDALEMUIR

The district which now forms the ecclesiastical parish of Eskdalemuir was, prior to 1703, part of the ancient parish of Westerkirk. Upper Eskdale was supplied with spiritual ordinances by the sub-chapel of Watcarrick.

Even after the re-arrangement of the Eskdale parishes in 1703, this old chapel was used for public worship until 1722, when a new church was built higher up the valley. The present building, seated for about 400 worshippers, was erected in 1826. Some restoration work was done in 1907 and further improvements were made in 1936. The earlier history of the parish is, of course, merged in that of Westerkirk.

ESKDALEMUIR KIRK
Photograph May 2000

Ministers since the formation of the parish[5] :—

JOHN LAURIE, AM.   1703
      Translated from Wauchope where he had been minister from 1691. He is buried in Eskdalemuir kirkyard, and on his tombstone is the epitaph:—
           "Here lyes John Laurie, neither rich nor poor,
           Last of Wauchope, first of Eskdalemoor."

JAMES McGARROCH, AM.   1724
JOHN SCOTLAND   1763
      Translated to Westerkirk, thence to Linlithgow.
ROBERT FOOTE   1768
JOHN RUSSELL   1774
JOHN LAWRIE   1785

WILLIAM BROWN   1792
     Afterwards DD. Writer of *the Statistical Accounts* of 1793 and 1841. Discoverer of the Roman Camp at Raeburnfoot in 1810. Compiled much valuable data of an archaeological and historical description concerning Eskdale. Through the courtesy of the late Mrs. Dobie, his valuable MS. diaries have been frequently consulted in the preparation of this volume. A faithful minister of the Gospel; of broad human sympathies and of great learning, Dr. Brown's memory is cherished in Eskdale.

ADAM CUNNINGHAM   1836
JOHN STRATHEARN, AM.   1843
J. C. DICK   1877
J. R. MACDONALD, MA.   1908
     Graduated at Edinburgh University. Licensed by Presbytery of Edinburgh. Ordained assistant in 1902 and succeeded to full charge in 1908. Chairman of School Board and Parish Council. Retired 1933.

ROBERT WILSON   1933
     Demitted office 7th September, 1955.
ROBERT HUGH DRUMOND   1956
     Inducted 18th July 1956. Translated to Kilmuir-Easter 23rd November, 1961.
JOHN CAMPBELL LOUGH
     In 1960 he became minister of Hutton and Corrie which was linked with Eskdalemuir in 1962.

    The Parish Registers have been regularly kept since the formation of the parish in 1703. The manse was built in 1783 but has several times been repaired and enlarged. The glebe consisted of 24 acres, including the manse, gardens and offices

    The Token of Eskdalemuir Kirk is similar to those of Ewes and Westerkirk.

       Obverse: ESKDALEMUIR around the edge, K in centre.

       Reverse: I Cor. / XI., 23.

    On 8th August 1962 Eskdalemuir was linked with Hutton and Corrie.

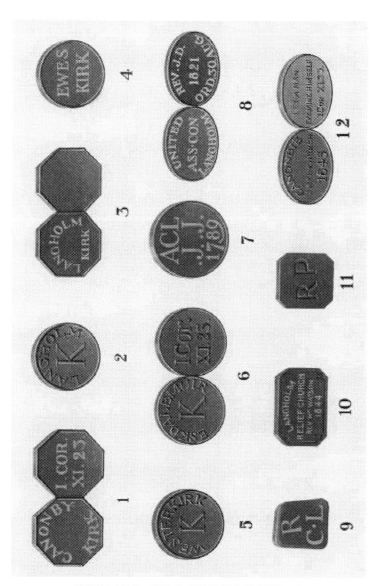

ESKDALE COMMUNION TOKENS

(Reproduced from, "The Communion Tokens of Dumfriesshire" by the kind Permission
of the Rev. H. A. Whitelaw, Dumfries.)

CHAPTER 23

THE COVENANTERS OF ESKDALE

The period between the Restoration, in 1660, and the Revolution, in 1688, was a time of darkest gloom in Scotland. The efforts of Charles II to destroy the Presbyterian form of church government in Scotland and introduce Episcopacy met with unbending resistance from the people, especially from those of the lowland counties.

The policy of the King found fitting expression in the decree of the Council of Glasgow, the drunken Council, in 1662, known as the Collation Act, which required every Presbyterian minister who had been ordained since 1649, as a condition of retaining his incumbency, to obtain nomination thereto and to submit to re-ordination by a bishop. These terms struck at a vital conception of Presbyterian church government, implying the invalidity of its Orders.

The decree was, therefore, regarded as a challenge, which no honourable man could ignore. Rather than accept the conditions it imposed, between three and four hundred ministers, or a third of the entire ministry, left their churches, manses and their congregations, one dreary November day in 1662.

It is a matter of pride to Eskdale people to know that several of their ministers were true to their ordination vows, and true to their own beliefs. The kirks of Eskdale were then, and until 1743, included in the Presbytery of Middleby, which comprised 11 churches. Of these, one was vacant, and of the other ten, six ministers remained staunch to their convictions and gave up what must have been very dear to them, apart altogether from mere worldly considerations.

The remaining four who conformed were, Allan of Wauchope; Laynge of Canonby; Graham of Kirkpatrick-Fleming; and Craig of

Hoddam. The ministers of Eskdale who went out at the call of conscience were Robert Law of Stapelgortoun, John Lithgow of Ewes and James Pringle of Westerkirk. All suffered long years of persecution.

ROBERT LAW

Robert Law was descended from the family of Laws Bridge in Ayrshire. He attained his degree at Glasgow University in 1646 and became assistant to Archibald Gibsone, minister in Stapelgortoun, and became parish minister on the latter's death in 1657. Little difficulty would have been experienced by him in obtaining episcopal nomination, but, rather than apply for it, he yielded up his charge at Stapelgortoun. He was 32 years of age, with a wife and family dependent upon him, but these considerations were not first with Law and, seeing the path of duty, he chose it without wavering.

His epitaph recounts that he was "a cheerful sufferer for religion"; and surely mention should also be made of his heroic wife, Mary, or Marion, Meiklejohne. The Session records of Langholm say that Mr. Law went to Ireland after leaving Stapelgortoun, but this lacks confirmation.

In 1674, or 12 years after his expulsion, Robert Law was in prison in Glasgow for the offence of preaching at conventicles and, in July that year, he was brought before the civil court on a charge of preaching in private houses. He had to enter security for 5,000 merks.

A Privy Council decree was issued as follows:— "The Lords of His Majesty's Privy Council do hereby authorise the Lord Chancellor to give orders to parties of that troop of horse under his command to pass to such places where field conventicles are to be kept, and to apprehend the persons who shall preach or pray at these field conventicles; as also to apprehend Mr. John Welsh, Mr. Gabriel Semple, Mr. Archibald Riddell", and, among others mentioned, is Robert Law.

It continues:—"To any who shall apprehend Mr. John Welsh and Mr. Gabriel Semple, they shall have for each of them £100 sterling, and for each one of the rest 1,000 merks, and it is hereby declared that those who shall secure the said persons and their assistants are indemnified of any slaughter that shall happen to be committed in the apprehending of them", a decree which might well be called murder made easy.

The events of the next fourteen years are clouded in obscurity, but after the Revolution the clouds lift and Robert Law is restored to his kirk and congregation. For 14 years he ministered in peace until, in 1702, he died aged 72. He is buried in Stapelgortoun kirkyard as is his wife who had died in 1694. Early in the 20th century his gravestone was rescued from obscurity, the stone restored and erected against the west wall of the mortuary chapel of the Maxwells.

JOHN LITHGOW

The minister of Ewes at the date of the decree was John Lithgow who had been ordained to the pastoral charge in 1646. As this was three years before the date given in the decree, Lithgow was not required to undergo re-ordination to retain his living. But he persistently refused to own the King's supremacy in matters spiritual.

His refusal to conform brought Lithgow under the suspicion of the emissaries of the Government and, in 1664, two years after the expulsion of Robert Law, a messenger from the Civil Courts appeared one day at the kirk of Ewes, met the minister as he came from the pulpit, and, before two witnesses, made intimation to him that he was suspended from the exercise of ministerial functions, at the same time putting into his hands a copy of the Act of Suspension.

Mr. Lithgow, like Mr. Law, did not hesitate, but left his home in the beautiful vale of Ewes and retired to a property he owned at Reidpath on the Tweed. While there he met and enjoyed the friendship of Henry Erskine, the father of Ebenezer and Ralph Erskine, the founders of the Secession Church. Erskine and Lithgow co-operated in field-preaching and other religious work and were frequently in great danger.

Both of these men were eventually apprehended, in 1682, and taken to Edinburgh for trial. There they were accused of holding conventicles in the shires of Roxburgh and Selkirk. On being charged, they refused to take the oath, and so "the Lords held them confessed", and fined "ilk ane of them in the sum of five thousand merks, and ordains them to be carried prisoners to the Bass", that dread prison in which the boom of the ocean and the cry of the sea-fowl only render more intolerable still the horror of the grim dungeon.

Neither of them, however, actually went to the Rock, as, on petition, both were permitted the alternative of "removing themselves furth of the Kingdom".

But in a few years the glorious Revolution came, which enabled the hunted ministers to return to their parishes in peace. In 1688, Lithgow was restored to the kirk of Ewes, where he continued his ministry until 1694, when he finally retired to his estate at Reidpath.

JAMES PRINGLE

He was minister of Westerkirk when the decree of expulsion was promulgated. He, too, refused to conform and left his manse and emoluments. In 1679 he returned to his parish under an indulgence offered by the Government, a form of testing, against which Richard Cameron passionately warned the Covenanters.

Pringle had to endure a second time of trial, when he was required to sign a document abjuring the Solemn League and Covenant. This he refused to do, and for a second time had to leave his manse. It is said that he owned Burnfoot, probably not the modern Burnfoot, but that shown on Blaeu's map as nearly opposite Dalbeth, and to have resided there after his expulsion.

Amongst the people of the hill districts the principles of the League and Covenant were held tenaciously. The Rev. Duncan Stewart quotes a minute of Council which records that "delinquents in the parishes of Westerkirk, Staple Gortoun, and others, were cited to appear", and mentions "Allison Buckie, spouse to Thomas Vair, a printed fugitive, and Elspeth Paterson, spouse to M'Alla", as being committed "prisoners till further orders". These were ladies from Langholm who were cast into prison whilst their families were at the same time dispossessed and ordered to remove from the district. In the Privy Council list of those who were sought after in 1684 by the Government for their fidelity to the Covenant were William Armstrong in Tomshielburn, Robert Elliot in Crookholm and Johnston of Barngleis.

ANDREW HISLOP

His name is often incorrectly spelt as Hyslop but the latter spelling did not become current in Eskdale until the early eighteenth century. At that time, of course, the spelling of names depended greatly on the whim of the parish minister in his recording of baptisms and marriages. Frequently one finds variations in spelling within the same family.

Undoubtedly, Andrew Hislop, the shepherd lad of Eskdale, is the most interesting of all the Covenanters. He suffered martyrdom at Craighaugh on 12th May, 1685, towards the end of the period known in Scotland as the *Killing Time*.

Various guesses have been made concerning the identity of the Martyr, but we think there can be little doubt that he was one of a Langholm family. Our information is derived from Mrs. Glendinning, who died in Langholm in 1903 at the age of 84. Her great-grandfather was born in 1686, the year after Andrew Hislop's death, and her grandfather 43 years later. Mrs. Glendinning was herself 20 years of age when her father died. It was from him she received the information, which had been transmitted orally in his family, that Andrew was the son of a farmer in Wauchope, and that a cousin was a farmer in Tarrasfoot.

So far as we can ascertain, there was, at that date, only one farmer of the name in Wauchope, and his son John is given in the Duke of Buccleuch's rent-roll of 1679 as tenant in Neishill. We have a record of the marriage in 1669 of John Hislop in the parish of Wauchope to Bessie Little in Hole, a farm on the side of Warbla near the western entrance of Gaskell's Walk, in the parish of Stapelgortoun, the witnesses being Andrew Little of Rigg, and John McVittie in Stubholm.

John Hislop and his wife went to live at the Hole, where one, at least, of their daughters was born. But by 1679 they were at Neishill, which John Hislop farmed in partnership with Andrew Little, whom we take to have been his brother-in-law. In that year Andrew Little became cautioner for the Testament of Bessie Hyslop. The will is in favour of Margaret and Bessie Hislop, and the estate, consisting of horses, cattle, sheep and plenishing, was valued at £386 13s. 4d.

In 1673 there is a record of the marriage of Robert Hislop to Janet Hewetson, both of Wauchope parish. This Robert Hislop appears to have been a younger brother of the above John. He went to Broomholm, and in 1681 he had a son baptised Andrew.

From these facts we conclude that the father of John Hislop of Hole and Robert Hislop of Broomholm was John Hislop, senior, of Neishill, who seems to have died between 1669 and 1679, and was succeeded in that farm by his son John. We also think that Andrew Hislop the Martyr was another son of John Hislop, senior.

Andrew Hislop, the Martyr, appears meanwhile to have done one of two things, both of which are recorded concerning him. One is that he went to the parish of Hutton and Corrie and commenced farming on his own account. The other, that he went to work on a farm in Eskdalemuir, and, on the death of his father, his widowed mother and her younger children went to him there, and were living under his guardianship when the shooting took place. If, as the tradition in Eskdale asserts, Andrew Hislop was aged 19 at the date of his death, then it is unlikely that at so early an age he would be farming on his own.

Of the different histories of the shooting of Andrew Hislop, the most consistent is that woven together by the Rev. Dr. Brown, minister of Eskdalemuir from 1792 to 1836, writer of the *Statistical Account* of the parish in 1793, and well accustomed to sifting fact from legend.

According to Dr. Brown, Claverhouse, who had been appointed by the Government to the command of a troop of horse, pitched his camp at Johnstone, in the parish of Eskdalemuir, with the object of hunting down the Covenanters, or rebels as they were called in the official documents.

For some time Claverhouse went about with a small party of troopers and met with little success. A Covenanter, however, happened to die at the house of Andrew Hislop's mother, and was buried at night in one of the adjoining fields. His grave was discovered and the news was quickly carried to John Graham of Claverhouse.

With him was Sir James Johnstone of Westerhall, himself once an adherent of the Covenant but who, for a reward of a knighthood, had renounced his faith and turned persecutor. Like that of all renegades his zeal was very bitter, more so even than that of Claverhouse.

On hearing of the discovery of the grave, Sir James Johnstone went with a party and barbarously dug up the body. Finding that it had come from the house of the widow Hislop, her name being on the sheet in which the body was wrapped, he first pillaged, then pulled down her dwelling, and drove herself and her children into the fields. Naturally, Andrew, who was not then present, at once came under the suspicion of the persecutors, and was thereafter carefully sought for, but he evaded their vigilance.

However, Claverhouse happened to be in Hutton parish, which adjoins that of Eskdalemuir, on his remorseless search for the hated Covenanters, and on 10th May, 1685, he accidentally came upon four of them resting by the Winshields Burn at a place called Dumlinns.

When the troopers appeared, each man ran for his horse, but Andrew Hislop's was young and hard to catch, and before he could reach it, Claverhouse and his men had seized him. They brought him over the hills into Eskdale to Sir James Johnstone, who, being apprised of their coming beforehand, went and met the party at Craighaugh. With characteristic cruelty and indifference to justice, Sir James Johnstone would have had him instantly shot, saying that "they would shoot the rebel on the rebel's land." (This reference is to Scott of Johnstone, to whom both Johnstone and Craighaugh belonged. He was a staunch Covenanter).

Claverhouse was averse from this indecent haste and urged delay, until, being pressed by Sir James he yielded, saying "the blood of this man, Westerhall, be upon you. I am free of it".

Whereupon they brought Andrew Hislop to the place where he is now interred, the low, sloping hillside, on the west of Craighaugh farmhouse. He was allowed some time for prayer, and for this purpose went into a kiln hard by, but Sir James Johnstone, growing restive at the delay, asked Claverhouse to "go and hear if he had done". Returning, Claverhouse remarked that "he had left off praying and begun preaching".

Dr. Brown then relates how Sir James ordered a Highland captain to shoot Hislop, but instead of obeying this command from a civilian, albeit one of the lairds, he refused and drew his men away.

Claverhouse, thereupon, ordered three of his own men to shoot Hislop, who was ordered to draw his bonnet over his face before they fired. This he disdained to do, declaring that he had done nothing to be ashamed of and could look them all in the face. Holding up his Bible he charged them to answer at the great day for what they had done and what they were about to do, when they should be judged by that Book.

Dr. Brown does not expressly mention it, but tradition affirms that on the soldiers hesitating to fire, Westerhall himself impatiently drew his pistol and fired, and in a swift moment Andrew Hislop lay dead on the green hillside.

In a further note on the murder of Andrew Hislop, Dr. Brown says he learned from his mother-in-law, Mrs. Moffat, that on the morning he was shot, Andrew left the Howpasley heights, where he had been hiding for some time. Mrs. Moffat's grandfather, William Borthwick, who was then tenant of Howpasley, urged him strongly to stay where he was. Hislop answered that he could not as he must go to the boreland on business. It is also said that Borthwick tried to dissuade him from taking his gun, and that it was his firing it at the troopers who were pursuing him, which caused him to be more harshly dealt with.

Mrs. Moffat told Dr. Brown that, after the murder, Claverhouse went down to Langholm Castle, where he spent the night as the guest of Mr. Melville, the Duke's chamberlain. Whilst there, his restless demeanour was noticed by his hostess. He seemed unable to find rest and kept walking about the room, until Mrs. Melville enquired whether he was ill. He did not immediately reply, but shortly afterwards turned to her and with great emotion said he had been the butcher of the Government long enough and he would be so no longer.

THE MARTYR'S GRAVE
Photograph May 2000

This was the last execution in which John Graham had a part. If these details are authentic, and we are sure we can relie upon Dr. Brown's discrimination and judgment, this scene at Langholm Castle presents Claverhouse in a somewhat new light.

Andrew Hislop was buried by the dalesmen, on the spot where he fell. His cold-blooded murder created a profound sensation in Eskdale, and an equally profound hatred of Sir James Johnstone. The hill-folk raised upon the spot a simple memorial to the Martyr and on it the following quaint but eloquent inscription:—

Here lyes Andrew Hislop
Martyr shot dead upon
This place by Sir James
Johnston of Westerhall,
And John Graham of C
laverhouse for adheri
ng to the word of God
Christ's kingly govern
     ment in his House and
ye covenanted work of
Reformation agst tyran
ny, perjury and prelacy
May 12 1685 Rev 12.II.* Halt p
assenger, one word wi
th thee or two why I ly
here would(e)st† thou tru
ly know by wicked han
ds, hands cruel and unj
ust without all law
my life fr(o)m† me they
thrust and being dead
they left me on this s
pot, and for burial this
sarne place I got. tr
uth's freinds in Es
kdale now triumph
then let, viz. the faith
ful for my seal they
     1702   got

*Rev. 12, II. "And they overcame him by the blood of the Lamb, and by the word of their testimony; and they loved not their lives unto the death"

†The letters in parentheses have been omitted and then inserted later *over* the words.

The text of the inscription was as it appeared on the stone when this book was originally published, the lettering has been renewed more than once, and, doubtless, some slips have been made. The words, "then let" in the third line from the end, are given by the late Rev. J.H. Thomson in his book, *The Martyr Graves of Scotland,* as "their lot". Instead of "viz.", which now appears on the stone, Mr. Thomson gives "to wit". The late Mr. Richard Bell, of Castle O'er, in *My Strange Pets,* gives the correct wording, though possibly Mr. Thomson rightly guesses what the original text was. In the last line but one the word given as "they" was very indistinct on the stone, but Mr. Bell read it "thus". Mr. Thomson read it "that". At the present time very few of the words, due to weathering, are decipherable.

Various efforts have been made by the descendants of Sir James Johnstone, to have this memorial of his perfidy and cruelty removed, but each attempt has been speedily frustrated by the indignation of the people of Eskdale.

MARGARET SCOTT

Mention must also be made of Margaret Scott of Rennelburn in Eskdale, one of the bravest maidens of the Covenant in Eskdale, who, rather than renounce her faith, suffered persecution, and was prepared to suffer loss both of worldly possessions and of life itself.

Margaret was thirteen years old when she was siezed and taken to Jedburgh for trial. The sole charge being that she had failed to go to the Episcopal service and had been found listening to Covenanting preachers. She was the young sister of the Laird of Rennelburn and was released on condition that her brother vouched for her good behaviour in future.

ALEXANDER PEDEN

Another association of Eskdale with the days of the Killing Time was through Alexander Peden the prophet of the Covenant. This strange preacher, gifted with the vision of the seer, exercised an enormous influence upon the hill-folk during the days of persecution. His prophetic words of doom pronounced against the murderers of Andrew Hislop, are still quoted in Eskdale. Many people are convinced that his doom-prophecies shall yet be accomplished, and they point to more than one already fulfilled in the history of Westerhall.

Peden the prophet would appear to have been intimately associated with Eskdale. We have the name Peden's View given to the conical hill which seems set like a sentinel on the road into Upper Eskdale. Tradition says that it was here the prophet lay watching the troopers of Westerhall scouring the opposite hills for him.

At the base of the hill is Peden's Well, where he would baptise the children of the Covenanters and where many of his services would be held. One can picture these mountain services, where the worshippers would be thrilled, both by the weird utterances of these grizzled fiery-eyed preachers and by the manifestations of natural phenomena, which they ever interpreted as a revelation of God's will or judgement.

There is a tradition that on one occasion whilst Peden was preaching to a congregation gathered in the hollow of Peden's View, the troopers of Westerhall were suddenly seen. The prophet prayed that God would throw His mantle over them according to the promise "In the time of trouble He shall hide me in His pavilion", when lo, as he prayed, the mists rolled down upon the hill and they were securely hid from the enemy!

ALEXANDER SHIELDS

In his MS. diary Dr. Brown mentions that Alexander Shields wrote the greater part of his well known book, *The Hind let Loose,* in the Yetbyre, now Castle O'er, plantation, where he was hiding from his pursuers. He, too, suffered imprisonment on the Bass Rock, but died in the West Indies.

CHAPTER 24

NON-PAROCHIAL KIRKS

THE NORTH UNITED FREE KIRK

This is the oldest of the non-parochial churches of Eskdale and was the name given to it after the Union of 1900 but was more commonly called the Town-head kirk. Its origin dates to the period of religious revival following the Secession of 1733, when four ministers, the Revs. Ebenezer Erskine, William Wilson, Alexander Moncrieff and James Fisher, were thrust out of the Establishment because of their outspoken condemnation of the Assembly's attitude towards Patronage and lax doctrine.

These four ministers resented the action of the Moderate majority of the Assembly in accepting the various Parliamentary Acts relating to Patronage, and the condemnation of the book called *The Marrow of Modern Divinity,* which had become the popular standard of the evangelical party, but an object of intense dislike to the Moderates.

The controversy thus raised was brought to a head by a sermon delivered at the opening of the Synod of Perth and Stirling by the Rev. Ebenezer Erskine, who had been joined in his protest by his brother Ralph. In his discourse he denounced the time-serving of the kirk, its "peddling in politics"[1] and pointed out that many of the heritors were Jacobites, opposed to the Protestant succession.

For this sermon Ebenezer Erskine and the ministers who thought with him were turned out of the Church and formed the Secession Church. In 1743, supported now by fifteen others, they had formed themselves into the Associate Presbytery and had issued, at Stirling, a Declaration of adhesion to the National and Solemn League and

307

Covenants and to the Subordinate Standards of the Church.

This stand for spiritual freedom and purity of doctrine was contemporaneous with the great revivals in England under Wesley and Whitfield, and before long these simultaneous religious movements had profoundly impressed the people of the two countries. It was in the flowing tide of this revival that a few men and women in New-Langholm united for spiritual conference and encouragement. The Session book of the North United Free congregation records that:—

"In New-Langholm on the month of August one thousand seven hundred and eighty years in a meeting of a Christian fellowship society, the conversation turned on the dreadful defections of the Church of Scotland and the constant course of Backsliding which is still carried on by her Judicaturies; in opposition to the principles of our Reformation and the pious practice of our reformer ancestors, for which they professed great grief of Heart.

Therefore, from a conviction of duty the members of the Meeting unanimously resolved to join with those who had lifted up a Testimony against the unscriptural Doctrines and practices either supported or connived at by the courts of the Established church. After mature deliberation concerning the different classes of dissenters from the Church of Scotland they resolved to make application to the Associate Presbytery of Edinburgh".

We are indebted to the kindness of the Rev. George Orr for a perusal of the original minute book of the Session, from which the above extract and others are taken. The early minutes of Session are signed by John Little who appears to have held the position of Session Clerk.

In answer to this petition, pulpit supplies were granted in 1781 and 1782. Amongst the ministers assisting to encourage the new cause were the Rev. John Johnstone of Ecclefechan, the minister and teacher of Thomas Carlyle and the Rev. Alex. Waugh, of St. Boswells, afterwards widely known as Dr. Waugh of London, who drew up the Constitution of the London Missionary Society.

For some time the services were conducted in the open air, for the most part, in a field at the north end of Eskdaill Street. In 1782 it was decided to erect a place of worship, a very heavy undertaking for a religious society so small numerically and so poor financially. But the leaders were men and women of firm faith and a strong purpose, and by the end of 1784 the walls were finished.

Now, however, it was found that the resources of the society were also finished, and no way seemed open whereby the money to complete the building could be found. Four of the members agreed to advance a sum to put on the roof, but could only guarantee about £37. Two of these four were Bailie Matthew Little and his brother Archibald. This was insufficient, the work ceased and all hope of an immediate completion of their purpose was abandoned.

To quote again:— "The persons chiefly concerned in this work now begun to despare of accomplishing their designs and begun to speak of the shell of their intended Temple being advertised for sale, since Providence seemed to forbid their persevering in the work but as some of them was not willing, this motion was not carried any further but it was resolved that they would still continue for the space of five or six weeks hoping perhaps The Lord might yet appear for them and command them to go forward."

Then a strange thing happened. One day, the 6th October, 1786, there came into Langholm on foot, a traveller whose destination was further north but who stayed overnight in the town. On leaving the town next morning, he observed the unfinished building and, pondering over it, had reached the top of the Chapel Path on his way to Hawick, when he resolved to return and make enquiry. He was told the story of the brave struggle those doughty Seceders were making for their faith. He at once sought out the chief men of the congregation and explained to them that he had money which he purposed devoting to philanthropic causes, and offered to give part of it to enable them to complete the erection of their little sanctuary.

"When the men heard this Generous proposal of their unknown friend and benefactor they were greatly astonished and believed not for Joy. He soon convinced them that he was in earnest. He assisted them in forming an Estimate of the necessary Expenses and Generously gave them in present a sum sufficient for finishing the Meeting house."

The gladness with which they received this offer of help, was soon dimmed when, in answer to their enquiries, the stranger declined to give his name and wished the gift to remain entirely anonymous. Then, they firmly replied they must decline his offer. Unless they could account to him for the proper disbursement of the money they would not touch it.

The stranger saw the reasonableness of the stipulation and agreed to give to these five men his name, on their solemnly promising that they would never divulge it. They willingly gave their word; the kirk was completed; an account was rendered to the benefactor, and these five men carried with them to their graves the secret of his name.

Conjectures have been made as to the identity of this mysterious stranger, who is described as having the appearance of a farmer, quiet and homely in his bearing, and living frugally whilst in the town. It has been confidently asserted that he was John Howard the great prison reformer, but it does not appear from his journal that he was anywhere in the neighbourhood at that date. The secret remains a secret still.

"This Extraordinary interposition of Divine Providence is here Recorded to the Honour of God and the encouragement of his people for whom he doth great things whereof they are glad. By this extraordinary Display of God's goodness the managers and members of the congregation were encouraged to present a petition to the Reverend Associate Presbytery of Kelso for further supply of sermon which they received accordingly."

SECESSION MEETING HOUSE, 1822

The completion of the building, which seated 310 people, enabled the congregation to proceed to the calling of a minister and the constituting of a Session. This was done in 1787, but it was 1789 before a minister was called. In 1886 the congregation celebrated its centenary, during the pastorate of the Rev. William Ballantyne, who was only the third minister in a hundred years, a feature in its history which can be equalled by very few congregations. At this meeting congratulatory addresses were delivered by the Rev. Principal Cairns, DD., LLD., Edinburgh; the Rev. James Brown, DD., Paisley; and the Rev. John Dobie, DD., Glasgow, whose father had been second minister of the congregation; and various local ministers.

The original church was replaced in 1822 by a more commodious structure which seated 500 worshippers. This in turn gave place to the present graceful edifice, the spire of which has become such a notable feature of Langholm. The new building seated 600 people, and was erected in 1867 at a cost of about £1,670. The contract for the masonry work was awarded to Robert Hyslop and his son, John, their estimate being £855. It will thus be seen that a new church has been built for each of the three past ministers.

In 1820 there was effected a union between the two wings of the Associate church, the Burgher (to which section this congregation adhered) and the Anti-Burgher, and the name was accordingly changed to that of the United Secession Congregation.

In 1847 a further union took place between the United Secession and the Relief churches which then became the United Presbyterian or U.P. church, the two congregations in Langholm being distinguished as North U.P. and South U.P.

On the union with the Free Church of Scotland in 1900, the united denomination adopted the title of United Free Church. There were, therefore, in Langholm three congregations of this larger communion, and by agreement they were designated North U. F., South U. F. and Chalmers churches.

The following have been ministers of this congregation[2] :—

JOHN JARDINE   1789

A native of Jedburgh. A zealous and faithful pastor, highly esteemed in the town. He began a Sunday school with three scholars in the Manse kitchen, the first in the south of Scotland, and lived to see it number 300, with a large staff of teachers. He lived in the corner house of Mary Street and Francis Street, New-Langholm, and his biographer relates how, as he felt his end drawing near, he took a tender farewell of the Esk flowing past his dwelling, of the old kirk with its romantic history, of his books, of all the rooms in his house wherein a happy and honoured life had been spent, and, last of all, of his Bible, saying "Farewell, blessed Bible, that has been so often my comfort and delight". He died in 1820 in his 71st year and the 31st of his ministry.

JOHN DOBIE   1821
From Loreburn Street congregation, Dumfries. Ordained 30th Aug., 1821. Died, prematurely old with his manifold labours, 6ᵗʰ Feb., 1845, in the 45ᵗʰ year of his age and 24ᵗʰ of his ministry. A man greatly beloved, pious, zealous, eloquent and witty, of active mind, ready perception and clear judgement. During his ministry the congregation greatly increased. The new church, erected in 1822, was regularly filled. Frequently, his hearers could find only standing room, even in the vestibule, and overflowed into the roadway. Refused many calls to other spheres of labour. His sons afterwards occupied positions of influence and importance. One was the Rev. Dr. Dobie, of Shamrock Street Church, Glasgow, a second, Dr. William Dobie, Keighley, and a third was Mr. Hugh Dobie, writer, Langholm, and for some years its acting-chief magistrate. The Rev. J. Dobie owned and occupied Greenbank as a Manse. After his death, his widow and daughters lived for many years at Stubholm.

WILLIAM BALLANTYNE   1846
A native of Lauder. Ordained 31ˢᵗ Dec., 1846, after 34 probationers had been heard as candidates. Of considerable repute as a scholar, especially in Hebrew, of delicate literary taste and much natural eloquence. Declined more than once to allow his name to go forward to nomination for the office of Moderator of the U.P. Synod. Reserved in temperament, constant in friendship, greatly honoured in Eskdale. Died 13ᵗʰ Nov., 1892, after a faithful and fruitful ministry of nearly 46 years.

GEORGE ORR   1893
A native of Glasgow and an alumnus of its University where he distinguished himself in Philosophy and English Literature. Received his theological training at United Presbyterian College, Edinburgh. Licensed by Presbytery of Glasgow in 1891. Elected immediately thereafter, assistant to the Rev. Thomas McEwan, Hope Park Church, Edinburgh. In August, 1892, chosen assistant to Mr. Ballantyne, on whose death he was unanimously elected to pastorate. Ordained by Presbytery of Annandale 26ᵗʰ Jan., 1893 and inducted. One of the founders and present secretary of the Eskdale and Liddesdale Archaeological Society. Founder of the Townhead Literary Society, Langholm, for the promotion of the study of literature, science, and art. In May 1926 he went to Borgue.

The first Manse was at the corner of Mary Street and Francis Street. During the ministry of Mr. Dobie, the Manse was at Greenbank which he owned. The third Manse was in Buccleuch Square, the house later occupied by Mr. Andrew Johnstone. At a Congregational meeting in December 1871 it was agreed that a Manse should be built. A petition was sent to the Duke of Buccleuch asking for a grant of land for this purpose and the following letter was received from the Duke's agent :—

Dear Sir, I am glad to say that His Grace the Duke of Buccleuch has granted the petition by the Managers of the North United Free Church, for a site on which to build a Manse. The site to be between Eskdale Road and Eskdaill Street. Lease 99 years. The rent to be in

312

proportion to the area at the rate of £20 per acre. I trust this will be agreeable to the Managers, Yours truly, Signed, Hugh Dobie. The Manse was finally built in 1876.

This congregation has had at least three issues of Communion Tokens during the 126 years of its existence.

1. The first was issued in 1789, on the ordination and induction of the Rev. John Jardine. It was given to the Session by the late John Hyslop, husband of Agnes Hotson. It is shown, numbered 7, on the Plate at the end of chapter 22. It is round in shape, with borders, and measures one inch.

Obverse: A C L J J 1789. *Reverse*: *Plain*.

2. An oval Token, in sixteenths 16 by 12, with light borders, not represented on the Plate.

Obverse: ASS CON LANGHOLM.

Reverse: REV. J. D. (for Rev. John Dobie).

3. An oval Token, measuring in sixteenths 16 by 12, with light borders, numbered 8 on Plate.

Obverse: UNITED around top segment, ASS CON in the field, LANGHOLM around the lower segment.

Reverse: REV J. D. 1821 ORD. 30th. AUG.

SOUTH UNITED FREE KIRK

So it became named, but originally it was the Relief Kirk, and after 1847 the South U.P., but has been more generally called the Town-foot kirk. Its early history gives evidence of a continual struggle, with many disappointments, but, withal, a highly honourable record.

The Relief Church originated in 1752 in a second protest against forcing a minister upon an unwilling congregation. This protest was in connection with the famous Inverkeithing case, and for refusing to assent to the forced settlement,— that is, for resisting Patronage,— the Rev. Thomas Gillespie of Carnock was deposed by the General Assembly. Instead, however, of joining the Secession denomination, Mr. Gillespie instituted a separate body, the Relief Church, which has borne its testimony in the struggle for religious freedom in Scotland.

The Town-foot congregation had its source in Canonby. On 21st August, 1797, a petition was presented to the Relief Presbytery of

Dumfries "from the people of Canonby for the supply of sermon", the immediate occasion apparently being dissatisfaction with a probationer who had been appointed as assistant to the parish minister, the Rev. John Russell. In reply to the petition the Rev. Decision Laing, of Wamphray, visited the congregation in October, 1797. For some years partial supply of sermon was granted, during which the congregation was styled as "of Canonby".

Their place of meeting was at Priorhill, on the rising ground between Canonby Bridge and the railway station. In 1800 these partial supplies were still being sent by the Presbytery, and the meetings were held, sometimes in Canonby and sometimes in Langholm, until in August, 1801, a joint petition for sermon was presented from "the forming congregation of Canonby and Langholm". After this date the name Canonby drops out and the congregation is recognised as of Langholm. The Relief people in Canonby for many years travelled regularly to the services at Langholm, some holding office in the congregation.

In Langholm the services were first held on a piece of ground at the foot of the Laird's Entry. In 1805 the Presbytery seemed to think that undue delay was being shown in erecting a church, but a plot of land had been secured at the Town-foot from Mr. Walter Young. The title-deeds are dated 1812 but there is a stone dated 1807 built into the wall, so the building of a church had at least been begun in that year.

The following names were recorded in the deed:— John Elliot, clogger, New-Langholm; Ninian Wilson, New-Langholm; James Young, New-Langholm; Walter Paisley, weaver, New-Langholm; Walter Young, Langholm; Andrew Elliot, Broomieknowe; Archibald Thomson, Langholm; John Williamson, Langholm; Hugh Hotson, Enthorn; Robert Johnstone, Thorniewhats; William Brockbank, Byreburnfoot; Francis Bell, Andrewsknowe; and John Stothart, New-Langholm.

In 1849 Dr. Archibald Graham of Holmfoot generously, commuted the feu-duty was and the site rendered freehold. The original church served the needs of the congregation until 1883, when another church was built and was opened free of debt on 28th August, 1884. The closing services in the old building were conducted by the Rev. Dr. Dobie, of Shamrock Street Church, Glasgow.

The preacher, at the opening of the new building on the Drove Road, was the Rev. Principal Hutton. The stained glass windows on either side of the pulpit were gifted by the late Rev. William Watson, minister of the congregation, and his brother, Mr. Thomas Watson Lanark. The window above the pulpit was the gift of the late Bailie Cranston of Edinburgh. The Manse was built in 1852, a later one in 1890.

The following is a list of the ministers[2]:—

THOMAS GRIERSON   1812
     Ordained 16th Dec., 1812. Deposed 1814.

PATRICK HUTCHISON PEACOCK   1820
     The congregation now passed through a period of great embarrassment and trial, and its condition was on several occasions discussed by the Presbytery. However, in November 1819, they sent one of their probationers to supply the pulpit, with the result that he so inspired the people that they called him, and he was ordained on 30th March, 1820. His pastorate ended in May, 1821. He thereafter qualified himself for the medical profession.

JAMES CROSS   1835
     Between the resignation of the previous minister and the ordination of Mr. Cross a long and trying vacancy intervened. In the meanwhile the spiritual interests of the congregation were attended to by the Rev. William Muir, until 1824, and from 1830 by the Rev. John Watson, of Waterbeck. Mr. Cross came from Dalkeith (West). Ordained 2nd June, 1835. Translated to Newcastle upon Tyne in 1843.

WILLIAM WATSON   1844
     Ordained 20th March, 1844. Founder of the Langholm Penny Bank. Active in temperance work. Died 13th March, 1890, a week short of 46 years of ministry.

JOHN WALLACE MANN   1890
     From Nairn. Educated Edinburgh University. Acted as assistant to foregoing, and at the date of his death was under "call" as colleague and successor. Ordained 20th March, 1890. Took an active share of public work on the Parish Council and School Board. Translated, 20th May 1901, to Shettleston, Eastbank Church.

THOMAS S. CAIRNCROSS, MA., BD.   1902
     From Lesmahagow. Graduated Glasgow University and proceeded to his BD. degree. A poet and author. In 1910 he published *From the Steps of the Pulpit,* a series of semi-humerous sketches of Scottish life. In 1907 he accepted a call to Kilpatrick in the Presbytery of Dumbarton.

JAMES B. MACDONALD, MA., BD.   1908
     Native of Inverness. Educated at Inverness Royal Academy and where he was Dux of the School. Graduated at St. Andrews University, taking both Arts and Divinity degrees with the highest distinction. First scholar of his year in Philosophy. Theological course at New College, Edinburgh, and Heidelberg University, Germany. Licensed by Presbytery of Inverness in 1892. In the same year, called to Contin, Ross-shire and Dornoch, Sutherland, and accepted the latter. Inducted to Langholm South, on July 17th, 1908 and remained there until Nov. 1925.

Two Communion Tokens were issued by this congregation:—
The earlier, number 9 on the Plate at the end of chapter 22, is a square
Token, measuring eleven sixteenths of an inch, with light borders.

Obverse: R C L. These letters may stand for "Relief Church (or
Congregation), Langholm", or, as the Rev. H.A. Whitelaw suggests,
"Relief Canonby (and) Langholm". If for the latter, then the token
would be cast about 1801. *Reverse*: Plain.

The second Token, number 10 on the Plate, is oblong, measuring
17 sixteenths by twelve, with cut corners, and was issued during the
ministry of the Rev. William Watson.

Obverse: LANGHOLM   RELIEF CHURCH   REV. WM.
WATSON 1844

Reverse: THIS DO IN REMEMBRANCE OF ME 1 Cor. II. 24.

In 1999 the Roman Catholic community acquired the church
building and are restoring it as a place of worship.

THE ERSKINE KIRK

In 1925 the congregations of the North United Free and the South
United Free were joined and continued to worship in the North United
Free's building.   Obviously a new name had to be found for the
combined Kirks and the name chosen was Erskine, a fitting tribute to the
memory of Ebenezer Erskine.

In October 1929 there took place in Edinburgh the Union of The
Church of Scotland and The United Free Church of Scotland.   The
Erskine Kirk then became known as Langholm Erskine and Langholm
Parish Kirk became Langholm Old.

On 1st October 1970 Langholm Erskine was linked with Ewes and
Westerkirk. This arrangement terminated 30th October 1974 to allow
for the union of the Erskine with Langholm Old.   On Sunday, 7th
September, 1975 the last service, attended by a large congregation and
conducted by the parish minister, the Rev. John Cairns, was held in the
Erskine Kirk.

All Church of Scotland services would in future be held in the
former Old Parish Church now renamed Langholm Parish Church.   A
side aisle has been converted into a chapel named *The Erskine Aisle,* as a
tribute to the previous congregations, and the Communion Table from

the Erskine Kirk has been placed there.

Meanwhile the Erskine Kirk became a listed building which means that its external appearance must be maintained. However, the building has been allowed to fall into a sad state of disrepair. It is to be hoped that this historic landmark in the middle of the town will soon be repaired for some other use.

The following have been ministers at the Erskine Church[2] :—

GEORGE BARLAS GILLIES	1926-32
ALEXANDER HUNTER WRAY, BA	1932-39
JAMES WALTER DICKSON SMITH, BD., EdB	1939-43
ROBERT BURNSIDE, MA	1944-51
KENNETH MILLER CAMPBELL	1952-54
MATTHEW J. C. DINWOODIE	1956-70
J. J. GLOVER, MA	1970-73

CHALMERS CHURCH

This church was known, until the Union of 1900, as Langholm Free Church. Its origin dates to the Disruption of 1843 when the Kirk presented to Parliament a Claim of Right, insisting that its historic spiritual freedom from interference by the Civil Courts, should be recognised by Parliament.

This Claim of Right was the voice of the Kirk of Scotland, not of a minority of it, and had the Government generally, and Sir James Graham particularly, been wise, or had the latter possessed any intimate knowledge of the religious life of Scotland, the Disruption might have been avoided; but when the Claim of Right was declined as unreasonable the die was cast.

On the Assembly meeting in May, 1843, the Kirk was rent in twain. More than four hundred ministers slowly left their places, following Dr. Welsh and Dr. Chalmers, whilst those who remained sat awe-struck and amazed.

"A vast multitude of people stood congregated in George Street, crowding in upon the church doors. When the deed was done within, the intimation of it passed like lightning through the mass without, and when the forms of their most venerated clergymen were seen emerging from the church a loud and irrepressible cheer burst forth from their lips, and echoed through the now half-empty Assembly Hall. In the city Lord

Jeffrey was sitting reading in his quiet room, when one burst in upon him saying, 'Well, what do you think of it? More than 400 of them are actually out'. The book was flung aside, and, springing to his feet, Lord Jeffrey exclaimed, 'I'm proud of my country; there is not another country upon earth where such a deed could have been done.'"[3]

The Disruption was an accomplished fact. The four hundred ministers had relinquished livings and manses for the sake of a principle, and, once more, Scotland had shown her utter disregard of worldly considerations when her faith was threatened.

During these events not one of the Eskdale ministers sided with the Evangelical party in the Kirk and, accordingly, they all retained their livings. This impaired somewhat the prestige of the Disruption in the Langholm district, but a considerable number of the people cast in their lot with the Disruption leaders and determined that an effort should be made to form a congregation.

MR. ROBERT SMELLIE

Mr. Robert Smellie, energetic young man of 24, was called upon to head the movement. He was cordially supported by such men as R.M. Rome, John Young, William Plattoff, Matthew Young, and Anthony Yeoman. Supply of sermon was obtained, and the Town-head and Town-foot kirks, were placed at the disposal of the new society. Interest in it was shown, too, by the great Disruption leaders. Dr. Cunningham, Dr. Candlish, and Dr. Guthrie all came frequently to preach, and Dr. Chalmers himself manifested sympathy and encouragement.

The statue in honour of Sir Pulteney Malcolm had recently been completed and the sculptor's workshop in George Street was vacant. It was purchased for a few pounds and turned into a temporary meeting-place. It thus became the first Free Kirk of Langholm, and was known as *The Wud Kirk*. The services were so successful that at length the congregation turned their hopes towards an ordained minister.

The Rev. William Brown Clark of Half-Morton, brother-in-law of Henry Scott Riddell the poet, had come out in '43, and thought he might be able to act as minister of the Free Churches of Langholm, Canonby, and Half-Morton, but, this was found to be impracticable. In a short time, however, the congregation had the satisfaction of calling a young licentiate of the Church, Mr. Alexander Johnstone Ross. The ordination was held in a field on Whita side and the first communion was celebrated in the field at Greenbank, where in summer time the Secession congregation was wont to communicate.

Not only did the Free Church leaders aim at having a church in every parish, but they adopted the national educational policy of John Knox and resolved to found a school as well. Following this wise course, the Langholm congregation engaged as teacher, one Alex. Giles, who held his classes in what later became the Buccleuch Hotel. Mr. Giles afterwards entered the ministry and was ordained to a charge at Ashkirk.

A site, in Charles Street (Old), whereon to erect both a church and school, was obtained from Mr. George Maxwell of Broomholm. The foundation-stone was laid on the 18th May, 1845, and the church opened for public worship in April, 1846. Twice after that date it had to be enlarged.

A gift of a garden was made by one of the lady members and in it, at the Town-head, a handsome Manse was built. For many years the congregation, in addition to its ordinary religious work, carried on a successful day school, erected in 1850. Two of the headmasters were Mr. W. Easton, who died in 1861, and Mr. J.W. Stephen, who succeeded him.

In 1874, the school was handed over free to the newly-instituted School Board, who incorporated it with the old parish school in the Gala-side. The deacons thereupon repurchased their own school buildings from the Board, and converted them into the Chalmers Hall, to serve for Sunday School and congregational work.

When the union of the Free and U.P. churches took place in 1900 a re-arrangement of names became imperative, and on the happy suggestion of Mr. Smellie, it was resolved to name the church the *Chalmers Church*, in memory of that great churchman, whose portrait hung on the walls of the vestry.

The following is a list of ministers of this congregation[2] :—

ALEXANDER JOHNSTONE ROSS   1844 - 1847

Ordained 10th May, 1844. Joined the Church of England a few years later and received the degree of DD.

CHARLES WATSON   1848 - 1864

Ordained in Langholm 23rd March, 1848 and afterwards DD. of Edinburgh University. Translated to Largs in 1864. Died there in 1908.

JOHN DAVIDSON   1864-1870

Formerly of Lochend and New Abbey. Inducted December 1864. Married Harriet Miller, daughter of Hugh Miller, geologist. Translated to Chalmers Church, Adelaide, South Australia, in 1870, and became Professor of Church History and English Literature in Adelaide University. Died in 1881.

JAMES EWING SOMERVILLE, MA., BD.   1870-1875

Ordained 7th July, 1870. Graduated Glasgow University. Translated to East Church, Broughty Ferry, in 1875, thence to the Scots Church, Mentone, France.

DAVID SIEVERIGHT SMITH, MA.   1876-1878

Graduated at Aberdeen University. Ordained 20th April, 1876. Went to America in 1878. Became a Professor in one of the colleges of the Western States.

JAMES PANTON   1879-1900

Native of Perthshire. Ordained 13th January, 1879. After 21 years of faithful ministry died 9th June, 1900, aged 50 years. Buried in Wauchope kirkyard.

JOHN ALEXANDER DUKE, MA., BD.

Graduated Glasgow University. Assistant to Dr. Ross Taylor, Kelvinside, Glasgow. Ordained in Chalmers Church December 1900. Translated to Morningside, Edinburgh, 1904.

DAVID WILLIAM INGLIS, MA.   1905-1931

Graduated University of Edinburgh, 1897. Theological training New College, Edinburgh. Licensed by Presbytery of Edinburgh, 1902. Ordained to Chalmers Church, 10th March, 1905.

Two issues of Communion Tokens seem to have been made by the congregation. Both are stock patterns in common use amongst the Free Churches of Scotland in the years following the Disruption.

First issue: an oval token with borders, 19 sixteenths by 13.

Obverse: Free Church / OF SCOTLAND, around the edge. Date,

1843, in centre. Two plain dots separate upper and under legends around the edge.

Reverse: LET A MAN EXAMINE HIMSELF I Cor. XI., 28.
Second issue: same shape and size as first
Obverse: Free Church / OF SCOTLAND, around the edge. Date, 1843, in centre
Reverse: same as in first issue but has a period after "HIMSELF."

In 1931 Chalmers Kirk united with Langholm Old.

CANONBY UNITED FREE KIRK

Like that of Langholm, the Free Kirk of Canonby originated at the Disruption. But its history was even more exciting and impressive than that of Langholm. In the years immediately following the Disruption, the story of the Canonby congregation became familiar throughout Scotland for the hardships it suffered during the winter of 1843-4.

They were refused a site so their first place of worship was a tent pitched in the corner of a peat moss, where tinkers were conceded the right of encampment but which was denied to this congregation against whom an interdict was obtained. In their predicament they betook themselves to the roadside, and from September 1843 until July of 1844, they worshipped there. This site was on the south side of the public road at the Hollows end of Gilnockie Bridge.

When the first communion was celebrated they were permitted to meet in a field. Dr. Gordon, of the Free High Church, Edinburgh, dispensed the sacred ordinance, assisted by neighbouring ministers and some elders from Edinburgh, amongst whom was Sir Patrick Maxwell of Springkell. Afterwards, they received permission to erect a tent in a gravel pit, under an oak tree, below Brockwoodlees farmhouse. They worshiped there for more than six years.

Such steadfastness had its reward. Public feeling throughout the country on this question of the refusal of sites became so strong that Parliament had to intervene. A Committee of Enquiry was appointed, before whom witnesses gave evidence on behalf of the Canonby congregation.

After the Committee had reported, the Duke of Buccleuch yielded. A site was granted and on the 2nd September, 1849 the foundation stone of the church was laid.[4] The church was opened on the first Sabbath of 1851, nearly eight years after the Disruption. During these years of trial the congregation a large amount of public sympathy.

Most of this information was given by the Rev. John Jamieson, minister of the Canonby United Free congregation, who obtained his facts from the following documents:—

1. Sermon preached in the Tent at Canonby by the Rev. George Innes, MA., with a short *Memoir,* of the author, published 1849.

2. Dr. Guthrie's *Autobiography* and *Memoire* by his son, Lord Guthrie.

3. *The Annals of the Disruption*; *The Witness* newspaper, edited by Hugh Miller.

4. Evidence given before the Parliamentary Enquiry on Refusal of Sites.

The following is a list of the ministers:—[2]

GEORGE INNES, MA.   1844-1847
    Ordained minister of Seafield Church, Portnockie, Banffshire, on 10th May, 1843 eight days before the Disruption. Came out on the 18th. Called to Canonby. Inducted in the Tent September 1844. Died Nov. 1847 in his 29th year, from consumption induced by exposure to hardships

ALEXANDER WATSON MILNE   1848-1885
    Also ordained in the Tent in August 1848. Died in July 1885 in his 65th year, and the 37th of his ministry. A tablet was placed in the vestibule of the church stating that he was the chief means of getting the church and manse erected. The Pulpit Bible bears a silver plate having an inscription that it was presented to him by the ladies of Grand Street Presbyterian Church, New York, in 1852.

JOHN SMITH WILSON, MA.   1885-1892
    Graduate of Edinburgh University. Theological training at New College, Edinburgh. Assistant to foregoing. Ordained in succession in October 1885. Resigned owing to ill-health in 1892. Removed to Trinidad, West Indies, where he occupied an important position under the United Free Church of Scotland.

JOHN JAMIESON, MA.   1892-1917
    Graduate of Glasgow University. Theological training in Free Church College there and at New College, Edinburgh. Ordained at Firth, Orkney, in 1880. Inducted to Canonby in 1892 and continued in pastoral charge until retirement in 1917.

JOHN BROWN MILNE, MA.   1917-20
JOHN EDWARD MCINTOSH, MA.   1920-26
FREDERICK SMITH, BD.   1927-29
CAMERON GRANT   1930-36
DUNCAN GILLIES   1937-39
GEORGE LEWIS   1939-45
MATTHEW TODD   1945-52

FRANK GARDEK	1953-54
ROBERT HUDSPETH AND TOM ROUTLEDGE, Joint Ministry	1955-60
JAMES WALLACE	1961-63
GEORGE THOMSON	1963-66
ROBERT HUDSPETH	1967-76
GEORGE WHITAKE	1976-79
W. GOODALL	1979-80
GEORGE WHITAKER	1981-83
WILLIAM SPIERS	1983-87
ERNEST GILMORE	1987-88
RON CAMPBELL	1989-

The Token issued by this congregation is oval with borders 18 by 14 sixteenths of an inch. Number 12 on the Plate.

Obverse: CANONBIE FREE CHURCH 1845
Reverse: LET A MAN EXAMINE HIMSELF I COR., XI., 28.

After the Uniting Act of October 1900 the congregation became part of the United Free Church of Scotland and has continued to the present day. In 1999 the congregation celebrated its 150th anniversary.

The Rev. Ron Campbell kindly supplied the list of ministers since 1929.

ESKDALEMUIR UNITED FREE

This congregation was formed in 1836. Some dissatisfaction having arisen in the Established Kirk of Eskdalemuir, a small section of the members broke off and, uniting with a band of Cameronians, formed a separate congregation. The Cameronians received their name from their adherence to the doctrines of Richard Cameron, most eloquent of the Covenanters who paid for his religious principles with his life.

When in 1836 the two parties united, they built a little kirk at Davington, the lease of which was granted by the grandfather of Mr. Thomas Beattie. Following the custom of that day the lease designated it a Meeting House.

It was not until 1847 that a regular ministry was obtained. The congregation was part of the Reformed Presbyterian Kirk of Scotland. In 1876 most of the congregations of that denomination, including Eskdalemuir united with the Free Kirk.

LANGHOLM AS IT WAS

The following is the list of ministers since 1847:—

JAMES MORRISON   1847-78
     Ordained June 1847 to the united charge of Eskdalemuir and Buccleuch, Ettrick. In the latter church he preached every, third Sunday.

JOHN T. FALSIDE   1879-1903
JOSEPH CLARK NICOL, M.A.   1903-12
     Ordained and inducted to Eskdalemuir in May 1903. Translated to Pelaw-on-Tyne in June 1912.

     The congregation was without a minister until 1919.
GEORGE RAMSAY Ordained missionary.   1919-23
JOHN McLEAN FLOCKHART Ordianed missionary.   1924-28

The Manse was built in 1849.

One Token has been issued by this congregation. It is numbered 11 on the Plate, and is a plain metal Token, square, with cut corners, but no borders, and measures 11 sixteenths of an inch.
     Obverse: R P incuse, for Reformed Presbyterian. *Reverse*: plain.

LANGHOLM CONGREGATIONAL CHURCH

This congregation originated in December 1862 and belonged to the Evangelical Union of Scotland until it joined with the Congregational Union in January 1897. A small number of men, impressed with theological views more liberal than those prevailing at that time, met to consider the best means of giving expression to their religious convictions, and the formation of this congregation was the result.

Its founders were Walter Scott of Holmfoot, John Warwick, Robert Black, William Borthwick, Robert Lun, James McVittie, Thomas Ellis, D. Conchie, Walter Reid, William Warwick, John Wells, James Bell, Andrew Little, William Telford, Robert Hiddlestone, and Archibald Kerr.

The new congregation met with considerable apathy, if not actual opposition, in the town, and they had much difficulty in obtaining a site for their church. For a time they met for worship in the bark-house of Mr. Walter Scott, tanner, who took an active share in all the work of the church from its commencement, and was, until his death, its most generous supporter.

The bark-house was situated on the south side of Buccleuch Square, next to the police station, into which it was later absorbed. The formal opening took place on 27th July, 1863, the officiating minister being the Rev. William Deans of York. The services were at first taken by students but in 1864 the Rev. James Cron was inducted.

Efforts were afterwards made to obtain a site in the New-Town, but failure met them at every turn. Eventually a site on the Drove Road at the head of the Kirkwynd was secured and the building of the church was made possible by the munificent gifts of Mr. Walter Scott, who very appropriately was invited to lay the corner-stone.

It was opened for worship on 27th November, 1870, by the Rev. Dr. Morison, founder of the denomination. In the vestibule there was a marble slab which bore witness to the regard in which Mr. and Mrs. Walter Scott were held. For 40 years they were members and liberal supporters of the congregation.

In the same year 22 members and adherents of the congregation emigrated to Australia where they instituted the first Lodge of Good Templars naming it The Outward Bound.

The Manse was acquired in 1892 and was situated at the Town-head, adjoining Clinthead.

The following is a list of the ministers since the inception of the congregation.[5]:—

JAMES CRON   1864-1865
     Ordained June, 1864. Retired April 1865. Died 18th July at Durisdeer.

JAMES CAMPBELL   1866-1873
     Ordained 12th October 1866. Emigrated to America in 1874.

ROBERT BORLAND, DD   1873-1877
     Ordained 16th October 1873. Left Nov. 1877. Joined the Established Church of Scotland. Author of *Border Raids and Reivers,* frequently quoted in this volume.

W. RICHMOND SCOTT   1878-1887
     Ordained in October, 1878. In June 1887, translated to Nelson Street E.U. Church, Greenock. In 1900 joined the Established Church of Scotland..

ANDREW RITCHIE, MA.   1888-1894
     Graduated Edinburgh University. Ordained October 1888. Left in March 1894 and went to Nelson Street E.U. Church, Greenock. Called to St. Petersburg, Russia, in 1903, to take charge of the Anglo-American Church there.

GEORGE McKENDRICK   1894-1900
     Resigned in 1900 to take up work on Lake Tanganyika, Central Africa, under the London Missionary Society, where he died of fever after a few months. The congregation and friends erected a stone to his memory in Staplegortoun Churchyard.

ROBERT MACQUEEN   1900-1913
     Educated at Troon Academy and Edinburgh University. Theological training in Glasgow. Ordained 1893. Inducted to Langholm, June, 1900.

RICHARD SMITH	1916-18
WILLIAM ROBERTSON MILNE	1920-21
NATHANIEL JOHNSTON	1922-24
JAMES CALLANDER DRIFE	1925-34
WILLIAM CRAIG COWAN	1935-40
BEATRICE DUNNET BONNAR	1941-66
HARRY ESCOTT	1967-70

The Church closed in 1971.

EPISCOPAL CHAPEL

The chapel is a private one, belonging to his Grace the Duke of Buccleuch.. It is picturesquely situated within the policies of Langholm Lodge, not far from the ruins of the old Castle.

It was built by the Duke, and opened for public worship on 9th September 1883, which happened to be the birthday of his son, the Earl of Dalkeith. A handsome brass cross and candlesticks were presented by his friends, in memory of the Earl, who met his tragic death whilst deer-stalking in the Highlands on 17th September, 1886, whilst his father and mother were at Langholm Lodge.

The chaplaincy has been held by the following:—

P. S. LOCKTON, M.A.   1886
     Later became Rector of Holy Trinity, Melrose.

W.W. WHITE, M.A.   1893
     Moved to Norfolk to be Rector at Brockdish..

J. A. SEATON   1903
Associate of King's College, London University. Ordained by Bishop Bardsley of Carlisle in 1900. Curate in Ireleth-cum-Askam then in 1902 to St. Paul's, Carlisle.

The building is now used by Clan Armstrong Trust for their museum.

CHAPTER 25

THE LANGHOLM FAIRS

Fairs were a necessary adjunct to the trade and commerce of the Middle Ages. In many districts they were the only means whereby the produce of the land and the loom could be sold or bartered. As the population of the country was more widely distributed, less centred in large towns, the Fairs provided the means to bring the buyer and the seller together. They were certainly taken advantage of for enjoyment and social reunion, but their primary object was to foster trade and commerce.

Generally speaking, the Fairs were the rights of the feudal baron. They existed for the convenience of his vassals, but, for his own benefit he could levy tolls upon the sellers and merchants who took advantage of the Fair. His rights were usually expressed in the charter granting him the lands but, where not expressed, they were, we believe, implied, and when the heritable jurisdictions of the barons were modified by the Act of 1747, special reservations were made in respect of Fairs and markets, the baron retaining the right to levy tolls.

Prior to the Nithsdale charter of 1621, we have no definite record of Fairs being held in Eskdale, though tradition tells of one held at Staplegortoun, and another at the junction of the White and Black Esks. To the latter, it is said, the itinerant priests came from Melrose to confirm the hand-fasting, and it is accepted as history that the Fair was held on Hand-fasting Haugh. There is nothing unlikely in these traditions, indeed the name Stapelgortoun seems to imply some such mart as a large Fair would provide.

But it was by the charter granted by the King to the Earl of Nithsdale in 1621 that the Fairs in Langholm received statutory sanction.

327

As the charter of 1610 to William, Lord Cranstoun, was only of "a free barony", no necessity existed of giving power to hold Fairs, but in 1621 the Earl of Nithsdale contemplated the extension of the town of Langholm, and Fairs would then become an economic necessity. The charter conferred the right "of having . . . . a weekly market on Thursdays (the market day was later changed to Wednesday, when and for what reason we have no information) with two free fairs yearly" on 29th June and 24th October.

These served the requirements of the town and district until 1672, when the Duke and Duchess of Buccleuch and Monmouth, being desirous of extending trade and commerce throughout their estates, petitioned Parliament for further powers. Their petition, "To the Right Honourable My Lord Commissioner his Grace and High Court of Parliament" asked for two additional Fairs "besyd the fair dayes already Granted to Langholm". (See Appendix 8)

It would appear that as the town increased in size, and the surrounding district grew more productive and prosperous, even four Fairs were not adequate, or their dates were not sufficiently suitable to the special needs of a pastoral community, for in 1701 Anne, Duchess of Buccleuch, and her son James, Earl of Dalkeith, presented to Parliament another petition for liberty to hold two additional Fairs. Thus, in 1701, there were in addition to the weekly market, no fewer than six statutory Fairs held in Langholm. They were apportioned over the year in this way:—

5 April. By the Act of 1672. This came to be known as the April Fair.

Last Tuesday in May. By the Act of 1701. This was the May Fair but after the re-arrangement of the calendar it fell in June.

29 June. By the Nithsdale charter of 1621.

15 July. By the Act of 1672. After the re-arrangement of the calendar it fell on July 26. This is known as the Summer or Lamb Fair, at one time perhaps the largest of all the Fairs in the south of Scotland.

First Tuesday in September. By the act of 1701. Known as the Ewe Fair.

24 October. By the Nithsdale charter of 1621. Known as the Winter Fair.

Both the charter and the Acts of Parliament gave the right to the holder of the barony to impose tolls and customs at each of these Fairs and this right was exercised as long as the Fairs were held.

The following is a summary of the Tolls as fixed by the Sheriff in 1795:—

Table of Customs, Langholm; payable to the Duke of Buccleuch. Taken from all Extract Decreet of the Sheriff of Dumfriesshire, dated 14th July 1795.

For each Horse Twopence Sterling.

For each Cow or Nolt Beast Sixteen pennies Scots.

For each Rough Sheep Four Pennies Scots.

For each Lamb Two Pennies Scots.

For each stand or Stall, whatever be exposed thereat whither on Fairdays or Hiring-days, One penny sterling and for each Lintseed stall or stand at the April fair, Twopence Sterling.

For each Load of Meal Threepence Sterling.

For Flour, or Meal of Wheat, the same as other Meal.

For each Load of Malt Threepence Sterling.

For each Load of Salt Twopence Sterling.

For each Load of Potatoes Two pence Sterling.

For Herrings each Barrel Twopence Sterling.

For Butter a penny Scots each pound Scotch weight.

For Cheese when brought to the Public Market the same Duty as for Butter. But found it not proved that any Duty or custom is payable for cheese sold or retailed in private Houses or Shops.

Regulations were made respecting stands and applied both to the Fairs and Hiring Days. The ordinary size of a stand to be 12 feet long by 6 feet wide, toll one penny sterling. Above 12 feet and not exceeding 15 feet, twopence. Above 15 and not exceeding 20 feet, threepence. All above the last size, one shilling. These rates applied to every kind of stand. The letting of sites and collection of tolls were part of the duties of the baron-bailie, who deputed them to the baron officer.

The Fair, held annually on "the 15th day o' July auld style", was not only the most important, but was also the most interesting. It was principally for sheep, lambs, and wool but, naturally, was not confined to these. In course of time it became associated with the Common-Riding though, as a matter of fact, there was no necessary connection between them. Proclamation of the Fair had to be formally made, before the officers of the baron could legitimately levy the customs and tolls to which his charter entitled him. This would most likely be done in the

Market Place, probably from the steps of the Cross, which, it will be remembered, the baron, by the charter of 1621, had the right to set up. The Cross, placed at a considerable height and surrounded by graded steps, would serve admirably for the Proclamation.

The text of this Proclamation has been corrupted, and, as will be seen on comparing that quoted below with the modern text given in Chapter 27, it has been completely altered in many important points.

"He e-0 Yes! that's ee time; 0 Yes ! that's twa times; 0 Yes ! and that's the third and last time:—

All manner of person and persons whatsoe'er let 'um draw near and I shall let them kenn, that their is a Fair to be held at the muckle Town of Langholm for the space of aught days; wherein if any Hustrin, Custrin, Land Louper, Dub Skouper or Gang the gate Swinger shall bread any Urdam, Durdam, Rabblement, Brabblement or Squabblement, he shall have his Lugs tacked to the muckle Trone with a nail of twal-a-Penny, untill he down of his Hobshanks and up with his muckle Doaps, and Pray to Hea'n neen times 'God bless the King' and thrice the muckle Loard of Relton, paying a Groat to me Jemmy Ferguson, Baily of the aforesaid mannor, so you heard my Proclamation and I'll awa hame to my Danner."*

The text of the Proclamation here given appeared in the *Gentleman's Magazine* in March, 1731 and was there referred to as *lately published* . The wording seems to indicate that the Proclamation did not relate to the Summer Fair, which dates from 1672, but to the earlier Fairs held by virtue of the powers conferred by the Nithsdale Charter of 1621.

This view is supported by the internal evidence offered by the text itself:—

1. The omission of a date in the text. In the Proclamation of the Fair of 15th July the date is given (though this may be due to the alteration of the calendar), and so is the fact of its being held on the *Duke* of Buccleuch's Merk-Land, the Dukedom dating to the year 1663.

2. The mention of "the muckle Laird o' Ralton". This personage has been sometimes described as an illegitimate son of Charles II, but this appears to be nothing more than a guess. It seems certain to the writers that he was William Elliot of Roan, in Liddesdale, which had the alternative designation of Ralton or Relton, third son of William Elliot of Larriston. William Elliot of Roan, or Ralton, is, by the family papers

supposed to have been factor for Buccleuch. His son, Robert Elliot of Unthank, was also factor and probably succeeded his father, but on his getting into debt to Buccleuch, the latter seized his estates.

He seems to have been succeeded by his cousin Gavin Elliot, whose father Gilbert, (Gibbie o' the gowden garters), went with Buccleuch to the rescue of Kinmont Willie in 1596. Gavin Elliot acquired Midlem Mill, and his descendant, Robert Elliot of Midlem Mill, was also factor for the Duke, and, as we have seen, removed from Branxholme to Langholm Castle about the year 1725.

If, as we think, "the muckle Laird o' Ralton" was William Elliot, then the date of the above text must certainly be *earlier* than the institution of the Summer Fair, for William Elliot would at that date — 1672 — have been nearly 100 years of age. The Laird o' Ralton appointed as his bailie, the above named Jamie Ferguson.

*   "He e." This is given in the text, but its meaning is now unintelligible.

"0 Yes", is doubtless a corruption of the French *oyez,* "listen".

"Hustrin", cp. "all auld *huister* o' a quean", a dirty housewife.

"Custrin", probably "quistron", a beggar.

"Land-Louper", one who flees the country for debt.

"Dub-Skoupetr", probably a variant of the old border term "dubskelper or dub-skimper", a bog-trotter, "one who goes through thick and thin". "Gang (or gae by) the gate Swinger" one who sets out on a journey i.e. (probably) a tramp or beggar, cp., the old Scots term, "a gan-aboot-body".

"Rabblement", a mob. "Brabblement", sometimes given as "bragglement", probably from the French *babibler,* to tattle or gossip.

"Squabblement" probably a disturbance of the peace.

"Urdam, Durdam" are not given by Jamieson, and may be only rhetorical flourishes.

"His Lugs tacked to the muckle Trone with a nail of twal-a-Penny", cp., "on Decr. 2, 1689, the magistrates of Edinburgh were ordered to put William Mitchell upon the Tron and cause the hangman nail his lug thereto . . . . and for words of reflection uttered by him against the present Government"[1].

CHAPTER 26

THE COMMON MOSS AND KILNGREEN

The Feu-contract of 1628 conveyed the Merk-lands of Arkinholm and Langholm to ten members of the Maxwell family. Reference to Appendix 4 will show that these tenants-in-common were to have certain privileges. They could, for instance, "win and lead stones of any part of the common quarries of the said lands of Arkinholm". This right passed to their heirs and assignees and was conceded, likewise, to burgesses of the town of Langholm. Originally confined to them, but by long custom it has become the right and lot of all residents in Langholm, whether they reside on the Ten Merk-lands or in New Langholm, which is not included therein.

Naturally, between 1628, the date of the contract, and 1759, when the Commonty was apportioned amongst the holders, there had been changes of ownership.

Several of the Maxwells had sold, or otherwise disposed of, their Merk-lands to John Maxwell of Broomholm, whose mansion house was nearest thereto, or to other heritors. So that in 1756 the new Ten Merk-lands were held as follows:—

John Maxwell of Broomholm's holding had increased from one to	5
He had also purchased the rights and enjoyment of the Common, attaching to the Merk-land held previously by Simon Little, Knittyholm	1
Making the Maxwell holding	6
John Little, Langholm	3
Duke of Buccleuch	1
Total	10

In 1628 the Earl of Nithsdale had reserved to his own use the woods and fishings. However the Earl of Nithsdale had forfeited his estates in 1643-44. These rights, which existed apart from the occupation or enjoyment of the Merk-lands, were then conveyed in 1643-44 to the Duke of Buccleuch, who, although holding only one of the Merk-lands, had thus acquired the right to cut and appropriate the timber upon the entire Commonty, a right which the Award of 1759 did not, and could not, affect.

The approximate area comprised in the Ten Merklands was not that of the town of Langholm alone, but included virtually the whole of Whita Hill and the lands lying along the eastern bank of the Esk. It therefore consisted of townland, arable land, woodland, hill pasture, the Common Moss and the Kilngreen.

It was not unnatural that, with the different interests involved, disputes should occur between the owners, both concerning the extent or location of their particular Merk-lands, and also concerning the extent and use of those rights and privileges which were held and enjoyed by them in common.

In order to settle such disputes an Act had been passed, during the reign of William and Mary, by which all common lands, except those belonging to the Crown or the royal burghs, could be divided at the instance of anyone having an interest therein, by a process before the Court of Session, which could then determine the various interests and, according to them, divide such common lands.

The Act also provided that where these common lands included mosses which could not conveniently be divided, they should remain common, and that free passage to them should be preserved.

Maxwell of Broomholm, who held five of the Ten Merk-lands and the Commonty rights of a sixth, appears to have attempted to obtain a mutual arrangement and apportionment, but the other owners refused consent. He thereupon, in 1757, brought an action in the Court of Session against the Duke of Buccleuch, then a minor, and his tutors and curators; John Little, merchant in Langholm; Simon Little in Nittyholm; and Archibald Little, feuar in Langholm, to have the Common divided according to the Act.

On his claim to sue being confirmed, Maxwell craved the appointment of a Commission, who should perambulate the bounds and take proof of extent, limits, and marches of the Common, collect evidence and report, fix and determine as to such marches and lands, and then have the Common divided between those having interest, according to the valued rents of the lands. This Commission was granted on 5th August, 1757, and consisted of John Boston, chamberlain to the Duke of Buccleuch, Bryce Blair of Potterflats, Provost of Annan, with John Elliot, clerk of the Baronies of Eskdale and Canonby, as their clerk. It met at Langholm on 9th November, 1757, and took evidence on oath.

In Appendix 5 we give an Abstract of the Award and Division, with the boundaries defined, together with a Plan of the Commonty, and also an Abstract of the evidence relating both to the Common Moss and the Kilngreen. It is therefore only necessary here to summarise the findings.

The Commission found that the ground lying within the boundaries quoted in the Appendix 5, with the exception of the Moss which, according to the Act of William and Mary, was not to be divided, belonged to the pursuer and defenders, and that the right of the Duke of Buccleuch to the growing timber still held good. They appointed as valuators to value the different divisions, William Corrie Carlyle of Bridekirk, John Armstrong in Sorby, Walter Borthwick in Enzieholm, and William Yeoman in Thorniewhats, who made the following Award:—

	a.	r.	p.
To John Maxwell of Broomholm	574	: 0	: 12
To John Little, Langholm	118	: 0	: 32
To the Duke of Buccleuch	58	: 3	: 26
Total	751	: 0	: 30

The Kilngreen was not included in this Award, and the Commissioners asked for a renewal of their appointment to complete the work relating to it. Owing, however, to the illness and subsequent death of Mr. Boston, the Commission had to be re-constituted, when the following were appointed:— John Craigie, chamberlain to the Duke of Buccleuch, Robert Irvine, Writer to the Signet, and Bryce Blair of Potterflats, with John Elliot as their clerk.

The new Commission sat at Langholm on 25th October, 1758, and took evidence as to the limits, extent, possession and enjoyment of the Kilngreen, which John Maxwell of Broomholm claimed to be part of the

Common, and therefore subject to division. The witnesses called gave evidence as to the use of the Kilngreen by the people of Langholm, and stated that the river Ewes formerly ran in a course much nearer to Langholm Castle, and that consequently the Kilngreen had been reduced in size. They declared further that, within the longest memory, the people of Langholm had pastured their cattle upon it, and that the Langholm Fairs had been held there, and that at these Fairs the Duke of Buccleuch had levied customs and tolls.

When the action came before the Court on 24th February, 1759, the following relating documents were put in, viz., (a) to the Feu-contract of 1628, showing the equal rights to the Common of Langholm of the holders of the Ten Merk-lands, and their tenants, (b) the Report of the Commission, (c) a plan of the Common, (see Appendix 5) as divided by them, made by James Tait, land surveyor, and (d) the valuation of the Ten Merk-lands by the Commissioners of Supply for the County of Dumfries. Maxwell also produced documentary proof of his right to the share of the Common attaching to the Merk-land held by Simon Little in Nittyholm.

The Court :—

I. Accepted the boundaries of the Common set forth by the Commissioners and they became their finding.

II. Found that the said land had been immemorially possessed as Common property by the proprietors of the Ten Merk-lands and their tenants.

III. Found that, with the exception of the Moss thereon, the Common should be divided among the parties in the action, in the proportion of:—

Six-tenths to John Maxwell.
Three-tenths to John Little.
One-tenth to the Duke of Buccleuch.

IV. Found that the Moss should not be divided, but should be reserved as common to all who had previously had interest in the Common in its intact form; and the boundaries (given in Appendix 5) were set forth.

V. Found that the market roads to Langholm throughout the Common must be reserved, and a road twenty feet in breadth was also reserved to the Common Moss.

VI. Adjudged that the reservation of the timber growing on the Common should be continued to the Duke of Buccleuch.

VII. Found that the rights and claims of the parties to that part of the Common called the Kilngreen were reserved as they existed before the application for the division.

VIII. Found that Mr. Maxwell was entitled to the custody of the decree of the Court, but was under obligation to produce the same to the other owners when necessary.

The demarcation of the areas of the Ten Merk-lands belonging to each of the heritors is of less importance to the town of Langholm than the Awards concerning the Common Moss and the Kilngreen. What the burgesses obtained by this legal decision may now be summarised. They had it declared by a Court of law:—

I. That the Common Moss belonged inalienably to Langholm.

II. That the tenants of the Ten Merk-lands and the burgesses of the town of Langholm possessed the right to lead stones and win fuel from the Common Moss; and they had also free access to it secured.

III That the Kilngreen, with rights of pasturage, had belonged immemorially to the town of Langholm.

IV That the limits and boundaries of these various Common lands should hereafter be as the Commission had awarded.

It is of importance to understand these Awards clearly, for they explain much that is distinctive in the history of the town of Langholm, and furnish the explanation of the events and ceremonies described in the next chapter.

CHAPTER 27

THE COMMON-RIDING

Riding the marches is, in many Border towns, a time-honoured annual custom and is popularly known as The Common-Riding. In Langholm the ceremony is attended by all the pomp and circumstance of an annual festival and the Common-Riding Day has become the chief date in the calendar of Eskdale. One of the stipulations in agreements of hiring was that the servant should have holidays at Canonby Sacrament and Langholm Common-Riding.

The Award of the Court of Session in 1759 recognised that the burgesses of Langholm had certain legal rights in the Commonty and pre-eminently in the Common Moss and the Kilngreen which, with their pasture rights, were a valuable possession to the community. It became, therefore, a public duty on the part of the burgesses to see that these rights were maintained in their entirety for themselves and their posterity.

The boundaries of the Common lands were set forth in the Award and were delimited by natural objects such as trees or ditches, but, where these were not found, beacons or cairns were erected and pits dug, all of which served to indicate the marches between the different owners.

To maintain these intact now became the duty of the inhabitants, who, accordingly, engaged a man to go out to the Common Moss and the Kilngreen once a year "to see gif a' the marches they be clear", report encroachments, clean out the pits, repair the beacons, and generally protect the interests of the people. This was done regularly for a long period.

About the year 1765 it was done by one Archibald Beattie, known as Bauldy Beattie, the town drummer or crier. No doubt it would be by

337

virtue of his holding this public office that the duty of protecting the Marches was assigned to him. For more than 50 years he walked the Marches, pointing out their limits and boundaries to all who cared to accompany him; and he also "cried" the Langholm Fair at the Cross. Up to the year 1814 Bauldy Beattie went over the Marches on foot.

In 1815 Archie Thomson, landlord of the Commercial Hotel on the High Street, seems to have perambulated the boundaries alone. In 1816 Thomson went over them on horseback. Soon he was accompanied by others, amongst whom, John Irving, baker of Langholm Mill, and Frank Beattie of the Crown Inn, were the principal. These men were the fathers of the Common-Riding and it was they who, in 1816, began the horse-racing which has since been one of the features of the programme during the Common-Riding afternoon.

Amongst those riding the marches, there sprang up, not unnaturally, a spirit of competition as to the mettle of their mounts and the races which resulted were at first confined to the animals which had gone round the boundaries. This is still a condition in certain of the races at the present day.

At first the races and sports were held on the Kilngreen, but in 1834 they were transferred to the Castle Holm, which was then, and for many years later, called the Muckle Kilngreen, part of it, indeed, being included in the lands given to the town by the Award of 1759. In 1939 the Castle Holm was requisitioned by the Army and the races were transferred to Milntown eventually returning to the Castle Holm in 1958.

Horse-racing formed only a small part of the Common-Riding programme. The old Border games were entered into then with much greater zest and emulation than now, wrestling, for which there were entries from all over the Border country, notably from Cumberland which sent famous wrestlers such as Wright, Steedman, and the Blairs, high-jumping, climbing the greasy-pole, chasing the well-soaped pig, and other old-fashioned country sports, which in our day of professional athletics show a regrettable decline.

With the introduction of horsemen came the selection of the leader or Cornet, who was also Master of the Ceremonies. His following was at first a small one, numbering probably not more than six or seven, but during the succeeding years, as enthusiasm became keener, the number of horsemen greatly increased, and it is no unusual spectacle to see 70 horsemen spurring their steeds up the steep Kirkwynd, as they make for the Common Moss, — and a brave appearance they present, with the town flag flying in the breeze, a sight which, almost more than any other, stirs the pulses of Langholm men.

At first the selection of the Cornet was made entirely from the residents of the Old-town of Langholm. This was natural, seeing that in a strictly legal sense the Common, and all the privileges and rights conferred by the Award, belonged to them alone.

In 1843 a departure was made from this practice by the choice of a Cornet from the New Town when Robert Anderson, blacksmith, was chosen, and to him belongs the distinction of being the first Meikleholmer, to use the name given to the people of New-Langholm, to fill the honourable position. Since 1890, in response to a public demand, the election of the Cornet and a committee of management has been decided in public meeting of the inhabitants. Mr. Robert McGeorge of Greenbank was the first treasurer and Mr. James Morrison, inspector of poor, was the first secretary of this committee.

In recognition of the corporate sanction, now set upon what was originally and for many, years done entirely on personal initiative, the Provost, each Common-Riding morning, formally hands to the Cornet the town's flag and receives it again from him at the close of the day. Since local government re-organisation in 1975 when the position of Provost ceased, there have been various *acting Provosts* who have handed over the flag. This person is appointed by the Common Riding Committee each year. The Cornets of the two previous years act as right-hand and left-hand man respectively to the new Cornet.

It is of interest to note the occupations of some of the Cornets:— Brewer, meal dealer, cooper, candlemaker, horse-dealer, miller, scourer, woolsorter, spinner, finisher, skinner, millwright, and weaver. The trades here represented were at one time of considerable importance in Langholm. Frequently, the occupation is mason, joiner, warehouseman, baker, painter, slater, and butcher.

In the procession, of which the Cornet is leader, there are carried, in addition to the Flag, the following emblems, most of them having some special significance, either in relation to the preservation of the marches, or to the Summer Fair, on the day following which the Common-Riding has invariably been observed:—

I.— A BARLEY-BANNOCK and a SALTED HERRING fastened by a large nail to a wooden dish.

GROUP OF CORNETS

Photograph reproduced from Robert Hyslop's original glass plate. Former Cornets who
were present at the Common-Riding celebration in July, 1896

Back Row
John Fletcher, 1884. Robert Stewart, 1895. Robert Wm. Reid, 1896.
Harry A. Scott, 1894. Robert Thomson, 1883.
Second Row
William Trotter, 1891. Christopher Weatherstone, 1881.
William B. Scott, 1892. James Turnbull, 1876.
William Douglas, 1874. Andrew Beattie, 1872.
William McVittie, 1870. John Beattie, 1867.
Third Row
John Hotson,1857. John W.J.Paterson,1850. Robert Lunn,1844.
Matthew Murray, 1840. Joseph Park, 1856.
Matthew Irving, 1864, Andrew Johnstone, 1865.
Front Row
James Fletcher, 1890. John T. Burnet, 1885. John lrving, 1887.
James Smith, 1886. Archibald Irving, 1893. James Reid, 1878.

The Bannock symbolises certain of the privileges of the baron, and therefore appertains to the Fair rather than to the Common-Riding itself. A bannock of barley, oats, or pease-meal, but usually of barley, was a perquisite of the servant of the baronial mill, due from the tenants and vassals under the obligation of thirlage.

It was one of the *sequels*, which were not merely voluntary gratuities, but were due in virtue of the astriction of a tenant to a particular mill. All of these rights and privileges were continued to the Duke of Buccleuch, even after the Heritable Jurisdictions Act of 1747. The Summer Fair, when so many of the Duke's tenants were in the town, would be a convenient time to pay this acknowledged perquisite.

The servant to whom it was due would be the executive officer of the baron-bailie, who collected the baron's multures as well as the customs and tolls at the Fair. The Proclamation of the Fair which preceded the collection of the tolls, would also be made by this officer, to whom is probably due the introduction of the reference at the end of the Proclamation to the fact that he was to have "a barley bannock and a saut herring" for his dinner for, of course no such engaging and personal detail would appear in the original text. Abundance of barley-meal bannocks at the Fair and the mention of one in later versions of the Proclamation, would readily suggest the symbol when the two events came to be so closely associated about the year 1817.

The presence of the Herring is more difficult of explanation. It may have had its origin in the simple necessity of the baron-bailie's officer requiring some relish, or as our Scots forefathers would have expressed it, some *kitchen,* to the decidedly dry fare of the barley-bannock. Or it may be that, just as the bannock is indicative of the baron's rights in the mills, so the herring indicates his rights in the fisheries as conferred by the Burgh charter of 1621.

Even though expressly mentioned in a charter, the rights of a baron in respect of the fisheries were often matters of dispute, and a title was as frequently obtained by the exercise of the rights for the prescriptive period as it was given by the charter itself. It may therefore have been in support of his claim to the whole of the fishery rights that the baron-bailie of the Duke first brought the Herring into conjunction with the barley-meal bannock at the Fair. But, the origin of its presence is, admittedly, only a matter of speculation.

The Bannock has been carried by the following:—

Thomas Hutton, John Beattie, who officiated for over 50 years, James Carlyle, Thomas Irving, George Armstrong, and Peter Thomson.

II.— THE SPADE. This is used for cutting the sod at different points of the Common and for clearing out the pits which originally marked the boundaries of the Common Moss. On the return from the hill it is usually bedecked with heather "lately pulled frae Whita side". For over 50 years the Spade was carried by William Armstrong, better known as Willie Dick. It was one of the incidents of the Common-Riding day to see Willie, disdaining the plank bridge, dash through the Water of Ewes. There was about it something of the old mosstrooping recklessness and unconcern which his forefathers often displayed. As one of the events of the day it ranked in interest next to the Cornet's chase. The bearers of the Spade have been:—

William Armstrong, William Jackson and John Jackson, who succeeded his father in 1906.

As a mark of the ancient boundaries of the Commonty of Langholm, over which the inhabitants have rights, there are sods *cast* at the following points:—

1.— Near the boundary fence at the entry of the Common Moss.

2.— Below the road leading to the Castle Craigs.

3.— Close to the Castle Craigs.

4.— Between the Castle Craigs and the monument onWhita top.

5.— At Bet's Thorn, which formerly grew in Walter Ballantyne's garden, between the office-houses of the Buccleuch Hotel and the lodge of Ashley Bank.

Since 1884 the ground on which this Thorn grew has been enclosed and it now forms part of the Ashley Bank grounds. Very grave doubt may be expressed concerning the reality of such enclosing of any portion of the Common lands of Langholm which were fixed by the Award of 1759 At one time the Common-Riding Procession perambulated *round* Bet's Thorn, implying that it was within the town's Common lands. Who Bet was is not definitely known but may have been old Bet Lawson.

6.— On the Little Kilngreen near Ewesfoot.

7.— On the Castle Holm near Ewes Bridge.

8.— On the Castle Holm near Ewesfoot.

We have set forth these landmarks in detail because of their great importance to Langholm. It is a matter of history that attempts at encroachments upon the Common lands have been made from time to time, and we have known more than one effort being made to prevent the free quarrying and leading of stone from the Common Moss. The necessity, therefore, for recording and preserving the ancient beacons and landmarks must be obvious to every inhabitant of Langholm.

WILLIAM ARMSTRONG

III.— THE THISTLE. This is a picturesque accompaniment of the Common-Riding, whose origin and purpose are alike obscure. For many years the thistle was grown in the Townfoot garden at one time owned by William Irving. In later years it was grown by Thomas Bell. It has been carried in the Procession by the following:— Samuel McMillan, Robert Jardine, John Thompson, Andrew Irving, and William Thompson.

IV.— THE FLORAL CROWN. This is probably a comparatively recent addition, and can have no historic significance. It has been carried by the following:—John Thompson, J. Jardine, James Telford, George Armstrong, John Thompson and William Thomson.

Undoubtedly the most interesting feature of the Common-Riding is the Crying of the Fair. The Fair and the Riding of the Common have no necessary or historical connection, beyond the fact that the latter was celebrated on the day following the Summer Fair.

From what we have already said, it will be easily seen how the two events were brought together. According to the text of the Proclamation already quoted, the Fair was to be held "for the space o' aucht days", the words "and upwards" being added later. Naturally the season was made the occasion of a general holiday.

When, therefore, Bauldy Beattie, who had probably proclaimed the Fair, both on the Kilngreen and at the Cross, required to go with his companions to see if the Marches were clear, no date for the duty would be found more suitable than the slack day following the great day of the Fair.

Even then the Proclamation would be regarded as the quaint survival of a past century and it would be a natural proceeding to beguile the resting time at the Castle Craigs with a repetition of its well-known phrases.

The custom, once formed, would soon gather around it the additional literature with which we are now familiar. As the sentiment of the proceedings began to make its appeal to the people, they would be enjoined to take part in it as a public duty and so, gradually, the whole function would evolve into its present shape and the verses given below would become attached to the original text.

The Crying of the Fair falls naturally into three parts. The prologue calls upon the townsfolk to go out in defence of their rights; the central theme is the ancient Proclamation and the epilogue expresses the satisfaction which comes from a duty faithfully performed.

The local poets have employed their gifts to enhance the honour of the occasion and their parts, too, are couched in the language of the period, even as is the Proclamation itself.

Regret must be expressed that recent criers have taken considerable liberties with the texts, both of the Proclamation itself and of the introduction and conclusion.

The following versions used by old John Irving, who "cried the Fair" for 25 years, were nearest to the historic text, both in the Proclamation and the accompanying verses, and we therefore quote them as given by him:—

PROCLAMATION OF THE LANGHOLM FAIR AND COMMON-RIDING.

After demanding "Seelence", John Irving said:—

"Gentlemen, the first thing that I am gaun to acquaint you with are the names o' the Portioners* grounds of Langholm, from whence their services are from.

*Portioner is no doubt "apportioner" abbreviated. It related to the proprietor of small feus or "portions" of a landed property. The designation and its equivalent "proportioner" occur frequently in Registers and other documents for the 17th and 18th centuries, but now seldom used. Probably at that date the names were recited.

Now, gentlemen, we are gaun frae the Toun,
And first of a', the Kilngreen we gan' roun'
It is an ancient place where clay is got
And it belangs to us by Right and Lot;
And then from there the Lang-wood we gan' thro',
Whar evry ane, ay Brekans cut and pou
And last of a' we to the Moss do steer
to see gif a' oor Marches — they be clear;
And when unto the Castle Craigs we come,
A'll cry the Langholm Fair —
and then we'll beat the drum.

Now, gentlemen, after what you have heard this day concerning gannin' roun' oor Marches it is expeckit that every ane wha has occasion for peats, breckans, flacks, stanes, or clay will gan' oot this day in defence o' their properties, and they shall hear the Proclamation o' the Langholm Fair upon the Castle Craigs."

*   *   *   *   *   *   *   *   *   *

On the return from the Hill, John resumed:—

345

"Now, gentlemen, we hae gane roun' oor hill
Sae now A' think it's richt we had oor fill
O' guid strong punch — 'twull mak us a' tae sing
For this day we hae done a guid thing.
For gannin' roun' oor hill we think nae shame
Because frae it oor peats and flacks come hame.
Sae now A' wull conclud and saey nae mair,
But gif ye're pleased A'll cry the Langholm Fair.

"Hoys yes! That's ae time.
Hoys yes!! That's twae times.
Hoys yes!!! That's the third and last time.

THIS IS TAE GIE NOTICE

that there is a muckle Fair to be hadden i' the muckle Toun o' the Langholm on the 15th day o' July, auld style, upon His Grace the Duke of Buccleuch's Merk-land for the space o' aucht days and upwards, and ony hustrin, custrin, land-louper or dub-scouper or gae-by-the-gate swinger, wha come here to breed ony hurdum or durdum, huliments or bruliments, hagglements or bragglements or squablements, or to molest this public Fair shall be ta'en be order o' the Bailie and the Toun Council and his lugs be nailed to the Tron wi' a twalpenny nail, until he sit doon on his hob-shanks and pray nine times for the King and thrice for the muckle Laird o' Ralton, and pay a groat to me Jamie Ferguson, bailie o' the aforesaid Manor; — and A'll awa' hame and hae a barley bannock and a saut herring tae ma denner be way o' auld style."

It is not difficult to detect the interpolations in this text. For example, the insertion of the date, 15th July, and the mention of the Duke of Buccleuch's Merkland, show that when the Summer Fair became the principal one in Eskdale, the original Proclamation, quoted in a previous chapter, was adapted to the new circumstances by these and other insertions.

The mention of the date would not be necessary either in the original or the later texts. But owing to the change, in 1752, from the Julian to the Gregorian calendar with the subsequent loss of 11 days, it would become advisable to mention that the Summer Fair had been originally fixed for the 15th and not the 26th July. Hence the emphasis on the *auld style.*

The reference to the Duke's Merk-land is rather misleading. From time immemorial the Fair had been held on the Little Kilngreen which, as the evidence given in 1759 proved, had never belonged exclusively to the Duke, and certainly was not his original Merk-land, but had been held in common, and freely enjoyed by the inhabitants of Langholm.

It is, therefore, in every way probable that the Fairs held under the Nithsdale charter had been held on the Kilngreen, and though, naturally, the charters granted to the Duke and Duchess of Buccleuch provided that the Fairs would be held on their land, it was found more convenient to continue to hold them on the Kilngreen.

The mention of the Town Council too was probably introduced by some one who could not separate the idea of a bailie from that of a municipal body. Of course there was no Town Council in Langholm until 1893. John Irving himself introduced current hits into his Proclamation, as for instance, when he came to the words "twalpenny, nail" he always touched the nail by which the herring and bannock were fixed to the platter, and added, "o' Jock the nailer's ain hand-making".

Most of the observances in connection with the Common-Riding are maintained strictly according to precedent, and it is therefore the more to be deprecated that the old words of the Proclamation, some of the old Scots and others pure Border words, and the quaint language of the verses, should be smoothed out and Anglified. The Crier should be instructed to preserve the ancient text, and keep it free from his own personal preferences.

The following are the names of the Criers of the Fair as far as can now be ascertained:——
JAMIE FERGUSON.

ARCHIBALD BEATTIE. He cried the Fair for over 50 years. Died at No. 19 Kirkwynd. On his gravestone in Langholm Kirkyard there is the following inscription:—"Interred here, Archibald Beattie, town drummer, who for more than half a century kept up the ancient and annual custom of proclaiming the Langholm Fair at the Cross, when riding the Common granted to the town, and pointing out the various boundaries of those rights which descended from their ancestors to posterity. He died in 1823, aged 90 years. The Managers of the Common-Riding for the year 1829 have caused his name to be here inscribed, as a tribute of respect justly due to his memory."

General Sir Charles Pasley has commemorated Bauldy Beattie thus:—

"First Bauldy Beattie, glorious chief appears,
Who joins to youthful force the sense of years
Majestic! how he moves, born to command
Heather his brow adorns, a sword his hand.

While other men by fashion led astray,
Too blindly follow where she leads the way,
He, against all her gaudy tricks secure,
Preserves the manners of our fathers pure."

ARCHIBALD BEATTIE'S GRAVESTONE
Photograph by Alan J. Booth in 1993

PETER GRAHAM. More popularly known as Pete Wheep. Succeeded Bauldy Beattie as Town-Drummer.

"Now let us hear the Fair proclaimed
By Peter Wheep wi' cockit hat
He tells us that they're no ashamed
To show the country what they're at."

DAVID HOUNAM.

JOHN IRVING. Cried the Fair for 25 years.

ANDREW JOHNSTONE.

ROBERT NISBET.

JOHN WILSON. Died in 1907. Buried in Wauchope Kirkyard.

CHRISTOPHER ELLIOT

JOHN IRVING

It may interest our readers, who are not Eskdale people, to learn how the Common-Riding is celebrated. It is the time when the good old town is seen at its brightest and best.

Langholm people all over the world turn their thoughts homeward on the "15th day o' July, auld style", and all who are able endeavour to be in Langholm over the great event.

It is a season of family reunions, of cordial meetings between schoolfellows of long ago, who may not have met since they sat on the same form in the old school; a time moreover, when Langholm looks her bonniest and charms once again the hearts of all her children. The dawning of the Common-Riding is eagerly anticipated, and every item on the lengthy programme is enthusiastically observed.

The proceedings begin at 5.30 a.m. when the Flute Band and the Pipers perambulate the town, playing popular airs and quickly assembling a considerable crowd, who follow them to the Hillhead, on the northern spur of Whita, to witness the Hound Trail. This is a race between foxhounds specially trained, which since its commencement in 1845, has excited much interest along the Borders. After the race has been determined there is but time for breakfast, before the more important features of the day begin.

At 8.30 the Cornet musters his supporters, generally between 60 and 70 horsemen, at the Town Hall, where the town's standard is formally handed to him.

Headed by the Langholm Town Band a Procession is formed which proceeds up High Street, across the Langholm Bridge, round the old Pump in Buccleuch Square; then back to the Townfoot and thence again to the Market Place.

On the way the Band plays certain Scots airs *O' a' the Airts the Wind can Blaw, Thou Bonnie Wood of Craigie Lea, The Flowers of the Forest,* and others, and the townspeople would jealously resent even the slightest alteration in the programme.

The Procession has as yet only the Spade and the Bannock with it. On arrival at the Market Place, originally called the Cross, the first portion of the Fair is cried, demanding the attendance of the burgesses to keep the marches clear.

The Cornet then leads his men up the Kirkwynd and over the flank of the hill to the Castle Craigs on the Common Moss. Here the Fair is again cried, and refreshments, barley bannocks and salt herrings, moistened, perhaps, with some favourite beverage, are served.

The horsemen having reached the top of the hill ride round the Monument to Sir John Malcolm, one of Eskdale's most notable sons, which forms so conspicuous a landmark. A wonderful sight it is, to see the horsemen on the hill, and to watch the perilous descent straight down its steep and rocky face. On their arrival at Mount Hooley, the Cornet and his merry men are met by the Band, bringing with them the great Thistle and the Floral Crown, and also by some hundreds of children with heather besoms, the complement of the Spade, which, now is also bedecked with heather pulled from Whita side or the Common Moss.

The Procession again forms and marches to the Townhead, then returns to the Townfoot, the Band still playing the familiar Scottish airs. On arrival in the Market Place the Crier mounts a horse, and proclaims the second part of the Fair.

On its conclusion, three cheers are given; there is a moment's silence, then, very softly, the Band plays *Auld Lang Syne,* which the people join in singing, then in quickstep the Procession moves off, once more up the Kirkwynd, and along the old Drove Road to the Kilngreen, where the last sods are cut and Langholm's Rights are again preserved against all encroachments.

Then the sports begin. The first event is the Cornet's Chase. The Cornet, carrying the Flag, is given a fair start, and at a given signal his followers are away in pursuit, a lingering suggestion of the old days of Border raiding making this event a popular one.

The rest of the day is spent in horse-racing and other Border games of the past, wrestling, running, and leaping. Though these races date only from 1816, Langholm was a prominent centre of horse-racing in the old days of Border warfare. It was at a race meeting here that the plans for the release of Kinmont Willie were made by Buccleuch and his dauntless men in 1596.

Towards evening, when the sports are over and the sun is slowly sinking behind the hills in the west, the lads and lassies repair to the enclosure where the wrestling contests had been held earlier in the day, and dancing is kept up with great spirit and enjoyment until the darkness has settled down on hill and vale.

Then the Cornet lifts his flag, marshals his thinned forces around him, and leads the way back to the Town Hall, there to deliver up to the Acting Provost the standard he had received twelve hours before. Once more the Band plays *Auld Lang Syne,* at intervals dancing is indulged in, until at last darkness has fallen and the Common-Riding is over for another year.

PROCLAMATION OF THE FAIR, 1882

THE COMMON-RIDING — AN IMPRESSION.

Long, long years have passed; many a flood has swept beneath Langholm Brig; many a time the heather has bloomed at the Round House since we saw the Common-Riding. But, like all Langholm folk, we return some golden Summer Fair night and await the morrow with mingled feelings, memories which are sensitive, which fill us with the old hope of boyhood; anticipations of the Day; wonder as to whom we shall see; the Common-Riding airs meanwhile humming themselves in our soul.

What a morning! Warbla top is clear, and on the Peat Road the lark already is a sightless song. A lovely freshness breathes from the cool hills, and in the Stubholm wood a heavy dew lies on the grass. Out by Scotts Knowe, there is a sound of the mower, some one hastening to get his work done early, against the crying of the Fair.

How charming is The Langholm on a Common-Riding morning! Soon the glory of the heather over at the Castle Craigs will be dimmed. Soon the bracken on Warbla will be brown, and the great beech trees by Glenfirra will be shaking off their withered leaves. Soon all the visitors will have gone and the rainy days have come when Langholm will be very quiet. But to-day is the Common-Riding Day, the most joyous of all the year.

Ah! there is the sound of fife and drum, the Common-Riding has commenced! Musical critics may find defects in this introduction of the Day. They may refer to lack of balance, or to a preponderance of the drum, but we have heart for no such cynicism. There is not in all the wide world anything *quite* the same to one who was once a boy in Langholm, as the strains of the Flute Band on the Common-Riding morning.

Changes must have come, we suppose, but the players look to be just the same men we saw so many long years ago . . . . We follow them to the Dog Trail. We do not now care which dog wins the race: yet thirty years ago it was a matter of life and death to us, we felt that if Rattler did not win, all the joy of life would be clouded over. But since then genuine Care has placed the Trail and Rattler in their rightful perspective.

Now we are in the old Market Place. What a crowd! How many kent faces! There is auld John Ir'in selling Proclamations — here is Willie

Dick. We were never in the habit of shaking hands with Willie, but we do so to-day — it is the Common-Riding, and he is a man of tremendous importance this forenoon. What would have happened, we wonder, had some irreverent youth sought to carry that spade?

We still secretly hope Willie will dash through Ewes as he did so long ago, but listen, the Langholm Band is coming. It is playing *Craigie Lea*, and we silently fall in and follow them round the Pump in the Square. On the Brig the air is changed to *O' a' the Airts*.

Lads and lassies, now laughing and blithesome because it is the Common-Riding Day, who have not yet built up memories are, unknown to themselves, absorbing food for wonderful thoughts in days to come, when they will have gone far beyond those heathery hills, when, in some big town, or on some distant shore, there will surge in their hearts that overwhelming longing for their "ain fouk" which ought to come to every one of us.

We have all felt it, and when we return home and miss the old faces . . . . Yes, this thought has been induced by the change made by the Band. They are now playing *The Flowers of the Forest Are A' Wede Awae*, and in the panorama of the years we see many dear familiar faces, now cauld in the clay, who on a far-off Summer's morning heard the Fair cried at the Cross.

There! the Cornet and his men are off to the Hill, and as the Flag flutters up the old Kirkwynd with the horsemen following, our pulses are stirred by yet another emotion, are not these men Armstrongs, Elliots, Beatties, Irvings, Littles, and Scotts? and thus, surely, it must have been that the clans ran their horse on the Langholm Holm as they spurred their way to Carlenrig, and thus that they cantered to Carlisle Castle to the release of Kinmont Willie.

See! John Ir'in is mounting the grey horse now, and we note with a pang how frail he is growing. The Market Place is crowded: Langholm as it is and Langholm as it was meet today and tell their separate stories. Old schoolfellows, who shared the toffee and the tawse with us, whom we have not seen for many years, are in the throng.

There is Sandie Dodd, we have not seen him since his campaign in Afghanistan. He was with Roberts in the glorious march to Kandahar. Now he is marching after the Langholm Band, with a brighter eye than he had on that famous march. Years ago we walked near him in the Procession. We bought our canes at the same time at Jamie Edinbro's, for our local prejudice was so strong even then that we gave preferential treatment to Jamie over Benson, who came from the English side.

Now we watch the bairns waving their besoms, but surely at those far-off Common-Ridings the heather was in fuller bloom than it is to-day! There were no new threepenny pieces for the boys then. What a godsend one would have been! Fancy one's savings suddenly rising from fourpence to seven pence! Once, by rigid self-denial on many a Saturday, we saved ninepence in coppers, but, alas! ere yet the Cornet's Chase was run we had lost a penny of it in a reckless gamble at the coconut stall!

We smile at the bairns now. We are at the top of the Brae of Life and are looking back while they, God bless them, are just beginning the climb. They wave their heather besoms in a sheer ecstasy of delight, for it is the Common-Riding Day.

But John demands "seelence", and we wish not to lose one word of his old Scots tongue, so pure, so unaffected, so absolutely lacking in nippy English words. He cries the Fair as ably as he did it 20 years ago. John is the personification of the Common-Riding. Take away him and Willie Dick, and perhaps Sam McMillan, and where would the Common-Riding be?

John's work is over. A strange quiet falls upon the holiday crowd; it lasts but a moment; from the bottom of the Kirkwynd the Band plays, low and slow, the old, old air, *Auld Lang Syne,* and we remember childhood, boyhood, the long summer days, the old home and the kindly eyes, the whitewashed cottages, the mint and southern-wood of the Sabbath morning, the Kirk bell, the dreams of youth, of love and friendship, of wealth and fame, high hopes and merry boyish hearts, and the Band is well into the Drove Road ere we awake from our reverie.

We see the sod turned at the Bar, see Willie Dick go through Ewes, as he did many years ago, see the Cornet's Chase, indulge in brandy-snaps and coolers, and sandwiches and mustard in the wrestling ring. We cannot now risk the toffee on the stands, but we visit them for auld lang syne and buy fairings for the bairns, nuts and jumping-jacks and sweeties.

All the slumbrous afternoon we wander about the Castle Holm, meeting old friends, admiring the beautiful scene, breathing deeply of the Eskdale air, so caller (fresh) and purer than that of the stifling town. But slowly the darkness falls. Clouds of crimson and gold have been spread over the top of the Timpen all the time of the dancing, but now the colours have changed to grey and blue.

The Cornet brings up his horse, again gathers his men about him, now a straggling and thinner array, and they march slowly townward, as one can fancy the few dalesmen returning to the Forests on the night that followed Flodden. The only air now played is *Auld Lang Syne,* it is the evening tune. *O' a' the Airts* is for the morning. Another memory has been added to the Past, and it will make the recollections of long-gone years sharper and more vivid still.

There is the new moon on Warbla, hanging lazily over the Resting Knowe, where, oft and oft, on similar nights it has been seen by our hallowed Dead, who, unconscious of this being the Common-Riding Day, sleep amid the shadows in Wauchope, and hear not the hoolet cry from the darkening beech gently moving in the night wind.

CHAPTER 28

RELICS OF THE PAST

Throughout the preceding pages we have mentioned and described discoveries of ancient relics in Eskdale. Others remain to be recorded which are not readily separated into the periods we had under review.

KILN AT WESTWATER

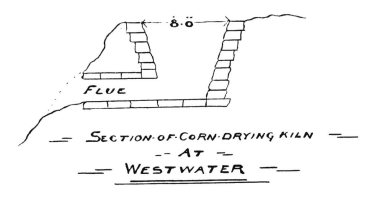

The accompanying drawing is of an old corn-drying kiln at Westwater. Concerning its date, we are unable to give any information. Such kilns were in use up to the beginning of the 19th century, but are obviously of a much earlier date. This one is situated in the plantation about 200 yards from Westwater House on the east side of the burn and, like others of the same description, at the top of a steep slope. Two Kilns were to be found on St. Bride's Hill, close to the continuation of the old Roman road from Calfield to Burnswark, where Mr. J.M. Elliot of Westwater also found a small Roman coin. A similar corn-kiln was situated further up the Logan Burn and another in Wauchope nearly opposite the footbridge at the Earshaw.

When in use, the kiln had, placed across the top, rafters covered with drawn straw on which the corn was spread out. Any grain falling through would be gathered from the bottom of the kiln when the drying was complete. The structure was enclosed, and covered with a conical thatched roof and chimney to cause a current of warm air to pass through the corn, peat or wood being used for fuel. Malt was also dried in these kilns, and the fuel gave to the spirit that original characteristic known as the peat or birch flavour.

THE GIANT'S GRAVE

This is the title given to an excavation found on the south side of Upper Dumfedling Hill. It is in the form of an ordinary coffin, measuring in length eight feet nine inches and in breadth three feet. In his MS. Diary Dr. Brown mentions that about 20 years before the date of his writing the grave was about 20 feet in depth, but it had since been filled up by the farmer to prevent the sheep from falling into it. What the excavation can have been has never been determined.

THE WESTSIDE STONES

At the hamlet of Berrycar in the parish of Dryfe there is an inscribed stone on one of the cottage doors. It bears a shield carved with the royal arms of Scotland, on one side of which there are a St. Andrew's cross and a holly leaf, and on the other side the letters "A.b.". This stone was brought from Tanlawhill, where tradition says there was a hunting lodge. Moll's map, published in 1745, shows a tower at Tanlawhill, but Dr. Brown says the stones were dug up on the farm of Westside by a cottar named Adam Marchbank, who found them whilst working in his garden.

The stone bore evidence of having been once built with lime into a wall, but the building at Westside has long since been entirely demolished. The suggestion that the building was used by some of the kings of Scotland, who, as we have seen, retained Eskdalemuir as a royal hunting ground, is not an unlikely one.

CARLESGILL URN

In 1860 a cist was found on the farm of Carlesgill. It was constructed of the rough undressed stone of the district. No skeleton was found in the cist but evidence existed that there had been an interment. On the floor were found powdery remains and fragments, possibly the dust of bones which had been wasted by the percolation of water into the cist. Lying on its side was an urn which contained nothing, but had probably been deposited for use as a food vessel with the body there interred. There is not sufficient data to warrant any opinion concerning the age of the cist.

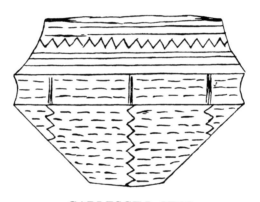

CARLESGILL URN

The urn is of the usual type found in cists of the neolithic and early bronze age. It is made of local clay, and the ornamentation is of the zigzag pattern, running round the widest part of the urn, and also lengthwise, dividing the surface into panels. The urn was in possession of the family of the late Mr. J. C. Little of Burnfoot, Ewes, tenant in Carlesgill at the time of the discovery.

LONGWOOD BRASS POT

Found at Longwood in 1862 and declared treasure-trove. It measures 13½ by 11 inches, and was deposited in the National Museum of Antiquities, Edinburgh but is now in The Museum of Scotland.

ARKLETON BRASS POT

Found by a shepherd at Lady Boodle's Cave on Arkleton Crags. It was kept for some time by the shepherd but was ultimately broken up for toe-plates.

COINS AT ARKLETON

In 1886 a considerable number of silver coins was found near Arkleton by a workman named William Jackson. Most of the coins were sent to the Museum in Edinburgh.

They were of the reign of Alexander III. and Edward I It has been suggested that they were dropped or deposited by some of the English army fleeing from Bannockburn.

SANDSTONE BASIN

A basin formed out of a block of red sandstone, found at Canonby in 1863, and presented to the National Museum of Antiquities, Edinburgh, by George Maxwell, Esq., of Broomholm. Now in The Museum of Scotland. On one side of the basin are the letters "T. A"., a tankard and drinking cup, a rose, part of an ornament, and the date 1660.

QUERN STONES

These were also found in Canonby in 1863 and given to the Museum by Mr. Maxwell. They consist of the upper and lower stones of quartz, about 20 inches in diameter, with three small sockets for handle.

Another quern, a bottom stone, was found by Mr. Andrew Aitchison in the bed of Irvine Burn in the year 1911. Curiously enough, it corresponds to an upper stone, which for many years has lain at the gable of Old Irvine farm house.

BRONZE AXE

A flanged axe of yellow bronze $4^{5/8}$ by $2^{1/8}$ inches in width, with semi-circular cutting edge; butt imperfect. Found in Canonby in 1885 and presented to the Museum by W. Scott Elliot, Esq.

RELICS OF THE PAST

SWORD

A sword was found in Tarras, possibly a relic of the old moss-trooping days. It was at one time in the possession of Mr. Peter Martin, Langholm.

DAGGER

A dagger, at one time in the possession of Mr. George Martin, Langholm, was found in the moss at Old Irvine.

URN

An urn found at Orchard, Canonby was in possession of the late Dr. Carlyle who died in 1894.

RAPIER

Whilst the property of Mr. Matthew Knox, in Caroline Street, was being rebuilt some years ago, an old rapier was dug up. It passed into the hands of Mr. Clement Armstrong, who presented it to the Museum of the Hawick Archaeological Society.

COINS AT CASTLE O'ER

Some years ago, whilst examining the hill fort at Castle O'er, the late Mr. Richard Bell found a coin of the reign of Charles II., dated 1672. It would be interesting to know how it came to be there. Was it dropped by one of the troopers who were in Eskdale after the Restoration, harrying the Covenanters?

COIN AT OLD IRVINE

Near the site of the old village of Cauldtown, Mr. Andrew Aitchison, in 1881, found two coins.

SILVER COIN

On 18th October, 1910, a silver coin, dated 1584, was found on the bank of the Capel Burn, near Capelfoot. It was in the possession of A. Hay Borthwick, Esq., of Billholm.

CHAPTER 29

SOME ESKDALE MEN

The biographies of Eskdale men whose life-story is worth preserving would require an entire volume. All that is possible in the space available here is to present a brief outline of the lives of a few of those whom Eskdale is proud to acclaim as her sons.

The name PAISLEY or PASLEY was well known in Eskdale in the 18th century through James Paisley of Craig who married Magdalen Elliot on 21st June, 1726. Their descendants distinguished themselves in public service and became famous and revered throughout Eskdale as *The Seven Knights of Eskdale*.

In 1329, this ancient family held the lands of Passelot, sometimes Passele or Passelees, in the Barony of Hawick under charter of Robert Bruce King of Scots. A tower was built, its date unknown, but it is recorded that in 1495 the brother of the Laird of Quithope was accused of stealing *iron yets, doors and cruiks from the Tower of How-paslot*.

The Paisley Family had its origins in Lochwinnock moving ultimately to the lands and Barony of Paisley and the great Abbey which bore its name in Renfrewshire. At the end of the 12th century a William Passlew appears on charters as a witness, and from him descends the chiefly line of Westerlea, currently represented by the 5th Laird and 16th Head of Family, Duncan W. Paisley of Westerlea, to whom we are indebted for so much new information.

Those Paisleys mentioned in Eskdale Parish Records who are identified with the family of Paisley of Craig, descend probably from John Paisley the elder, in Langholm, circa 1599-1672. His son James Paisley, younger, merchant in Langholm, married Helen Macvitie. They are the parents of James Paisley of Craig and Robert Paisley (page 261).

SOME ESKDALE MEN

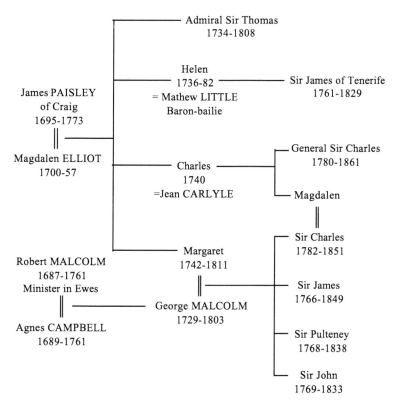

THE SEVEN KNIGHTS OF ESKDALE

ADMIRAL SIR THOMAS PASLEY

Thomas Paisley, (later Pasley), fifth son of James Paisley of Craig and Magdalen Elliot, was born in 1734 at Burn in Westerkirk. He entered the Navy and gradually rose in the service until he attained the rank of Rear-Admiral of the Red. In this position he was on the *Bellerophon* and fought, under the command of Admiral Howe, off Ushant, on the *Glorious First of June* 1794. In this action he had one of his legs shot off and also lost an eye. As a token of respect to Viscount Nelson, who lost an eye in the same year, he dropped the "I" and became Pasley.[1] Many of his descendants adopted this form of spelling.

For his "distinguished share . . . . in the glorious operations" he was created a baronet of Great Britain, received a pension of £1,000 a year, and was given the post of Commander-in-Chief at Plymouth.

His daughter Maria, who kept house for him and also wrote his biography, showed on one occasion that she had sailor's blood in her veins. One day she was out in her father's cutter, and, running outside the Eddystone, was seen and chased by a French cruiser. Instead of at once seeking safety the young lady made a fight, and kept firing at the Frenchman with the cutter's two brass guns, until a frigate was sent out to her assistance. Maria married Major John Sabine, and their son Thomas succeeded to the baronetcy.

GILBERT PAISLEY

He was the fourth son of James Paisley of Craig and Magdalen Elliot. Subsequently the spelling of his name became Pasley. His descendants, now living in New Zealand, are the senior representatives of line of Craig.[1] Gilbert was Assistant-Surgeon with the Army in Madras in 1756 but took a civilian post as Surgeon with the East India Company. He was later promoted Surgeon-General. He died in his forty-eighth year.

GENERAL SIR CHARLES W. PASLEY

He was born in Eskdalemuir on 8th September, 1780, the son of Charles Paisley, merchant in London and seventh son of James Paisley of Craig.[1] His mother was Jean (or Jane) Carlyle. In his early years his nurse was Elizabeth Little, daughter of Simon Little in Terrona and wife of Walter Hyslop in Old Irving. This information is contained in a letter dated October 1824, still extant, which Charles wrote to Elizabeth's daughter-in-law, Agnes Hyslop.

Educated first at the school of Miss Chattie Smith in Langholm and afterwards at the parish school, where John Telfer was the schoolmaster. Here, and afterwards at the school of Dr. Little in New-Langholm, Charles Paisley had as schoolfellow and friend David Irving, to whose well known book, *The History of Scottish Poetry*, he afterwards wrote the preface. At this time he boarded with Miss Easton, the postmistress of Langholm, to whose memory, as well as to that of Miss

Chattie Smith, he erected a tombstone in Langholm kirkyard. Charles Pasley afterwards went to a school in Selkirk where his cousins, James, Pulteney, John and Charles Malcolm, and James Little had also been educated.

In 1796 he entered the Royal Academy at Woolwich and, in 1797, received his commission in the royal artillery. In 1798 he transferred to the royal engineers.

Young Pasley saw considerable foreign service and his aptitude for acquiring languages, trained no doubt under Dr. Little, obtained for him rapid promotion. He was attached to the staff of Sir John Moore during the Peninsular campaign. At the battle of Coruña when Sir John was fatally wounded it was Pasley who carried him off the field and was at the burial that night. Sir John Moore was a cousin of the Paisleys of Westerlea[1] As Captain in the Marquis of Huntly's division Charles took part in the Walcheren Expedition, in which he rendered conspicuous service, and was wounded.

He was appointed director of military engineering instruction at Chatham and remained there for nearly thirty years. In 1834, almost 150 years ahead of his time, he completed a volume on the expediency and practicability of simplifying weights, measures and money and advocated the adoption of decimalisation. He was a prolific writer on military subjects and the training of engineers and was the pioneer of electronic detonation.[1] The duty of blowing up the *Royal George* fell to him, some of the timber of which he sent to Mr. Irving, the builder at Kilncleuch, who made some articles of furniture from it.

In 1841 he was promoted Major-General when he was appointed inspector-general of the railways. He was also an examiner at the East India Company's military school. In 1846 he received his K.C.B. and in 1851 he was made Lieut.-General and two years later Colonel Commander of the Royal Engineers. In 1860 he became General in the army.[2] He died in April 1861 and is buried in Kensal Green cemetery in a special section for engineers.[1]

LIEUTENANT COLONEL SIR JAMES MALCOLM

James Malcolm, the second son in a family of ten sons and seven daughters, was born on 23rd January, 1767. His parents were Margaret, or Bonnie Peggy, Paisley of Craig and George Malcolm, son of Robert

Malcolm, minister of Ewes. He and three of his brothers each received the honour of knighthood, probably a unique circumstance in any family.

He entered the Marines in which he served for 48 years. He saw active service first in Spain and later in America in the War of 1812. In August 1814 he was with the British force which landed in Chesapeake Bay.[1] They reached the Federal capital of Washington on the 24th and burnt The White House and the Capitol in reprisal for the conduct of American militiamen in Canada.[2]   (The House was painted white to cover up the scorch marks.)   For his services in these campaigns he received his knighthood. On retirement he came to live at Milnholm in Eskdale. He died on 27th December 1849, aged 82.

SIR PULTENEY MALCOLM

Pulteney, born in 1768, was the third son of George Malcolm. Entering the Navy at an early age he joined the war ship, *Sybil*, under his uncle, Admiral Sir Thomas Pasley.

He took part in the French wars and acquitted himself with great distinction. After a period of much active service, which brought him quick advancement, he was appointed to the *Donegal.* By a very short time he missed being engaged with his ship in the Battle of Trafalgar, arriving, to his intense chagrin, just too late. His ill-luck was deplored by every one of his brother officers, and Admiral Collingwood voiced this feeling in a letter to Captain Malcolm's uncle, Sir Thomas Pasley.

For his services in the battle of San Domingo, in which his brother James was also engaged, he received a gold medal and the thanks of both Houses of Parliament. In 1813 he was made Rear-Admiral. He was engaged in the American War of 1812 and in 1815 in co-operating with Wellington.

After the battle of Waterloo, Sir Pulteney, as he now was, was entrusted with the conveyance to St. Helena of the defeated Emperor Napoleon and was commended by Napoleon for his chivalrous conduct towards his former foe. He died in 1838 and was buried in the Church of St. Mary-le-Bone in London.

The statue to Sir Pulteney was, in 1842, erected in the Market Place of Langholm on the site of the old Mercat Cross. The foundation stone was laid, with masonic honours, on 20th August, 1841 by His Grace the Duke of Buccleuch, under the direction of Mr. John Babington

SIR PULTENEY MALCOLM

This portrait, in the Town Hall of Langholm, is incorrectly labelled as Sir John Malcolm and as such was printed in the original edition. The error was pointed out to Robert Hyslop in a letter from Colonel Leckie, a descendant of the Malcolm's of Burnfoot. This was confirmed by Mr. George Irving historian in Langholm.

Past Grand Master of Dumfriesshire. The sculptor of the statue was Mr. David Dunbar. In 1886 the statue was removed to within the grounds of Langholm Library where it still stands.

Sir Pulteney's residence was at Irvine House, which, prior to and during his occupancy, was called Peel Holm after the Border peel-tower of Stakeheuch, which stood on the eminence overlooking the mansion.

Sir Pulteney's son, William Elphinstone Malcolm Esq. of Burnfoot, was for very many years one of the most beloved and reverenced residents in Eskdale. In religious and philanthropic work of all kinds he took a foremost part. At his own expense he built the Temperance Halls and Reading Rooms for the benefit of the working men of Langholm to whom he delegated their management.

As Lieut.-Colonel of the Dumfriesshire Volunteers he manifested the keenest interest in the movement and raised the Langholm corps to a high standard of efficiency. On Saturday 28th December 1908 Mr. Malcolm was presented with his portrait in oil, painted by Mr. Alex. Roche, R.S.A., and subscribed for by 700 admirers throughout Eskdale and the Borders. On the following Monday he was found dead in bed, having quietly passed away in his sleep, at the advanced age of 90.

SIR JOHN MALCOLM.

The most distinguished of the sons of George Malcolm and the most eminent native of Eskdale was John, fourth son, who was born 2nd May 1769, the day after the birth of Wellington and the birth-year of the first Napoleon. In his boyhood John Malcolm showed no special aptitude auguring his brilliant career as scholar, soldier, and diplomatist, excepting a love of boyish mischief, which caused his schoolmaster to say, when any pranks were played: "Jock's at the bottom o't".

Whilst yet a mere child he was sent to London. It is said, with what truth we know not, that the last words of advice given him by his old nurse were: "Now Jock, my man, be sure when ye're awa' to kaim yer head, (comb your hair), and keep ye're face clean!" To which the the future Knight replied, "Tut, woman, ye're aye sae fear't. Ye'll see if I were away amang strangers I'll do weel eneuch!

Young John Malcolm entered the service of the East India Company at the age of 13. Later he was appointed a Cadet in Madras, and saw active service against Tipu Sahib, Sultan of Mysore. In 1798 he was made, by Lord Wellesley, assistant to the Resident at Hyderabad. There he obtained great praise for his resource and coolness in the suppression of a mutiny. Shortly afterwards he was sent on an important mission to Persia, where he was sent a second time after he had filled the office of secretary to the Governor-General, and later he was made Minister-Plenipotentiary to that country.

In 1815 he was made K.C.B., as his brothers James and Pulteney had been before him. On returning from India, in 1817, he received the thanks of Parliament for his distinguished services. He was also given the rank of Major-General, and a pension of £1,000 a year from the East India Company. Sir John was appointed Governor of Bombay in 1827, but soon resigned the position. Returning to Britain he became M.P. for Launceston and vigorously opposed the Reform Bill of 1832.

SIR JOHN MALCOLM

We are indebted to Mr. George Irving for a copy of this portrait which is in the Town Hall of Langholm but at present it is un-named.

Not only was Sir John Malcolm a brave and distinguished soldier, but had several literary achievements. His *History of Persia*, published in 1815, is perhaps his most notable literary achievement, but, in addition, he wrote a *Sketch of the Political History of India*, *Sketches of the Sikhs*, and a *Life of Lord Clive* — the last, published after his death in 1833, was made the basis of Macaulay's famous Essay on Clive.

Monuments to the memory of Sir John were erected at Bombay, in Westminster Abbey and on Whita Hill. The foundation-stone was laid by Sir James Graham on the 16th September 1835. It is a plain obelisk, built of the freestone of Whita Hill. Its height is 100 feet, and standing on the lofty hill it can be seen from a distance of thirty miles. He who knows not Langholm Monument knows not the western Borderland.

John Hyslop, in his remininscences describes the building of the Monument as follows:—

369

THE MONUMENT TO SIR JOHN MALCOLM

"The building of the Monument formed one of the landmarks of my boyhood, even as itself is to-day a land-mark along the Borders. I was present at the laying of the foundation stone by Sir James Graham of Netherby, and also when the work was completed. For a short time my father and, I believe, some of my uncles and great-uncles (for most of them Hyslops and Hotsons alike were builders) helped in its erection. Very naturally, therefore, it formed the subject of many an interesting talk at our fireside. The building was begun in 1835 and completed within a year.

Designed by Robert Howe, the Monument was built entirely by local men. Naturally, there were very serious difficulties to be faced in the erection, but they were all successfully overcome by the practical genius of Mr. Thomas Slack, who, in recognition of his achievement, received a gold medal from a Society in London. Mr. Slack was a man of remarkable genius, amongst other important inventions of his being that of the skew-bridge.

The first course of the building is 17 feet 6 inches high and is solid. Then it is built in walls of four feet in thickness, until it reaches the moulding 20 feet higher. The space then left inside for the workman is three and a half feet. Here the thickness of the walls is three feet, which is gradually reduced two. At a distance of seven feet from the apex the solid building is resumed. The monument was built to a height of 93 feet without any outside scaffolding.

The appliance used for lifting the heavy stones into position consisted of a pole, about 40 feet in length, from the top of which extended two arms with pulleys, with a travelling contrivance along the beam. The pole revolved on ball bearings in a large iron collar. It was supported on blocks of stone projecting from the side of the wall. As the obelisk lengthened the pole was raised by an ingenious device worked by a winch on the ground. The outside scaffolding at the top of the column, after the pole was dispensed with, was in two sections held together by four iron bolts, two of them screws and nuts, the other two being cotterils, a wedge in the slit of a bolt.

I remember that when the top stone was laid into its bed some of the spectators raised a cheer. I was beside Mr. Slack at the moment and heard him sternly rebuke the onlookers, saying there must be no cheering until the workman was safely down. The last man to come down was Mr. Slack's assistant, John Clark, to whom a share of the credit is due. He descended safely in the bucket, and then came the task of bringing down the scaffolding without injuring any one or damaging the Monument.

Here again Mr. Slack's ingenuity overcame the difficulty. A rope was attached to each of the cotterils and by it they were pulled out. Ropes were fastened to each of the two sections of the scaffolding, and when the bolt was drawn the men in charge of the ropes ran outward. Down came the scaffolding with a crash, no one was hurt, and not a chip was made in the Monument. The work was successfully accomplished, begun, executed and completed by Langholm men. Then there arose a cheer which resounded across Tarras Moss and penetrated into Ewesdale, Eskdale, and Wauchopedale. I have always felt gratified that I was present on an occasion so memorable and historic."

SIR CHARLES MALCOLM

He was the tenth and youngest son of George Malcolm. Born in 1782, he entered the Naval Service at the age of fifteen. He served under his brother Sir Pulteney in the *Fox* and was afterwards promoted to the command of the *Narcissus*, 32 guns. During this and subsequent commands in actions in the West Indies and other waters he took no fewer than 20 Spanish privateers, carrying 168 guns and 1,059 men, and also captured many merchantmen.

After the Napoleonic Wars were over Malcolm was given the command of the Royal yacht in attendance on Lord Wellesley, Lord-Lieutenant of Ireland, from whom he received the honour of knighthood. In 1837 he was made Rear-Admiral, and 10 years later Vice-Admiral. The first wife of Admiral Malcolm was his cousin Magdalen Paisley. He died at Brighton in 1851, aged 69.

SIR JAMES LITTLE OF TENERIFE

He was the son of Matthew Little, baron-bailie of Langholm, and Helen Paisley, daughter of James Paisley of Craig. Sir James was therefore a cousin of the Malcolms and of Sir Charles Pasley. He was a wine merchant in Tenerife and, for his outstanding services rendered during a yellow fever epidemic, he was made a Knight of the Most Illustrious Spanish Order of Charles the Third, Sacred to Virtue and Merit. As he could not use this title in Britain some of his friends prevailed upon King George III to award him a British Knighthood. He was born in 1761 and died in 1829 at Shabden Park, Surrey.

WILLIAM JULIUS MICKLE

He was born 28th September 1735, in the manse at Wauchope Waas the third son of the Rev. Alexander Meikle, A.M., minister at Langholm. His mother was Julia Henderson, of Ploughlands in the parish of Dalmeny, a cousin of Sir James Johnstone of Westerhall. Educated first at Langholm parish school and then at the High School of Edinburgh. At the early age of 13 he read Spenser's *Faërie Queene,* and formed the ambition to emulate the achievements of its author.

For no obvious reason he changed the spelling of his name from Meikle to Mickle. Having obtained a post as corrector for the Clarendon Press at Oxford, he cultivated his literary tastes, and zealously contributed to periodical publications.

From stray contributions of verse he proceeded to more exacting work, and in 1762 published his poem *Providence,* which brought him under the notice of Lord Lyttleton. Other poetic pieces followed: *Pallio* in 1764, *The Concubine* in 1767, *Voltaire in the Shades* and *Mary, Queen of Scots* in 1770.

In 1775 Mickle published his great translation of *The Lusiad* of Camoëns, the Portuguese national poet, and it is principally upon this work that his reputation as a poet rests. It not only placed him amongst the best British poets but created much enthusiasm in Portugal. When later he visited Lisbon he was received with the greatest cordiality and admitted a member of the Royal Academy of Portugal. Whilst in Lisbon he wrote his poem *Armada Hill*.

His ballad *Cumnor Hall*, which was originally published in Evans's *Collection of Old Ballads*, is admitted by Sir Walter Scott to have suggested to him the groundwork for *Kenilworth*; indeed, Sir Walter originally intended to name his romance after Mickle's poem, but was dissuaded by his publishers.

Perhaps the best known amongst Mickle's shorter pieces is the song, *There's nae Luck aboot the Hoose*. Some controversy arose concerning its authorship, a claim being put forward on behalf of Jean Adams, one of the minor writers of Scottish verse, but the weight of evidence is on the side of Mickle. Sir George Douglas, perhaps the greatest authority on Border literature, strongly favoured Mickle's authorship, as also does Palgrave in his *Golden Treasury*.

The poet died in 1788 and was buried at Forest Hill near Oxford. A M*emoir* of the poet by the Rev. John Sim was published in 1806.

In April 1925 the Townhead Literary Society erected, on the front of the Town Hall, a memorial plaque which was unveiled by the above Sir George Douglas. The London Eskdale Society gave the drinking fountain at the Town Hall in his memory.

COLONEL JOSIAH STEWART, C.B.

He was the son of John Stewart of Langholm. His mother was a descendant of the Scotts of Davington and Thirlestane. He was educated at the school of Dr. Little in New-Langholm, two of his school-fellows being Sir Charles Pasley and Dr. David Irving. Sir Charles mentions, in his preface to Dr. Irving's work on the *History of Scottish Poetry*, that Stewart was one of the boys whom Irving drilled on the Kilngreen to meet their sworn trans-Esk enemies, the Meikleholmers. After a period

373

at Kelso, Stewart entered the University of Edinburgh where he graduated M.A.

He became a Cadet of the East India Company and saw active service in the Persian Gulf, where he lost his right arm and was in other ways severely wounded. When Sir John Malcolm went to Persia Stewart accompanied him as first Assistant. Later, he held the position of Political Resident at the Courts of Jeypore, Gwalior, and Hyderabad, and on several occasions received honourable mention from the governing authorities of India. He returned to Britain in 1838 and died at Cheltenham in 1839.

DAVID IRVING, LL.D.

David was the fourth son of Janetus Irving who, in 1768, had started a bakery business at the Townhead, Langholm. David was born 5th. December, 1778 in the house, then just a thatched cottage, adjoining the land on which, a few years later, the Secession Meeting House was built and where the Erskine Church still stands. The cottage was rebuilt in 1816 by David's older brother, John.

David Irving, who became probably the most learned man whom Eskdale has ever sent forth, received his early education in the school of John Telfer and afterwards in that of Dr. Little.

In 1796 he went from Langholm to Edinburgh, where he attended the University classes. He took up literary work and began to produce the notable books associated with his name.

The following list will convey some idea of the versatility of Irving's genius: *Ferguson's Life, Lives of Scottish Poets*, *Elements of English Composition*, which became a text-book in many schools. In 1805 he produced his greatest work the *Life and Writings of George Buchanan*.

In 1808 he received from Marischal College, Aberdeen, the degree of LL.D. He was elected in 1820 to the position of Librarian to the Advocates' Library in Edinburgh, which he held until 1849. During his occupancy of this eminent position he edited various works for the Maitland and Bannatyne Clubs and contributed several articles to the seventh edition of the *Encyclopaedia Britannica*.

Dr. Irving died in 1862 in his 82nd year. He was twice married, first to Annie, daughter of Dr. Anderson, Edinburgh, and secondly to

Janet, daughter of Mr. Charles Laing of Canonby. He was a man of great learning, his knowledge of ancient and modern literature being profound and extensive.

THOMAS TELFORD

The father of Thomas Telford was a shepherd on the farm of Glendinning in Westerkirk on the Westerhall estate. The humble cottage in which he lived was of the class known in the pastoral districts of the south of Scotland as *shielings*, from the Norse *skali*, a shepherd's hut. Here in this lonely spot, where once the Kings of Scotland hunted, was born one of the greatest engineers our country has produced — born in this cottage in August 1757, but buried in Westminster Abbey.

His father died within a few months of his birth leaving his widow to face a bitter struggle. Mother and son removed to the Crooks, where she took a cottage and set herself to train the lad. His early years were spent herding sheep amongst the hills of Eskdale, on the land of Overcraig owned by the Laird of Craig, and attending the parish school of Westerkirk. Miss Elizabeth Paisley took a keen interest in his education and it was she who gave him his first book on bridge building.

Telford was apprenticed to a mason in Lochmaben, on whose death he came to Langholm and finished his apprenticeship with Andrew Thomson, himself a native of Westerkirk. At that time the Duke of Buccleuch, known as *Good Duke Henry*, was engaged in the building of the New-Town of Langholm.

In the work of building the cottages Telford took a share, and possibly it was at this time that he worked the sundial, of which a print is here given. Telford worked the dial only, the fluted pedestal being of recent date, and wrought by the late Andrew Park. It is one of the few genuine pieces of Telford's handicraft extant in Langholm, and was in the garden of Mr. William Park, Buccleuch Square, in the possession of whose family it remained for very many years. Its whereabouts now is unknown.

Two other authentic examples of Telford's workmanship can be seen. One is the Doorway, now appropriately erected within the grounds of Langholm Library which Telford's liberality helped to endow. This Doorway was probably that of the old Kings Arms Inn, shown on the right of the print of Langholm Market Place on page 242.

THOMAS TELFORD

The other is the carved wall headstone for James Paisley of Craig in the kirkyard at Westerkirk. Telford did this in 1780 at the request of Charles Paisley, son of James.[1]

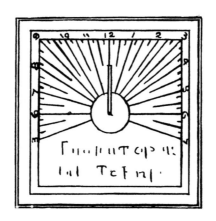

TELFORD'S SUNDIAL

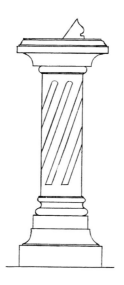

ANDREW PARK'S PEDESTAL

DOORWAY WORKED BY THOMAS TELFORD

377

As already mentioned, when Langholm Bridge was being built by Robin Hotson during the years 1775 to 1778, Telford, having finished his apprenticeship, was employed as a journeyman and there received his first lessons in bridge-building, with which his name and fame were to be inseparably connected.

In 1780 he went to Edinburgh and thence to London, due to the influence of John Paisley, to work on the building of Somerset House. John Paisley, merchant living in Gower Street, London, was the third son of James Paisley of Craig. Telford also enjoyed the patronage of Sir James Johnstone of Westerhall who was a cousin of the Paisleys of Westerlea. He became Surveyor for the county of Shropshire and in 1793 was appointed engineer for the Ellesmere Canal at a salary of £500 a year. From this moment he quickly ascended to fame and fortune.

Some of his principal works were the Ellesmere Canal, the Caledonian Canal, the Tubular Bridge over the Menai Straits, and St.Catherine's Docks, London. He was elected a Fellow of the Royal Society and President of the Institute of Civil Engineers. He never married and died in London, 2nd September 1834, aged 77.

By his will he left £1,000 each to Westerkirk and Langholm Libraries and amongst other bequests he left £500 to Southey, then Poet-Laureate, and a like amount to Thomas Campbell, the poet.

As well as a distinguished engineer Telford was a writer both of prose and verse, one of his best-known poems being *Eskdale*. He was conversant with the Latin, German, French, and Italian languages, all of which he acquired by self-tuition. His writings on engineering subjects were published, but are now extremely scarce.

Samuel Smiles included a biography of Telford in his *Lives of the Engineers* but there are many inaccuracies. Sir Alexander Gibb, great-grandson of John Gibb, colleague and friend of Telford, wrote *The Story of Telford*. In his introduction Gibb is very scathing of Smiles's account of Telford's early years, being for the most part of doubtful authority and should be taken as fiction rather than fact.

WILLIAM PARK

William was born on the farm of Effgill in 1788, son of William Park, R.N. He became servant to the Rev. Dr. Brown, minister of Eskdalemuir, and whilst in this position contributed to periodicals. He devoted his spare moments to literary pursuits, and ultimately attained a position in letters which, though not exactly distinguished, was yet highly creditable.

In 1833 he published, through Blackwood, a modest little volume of verse dedicated to Sir John Malcolm, entitled *The Vale of Esk*. Some of the compositions display very high and refined powers, notably his *Ode to Poverty*, to which attention was drawn by a writer in *Chambers's Journal*.

When Dr. Brown died in 1837, Park became tenant of the farm of Holmains in the parish of Dalton on the Solway. He came out in the Disruption in 1843, and by his writings advocated the claims of the Free Kirk. He became editor of the *Dumfries and Galloway Standard*, but only held the position for three weeks, dying in June, 1843, aged 55.

Appended to his volume of poems is a note on the poems of William Park, R.N., his father, of the parish of Hutton, editor of the *St. George's Chronicle*, Grenada, to which place he had gone as overseer of an estate belonging to the Johnstones of Westerhall. William Park, senior, was for a time in Lisbon where he met William Julius Mickle.

One of the poems is on the death of Governor Johnstone, and another on the death of William Telford, Surgeon, R.N., who was a surgeon on a 74 gun ship-of-the-line in Lord Rodney's action in the West Indies, and whose father had farmed on the Westerhall estate.

HENRY SCOTT RIDDELL

He was born at Sorby in Ewes on 23rd Sept., 1798, in a cottage, no longer extant, near the bridge. A memorial stone has been erected at the roadside. It is remarkable that the songs of the Scottish people, and the singers who obtain from the latter the readiest response, have so often come from such humble cot-houses as that wherein the author of *Scotland Yet* was born. His father went to live at Langshawburn in Eskdalemuir, where his son became acquainted with James Hogg, the Ettrick Shepherd.

Henry Scott Riddell worked first as a shepherd, but then went back to school and then to university. He eventually became a minister in the Church of Scotland. He was appointed by the Duke of Buccleuch to the *quoad sacra* church of Teviothead. Resigning this, he retired on a pension granted by His Grace.

MEMORIAL TO HENRY SCOTT RIDDLE

He is, of course, most widely known by his song entitled *Scotland Yet,* the popularity of which in Scotland is second only to *Auld Lang Syne.*

> "The heath waves wild upon the hills
> And roaming frae the fells,
> Her fountains sing o' freedom still
> As they dance down the dells;
> And weel I lo'e the land my lads,
> That's girded by the sea,
> Then Scotland's dales and Scotland's vales
> And Scotland's hills for me, —
> I'll drink a cup to Scotland yet
> Wi' a' the honours three."

The profits derived from the publication of this song were devoted by Riddell to putting a parapet and railing round the monument to Burns on the Calton Hill, Edinburgh.

He wrote a great deal , not only in verse but in prose, and many of his writings became extremely popular in Scotland. Some of his more notable poems are *Songs of the Ark; The Crook and the Plaid; The Wild Glen sae Green; The Emigrant's Wish;* and *the Hames o' oor Ain Folk*.

Henry Scott Riddell died on 30th July, 1870 and is buried in Teviothead kirkyard.

In 1898 the centenary of his birth was celebrated at Sorby by a company of admirers from Langholm, headed by the Provost, Mr. J.J. Thomson, who delivered an eloquent eulogium on the poet.

On Sunday, 20th September, 1998, a further celebration, to mark the bi-centenary, was held at the memorial cairn on the hilltop above Teviothead Kirkyard.

MATTHEW WELSH

Matthew Welsh, like Henry Scott Riddell, was born in the lovely vale of Ewes. At an early age he devoted himself to improving his meagre education, and to that cultivation of the higher graces of the intellect, which has ever been one of the boasts of the Scottish peasantry.

MATTHEW WELSH

That he was successful in this gentle ambition is attested both by the large output from his pen, and the excellence and taste which characterise all his writings, whether verse or prose.

Mr. Welsh worked on the Arkleton estate until, at the age of three score years and ten, he retired to Langholm. He devoted his days of ease to literary and archaeological work, and in all matters of local lore he was an acknowledged authority.

His chief publication is a volume of verse entitled *Maggie Elliott and other Poems*, a Romance of Ewes. He has also written, but not published, *Thoughts on Redemption*, an epic in three books. His contributions to periodicals have been many and popular, and have embraced a large variety of themes and treatment and include lyrics, sonnets and odes.

He also lectured on literary and archaeological subjects such as the *Border Ballads*; *James Hogg the Ettrick Shepherd; The Lady Balladists of Scotland; Roman Roads* and kindred topics.

PRIVATE ROBERT MCVITTIE

Private Robert McVittie of Langholm was, for a quarter of a century, known throughout the world as one of the most famous rifle-shots in the British Isles. He early distinguished himself with the rifle and won many important prizes at rifle meetings such as Wimbledon, Altcar, Lanark, and Edinburgh.

As early as 1869 Private McVittie was selected as a member of the Scottish Twenty to shoot for Scotland in the International Matches. He was also for many years a member of the Scottish Eight, to compete against England and Ireland for the Elcho Shield.

In 1876 he was one of the representatives of Scotland in the great Centennial matches at Creedmoor, New York, when America, Scotland, Canada, Ireland, and Australia competed for the Centennial Trophy in what was perhaps one of the most famous rifle-matches in the history of long-range shooting. On the first day's shooting Scotland led, and McVittie was top scorer with a score of 209 out of a possible 225. This was the biggest score which had ever been made in a long-range rifle match, and the third largest score on record.

The portrait was taken on that occasion, the rifle being the one with which the score was made.

PRIVATE McVITTIE

In 1882, he was a member of Sir Henry Halford's team, which represented Great Britain against America in the military breech-loading matches. His scoring on that occasion surpassed all records, and on the average of the aggregate scores, he was some four points ahead of his nearest competitor. It is an evidence of the reliance placed by the team-captains on McVittie's judgement, that he was invariably selected to lead off the firing, and from him the team received guidance as to windage and elevation.

During his various visits to America, the inventive press of that country contained much apocryphal matter relating to him, interviews which never happened, and photographs of him for which he never sat! One paper having described him as an English-man and the best shot in England, *The Scottish-American Journal,* with national pride, at once corrected the statement, saying that McVittie was not an Englishman, but a Scotsman, and the best shot in Great Britain.

383

In 1885 the *Volunteer Record* took a plebiscite of its readers as to who was the best all-round shot in the shooting world, and McVittie headed the list by an enormous majority. In 1874 he won the St. George's Vase and Dragon Cup at Wimbledon, with the highest possible score at 500 yards with the Snider rifle. He also won the Bass, the Olympic, the Albert, and many other notable prizes. Albert Place in Langholm, was so named in commemoration of his success in the Albert competition.

In the famous Queen's Prize competition he was three times second for the silver medal, and has been third and fourth in the final stage, only losing the great prize, in 1881, with his last shot. By it he scored an outer, counting two, but had it been an inner, which counted four, the *Blue Ribband* would have been his. His successes are too numerous to mention here, but he won distinction with every rifle he tried. In the famous *Wimbledon Ballads* the following reference to McVittie is made:—

> "From near the Border-land comes Nestor sage,
> For skill, esteemed the wonder of the age.
> May Heaven protect him and reward him still,
> Preserve his eyesight and his snuffbox fill."

During the period of which we write, the Langholm Volunteer Corps possessed not a few first-class shots in addition to McVittie, and its fame was known throughout the country. The team embraced such veteran and cool shots as John Cowan, Samuel Hounam, James Bell, Thomas Wintrope, George Duncan, Gilbert Byers, C. Weatherstone, Thomas Bell, Sergeant Pearson and his son Albert, Ackroyd Bowman, and others, who well maintained the honour of Langholm at the rifle-butts. In 1886 Private McVittie produced a manual entitled *Hints and Advice on Rifle Shooting*, which had a very large circulation both in this country and America.

Robert McVittie was born in 1839, son of John McVittie in Ewes and his wife Jane Thomson. He married, on 11th November, 1869, Elizabeth Hyslop, younger sister of John Hyslop. His children were born in Langholm and they lived in Charles Street (New). He worked as a builder and joiner.

He emigrated to Canada in 1888, living first at Wingham, Ontario before finally settling in Toronto. In Canada he continued to distinguished himself at the great rifle meetings.

Robert's wife died in Toronto in 1906. He had a longing to return to Langholm again and was staying there at the outbreak of war in 1914 and was unable to return to Canada. He was living with his cousin William Hyslop and his wife, Janet, in Caroline Street when he died on 21st January, 1918. He is buried in Wauchope Kirkyard.

JOHN MAXWELL

He was the Laird of Broomholm circa 1770. Mr. Maxwell was a correspondent of Pennant, the antiquary, and furnished him with certain data during his *Tour*. He also furnished the Rev. Dr. Brown with a sketch of the ancient practice of hand-fasting in Eskdale, and a summary of the Roman remains which had been discovered in the district.

THOMAS HOPE

Thomas, son of Matthew Hope, was born on 3rd March, 1809, in Charles Street (New), Langholm. His father had had a cotton mill, with a field attached, but was not successful in business. His mother was Grace Corrie of Corrie Common, near Lockerbie. Thomas was named after his uncle, Thomas Hope, at one time farmer in Bomby, now Hopsrig.

An amusing story is told that when a letter addressed to "ThomasHope, Bombay" could not be delivered in that city, it happened to be seen by a clerk who came from Eskdale, who wrote across it 'Try Langholm'!

In 1817 the father and his son James emigrated to New York, and two years later his wife, with the rest of the children, joined them after a voyage taking nine weeks. Owing to the straitened circumstances of the family, they had to leave Langholm without paying some school fees. Many years afterwards when Thomas Hope, a rich man, returned to his native town, he at once sought out his old schoolmaster and more than repaid him.

Thomas Hope and one of his brothers began business as grocers in a small way in New York, but by their integrity and hard work they succeeded in establishing a very large enterprise, comprising three main stores in Chambers Street, with about 30 branches in various parts of the country. On retiring with ample fortunes, the brothers conveyed their business over to their clerks who presented them with a silver testimonial which is now in the Hope Hospital, Langholm.

THOMAS HOPE

Thomas paid three visits to his native country, the first in 1844, the second a year or two later and the last in 1888. It was on this last occasion that he made public his intention of benefitting his native town.

His first idea, to erect cottage homes for aged people near Holmfoot, was abandoned. Instead he decided to build and endow a hospital in Langholm, now known as The Thomas Hope Hospital, for the care and relief of the sick, infirm and aged persons, natives of Langholm, in reduced circumstances.

In 1896 the memorial stone of the Hospital was laid by his sister and the Hospital was opened on 28th May 1898. In the Hope Hospital there are many very interesting memorials of the generous donor, whose name will ever be gratefully cherished in Langholm and Eskdale.

Thomas Hope was a man of singularly benevolent disposition, delighting to help his less prosperous fellowmen, yet his liberality was always controlled by a wise judgement.

In May 1998 the hospital celebrated its centenary with a birthday party for the patients, a garden party for invited guests and an impressive exhibition of the town's medical history.

RICHARD BELL

Richard Bell of Castle O'er, laird, naturalist, and author, came of one of the oldest families in Eskdale. In 1764 George Bell of Woodhouselees purchased Burncleuch from Robert Scott, of Davington, but later it was exchanged by his descendants with the Duke of Buccleuch for Castlehill.

However, the Bells were in Eskdalemuir earlier than this date, for the Rev. Dr. Brown in his version of the legend of *Gilpin Horner* gives the name of "Thomas Bell from Westside" as certifying that the "bogle of Todshawhill" was possessed of both flesh and blood. This Thomas Bell, was the grand-uncle to Thomas Bell Esq. of Crurie.

The family had purchased Crurie from Scott of Tushielaw, and later they also came into possession of Yards and Yetbyre. The name of Yetbyre was changed to Castle O'er by George Graham Bell, who was succeeded as laird by his son, the late Richard Bell. George Graham Bell was an advocate of much renown throughout the south of Scotland, where he was known as *Advocate Bell*.

In addition to his interests at the Parliament House, the Advocate farmed his ancestral acres in Eskdalemuir, and it is said of him that he would walk from Castle O'er to Edinburgh — a distance of 60 miles by road — and perhaps dance at a ball in the evening! In 1848 his eldest daughter Eliza married John Wilson, tenant of the neighbouring farm of Billholm. He was the elder son of John Wilson, Professor of Moral Philosophy in Edinburgh, known to all the world as *Christopher North*, whose premier place in the literary life of Edinburgh was unchallenged, and who was brought into close touch with Eskdale by his son's tenancy of Billholm.

The late Richard Bell devoted himself largely to the oversight of his estates, but his interests were not limited to these. In 1905 he published *My Strange Pets,* a book of fascinating interest, dealing mainly with the wild life of Eskdale. As a naturalist, Richard Bell had few equals, and the volume reveals not only his intimate knowledge of bird and animal life, but the keen observation of all the interesting phenomena of the country side. He died in 1910.

CHAPTER 30

THE GEOLOGY OF ESKDALE.

The geology of Eskdale follows, with certain variations, the characteristic features of that of the entire southern uplands of Scotland. The scenery of the valley has been, in the main, determined by its geological structure. As the rocks have yielded to, or resisted, the destructive agencies which have been unceasingly at work upon them, so they have received that sculpturing and carving which now give to Eskdale a charm all its own.

It is one of the most noteworthy features of the rocks of Eskdale that they are folded, contorted, or broken into wonderful and picturesque disorder by the slow-moving lateral pressure which is ever at work upon the rock systems of our globe. And yet the tops and sides of the hills have been planed and smoothed into one common type, by ice-action and other forces acting from without, though here and there a bold escarpment remains, such as Whita Hill, Warbla Knowe, or Arkleton Crags, to give a pleasing variety to the landscape.

The Esk is not a long river, yet in its course it flows over at least four distinct geological systems:—

I. North of Stennies Water the rocks are lower Silurian.

II. Southwards to Skipper's Bridge they are upper Silurian.

III. Between Langholm and Canonby we have the Calciferous Sandstone rocks of the Carboniferous system.

IV. Southwards to where the Esk crosses the Border and becomes an English river, there is found a system which by some is called Permian, by others Triassic, or, as some name it, the New Red Sandstone. But the unfossiliferous nature of this series leaves its classification an open question. Thus, from the source of the Esk to its

388

junction with the Solway, the rock systems are in a regular and ascending series, save that there is one system missing, viz., the Old Red Sandstone. A few isolated patches of it, however, remain, mostly on the higher ground, to tell us of an age of enormous waste and denudation.

These rock-systems, being all stratified, indicate that once upon a time, there rolled a sea whose depth varied with successive upheavals and depressions, until, by some steady force acting throughout many ages, the sea-bed was raised, and what was once the home of star-fishes and sea-worms became the haunt of the plover and the lark.

I.   North of Stennies Water the rocks are of the lower Silurian system.   The line of separation in Eskdale between the upper and the lower Silurian, which consist of shales or friable compressed mud, and greywacké, the angular grained sandstone of the period, runs from Stennies Water in a south westerly direction, touches Enzieholm Bridge and Crossdykes, then runs over towards Hartfell.

II.   The boundary between the upper Silurian and the Calciferous Sandstone is an irregular line running east and west from Whita Hill towards Winterhope Head.   The upper Silurian rocks predominate in Ewes, but after passing the Terrona Burn they are mostly confined on the left bank of the river to a narrow belt along the water's edge.   This narrow belt runs through the Old-town of Langholm, along the side of Whita as high up the hill as the gate, and gradually tapers off as it approaches the Skipper's Bridge.   The upper Silurian, which can be easily detected as the greywacké, locally known as the hard whinstone, then crosses the Esk a few yards south of the Skipper's Bridge, where the division between it and the Carboniferous can be easily traced through the river to the mouth of the Skipper's Burn.   It then runs up to Warbla Hill, on the lower flank of which it gives place to a broad band of the Old Red exactly as it does on Whita, opposite.   In both places a sheet of porphyrite has been intruded into the latter rock, and the escarpment of Warbla Knowe, like that of Charteris Crags, is thus of volcanic origin, and is contemporaneous with the adjoining sandstone. These two cliffs, therefore, stand as it were like sentinels placed, many ages ago, by volcanoes, long since extinct, to guard the entrance to Eskdale.

Tracing it now from the west, the upper Silurian crosses from Winterhope Head to the neighbourhood of Cleuchfoot, then runs down Logan Water and the left bank of Wauchope and, about two miles west of Langholm, crosses to the right bank of the Wauchope and continues to

Langholm and up along the side of Warbla, where, after forming the escarpment already referred to, it dips down into the Skipper's Burn. The town of Langholm is therefore built on an isthmus of upper Silurian rocks, with the crags of Whita and Warbla towering above.

These Silurian rocks furnish evidences both of animal and plant life. The animal life of the period was elementary, consisting largely of graptolites and foraminifera. Many beds of shale contain these fossils, some being found near the top of Garwald Water. This bed is probably part of the great shale deposits which lie along the course of Moffat Water. The Silurian plant life, at least what the rocks retain of it, seems to have been meagre, consisting largely of seaweeds.

III. The line of separation between the upper Silurian and the Calciferous Sandstone of the Carboniferous system passes along the ridge of Whita Hill. So far as Eskdale is concerned this series begins on Arkleton Hill, which is an isolated patch of White Sandstone set in a frame of Old Red. The boundary line between the Silurian and the Calciferous is dotted with such patches from Whita Hill, up Ewes and over into Hermitage Water. Whita Hill is thus composed of three distinct series of rocks:— (a) Up to near Whita Gate the rocks are Silurian, (b) with a belt of Old Red stretching from Hillhead over to St. Thorwald's, in which is an intrusive sheet of porphyrite, extending from near Hillhead, past Whita Well and along Charteris Crags almost to the old quarry and (c) higher up the hill than the Crags and forming its main mass is the Sandstone rock of the Carboniferous age.

On the opposite side of Esk, the Sandstone begins in the Skipper's Burn and the Middlehams Hill, then stretches down beyond Canonby Bridge. The southern boundary line of the Sandstone runs from the west of the county, past Cadghillhead, crosses the Esk at Canonby Bridge, and terminates within the angle formed by the old railway and the road leading from Canonby Bridge to the station.

IV. Here it gives place to the Sandstones whose reddish colour is so marked a feature of the landscape at Riddings and southward to Carlisle.

More detailed mention must be made of the appearance of the Old Red Sandstone, with whose lower group the writings of Hugh Miller are so inseparably associated. Its most noteworthy feature in Eskdale is that it seems to exist only along the lines of separation of the Silurian and Carboniferous rocks. It runs in patches, more or less prominent, from

Birrenswark in Annandale to Arkleton Crags in Ewesdale. Tracing it from the west it forms a belt, — lessening in width as it comes eastward, and accompanied on its southern edge by a parallel band of porphyrite,— past Dunaby and Kirtlehead in a north-easterly direction to Falford and Calister Ha'. Here it has been considerably faulted, but re-appears opposite Cleuchfoot and ends in Logan Burn.

Its next outcrop is a broad wedge running between Warbla and Earshaw Hill. The old Peat Road along Warbla runs across this wedge at the "Ellers", where, as so frequently happens in the Old Red, there is a patch of porphyrite, easily traceable in the heavy purple-coloured pieces of rock lying in the syke. These bands of porphyrite are igneous rock injected into the Old Red. This one continues in a south-easterly direction right across the front of Warbla Knowe and down into the Skipper's Burn.

From the face of Warbla Knowe there has been a big landslip, when masses of rock and soil fell from the front of the hill on to the land below. From Arkleton Crags there has also been a landslip. The huge portions of the sandstone rock scattered on the hillside, known locally as tumblers, are no doubt the broken fragments of this fall.

Another isolated patch of Old Red crops out at Ha'crofts. It is well seen in the Becks Burn, at the end of what was once the highway into Wauchope and Annandale. It is a small piece extending from the Burn a few hundred yards past the farmhouse and it may be seen crossing the road half-way between the latter and the Curling Pond.

Coming now to the east side of the Esk valley, we find the largest remnant of the Old Red on Arkleton Crags, whose sides are of this series, whilst the summit is of the same sandstone as Whita Hill. The crags are thus a patch of White Sandstone set round with Old Red and separated from the Sandstone of Terrona Hill by a wedge of upper Silurian which, crossing the Ewes at the Kirk Style, runs over into Tarras near the Cooms. This Old Red also is edged with porphyrite, especially on the Liddesdale side, and where it stretches up into Hermitage Water. Occasionally, as on Cooms Fell, there is seen a volcanic vent filled with broken lava.

All over Ewes and Hermitage the Old Red is greatly disturbed by faults, some of them with a very considerable downthrow. Tracing the belt of Old Red from the hill just above the Howgill, we find it thinning out as it runs down the left bank of the Ewes. It proceeds by a rapid series of faults along the flank of the Terrona Hill. Between it and Hillhead, it suffers a fault whose downthrow is no less than 300 feet. As we have shown, it reaches to the old quarry on the face of Whita, where, by another fault, it is thrown down some 400 feet into the Skipper's Burn where it terminates.

Geologists tell us that the scenery of Eskdale and of Dumfriesshire generally, has been determined more by the agencies of ice, rivers, rain, and frost than by igneous or volcanic action, yet the whole district is studded with evidences that in some far-off age, chiefly in Carboniferous times, volcanic action was very powerful in the neighbourhood of Eskdale. One of the most distinct indications of it is seen in Tinnis Hill, on the borders of Tarras and Liddesdale, both of which watergates, right up to Hermitage, are studded with old volcanic vents or craters.

Only a little smaller than Tinnis Hill is the Perter Hill in Tarras, which, as well as the Perter Rig, is an ancient volcanic vent which has been filled up by broken rocks. A larger one still is seen at Cooms Fell. Nearer Langholm we find a volcanic vent on the left bank of Ewes, extending for some 500 yards, from the Whitshiels Burn to Arkinholm. There is also a small one in Arkleton Burn and another on the Mid Hill, above Unthank. These vents are filled with broken lava, *i.e.* agglomerate, which was shot out of the vent at the time of the eruption, and fell back into the neck of the crater.

Other interesting evidence of such volcanic activity is found in the various intrusive dykes of igneous rocks, which form a fairly conspicuous feature of the scenery of the Border counties. These dykes, which are for the most part of basalt, have been forced into the overlying strata by eruptive agencies.

The most noteworthy local example is the Great Dyke, which, appearing in the Lead Hills, runs past Moffat over into Eskdale, which it enters near the source of the Black Esk It crops out in the prominent crag of Wat Carrick, a mass of basalt, or as some authorities call it, diabase or dolerite (a medium grained basalt). Crossing the Esk near Crurie it pursues a zig-zag course over Meggat Water then through the policies of Westerhall into the Back Burn, near Burnfoot, where it is lost. It re-appears on the left bank of the Esk near Staneholm Scar, and runs through the Langfauld Wood and across the flank of the Castle Hill, where it seems to terminate. Here, as at many places along its course, it has been quarried for road metal and also for building material.

Its lithological structure makes it well adapted for curling-stones, and the curlers of Eskdalemuir, Westerkirk, and Langholm have frequently obtained their stones from its hard, black rock. Between the Back Burn and the Langfauld the Dyke has been cut through by the persistent action of the Esk, which, for many centuries, has been carving its way through this stubborn barrier.

From its first outcrop among the Leadhills to its disappearance at Langholm, the Dyke runs a course of almost 50 miles. The similar dyke of basalt which crops out at the Orchard in Canonby, and then runs past Liddlebank into Cumberland, is almost certainly a continuation of it. These dykes were intruded into the strata along the fissures of the rocks long after they had been deposited, viz., in Tertiary times.

Other isolated pieces of intrusive dyke are scattered about Eskdale. Near to Eskdalemuir Manse there is an outcrop similar to that at Wat Carrick, both probably branches of the Great Dyke. On the right bank of Meggat Water, near Dorniegill, a smaller dyke appears, which, running in an easterly direction, ends in the Stennies Water. Near to Enzieholm, at the foot of the Shiel Burn, there is an outcrop of mica-trap or minette. At Over-Cassock and in Fingland Burn, and at the head of Garwald Water, small lengths of basalt crop out, whilst at Burncleuch there is an outcrop of felsite.

Among the hills between Eskdale and Ewesdale there are several small dykes, intruded during different ages, of basalt, felsite, and mica-trap. On the hill behind Fiddleton wood there is a dyke of basalt nearly half a mile in length. At the head of Meikledale Burn there are intrusions of porphyrite, and another is seen striking across the burn at the entrance to Mosspaul Pass. In the Dean Banks, nearly opposite Longwood, a small piece of porphyrite crops out, running across the road through the plantation and down into the bed of the Esk.

In Canonby one of the most noteworthy geological features is a band of volcanic ash. It appears in the Irving Burn, divides into two at Auchenrivock, then crosses over to the left bank of the Esk. Occasionally volcanic bombs are found imbedded in the ashes. The two bands re-appear at Mumbiehirst, and then bend off in a north-easterly direction. They then pass under the old railway line and again unite about half a mile from the Mumbie Cottages. The united band then runs up towards Bruntshiel Hill, where it is highly faulted, down to the Broomieknowe, then pursuing a course parallel to the original band, runs into Liddesdale.

As already noted, the rock system of Eskdale changes at Langholm, where the Silurian gives place to the Sandstone of the Carboniferous period. This stone of which the town of Langholm is built, is a white freestone of great durability. It has been deposited in masses probably many hundreds of feet thick, on Whita and the Middlehams Hill. In Irvine Burn it occurs in the well known cement stones. It is to this group of the lower Carboniferous, and not to the Coal Measures proper, that the coal seams of Canonby belong. These number no fewer than thirteen and vary in thickness from seven inches to nine feet. The main seams measure respectively three, five, six, seven, and nine feet. In the lower strata the coal appears in thin bands interbedded with limestone. All the seams are much faulted, especially as they proceed eastward.

Limestone of the Carboniferous age is deposited in considerable masses in the hollows of the old Silurian rocks, where its position seems to have preserved it during the times of great denudation. In several places, notably at Harelawhill, the limestone has been successfully worked. The Statist of 1842 mentions as a curious fact that "within the space of 200 yards in one particular place, coal, peat, limestone, and freestone may be digged".

Near Tarras distillery is what is locally known as "The Marl Well", a petrifying spring similar to the famous one at Knaresborough in Yorkshire, the water being heavily charged with carbonate of lime. In Wauchope there are two chalybeate and one sulphureous spring. The larger chalybeate spring is known as the Grains. The water contains a very strong solution of iron, thought at one time to be of great medicinal value. The sulphureous spring is on the peaty soil at Bloughwell, and its efficacious properties were held to be the equal of the famous springs of Harrogate and Cheltenham.

Several minerals have been found in Eskdale. Lead has been found at Westwater in Wauchopedale, and also at Broomholm, but at neither place has there been any attempt made to work the ore. By the researches of Sir James Johnstone, antimony was discovered in 1760 on his estate of Glendinning in such quantities that at one time it was regularly worked. Some 40 men were employed in raising and smelting the ore, which was manufactured into sulphurated antimony. From 1793 to 1798 there were produced from the Glendinning mine 100 tons of regulus of antimony, realizing about £84 a ton. It was said to be the only antimony mine in Great Britain. The vein also yielded blende, calcareous spar, and quartz, but the great difficulties of transit operated against its commercial success.

Traces of copper have also been found near Broomholm, but generally it may be said that the Silurian rocks of Eskdale are singularly free from metallic veins, iron especially being almost entirely absent. It was mainly this fact which determined the selection of the Eskdalemuir site, when the Magnetic Observatory was removed from Kew on account of the interference with the instruments caused by the proximity of electric tramway lines.

Though volcanic action has had only a subordinate share in determining the general scenery of Eskdale, some of the most picturesque features of the valley are, nevertheless, due to its agency. The escarpment of Charteris Crags on the brow of Whita, Warbla Knowe, and the more rugged hills of Ewesdale, owe their boldness to the resisting power of the hard volcanic rocks.

However, in their main outlines, the hills have been moulded and shaped into their present forms by sub-aerial agents, such as ice and frost, floods and winds, rain and sunshine, more than by any violent volcanic action. Scotland, at one time, was buried under an ice-field as extensive and as thick as that which covers Greenland to-day. The ice has smoothed down the crags and rounded off the sharp angles left on the hills and rocks by the violent and long continued denudation of the period preceding the glacial age. The rounded summits of the Eskdale hills have thus been slowly chiselled and planed by ice.

The valleys, now covered over with corn, were once upon a time wholly filled with glaciers, which have left their magic writing upon many a hillside and many a rock. Many of these marks are as fresh to-day as when the glaciers first cut them, and it is by them that the movements of the ice-field are traced. Not only were the valleys, where birk and hawthorn now grow, filled with ice, but even the tops of the highest hills of Eskdale were covered by it to a great depth. This mass of ice was not fixed and inert, but flowed with a persistent movement towards the sea or lower ground. The general direction of the ice-flow through Eskdale was south-easterly, but the striation marks seen higher up in Eskdalemuir and in Ewes indicate that there was also an easterly flow. Round about Meikledale they point almost due south, but at the Burnfoot of Ewes the trend is straight over into Liddesdale.

The main flow of the Eskdale ice was towards the English border, and its course may be traced, by both ice-markings and by the perched blocks which dot the course of the Wauchope Water. The ice which came down the Wauchope valley, or over its hill tops, appears to have broken up somewhere about Carpshairn on the borders of Dumfries and Galloway, helped possibly by the pressure of the ice moving down from the Highlands.

It was this Galloway ice which travelled across Annandale towards Eskdale. It carried with it boulders, pebbles and detritus broken off from the surface of the rocks over which it slowly pushed its way. These stones, left behind as the ice slowly melted when the climate became warmer, form both an interesting feature of the scenery, and scientific evidence of the climatic conditions of Eskdale in those far-off times.

The Wauchope Water contains hundreds of large granite boulders, all of them planed and polished by the grinding they received in their journey thither, as well as by the friction to which they have been and are daily subjected in the river bed. The largest in the district is the Big Dowie Stane, (Dowie being the commonly applied term in Eskdale to granite stones), lying in the bed of the Wauchope at Earshaw, some two miles west of Langholm. It is of the grey granite characteristic of Galloway and its weight is estimated at 60 tons. Large numbers of these granite boulders lie scattered about the tops of the hills around Westwater and over the Becks Moss.

Glacial drift or boulder clay, the *moraine profonde* of the ice-sheet, is also thickly spread over the valleys of Eskdale and on the slopes of its hills. Instances of these thick deposits being partly washed away by the rivers are seen in the Corsholm in Wauchope, and the Staneholm Scar in Esk, where the floods of many ages have eaten into the mass of glacial clay.

Reference has been made to the effect of agencies, such as rivers, rain, and frosts, in chiselling out the scenery of the Eskdale valley. Interesting evidences of this sculpturing are the so-called "letter-stones", of which several series exist. The best known are on the road from Eskdalemuir Kirk to Lockerbie, near to Fauldbrae. The appearance of lettering is due, of course, to the unequal weathering of the hard and soft amygdaloid strata, but concerning their significance there was no little superstition existing at one time in Eskdale. Similar effects are seen on

BIG DOWIE STANE

the rocks at Watch Craig, about a mile nearer the White Esk than the above, but in the same range of rocks, and also near to Twiglees, Burnhead, and Black Esk-head Pikes, and we believe also on the Shawrig and Castlehill Crags.

The effects of water action on the rocks are well illustrated at the Linns of Garwald, about half a mile from the high road, where a cascade of eight feet is formed in a deep-cut gorge overhung with birk and fern, through which the Garwald threads its way among masses of broken rocks. In the Byreburn, Canonby, there is a similar waterfall known as, "The Fairy Loup". But finer still is the cascade of Wellsburnspout at the back of Fingland Hill.

Noticeable features, almost everywhere in the valleys of Eskdale, are the old river-terraces, which have been cut since the glacial period, and which indicate where the rivers ran in days gone by. As the Esk, Wauchope, and Ewes are all rapid-flowing rivers, they have possibly cut out their present courses in a shorter time than most rivers take, so some of these old terraces may not be of very great antiquity, but many undoubtedly are, for a series of three, and occasionally four, distinct terraces may be traced along the rivers in Esk, Wauchope, and Ewes. Good examples of these terraces are the holms in front of Terrona House and at Murtholm, and in Wauchope at the Big Dowie Stane.

397

Perhaps the most interesting of all these is that on which the town of New-Langholm is built. This land once formed the old river course of both the Esk and the Wauchope. In some far-off age, the Esk turned west-ward near the Academy and flowed across the New-town. Then it altered its course and left behind it gravel and soil, even as it did in the opposite direction when it flowed close by the base of the Castle Hill.

Wauchope, too, has greatly changed its course. Formerly it turned off at the Auld Caul and swept round the pasture fields which lie on the east and west of the Wauchope Road. It then flowed over the field to the west of Meikleholm toll-bar, and, when near Moodlawpoint, it united with the Esk. The united river then ran across what is now called the Eldingholm, the site of the Established Kirk, and joined the present bed of the river at Codgie.

The Kilngreen, as well as the Castle Holm, is an old river terrace. Arkinholm, the fertile stretch of holm land in front of Terrona, and the field on the right bank of the Ewes near the Bridge, once known as the Lint Dub, are also indications of where that river once flowed. These holms, with the New-town of Langholm, and the land whereon Stapelgortoun Kirk stood, and the land on both sides of the Byken Burn, at its junction with Esk, are perhaps the oldest river terraces in the Eskdale district.

Later terraces, which the rivers have vacated within a comparatively recent date, may be seen both in Esk, Wauchope, and Ewes, such as those at the Enzieholm, Hopsrig, Potholm, Milnholm, Brackenwrae in Esk; Flaskholm and the Kilngreen in Ewes; and near the Big Dowie Stane in Wauchope.

Wauchope Water presents a very interesting study to the physiographer. In addition to its boulders of granite and its old terraces, its course affords an excellent illutration of how a river, though comparatively small, may affect the scenery of a district by carving its way through hard belts of rock. To eat out a course for itself through hard Silurian rock, a river requires long periods of time, far beyond the reach of history, whilst to carve out the softer boulder-clay is an easier and quicker process. This inequality produces a succession of small lakes, which form just above the rocky parts in the river's course. As the action of the river prevails over the hard barrier, a gorge is slowly cut through the rock, and these small lakes are drained away, only, in the case of the Wauchope, to form others farther on.

In its short course from the Schoolhouse to Langholm, the Wauchope has had to overcome this hard rock barrier at three different points. The first of any great importance is met with just at the bend where the river receives the Blough Burn. Whilst, with long continued patience, it was cutting its way through this mass, the water was dammed back and covered the large holm at Bloughburnfoot. The small outflow from this lake again accumulated above the bend at Besse Bell's Brae, where again a lake was formed. From the overflow of the second lake a third was formed, extending from Besse Bell's Brae to the Auld Stane Brig.

Naturally, the Wauchope took longer to cut for itself a passage through the third mass of rock, that lying between the Brig and the Plump, and so the lake which formed on the glebe land was of longer duration. But in course of time it overcame all its obstacles, with the result that this gorge, along which runs the charming woodland path known as Gaskell's Walk, overhung with trees through which the summer sun can scarcely pierce, its steep side abounding in ferns, mosses, and wild flowers, forms one of the most picturesque landscapes in Eskdale. The same method of work is seen in the Esk. Whilst it was cutting a course through the rocks at Skipper's, a lake was formed, which covered not only the holms about Murtholm, but extended back even to Langholm itself.

Wauchopedale is richest in relics left by the Great Ice Age. Besides the granite stones and the boulder clay, the ice has left in Wauchope the solitary example in Eskdale of a kame, a huge mound of sand or gravel. This was probably by slow degrees heaped up under the ice by a stream that flowed beneath. When the ice melted the kame was left.

This local example is seen just above the old Wauchope School house, in the huge mound through which the Bigholms Burn has now cut its way. It consists of sand, gravel, and water-worn stones, upon some of which striation marks are discernible.

In some of the sedimentary rocks both animal and vegetable fossils have been found. Here and there in the Silurian rocks are deposits of shale bearing graptolites, considerable quantities of them being found at the head of Garwald Water. They are probably connected with the immense beds of Birkhill Shale running along both banks of Ettrick Water. Other beds of graptolitic shale lie up Carlesgill Burn and its way. It consists of sand, gravel, and water-worn stones, upon some of which striation marks are discernible.

In some of the sedimentary rocks both animal and vegetable fossils have been found. Here and there in the Silurian rocks are deposits of shale bearing graptolites, considerable quantities of them being found at the head of Garwald Water. They are probably connected with the immense beds of Birkhill Shale running along both banks of Ettrick Water. Other beds of graptolitic shale lie up Carlesgill Burn and on the left bank of the Stennies Water.

Some years ago a notable discovery of *Scorpionida* fossils was made in the Carboniferous rocks in the bed of the Esk at Glencartholm, whose existence in these strata had not hitherto been known. Such scorpions have, so far, not been found complete, but those discovered at Glencartholm, though not absolutely complete, were the best which had yet been found. The best specimen is without its tail or sting.

A number of new fossils were found in 1882-3 both at Tarrasfoot and Glencartholm, the most valuable being amongst the Arthropoda. These groups were named by Mr. B. N. Peach, one of the officers of the Geological Survey. He it was who discovered that the Silurian group, which predominates in Eskdale, rests on a base of volcanic rocks. The following fossils, several of which have not been found anywhere else, have been obtained at Glencartholm.

ARTHROPODA

1. *Perimecturus Parki*, (named after the late Mr. Walter Park of Brooklyn Cottage, Langholm, as is also the fish, Holrus Parki), varying from five inches in length down to about an inch; 2. *Perimecturus elegans*; 3. *Perimecturus communis*; 4. *Palæocaris Scotica*; 5. *Acanthocaris scorpioides*; 6. *Acanthocaris elongatus*; 7. *Crangopsis Eskdalensis*; 8. *Crangopsis elegans*; 9. *Tealliocaris Etheridgei*; 10. *Pseudo-Galathea Macconochiei*; 11. *Eoscorpius eulglyptus*; 10. *Eoscorpius glaber*; 13. *Glyptoscorpius personatus*.

Numbers 1 to 9 may be popularly described as shrimp-like in appearance.

Numbers 10 and 11 are probably the true land scorpions, and too closely resemble their living descendants to be mistaken.

Number 12 differs in appearance from 10 and 11 and was probably their water variety. It is found at Tarrasfoot as well as at Glencartholm.

FISHES

1. *Rhadinichthys tuberculatus;* 2. *Rhadinichthys fusiformis*; 3. *Canobius elegantulus*; 4. *Canobius Ramsayi*, these two species of *Canobius* are about two inches in length; 5. *Holurus Parki*; 6. *Cyclotychius concentricus*; 7. *Platysomus superbus.*

PLANT FOSSILS

The newest discoveries in plant fossils are 1. *Sphenopteris Hibberti;* 2. *Sphenopteris decomposita,* (Ferns); 3. *Bythotrephsis carbonaria;* 4. *Bythotrephsis plumosa,* (Fucoids).

Among the mollusca the Pteropod *Conularia quadrisulcata* is the commonest here, as in many other districts. Corals have been found between Tarrasfoot and the Hollows Mill, amongst them Lithostrotion and Zaphrentis, and in the limestone outcrop in the bed of the Esk near the Tower numerous examples of the Productus giganteus occur.

GEOLOGICAL SUMMARY

Recent.	River terraces, peat, &c.
Glacial.	Boulder clay, boulders, glacial striations, kames, &c. Great period of denudation, &c.
Tertiary.	Tertiary basalt dykes intruded.
Permian.	Red sandstones.
Carboniferous.	Calciferous sandstone series, with limestones and coals. Much volcanic activity.
Old Red Sandstone.	Red sandstone.
End of Silurian.	Silurian rocks folded and denuded. Mica-trap dykes intruded.
Silurian	Greywacké, shales, and graptolitic shales.

401

CHAPTER 31

STORMS AND FLOODS

It is a frequent remark of older inhabitants that the climate of Eskdale, within the last two or three generations, has become more temperate. No doubt this change has been helped by the irrigation and cultivation of the land, and the smaller area now covered by woods and forests.

Some of the place-names of the Esk valley give indications of the existence of those large forests e.g., Blackberry-wood, Woodslees, Brockwoodlees, Langshaw, Braidwood, Timmerwood, and others. Placenames derived from the presence of wild animals have already been mentioned. In the heights of Eskdale is a place called Wolfstane, where tradition says, the last wolf was killed.

The late Mr. Richard Bell describes, in *My Strange Pets,* many species of animals now extinct in Eskdale, for whose preservation extensive forests were a necessity. Observations made by Dr. Brown, the parish minister, showed that rain or snow fell in Eskdalemuir on about two days out of every five from 1800 to 1810, and the average temperature throughout the period was about 44½° Fahrenheit or 5° Centigrade.

1674

Perhaps the most severe snowstorm ever experienced at that time in the south of Scotland occurred at the end of February and beginning of March, old style, 1674 and became known as *The Thirteen Drifty Days* Nine-tenths of the sheep were destroyed, and in Eskdalemuir alone, which was capable of sustaining 20,000 sheep, only 40 dinmonts, the Border name for young male sheep, were saved. These were on the farm of Westside and there were also five old ewes saved on another. The cold was intense, and on about the fifth or sixth day of the storm the young sheep began to die. On the ninth day the shepherds built up circular walls of the dead to safeguard the living, but this gruesome remedy came too late to be of much use. When the storm abated, on scarcely one of the high lying farms was there a sheep left alive. It was under these circumstances that the Duke of Buccleuch and Monmouth received license to import stock from Ireland.

1740

Snow began to fall on New Year's Day, 1740, and it lay on without decrease until it was melted by the sun in the spring. Even on May 20, new style, the frost was so keen that people were unable to cast their peats.

1746

A snowstorm began on 25th January, 1746, and lasted six weeks, destroying practically all the stock in Eskdalemuir. Every farmer save six was ruined, the fortunate six being Thomas Bell, Westside; John Grieve, Kilburn; William Curle, Moodlawknowe; William Graham, Cot; William Beattie, Watcarrick and John Beattie, Upper Dumfedling.

1748

In the *Gentleman's Magazine* for March 1748, a correspondent described how certain Border rivers, notably the Teviot, had suddenly ceased flowing on 25th January, and had continued in this condition for about nine hours. On 19th February the river Kirtle also went dry for six hours, and Sir William Maxwell rode along its banks for seven miles and attested the fact. On 23rd February the river Esk itself stopped its course and the channel was quite dry for the space of six hours. On this occasion quantities of fish were gathered from the dry river-bed and sold at Longtown and other places.

In the April issue of the *Magazine* there appeared a letter, dated Carlisle, April 16th attempting to explain the phenomenon. The explanation given was that the previous autumn had been hot and dry, and these rivers had then been lower than ever was known before, and that the earth, being heated to an uncommon degree, affected the melting of the snow on the hills. "The different courses of the freezing air and the situation of the mountains with respect to the several rivers were the cause, and this circumstance did not happen to all on the same day. And that several adjoining rivers did not freeze, must be attributed to their running through a more level and therefore a warmer country; and for the same reason some parts of the Esk might have little ice, as it is not surrounded by mountains".

1751-5

These Years were memorable in Eskdale because of the calamities which again befell the farmers. For five years one disaster followed quickly upon another. The old sheep were destroyed by the inclement seasons and the lambs by the frost and snow. For many years afterwards this period was always spoken of with horror.

1765

A severe drought occurred in 1765 which did great damage to sheep and cattle. A species of worm, of a green colour and about one inch in length, destroyed the grass, by cutting it away at the roots. The worms appeared first in May and continued till the beginning of August, when they were destroyed by large flocks of crows helped by heavy rains. Great quantities of the worms were found at the sides of the burns and rivulets after the rains ceased. The neighbouring dales of Liddle, Annan, and Teviot were similarly visited.

1772

More than one-third of the sheep and lambs in Eskdalemuir perished by a severe storm of frost and snow.

1785-6

An almost continuous storm lasted from 26th November to the end of March, but fortunately very little loss was sustained, as the snow was accompanied by high winds which cleared the ground and enabled the sheep and cattle to get sufficient food. The years succeeding this storm were good and farmers were enabled to recoup themselves for their previous severe losses.

1794

The storm which began on 23rd January, 1794 and became known as *The Gonial Blast,* was so named because of the extraordinary number of sheep that perished, gonial, or goniel, being a term applied to the mutton of sheep found dead, from which the smoked mutton-hams are produced. The storm continued for several days, snow, rain, and frost alternating and following each other in quick succession. The sheep were either smothered, drowned, or frozen. The melting snow washed them into the sykes and burns, where hundreds were afterwards found frozen to death.

An especially heavy fall of snow was followed by a deluge of rain, and the Esk had never before been known to rise to such a height. When the storm abated and the rivers fell, there were found thrown up on the bed of the Esk at the Solway, the bodies of two men and one woman, and the carcasses of 1,840 sheep, nine black cattle, three horses, 45 dogs, and 180 hares. In Eskdalemuir 4,006 sheep and seven black cattle were killed. The only farms which escaped the disaster were Yetbyre and Tanlawhill. Burncleuch lost one stirk, but Upper Cassock lost 540 sheep, Nether Cassock 240, Garwald 440, Langshawburn 300, Black Eskhead 254, Kilburn 280, Fingland 250, and Rennelburn 200.

ICE FLOODS

Towards the end of December, 1870, a severe frost set in throughout Eskdale, and continued for about ten days. On 4th January, 1871, a thaw came and the ice broke up. Huge blocks of ice, thirty to forty feet square, were thrown high up on the banks, where hundreds of tons were soon deposited. A similar flood occurred in January 1881, following a prolonged frost, during which curling had been played on the Skipper's Pool. The scene presented by the ice-flood when it broke away on the night of Sunday, 30th January, was a memorable one.

One of the heaviest floods ever known in the Esk occurred on 2nd November 1898. A heavy rainfall brought all the rivers down in flood, and at the Boatford Bridge the water was only some two feet from the bridge level. The Souter Stane, an isolated stack of greywacké, which

THE SOUTER STANE

which from time immemorial had served as the town's flood-gauge, was toppled over and broken up. The enormous volume of water had found an opening at the base of the rock, the bedding of which so favoured such an occurrence that it is wonderful that the stone had resisted so long. To the great regret of the people of Langholm, the sustained force of water at last destroyed this famous landmark.

Discussion has frequently arisen concerning the derivation of the name Souter Stane. Perhaps the simplest and most probable explanation of its origin is that on it, the souters, i.e., the shoemakers, cobblers, and cloggers of the town, were accustomed to sharpen their knives. Its hard and polished surface provided an excellent whetstone, and through serving this practical purpose the rock came to be designated the *souters'* stane. Whether this is historically correct, we are unable to say, and we quote the explanation with reserve.

CHAPTER 32

MISCELLANY

ESKDALE CHARITIES

The following Charitable Trusts, for the benefit of education in Langholm, were administered by the School Board, in terms of an Order in Council, dated 28th November, 1887.

REID'S MORTIFICATION

A sum of £50 was mortified by one John Reid, schoolmaster in Langholm, for teaching poor scholars to read and write. The date of the bequest appears to have been 27th June, 1727. Mention of it is made in a minute of the kirk session of 12th July, 1749:—

"- - - - Reid's mortification for teaching poor scholars to read and write, together with the Instrument of Seisine thereupon, in the lands of Burnfoot, formerly designed Cannel-Shiels, being part of the Barony of Westerhall".

There is also mentioned in the same minute a legacy of £10 sterling as having been made by Jno. Little, junr., merchant in Langholm and member of the Session, for buying books for poor scholars, and some concern is expressed about the wasting of the capital sum.

This John Little, who died in 1733, was the father of Laird Little. Another legacy of £3 is noted as having been made in 1732 by Mrs. Meikle, wife of the parish minister, for teaching poor scholars in Wauchope.

BROOMHOLM TRUST

This Charity consisted of the free school known as the Broomholm School in the Drove Road, for the benefit of poor scholars. It was established by Captain Geo. Maxwell of Broomholm, on 24th July, 1827. A sum of £500 was mortified for the support of the teacher and a tack, granted from Whitsunday 1828 for 1,000 years at the nominal duty of 6d. annually, of two houses on the east side of Drove Road.

In his letter intimating the Charity, Captain Maxwell made the interesting suggestion that "each of the scholars should be required to bring each day they attend the school a single Peat of at least one foot in length and of a proportionate thickness for the supply of the fire in the schoolroom". Certain feuars "in Langholm or those parts of the ten merk-land of Arkinholm" are nominated, along with the parish minister, as trustees. To the above Mortification the kirk session added £100 which they had received in trust for the education of the poor from one David Park in London.

MAXWELL'S TRUST

By a codicil of will dated 13th January 1866, William Maxwell, surgeon in Langholm, bequeathed a sum of money sufficient to yield an annuity of £10 for providing "a good plain English education for 10 orphan children", natives of Langholm, five to be educated at the Parish School and five at the Free Church School.

The scheme sanctioned by the Order in Council provided that there should be "at least one School Bursary, to be called the Maxwell School Bursary - - - - of the yearly value of not less than £5 nor more than £10".

The following three Mortifications were administered by the Parish Council of Langholm for behoof of the poor:—

(1) THE IRVING BEQUEST
Dated 21st March 1866, by John Irving, secretary, Royal Navy, Oak Cottage, Langholm, interest on a legacy of £401 16s. 3d.

(2) THE PASLEY BEQUEST
By William Pasley, The Lindens, Effray Road, Brixton, London, who died 8th Sept. 1906, the sum of £300.

(3) THE MAXWELL BEQUEST

A sum of £200, left by Captain George Maxwell. The date of the bequest is uncertain, but it was probably made about 1830.

There are two other Charities which do not appear to be included either in those administered by the School Board or in those by the Parish Council.

On 20th January 1839 there died at Rosevale Mrs. Agnes Little, or McKinley, who by her Will bequeathed to the parish minister and kirk session, for the infant school, the sum of £50. Also a sum of £100 for behoof of the poor of the parish of Langholm to the Rev. W.B. Shaw and Mr. Alexander Stevenson.

THE WILLIAM MAXWELL BEQUEST

Of £50, less duty, by the late William Maxwell, Townhead, Langholm, paid 9th November, 1910, to the parish minister, to be used at his discretion for behoof of the poor of the congregation of Langholm parish church

THE HOPE TRUST

This is the most important Charity in Eskdale. The late Thomas Hope of New York, left in trust the sum of £100,000 for the benefit of his native town of Langholm.

Part of the money was expended in the erection and equipment of the Hope Hospital, Langholm, for the treatment of surgical cases, and part was used to afford assistance, by way of regulated pensions, to deserving and necessitous inhabitants, at the discretion of the Trustees, by whom the Trust is administered. When first established, the joint secretaries of the Charity were Mr. Robert Smellie and Mr. William E. Elton, solicitor.

In the other Eskdale parishes there are no charitable or educational trusts of any importance. In Westerkirk the kirk session has the disbursement of some small Charities.

At one time there existed in Canonby a small charity known as THE YEOMAN BEQUEST, by which the schoolmaster at the Tail school benefited to the extent of £1 yearly, but the payment has been discontinued.

THE LIBRARIES

Very excellent Libraries, well stocked with carefully-selected books of wide and varied interest, exist both in Langholm and Westerkirk. In 1800 Langholm Library was established, and in 1813 another known as the New Library was formed by tradesmen and others. Some time after 1850 the latter ceased to exist, but its members were received by the older institution, under certain conditions.

Under the will of Thomas Telford a sum of £1,000 was left to the parish minister of Langholm, in trust for the Library, the interest to be annually expended in the purchase of books.

Both Langholm Library and the New Library laid claim to this bequest. In order to enable the parish minister to obtain the legacy, certain arrangements were agreed upon by the two societies, but at the instance of the Trustees a suit was instituted to determine the rightful legatee. The Court decided that the Langholm Library was intended by the testator, and the sum of £1,349 15s. 3d. was thereupon paid to the Rev. W.B. Shaw. This was augmented by further amounts which made together a sum of £3,119 15s. 11d.

Suitable accommodation being urgently needed for the proper housing of the books purchased under the Telford Legacy, His Grace the Duke of Buccleuch, on being approached, very generously gave a site free of all conditions, excepting a nominal feu-duty of 5/- and the late Alexander Reid gave £1,000 towards the erection of the building on condition of a like sum being raised by the members.

Under Telford's will the sum of £1,000 was also left to the parish minister of Westerkirk in trust for the parish Library. The legacy accumulated to the amount of £2,729 1s. 3d. which produced an annual revenue for the purchase of books. Through this munificent provision the parish of Westerkirk has been enabled to acquire a Library such as few villages in Scotland possess.

THE ESKDALE KILWINNING LODGE OF FREEMASONS

This Lodge stands third as to age in the chronicles of Craft Masonry in the county of Dumfries. Dumfries Kilwinning No. 53 was founded in 1687, Sanquhar Kilwinning No. 194 in 1738, and Eskdale

Kilwinning No. 107 on 16th September 1747, though the Sanquhar Lodge is the only one of the three which holds a charter from the original Lodge at Kilwinning. Twenty years after the foundation of Lodge Eskdale Kilwinning, No. 107, it was decided to obtain a charter from the Grand Lodge of Scotland. This was duly granted on 10th November 1767, with the number 134, which in 1816 was altered to 103, and in 1835 to 107.

A society to assist distressed brethren was instituted in connection with the Lodge in 1786, and in 1788 a joiner was granted £13 as indemnity for the loss of his tools by accidental fire at Langholm Lodge, which was destroyed by fire, when in process of erection. In 1816 the Lodge interested itself in the formation of a Band of Music in Langholm, contributing five guineas, in return for which the Band agreed to play gratis on St. John's Day. For a period of about 10 years, from 1860 to 1870, the Lodge was dormant, but interest being then revived, the Craft was again followed with enthusiasm. A list of the Past Masters of the Craft is in Appendix 10.

The foundation-stone of the present Masonic Hall was laid on 17th October 1894 by Mr. A.H. Johnstone Douglas, P.G.M., and it was consecrated on 23rd August 1895 by Sir Charles Dalrymple of Newhailes, Bart., M.P., M.W. Grand Master Mason.

Royal Arch Masonry has also been practised in Langholm, but its origin is of much later date than Craft Masonry.

In 1800, the Grand Lodge of Scotland, from which the Eskdale Kilwinning held its charter, prohibited its daughter lodges from holding any meetings above the degree of Master Mason. Application had already been made to "The Grand and Royal Chapter of the Royal Arch of Jerusalem", in London, and in 1797 a charter of erection had been granted by it to the Lodge, which was designated the "Loyal Scots", No. 106.

Later, in 1803, another charter to the "Mount Sinai", No. 123, was granted. This charter was signed by Lord Mount-Norris, Z., Sir Ralph Milbanke, H., the father-in-law of Byron, and Walter Rodwell Wright, J., to "our Excellent Companions William Johnstone, Matthew Hope, (presumably the father of Thomas Hope, the founder of the Hope Hospital), and Walter Forrester". Suitably framed, it forms one of the wall decorations of the present Masonic Hall, Langholm.

The Lodge continues to play an active role in the town. In 1997 it celebrated the 250th anniversary of its first meeting. In 1999 Brother Peter Irving Stuart, Past Master, had the honour of being installed as Provincial Grand Master of Dumfriesshire.

ESKDALEMUIR OBSERVATORY

In the summer of 1903, owing to the laying down of an electric tramway near the Kew Observatory, and the consequent disturbance of the instruments, it became necessary to look for a site to which could be removed the Magnetic part of the Observatory work. It was essential that the site should be remote from railways and tram lines and be where there existed no trace of iron which might disturb the extremely sensitive instruments. After much enquiry the site was selected on the farm of Cassock in Eskdalemuir.

The Observatory was opened in 1908 as a branch of the National Physical Laboratory. The primary object of the Observatory is the investigation of the Science of Terrestrial Magnetism, but the work in other branches of Geophysics developed rapidly. The Observatory became a first order station for Meteorology, while in earthquake investigation there were in regular operation the following seismographs:— Milne two horizontal components, Galitzin three components, Wiechert two horizontal components, and Omori one component.

On 1st July 1910, the administration was transferred to the Meteorological Office, while the Gassiot Committee of the Royal Society acted as an advisory scientific committee. Complete publication of all observations commenced on 1st January 1911, and these will be found in the *British Meteorological and Magnetic Year Book*, published by H.M. Stationery Office for the Meteorological Committee. The Superintendent of the Observatory, at that time, was Mr. George W. Walker, formerly Fellow of Trinity College, Cambridge.

THE ESKDALE AND LIDDESDALE ADVERTISER

No history of Langholm can be complete without mentioning the local paper, *The Eskdale and Liddesdale Advertiser,* known locally as *The E. & L .A.* It was founded in May, 1848, by Mr. Thomas L. Rome and soon developed an importance in the intellectual, social and corporate life of the town. Distributed gratuitously at first, it had the distinction of being the first penny newspaper to be issued in Scotland, a fact of which we are all proud. It helped very speedily to stimulate the intellectual life of the district, and was soon taken advantage of by people with poetic and literary ambitions. For several generations it has served almost as a home letter to Langholm's exiles scattered the world over. Since then the paper has gone from strength to strength and in May 1998 it celebrated its 150 years with an exhibition of publishing. Many were the congratulations it received on its continuing to be such a vibrant publication.

POPULATION

The table shows the population of each of the civil parishes of Eskdale from the institution of the Census in 1801. The figures prior to this date are those of the ecclesiastical parishes, as ascertained by the parish ministers.

In the 1811 Census the Parish of Half Morton was included with Langholm which accounts for the apparent increase in the population of Langholm since 1801 and subsequent decrease in 1821.

In the original edition of *Langholm As It Was* the figures given for the population of Langholm for 1801 and 1821 included the figures given for Half Morton.

It is sad to see that the population has almost halved in the last hundred years, reaching its lowest in 1971 although there is a very small increase in 1981 and 1991.

Year	Langholm	Eskdalemuir	Westerkirk	Ewes	Canonby	Total
1755	1,833	675	544	392	1,733	5,177
1791	2,540	619	655	325	2,725	6,864
1801	2,039	537	638	358	2,580	6,649
1811	2,636	581	698	338	2,749	7002
1821	2,404	651	672	314	3,084	7,678
1831	2,676	650	642	335	2,997	7,300
1851	2,820	646	638	328	3,032	7,464
1851	2,990	672	658	354	3,163	7,837

Year	Langholm	Eskdalemuir	Westerkirk	Ewes	Canonby	Total
1861	2,979	590	537	356	3,219	7,681
1871	3,735	551	540	338	3,055	8,219
1881	4,612	543	478	337	2,723	8,693
1891	3,970	488	454	299	2,476	7,687
1901	3,500	441	415	261	1,959	6,576
1911	3,302	392	393	247	1,838	6,172
1921	2,981	385	368	235	1,756	5,725
1931	2,770	378	372	241	1,498	5,259
1951	2,750	360	322	193	1,455	5,080
1961	2,625	336	275	183	1,354	4,773
1971	2,567	288	196	164	1,218	4433
1981	2,742	240	189	148	1,140	4,459
1991	2,728	404	190	91	1,144	4,557

The above figures have been supplied by and are reproduced by courtesy of the General Register Office for Scotland. Crown Copyright.

REFERENCES

Chapter 2	1	*My Strange Pets* by Mr. Richard Bell p. 305.
	2	*Prehistoric Times* by Lord Avebury.
Chapter 3	1	*Prehistoric Times*, p. 106.
	2	Lockyer's *Stonehenge*, p. 161.
Chapter 4	1	*Prehistoric Times*, p. 103.
	2	Lockyer's *Stonehenge* p. 35.
Chapter 5	1	Dumfries Journal, June 24th 1828. MS communication Soc. Antiq. Scot., Andrew Brown, Esq. and read March, 1829.
	2	*My Strange Pets*, p. 307.
Chapter 6	1	Hutchinson's *History of Cumberland*, Vol. III., p. 529.
	2	*My Strange Pets*, pp. 297-8.
Chapter 7	1	*Journal* of Anthropological Institute, N.S. III., 1900.
	2	See *The Scottish Gael*, Vol. II., p. 7.
	3	*Prehistoric Annals*, Vol. II., p. 338.
	4	See Sir Walter Scott's *Minstrelsy of the Scottish Border*, Vol. II., p. 337.
Chapter 8	1	Mr. Alex. McCracken.
	2	Hutchinson's *History of Cumberland*, Vol. II., p. 534.
Chapter 9	1	*Bloodline of the Holy Grail* by Laurence Gardner, pp. 192-3.
	2	Skene's *Celtic Scotland*.
	3	Bogg's *Border Country*, p. 317.
	4	Anglo-Saxon Chronicle.
	5	*Scotland from the Earliest Times* by W C. Dickinson p. 53-55.
	6	*Scottish Kings* by Gordon Donaldson p. 13.
	7	Wilson's *Prehistoric Annals of Scotland, Vol.* II., p. 397.
Chapter 10	1	Skene's *Celtic Scotland*, Vol.II., p. 19.
	2	Armstrong's *History of Liddesdale, Eskdale &c.* p. 152.
	3	Armstrong's *History of Liddesdale, Eskdale &c.* p. 107.
	4	Scott's *Border Minstrelsy*, p. 12.
	5	Armstrong, p. 99.
	6	*Catalogue* of the National Museum of Antiquities, 1892 ed. p. 358.
Chapter 13	1	Canon Taylor's *Words and Places*, c. viii.
	2	R.B. Armstrong's *History of Liddesdale, &c.*, p. 151.
	3	R.B. Armstrong, p. 192.
Chapter 14	1	R.B. Armstrong's *History of Liddesdale*, p. 152.
	2	R.B. Armstrong, p. 153.
	3	New Statistical Account, 1841.
	4	R.B. Armstrong, p. 168.
Chapter 15	1	R.B. Armstrong's *History of Liddesdale &c.* p. 152, note 5.
	2	Sir Herbert Maxwell's *History of the House of Douglas*, Vol. I.
	3	*History of the House of Douglas*, Vol.1., p. 181.
	4	R.B. Armstrong, Appendix X11 and XIII.
	5	*Privy Council Records*, 1578.
	6	W. Riddell Carre's *Border Memories*, note, p. 51.
	7	*Border Memories*, p. 52.
	8	R.B. Armstrong, pp.158 and 165.

	9	*The Historical Families of Dumfriesshire.*
	10	*The Historical Families of Dumfriesshire,*
	11	Border Memories, p. 62.
Chapter 16	1	*The Historical Families of Dumfriesshire*, p. 7.
	2	R.B. Armstrong's *History of Liddesdale &c.*, p. 178.
	3	Pitscottie's Chron., edition 1814, Vol. I., pp. 342, 343. quotes as follows :- "Efter this hunting the king hanged Johne Armstrong, laird of Kilnockie". Pitscottie is quoted by R. B. Armstrong p. 275.
	4	R.B. Armstrong, p. 274.
	5	Calendar of Border Papers, Vol. I., p. 76.
	6	Echoes from the Border Hills Chap. 3 & 4.
	7	*The Elliots* p. 3 by The Dowager Lady Eliott of Stobbs and Sir Arthur Eliott, 11th Baronet of Stobbs.
	8	Dr. J C. Little. 1987 lecture to the Scottish Genealogy Society.
	9	R.B. Armstrong, p. 164.
	10	Personal communication from Mrs. Edith van Driel.
	11	Privy Council Records, Vol. II., p. 42.
	12	Story of the Surname of Beatson.
	13	William Park, *The Vale of Esk.*
	14	*The Irvings of Bonshaw*, A M.T. Maxwell-Irving, BSc., F.S.A. Scot.
	15	Nat. Dict. of Biography.
	16	T.J. Carlyle, *The Scotts of Ewisdail.*
	17	Craig-Brown's *History of Selkirkshire*, Vol. I., p. 164.
Chapter 18	1	R.B. Armstrong's *History of Liddesdale &c.*, p. 214.
	2	R.B. Armstrong's *History of Liddesdale &c.*, p. 3.
	3	MS. by the late Geo. R. Rome.
	4	Royal Commission on the Ancient Monuments of Scotland, 1981.
	5	Chronicles of the Armstrongs, p. 138 of 1st Edition published 1902.
	6	The Book of Caerlaverock Vol. II., p. 465.
	7	Major T.C.R. Armstrong-Wilson letter to Eskdale and Liddesdale Advertiser 27th Aug. 1998.
	8	Pennant's *Tour*, Vol. I., p. 87.
	9	Sir Walter Scott's Introduction to "Johnie Armstrong" in *Border Minstrelsy.*
	10	Mr. Alex. McCracken in The Eskdale & Liddesdale Advertiser, 12th January, 1977.
	11	*The Irvings of Bonshaw*, A. M. T. Maxwell-Irving, BSc.,FSA Scot.
	12	Statistical Account, 1793.
	13	Dr. Borland's *Border Raids and Reivers*, p. 171.
Chapter 19	1	From Teribus, the Common Riding song of Hawick.
	2	Tytler's *History of Scotland*, Vol. II., p. 275.

REFERENCES

	3	Sir H. Maxwell's *History of Dumfries and Galloway,* p. 958.
Chapter 20	1	Green's *Encyclopaedia of Scots Law.*
	2	Sir William Fraser's *Scotts of Buccleuch.*
	3	Paper read to the London Eskdale Society on 12th January 1883, Mr. Geo.R. Rome.
	4	The Macmillan Encyclopaedia.
Chapter 21	1	Statistical Account 1793.
	2	Echoes from the Border Hills p. 114.
	3	The Journal of the Paisley Family Society, Vol 10, p. 54.
Chapter 22	1	R.B. Armstrong's *History of Liddesdale,* &c. p. 101.
	2	Taken from reprints which appeared in the Eskdale & Liddesdale Advertiser.
	3	R.B. Armstrong's *History of Liddesdale,* &c. p. 96.
	4	Acta. Parl. Scot. (1615).
	5	Fasti Ecclesiae Scoticanae.
Chapter 24	1	*Scotland's Battle for Spiritual Independence,* by Hector Macpherson p. 950.
	2	The Fasti of the United Free Church of Scotland up to 1929.
	3	Scotland's *Battles for Spiritual Independence,* pp. 221-2.
	4	Report in the Eskdale & Liddesdale Advertiser.
	5	*The Scottish Congregational Ministry, 1794-1993.* Copyright W.D. McNaughton.
Chapter 25	1	Privy Council Records.
Chapter 27	1	*The Common-Riding* by Francis Bell.
Chapter 29	1	The Much Hon. Duncan Paisley of Westerlea.
	2	*A History of the English-Speaking Peoples*, Vol. 3, p. 294 by Winston S. Churchill.

APPENDIX 1

LOWLAND WORDS

In Chapter 12 there are given lists of place-names in Eskdale which are Celtic or Norse in their form, and some of which may possibly date back to the coming into Eskdale of these races. Subjoined are lists of words now, or until recently, in common use in the south of Scotland, which are traceable to Celtic, Norse, or Norman French influence.

CELTIC

Many words of Celtic descent are in daily use throughout the British Isles, e.g., *button, cart, bogie, gown, rug, darn, trap, whip, wicket, clan, flannel, kill, tartan, whisky, plaid,* &c.

Others are more commonly found in the dialects of the north of England and south of Scotland:— *brat,* an apron; *cam,* meaning crooked, as in the Scots word *camsteerie,* or in the Northumbrian word *cammeral,* crooked (cp. "a game leg"); *peel,* a castle, applied especially to the towers on the Borders. A word once in regular use in Eskdale but now rarely heard, was *ker-handed,* meaning left-handed. The term is said to be derived from Kinnath-Ker, an ancient Pictish King who was left-handed. The name *ask,* applied in Eskdale to the water-newt, is from the Celtic *asc; airs* is Celtic *aird; bannock* is from the Gaelic *bonnack; brae* from *bre,* a hill; *dub* from *dubh,* the gutter; *duds,* meaning rags, from *dud; angle,* the fireside, from *aingeal; lum,* the chimney, from Cymric *llumon; spate,* a flood, from *speid; whin,* gorse, from Cymric *chwyn.*

NORSE

The number of Norse words in the speech of the Lowlands is naturally very large, and many of them show very little modification. The following list might easily be augmented :—

Lowland Words	English	Norse
Bairn	Child	Barn
Byre	A cow-shed	Byr
Clip	To cut	Clippe
Drucken	Drunken	Drukken
Frem Folks	Strangers	Fremmede Folke
Fou	Drunk	Fuld
Gar	To make	Gjöre
Glaikit	Stupid	Glaikit
Greet	To weep	Grœde
Gudeman	Husband	Gudeman
Hansel	Gift	Hansel
Hass	Throat	Hass
Hogmanay		Hogmanay
Kame	To comb	Kœmme
Kail	Cabbage	Kaal
Kirn-milk	Churn-milk	Kjernemelk

Lowland Words	English	Norse
Liester	Barbed fish-spears	Lysters
Kirkyard	Churchyard	Kirkgård
Lowe	Flame	Lue
Nieve	Fist	Nief
Rigging	Ridge of a house	Ryging
Rive	To split	Rive
Sackless	Worthless	Sageslös
Sark	Shirt	Sœrk
Slocken	Quench or Slake	Slokke
Smiddy	Smithy	Smedja
Stey	A steep ascent	Stiga
Starn or Sterne	Star	Stjerne
Toom	Empty	Tom
Yin	One	Een
Thole	To endure	Tåla
Trumf	Trump	Trumf

NORMAN FRENCH

It is impossible to trace definitely how many of the Norman-French words came into the Scots. The settlement of the barons in the time of David I; the intercommunication between Scotland and France in commerce, and the interchange of soldiers in the sixteenth century, were all favourable occasions. The words relating to feudalism, war, and sport, such as *chivalry*, *warden*, *truncheon*, *forest*, *quarry*, *banner*, *joust*, *falconer*, probably were introduced by the barons. Others still in use are *ashet*, from *assiette,* a plate; *jigget*, from *gigot*, a leg of mutton; *grosel*, or *groser*, from *groseille*, a red currant; *gean*, or *geine*, a wild cherry; *gou*, an after-taste; *corbie*, from *corbeau*, a crow; *boule*, a ball; *dour*, from *dur* hard; *douce*, from *douce*, sweet; *brulliment*, from *brouiller*, to quarrel; *cundy*, from *conduit*, a pipe; *muillings*, crumbs, from *moulin,* mill; *fash*, from *fâcher*, to vex; *hoolet*, from *hulotte*, the wood-owl; *raw*, from rue, a street; *tue*, from *tuer,* to tire.

LORD WILLIAM CRANSTOUN'S CHARTER OF 1610

Apud Regiam de Roistoun, 15 Jan., 1610

Rex,— in memoriam revocans servitium sibi prestitum per D. WILLELMUM CRANSTOUN de eodem equitem auratum ducemque sui satelitii constituti subire illud servitium ad pacandos incolas limitum regni Scotie *lie lait borderris* continuo post suam corone Anglie successionem, non solum ejus magnis sumptibus verum etiam ejus, amicorum et servorum in varia damna et pericula expositioni, quod servitium recompensationem meritum est cum digno premio ei in verbo principis promisso, — concessit dicto Wil., heredibus ejus masc. et assignatis quibuscunque, — terras de Langholme, cum fortalicio, manerie, molendinis, piscariis, terras de Brwmeholme, Arkinholme, Taviotscheillis, Quhytescheillis, Balgray, Arkin, Brakinuray, Over et Nether Mylneholme et Tympen, Stablegortoun, Burnefute, Strankgait et Fingland, Carnisgill, Bombie, Glenberten, Cowcherland, Loganeheid, Bowineis, Enzieholme et Milgilheid, Apiltraquhit, Harberquhit, Lyneholme, Dabeth, Monksyde, Bailyiehill, Earshud, Crunzertoun, Scheill cum molendino, Littil et Meikill Megdaill, Braidheid, Glenkeill, Massiesait, Wyndieleyis, et Stanereis, Auchingavill, terras dominicales de Logane, Knok cum molendino, Boukin, Rig, Craig, cum fortaliciis, maneriebus, molendinis, moris, piscariis, tenentibus, etc., omnium suprascriptorum, vic. Drumfreis:— que regi devenerunt ob forisfacturam Joannis olim dom. Maxwell (Jun. 1609):— et quas rex incorporavit in liberam baroniam de Langholme, ordinando fortalicium de L. principale fore messuagium:— REDDEND unum den. argenti nomine albe firme:—Test. ut in aliis cartis *etc.*

TRANSLATION:— *At the Palace of Royston, 15 January, 1610*

The KING,— calling to remembrance the service discharged for him by SIR WILLIAM CRANSTOUN of that ilk, Knight of the Bath, and commander of his guard constituted to undergo that service for the pacifying of the inhabitants of the boundaries of the kingdom of Scotland *the late Borders* immediately after his accession to the crown of England — not only for his great expenses, but also for the venturing of himself, his friends and his servants into various losses and dangers — which service hath earned recompense and therewith a worthy reward promised on the word of a Prince — has granted to the said William, his heirs male, and assignees whatsoever the lands of Langholm with its fortress, manor, mills and fisheries, the lands of Broomholm, Arkinholm, Teviotshiels, Whitshiels, Balgray, Arkin, Brackenwrae, Over and Nether Milnholm and Timpen, Stapelgortoun, Burnfoot, Strankgate and Fingland, Carlesgill, Bombie, Glenberton, Coucherland, Loganhead, Bonese, Enzieholm and Millgillhead, Appletrewhat, Harperwhat, Lyneholm, Dabeth, Monkside, Bailie Hill, Erschewood [Airdsmoss], Crunzertoun, Shiel with its mill, Little and Mickle Megdale, Braidhead, Glenkeill, Mossieseat, Windylees and Staneries, Auchingavill, the demesne lands of Logan, Knock with its mill, Boyken, Rig, Craig, with the fortresses, manors, mills, moors, fisheries, tenants, &c., of all above written, in the sherifdom of Dumfries — which were escheated to the King by the forfeiture of John, sometime Lord Maxwell (June 1609) — and which the King has incorporated into the free Barony of Langholm, appointing the fortress of Langholm to be its principal messuage:— RENT, one silver penny, in the name of blencheferme — Witnesses, as in the other charters of the same date.

THE BURGH CHARTER OF 1621

(GRANTED TO THE EARL OF NITHSDALE)
Apud Theobaldis in Anglia,. 19 Sept. 1621

REX,— cum consensu Joannis Comitis de Mar, Domini Erskene et Garioch, Thesaurarii, Computorum Rotulatoris et Collectoris,— et Carolus princeps et senescallus Scotie et Vallie dux Rothesay, Albanie, Cornubie et York comes de Carrick dom. Insularum baro de Renfrew,— concesserunt ROBERTO COMITI DE NITHISDAILL domino Maxwell, Eskdaill et Cairleill &c. heredibus ejus masc. et assignatis quibuscunque.......10 mercatas terrarum de Arkiltoun, 20 librat. de Mekildaill, infra bondas de Eskdaill, vic. Drumfreis; 12 mercat. de Wraithis vocat. Over and Nather Wraithis in parochia de Nather Ewis, vic. de Drumfreis; cum molendinis et piscationibus earundem:......advocationem ecclesie parochialis de Nather Ewis et terrarum ecclesiasticarum ejusdem, decimas garbales et alias decimas et devorias rectorias et vicarias dicte ecclesie et parochie ejusdem, advocationes ecclesiarum et parochiarum de Wauchope et Sibbelbie, decimas garbales aliasque decimas et devorias rectorias et vicarias earundem, vic. Drumfreis......necnon terras de Flask alias Flaskholme, Howgill et Glendoven, Burnegranis (vel Burnegrange), Woufhoip (vel Wolfhoip), Park alias Busis, cum turribus, vic. Drumfreis 53 solidat. 4 den. terrarum de Murthum, 5 librat. de Gallowsyd, 40 sol. de Nes, 26 sol. 8 den. de Wattirgranis (vel Wattergrange), 40 sol. de Brigholmes, 53 sol. 4 den. de Glencorff, ant. ext. que fuerunt partes de Wauchopdaill, terras de Torronnane extenden. ad 3 librat. 6 sol. 8 den. ant. ext. cum salmonum aliisque piscationibus, vic. Drumfreis;— quas D. Gedeon Murray de Elibank miles eum consensu D. Patricii M. de Langschaw militis filii sui natu maximi et heredis apparentis resignavit;— necnon terras de Dewscoir, Willieholme et Cruholme, Townisteidis, Hallieschaw, Sanctbryd-hill, ter de Quhittingstounholme (vel Puttingstounholme), Raeknowis, Glentenmonthheid, Tannalie, Waterholmes et Birslandis, Bloche, Brokinheidishoill, Blocheburnefute et Corsmungo, Irishauch, Thomishoill, Newlandis, Beckeis, Birnlie, Calffeild cum molendino, Middilholme, Staikheuch, Stobholme, Rowntrielie et Monkreland, cum advocatione rectorie et vicaric ecclesie parochialis de Wauchop, cum salmonum et aliis piscationibus in aquis de Esk et Wauchop, jacentes in Wauchopdaill, terras de Blisses in Ewisdeall, terras de Park, Craigielandis, Carrutheriscroft, Crosie, Craigie, Hotcroftis et Middingknowis, terras, vocatas Inter aquas *(Betuix-the-watteris)* terras de Tannasyd, Quhitleis, Bogthropill, *the Chaippell*, Patrikholme, omnes in Carrutheris, vic. de Drumfreis; cum advocatione rectorie et vicarie ecclesie et parochie de Carrutheris ; terras de Dryisdaill et Pengaw......necnon terras de Langholme, cum turre, manerie loco, molendinis, piscariis, terras de Brumholm, Arkinholm, Teviotscheillis, Quhytscheillis, Balgray, Ardkin, Breckanewrae, Over et Nether Mylneholme, Timpen, Staplegortoun, Burnfute, Stainkgatt (vel Strongait) et Fingland, Carnisgill, Bombie, Glenberten, Coucherland, Loganheid, Boineis (vel Bowineis), Enzieholme et Mylngilheid, Apiltriequhat, Harperquhat, Lyneholme, Dalbeth, Monksyd, Bailliehill, Ershuid, Crunzertoun, Scheill cum molendino, Litill et Meikil Megdaill, Braidheid, Glenkeill, Massieseat, Windieleyis et Stanreis, Auchingavill, *lie* Maynes de Logan, Knok cum molendino, Boykin, Rig, Craig, cum castris, manerierum locis, molendinis, moris, piscariis, tenentibus, &c., vic. de Drumfreis;— quas Wil. dom. Cranstoun de eodem et D. Jo. Cranstoun ejus filius et heres apparens similiter resignaverunt;.....terras vocatas *the Birrages* aut acras burgales *lie Burrow-aikeris* de Stapilgortoun, terras de Absterlandis et Dornokgillis in parochia de Watstirker, 5 libratas de Langriggis in parochia de.....et senesc. Vallis Annandie......Preterea rex creavit urbem et villam de Langholme, partem terrarum de L. existentem, — in liberum burgum baronie, BURGUM DE LANGHOLME nuncupand; cum potestate dicto com. eligendi ballivos, burgenses, &c. ; cum potestate comburgensibus *lie pack* et *peill* emendi et vendendi, &c., cum potestate dicto comiti habendi pretorium et crucem foralem, et forum hepomadatim die Jovis, cum duabus liberis nundinis annuatim, 29 Jun. et 24 Oct., cum tolloniis, &c.: REDDEND.........pro Flask, &c. (usque ad

Torronnane) 2 den., nomine albe firme; pro Deuscoir, &c. (usque ad Pengaw) 40 sol. feudifirme, cum duplicatione feudifirme in introitu heredum; pro Langholme, &c. (usque ad Craig) unum den. argenti, cum administratione justicie in dicto burgo. Test. ut in aliis cartis, &c.

TRANSLATION:—*At Theobald's in England,* 19 Sept. 1621

The KING,— with consent of John, Earl of Mar, Lord Erskine and Garioch, Treasurer, Enroller and Collecton of Accounts, and Charles, Prince and Steward of Scotland, and of Wales, Duke of Rothesay, Albany, Cornwall, and York, Earl of Carrick, Lord of the Isles, Baron of Renfrew,— have granted to ROBERT, EARL OF NITHSDALE, Lord Maxwell, Eskdaill, and Cairleill, &c., and to his heirs male and assignees whomsoever, &c., &c., the ten merk-lands of Arkiltoun, the 20 pound lands of Mekildaill within the bounds of Eskdaill, in the county of Dumfries; 12 merk-lands of Wraithes, styled "Over and Nether Wraithes", in the parish of Nether Ewes, in the county of Dumfries, with the mills and fisheries of the same, &c., &c., the advowson of the parish church of Nether Ewes and of the glebe land of the same, the corn tithes, and other tithes and dues, rectorial and vicarial of the said church and parish of the same, the advowsons of the churches and parishes of Waucbope and Sibbelby, the corn tithes and other tithes and dues rectorial and vicarial of the same, in the county of Dumfries, &c., &c.: moreover the lands of Flask, otherwise Flaskholme, Howgill, and Glendoven, Burngrains (or Burngrange), Woufhope (or Wolfhope), Park, otherwise Buss, with their towers, in the county of Dumfries ; the 53s. 4d. lands of Murtholm, the £5 lands of Gallowside, the 40s. lands of Neis, the 26s. 8d. lands of Watergrains (or Watergrange), the 40s. lands of Brigholmes the 53s. 4d. lands of Glencorff of old extent, which were parts of Wauchopedale; the lands of Torronnane, extending to 3 pounds 6sh. and 8d., of old extent, with salmon and other fisheries in the county of Dumfries — which Sir Gideon Murray of Elibank, knight, with consent of Sir Patrick Murray of Langschaw, knight, his eldest son and heir apparent, resigned;— moreover the lands of Dewscoir, &c., &c.; Calfield with its mill, &c., &c., with the advowson of the rectory and vicarage of the parish church of Wauchope, with the salmon and other fisheries in the waters of Esk and Wauchope, lying in Wauchopedale, the lands of Blisses in Ewesdale, the lands of Park, Craiglands, Carutherscroft, Crosie, Craigie, Hotcrofts, and Middingknowes, the lands called *Betwixt-the-Waters*, the lands of Tannaside, Whitelees, Bogthrophill, The Chapel, Patrickholme, all in Caruthers in the county of Dumfries ; with the advowson of the rectory and vicarage of the church and parish of Carruthers; the lands of Dryffesdale and Pengaw, &c., &c., moreover the lands of Langholm, with the tower, the manor place, mills and fisheries, the lands of Broomholm, &c., &c.; the mains of Logan, Knock with its mill, Boykin, Rigg, Craig, with their castles, manor places, mills, moors, fisheries, tenants, &c., in the county of Dumfries — which William, Lord Cranston of that ilk, and Master John Cranston, his son and heir apparent in like manner resigned, &c., &c. The lands called the Burages, or Burgh-Acres of Stapelgortoun, the lands of Absterlands and Dornockgills in the parish of Watstirkir, £5 lands of Longriggs in the parish of......and the stewartry of Annandale......moreover the King has created the town and house of Langholm, the existing part of the lands of Langholm — into a free burgh of barony, to be styled THE BURGH OF LANGHOLM, with power to the said Earl to choose bailiffs, burgesses, &c., with power to the fellow-burgesses, "the pack and the peel," of buying and selling, &c., with power to the said Earl of having a public hall and market cross, and a market weekly on Thursdays with two free fairs yearly (29 June and 24 Oct.), with tolls, &c. RENT for "Flask, &c." — (to Torronane,) 2d. in the name of blencheferme; for Dewscoir, &c.-(to Pengaw,) 40s. fee-ferme, with a double fee-ferme in case of entrance of heirs for Langholm, &c. (to Craig,) one silver penny; with administration of justice in the said burgh. Witnesses as in the other charters, &c.

422

THE NITHSDALE CONTRACT OF 1628

Contract between the Earl of Nithsdale and the Heritors of Langholm, 1628

Ane contract to be drawn betwixt my Lord Nithsdale on the one part and James Maxwell of Kirkconnell, Master of Maxwell, James Maxwell of Tinwald, Archibald Maxwell of Cowhill, George Maxwell of Carnsalurth, Robert Maxwell of Dinwoodie, John Maxwell of Middlebie, Herbert Maxwell of Templand, Robert Maxwell, brother to the said James Maxwell of Tinwald, John Maxwell of Holms, John Maxwell of Broomholm, brother to the said Archibald Maxwell of Cowhill, on the other part, as follows — That is to say, the said Earl dispones heritably in fee to the forenamed persons equalie amongst them, their heirs and assignees, all and haill the lands of Arkinholm, with the pertinents, except the woods and fishings within the same preserved to the said Earl, holden of My Lord, his heir, and successors, in feu farm, for payment equalie amongst them for the sum of 250 merks Scots, at Whitsunday and Martinmas proportionaly, and doubling the feu farm the first year of the entry of each heir and successor, as use is of in feu farms, and My Lord still warranting the said lands free of all inconvenienceys, and because the forenamed lands on ane part of the lands and Lordship of Langholm pertaining to the said Earl, and that he has procured of His Majestie the erecting of ane Burgh of Baronie at Langholm, to be called the Town of Langholm, and that the said Earl be of mind and be thir present consents that the said Burgh of Baronie called the Town of Langholm, shall be builded within the said lands of Arkinholm, as ane part of the said land and Lordship of Langholm; therefore the haill forenamed persons binds and oblidges them, their heirs and successors, ilke ane of them for their own part, to build and conform upon the most convenient part as they shall design within the bounds of the said lands of Arkinholm, ilke ane of them a sufficient stone house on the fore street, builded with stone and lyme, of two houses height at the least, containing fourty foots within the walls of length, eighteen foot of breadth, twelve foot of height, with power to them to build higher, longer, or broader, or more houses within their own bounds designed to them as they shall think expedient on the said persons their proportion of bounds designed to them shall allow conform to their gavall. These shall bigg upon each side of the High Street of the said Burgh of the quantitie and quality foresaid — to wit, five of the said persons on the ane side thereof and the other five on the other side of the same, and that within the space of three years of the date hereof, and the said persons, and ilke ane of them, oblidges themselves, their heirs and successors, that ilka ane of their buildings so to be constructed within the said space shall be worth at least the sum of 500 merks Scots money, and if they shall faill therein they oblidge them and ilke ane of them to pay to the said Earl the sum of 500 merks, and that by and attour and without prejudice of the fullfilling of the premissies like as the said persons oblidges them and ilka ane of them and their foresaids, that if they shall dispone any part or portions of the properties disponed to them, that they shall build and confront upon the said High Street ane sufficient stone house with stone and lyme of the like height with the rest and breadth and of length so far as shall be proportionable to their parts alike; and they shall dispone under the aforesaid pains, and the said persons oblidges and ilke ane of them to leave ane *patent* and High Street to be the High Street of the said Burgh of thrittie foots of breadth at least in all parts thereof, and it is proceeded (or provided) that the Tolbooth of the said Burgh in the same shall be constructed and bigged and the same shall be in the High Street, part foregainst or next adjacent to the proportion which shall belong to the said George Maxwell of Carnsalurth and his foresaids, and My Lord oblidges to make the said haill ten persons Burgesses of the said Burgh of Langholm in due form as officers, with power to them to use all kinds of trade and traffique within the said Burgh as any Burgh of Baronie uses now or may do within this kingdom, and the haill forenamed persons oblidges them and ilka ane of them that they shall nowise sell or dispone or woodset the said lands, houses, and pertinents thereof, or any part of the same, or yet sett any longer tack whereof than nynteen years without the special consent and assine of the said Noble Earl and his foresaids first had and obtained thereto, otherwise to be null and ineffectual, and it is specially provided betwixt the haill parties or his presents that it shall be lesum to them their heirs and successors, or any other persons dwelling within the said town, who shall have the said Earl and his foresaids' consent and be burgesses therein to win and lead stones of any part of the Common quarries of the said lands of Arkinholm, and for grassings to be made to the persons and ilka ane of them for then own parts equally as said is in the said lands of Arkinholm, upon the provisions and conditions above specified, the said Noble Earl make and constitute conjunctly and severally his bailleys committing to them or any of them his full power, to give state seasing heritable, actual real, or corporall possession of the said lands of Arkinholm, with the pertinents, excepting the woods and fishings thereof, as said is to the said persons equally, or to their attorneys their name to deliverance, of earth and stones of the said lands as use conform to the tenor hereof, and the said persons oblidges them their heirs and successors *nunc inde* to others for extension of this minute of contract in ample form keeping the substance herein contained, and to observe and fullfill the same aither of them to others conform to the tenor hereof in all points and the said parties are content thir presents be insert and registrat in the books of Councill and Session, or in the Sheriff Court books at Dumfries; and ilka ane of them conjunctly and severally their procurators respectively, in witness whereof the said partys have subscribed these presents with their hands, written by Martin Newall, writter to His Majestie's Signet at Dumfries, the fourth day of February, 1628 years, before these witnesses — Matthew Hairstens of Craigs, J ohn Maxwell of Thornieland, and John Maxwell of Shaws, and the said Martin Newall, writter hereof, *sic subscribitur.* (Signed)

JAMES MAXWELL, Nithsdale.	ROBERT MAXWELL of Dinwoodie.
ARCHIBALD MAXWELL, Cowhill.	ROBERT MAXWELL.
JAMES MAXWELL, Tinwald.	JOHN MAXWELL of Middlebie.
GEORGE MAXWELL, Carnsalurth.	JOHN MAXWELL of Broomholm.
HERBERT MAXWELL	JOHN MAXWELL of Holm.
JOHN MAXWELL, 3 Merkland, *Witness.*	MATTHEW HAIRSTENS, *Witness.*
JOHN MAXWELL of Shaws, *Witness.*	MARTIN NEWALL, *Witness.*

Season was given to the within-named persons at Dumfries, April, 1628, at four in the afternoon by Martin Newall.

DIVISION OF THE COMMONTY OF LANGHOLM IN 1757-8

THE COMMONTY of Langholm, the division of which is referred to in Chapter 26, was bounded as follows:—

Beginning at the Kilnsyke ford goes down the said syke till it joins the water of Esk, and then goes northward by the side of an enclosure belonging to John Little, defender; along the dyke and hedge of said enclosure to the old Mercat Road at the head of the said hedge, and from thence to the side of the water of Esk, and down the water side to the foot of the aforesaid Kilnsyke, and from thence along the side of the said water to the foot of the Longwood Gill, commonly called the North Gill or March Gill, which is the march betwixt the property lands of Broomholm, belonging to the pursuer, and the said Commonty, and the march of the said Commonty goes from thence eastward up the aforesaid Gill to the head thereof, where a pit is made at the sample of a syke, and from thence up to the said syke or sample of a syke by pits made to a pit made with wings, and from thence in a line to a rush bush at the Peat Road, where a Pit is made, and thence goes northward by pits to a pit where a line going northward cuts a line coming westward from the Saugh Bush at the head of the Haresyke till it comes to a stone at the Beacon end, where a pit is made at the waterfall, and then the march goes straight east to the said Saugh Bush on the Haresyke head, and down the said syke till it join the Water of Tarras, and from thence up the side of the said water to the foot of a little syke or runner, and up the said runner to a pit made at the root of an old alder tree, and from thence by heaps of stones until it join the Water of Tarras again at the Willow Bush, a little above a big stone called the Hackyd Stone, and goes from thence by the side of the said water to Little Tarras-foot, and up Little Tarras to the foot of Birch Syke, where a piece of ground lying between Birch Syke and Black Syke, bounded on the east side with the Black Syke and on the west with the Birch Syke until the same joins the Mercat Road is called the Pleafields, and that the march of the said Commonty goes from thence along the said Mercat Road to a place called Clatteringfoord, where the march joins with the Black Syke, and then goes up Black Syke to the head thereof, where a pit is made, and goes from thence northwards through a flow moss in a straight line to a pit made at the head of a syke at the east end of the Donks, and down the said syke or runner to the Turner Cleuch head, where another pit is made, and from thence the march goes up Slatyford Syke to the Slaty Ford, where it joins the corner of a stone dyke belonging to John Little, defender, and goes from thence along the said dyke to the head of Langholm Loaning, and from thence along another dyke belonging to the pursuer to Kilnsyke-head, and down Kilnsyke to Kilnsyke Foord, where the march began.

. . . .

On the suit of 1757, by Maxwell of Broomholm against the Duke of Buccleuch, John Little, Simon Little and Archibald Little, the Court made the following AWARD:—

"That the whole bounds comprehended within the said limits and marches do belong in common property to the pursuers and defenders, proprietors of the Ten Merk-lands of Langholm and pertinents and have been immemorially possest as such by them and their tenants and that the whole of the said Commonty within the foresaid limits excepting the Moss after mentioned is to be divided amongst the defenders the Duke of Buccleuch and John Little and the pursuer and that the valuation of each of the Ten Merk-lands of Langholm is 70 merks Scots and that the pursuer John Maxwell's share in the said division as proprietor of five of the said Ten Merk-lands and as having rights by the writes produced to the share of the said Commonty falling to the other merk-land which belonged to Simon Little is to be conform to 420 merks Scots and that the said John Little's share of three of the said Merk-lands is to be conform to a valuation of 210 merks Scots and that the Duke of Buccleuch's part is to be conform to 70 merks Scots valuation."

The witnesses summoned before the Commission were Archibald Paterson, weaver, Langholm; William Plenderleith, labourer, Langholm; Archibald Scott in Hopsrig; and John Irving and John Murray in Milntown. These, with the Commissioners, passed to the Kilnsykeford, the first-mentioned point on the boundary of the Common, and being solemnly sworn, proceeded along the marches of the Common as far as they could till darkness set in. The company then returned to Langholm and the examination of the witnesses began, their evidence being put down in writing and signed by the Commissioners, the clerk, and the witnesses, except John Irving, who could not write. The evidence of the witnesses, who were all men of advanced age, embraced statements as to the correctness of the description of the bounds of the Common and who possessed rights to it. One witness, Archibald Little, merchant in Langholm, stated in regard to the latter point that "the tenants within the Ten Merk-lands had been in use to cast their peats and lead home the same, and that the tenants and inhabitants of Langholm had a right and had always been in use to quarry and lead home stones the same as the peats." Plenderleith concurred with the evidence by Little that the whole Common was very stony, and that building stone might be had in any part of it.

PLAN OF THE COMMONTY OF LANGHOLM DIVIDED
According to the Interlocutor of the Commissioners for that end
27 Oct. 1758.
by JAMES TAIT Edinburgh.

426

The Court found that the Common Moss lying within the limits of the said Commonty must not be divided, but was to be reserved as common for the use of those having interest therein. The boundaries of the Common Moss were defined as follows:—

"Beginning at a pit made at the Castle Craigs on the east side of the hill, and from thence westward in a line to a two-pointed pit near a gray stone at the south corner of the said Moss, and from thence westward by another two-pointed pit near a well, and from thence northwards by pits to Maxwell's Cairn, and from thence north-eastwardly by another pit near a cairn, till it strikes the common march, and along the same to the head of Grey Bannock or Black Syke, and down the same to a two-pointed pit a little above the Clattering Foord, and from thence in a straight line to the said pit at Castle Craigs where it began."

THE KILNGREEN was not included in this Award, but was made the subject of a separate enquiry. The witnesses examined regarding this part of the Commonty were:—

John Irving in Milntown; William Paisley, innkeeper, Langholm; and John Murray in Milntown, and they pointed out its marches and gave evidence as to its possession by the people of Langholm. The statements of these witnesses included a description of the marches of the Kilngreen, and showed that at one time the Ewes ran in a course nearer to the old Castle than that in which it ran at that date, and consequently the Kilngreen had been reduced in size. The course of the river had been changed by a bank of stones laid down at the foot of the mill dam by Mr. Melville, the Duke's Chamberlain, and a big flood occurring, the Kilngreen was broken into by the river. The witnesses also declared that ever since they could remember the Kilngreen had been pastured upon by the cattle of the inhabitants of Langholm, and that at one time this right extended to the ground on the right bank of the Ewes, and was only interrupted after Elliot of Middleholm Mill went to Langholm Castle [1724], and it was by his orders that the miller of Langholm Mill interfered with these pasture rights, and that Langholm Fairs had been held upon it, the Buccleuch family levying tolls at these Fairs.

The following is a description of the bounds of the Kilngreen as pointed out and sworn to by the witnesses to the Commissioners:—

"The march begins at the little Clinthead, where a pit was made, and from thence to another pit made at the corner of Johnathan Glendinning's park nook, and from thence to another pit made at the side of a dyke at Janet Bell's pathhead, and from thence along the dyke on the head of the Green Braes to a pit made opposite to the bridge, and from thence down the brae to a pit made at the lower ledge of the bridge, and along the said bridge to another pit made where the old watercourse was, and from thence to another pit near the foot of the mill dam, and from thence by pits made along the old watercourse, until it join with the water of Esk at the foot of the old Castle garden, and down Esk till it join with the water of Ewes at the little Clinthead, where the said marches began." The accompanying plan is a copy of that prepared, in accordance with the Award of the Court, by James Tait, land surveyor, Edinburgh.

REGISTER OF BAPTISMS OF STAPELGORTOUN

(This appendix is not included in the subjoined indices.)

A Copy of Register* — of all the names of the Children in the parish of Staplegortoun — and some other Children, in some other parishes that was Baptized by me; since the 8 of May 1668, all thesse in the parish of Staplegortoun, that was Baptized, in my absence, by some other Ministers, all having this mark in the hinderend of the line. ∞

*The writers are indebted to Miss Janet Scott Hyslop, Mount Gardens, Langholm, for the use of this document. The entries appear to have been copied by the late Simon Hyslop, Market Place, Langholm, from an imperfect copy of the original Register, made by the Rev. Robert Allan episcopal minister of Stapelgortoun, for his own use. The story is told of one of the lairds of Broomholm that, riding one day in Nicol Forest, he noticed some children playing at a cottage door with a MS. book. On examining it he discovered it to be one of the Registers of Stapelgortoun, and later he succeeded in obtaining possession of it. Possibly it was from this copy that Simon Hyslop obtained his.

The entries have been carefully compared with the original Register in the Register House, Edinburgh, and corrected by Mr. John Reid.

1668.

June	11.	The Foresaid day John Thomson, *s. naturall* to James Thomson in Winterhope-head, in the parish of Middlebie. *Wit.* Thomas Armstrong of Over-Crage and Matthew Lyttle elder....in the foresaid Over-Crage.
July	19.	The fd. day, Janet Graham, *d.* to William Grahm in Brekanwrae. *Wit.* Walter Scot in Talend and Andrew Little in Brekanwrea.
	19.	The fd. likewise, William Mackintosh, *s* to James Mackintosh in Miltown. *Wit.* Patrick Scon at Miltown and John Huggon at Langholm Castle.
	26.	The fd. day Besse Lyttle, *d.* to John Lyttle in Dowglandholme. *Wit.* John Irving, Dowglandholme and John Lyttle in Overdowgland. ∞
Aug.	2.	The fd. day John Talphor, *s.* to Stephan Talphor in Rushill. *Wit.* John Pasley in Longholme and Willm. Macvitie, yr.
	6.	The fd. day Margaret Allet, *d.* to Robert Allet in Longholme. *Wit.* Adam Glendining in Longholme and Willm. Macvitie, yr.
Oct.	7.	The fd. day Janet Hope, *d.* to John Hope in Over-crage. *Wit.* Thomes Armstrong of Crage-burne and Matthew Little elder in Over-crage.
	9.	The fd. day John Lindsay, *s.* to John Lindsay, in Langh. *Wit.* John Maxwell of Broomholme and Robert Wright in Ld.
	2.	The fd. day Andrew Bettie, *s.* to Walter Bettie in Bombie. *Wit.* John Allet in Bombie and John Little in Hole.
Nov.	3.	The fd. day Andrew Gowenlocke, *s.* to Thomas Gowenlocke yonger in Whichshields. *Wit.* John Scott in Whichshields and Andrew Lyttle yr.
	10.	The sd. day William Pasley, *s.* to John Pasley in Langh. *Wit.* William Macvite in Longholme and James Oliver yr. ∞
	22.	The fd. day Adam Dalglish, *s.* to Walter Dalgliesh in Longh. *Wit.* George Thomson in Longholm and John Pasley, yonger yr.
Dec.	17.	The fd. day Nans Irving, *d.* to Thomas Irving in Carlesgill. *Wit.* William Irving in Carles-gill and Archbald Irving, yr.
	27.	The sd. day Isabell Murray, *d.* to John Murray in Timpen. *Wit.* William Armstrong in Nether-Crage and Andrew Little in Brekenwray.

Jan.	7.	The sd. day Nans fforsythes, *d.* to John Forsythes in Longholme. *Wit.* Anthony Brown in Longholme and John Lindsay, yr.
Jan.	10.	The sd. day William Lambe, *s.* to James Lambe in Pott-holme. *Wit.* Thomas Wilson in Pott-holm and John Scott in Bank-howse.
	14.	The sd. day Willm. Blackloke, *s. natrull* to George Blackloke in Longholme. *Wit.* George Wyilie at Miltown and Robert Blackloke in Calf-field.
	17.	The sd. day Simeon Wilson, *s.* to Thomas Wilson in Pottholme. *Wit.* John Scott in Bankhouse and William Scott, yr.
	22.	The Anna Allet, *d.* to John Allet in Bombie. *Wit.* Walter Bettie in Bombie and John Lyttle in Hole
	15.	The sd. day Mary Armstrong, *d.* to William Armstrong, of Nether-Crage. *Wit.* Thomas Murray in Nether-Crage and Walter Hope yr.
	23.	The sd. day George Irving, *s.* to Mungo Irving in Aughengile in the half P. of Morton. *Wit.* Maxwell in Aughengile and James Rae yr.
Mar.	18.	The sd. day Nans Scot, *d.* to Walter Scot in Taillend. *Wit.* John Scot of Rennelburn and John Maxwell of Broomholme.
	18.	The sd. day likewise Bessie Fletcher, *d.* to Thomas Fletcher in Longholme. *Wit.* Thomas Lyttle in Longholme and James Johnston yr.
	28.	The sd. day Margret Irving, *d.* to William Irving in Carlesgill. *Wit.* John Armstrong in Crage-burn and John Hope in Over-Crage.
April	3.	The sd. day Patrick Maxwell, *s.* to the deceased John Maxwell of Broomholme. *Wit.* Sir James Johnston of Westerhall and Frances Scott of Erkelton. ∞
	9.	The sd. day Helen Scot, *d.* to John in the P. of Waughope. *Wit.* Andrew Hewetson in Bigholme and Alexander Armstrong, Bloughburnfoot.
	11.	The sd. day Jeane Lyttle, *d. natural* to Willm. Lyttle, Overdowgland. *Wit.* John Lyttle in Overdowgland and Archbald Lyttle in Middowgland.
	15.	The sd. day Hugh Reid, *s.* to William Reid in Longholme. *Wit.* Thomas Lyttle in Longholme and James Johnston yr.
	22.	The sd. day, George Lyttle, *s.* to Archbald Lyttle in Middowgland. *Wit.* John Lyttle in Overdowgland and John Bettie Dowglandholme.
May	13.	The sd. day John Allet, *s.* to Walter Allet in the P. of Wachope. *Wit.* Andrew Hewetson in Bigholms and William Young in Shaw.
	18.	The sd. day Margret Wright, *d.* to William Wright in Longholme. *Wit.* Adam Glendining in Longholme and James Oliver yr.
	31.	The sd. day Janet and Jeane Macvites, *drs.* toWilliam Macviti in Longholme. *Wit.* Robert Allet in Longholme and William Wright yr.
June	13.	The sd. day John Murray, *s. natural* to William Murray in Broomholme. *Wit.* John Murray in Timpen and David Murray yr.
July	14.	The sd. day John Wright, *s. natural* to Andrew Wright in Longholme. *Wit.* John Wright in Longholme and Thomas Byres, yr.
Aug.	4.	The sd. day Margaret Macvitie, *d.* to Thomas Macvitie in Longholme. *Wit.* James Oliver in Longholme and Thomas Byres yr.∞
	15.	The sd. day William Hewetson, *s.* to William Hewetson in Holmhead. *Wit.* Andrew Irving in Holm-head and George Scott, yr.

| Sept. | 12. | The sd. day John Scott, *s. natural* to Robert Scott in Byking, Wester-kirk P. *Wit.* William Armstrong of Nether-Craige and Andrew Irving in Holm-head. |

Sept. 12. The sd. day John Scott, *s. natural* to Robert Scott in Byking, Wester-kirk P. *Wit.* William Armstrong of Nether-Craige and Andrew Irving in Holm-head.

28. The sd. day Janet Gibson, *d.* to Mr. Thomas Gibson in Longholme. *Wit.* Adam Scott in Longholme and James Pasley yr.

Nov. 2. The sd. day Helen Allet, *d.* to Robert Allet. *Wit.* George Thomson in Longholme and William Wright yr. ∞

Nov. 7. The sd. day Grissle Henderson, *d.* to John Henderson in Crage-Hope. *Wit.* Mathew Lyttle in Over-Crage and Thomas Hope, yr.

25. The sd. day John Lyttle, *s.* to Andrew Lyttle in Westerkir. *Wit.* George Dixon in Linholme and Simon Lyttle yr.

Dec. 4. John Scott, *s. nat.*to John Scott Longholme. *Wit.* G Thomson and James Pasley.

7. The sd. day Margret Scott,* *d.* to John Scott in Bankhous and laird of Rennelburn. *Wit.* John Scott in Bankhous and David Scott yr. ∞

*This is probably the Margaret Scott referred to on page 305

1670

Jan. 14. The sd. day Janet Lyttle, *d.* to Archbald in Longholme. *Wit.* Thomas Lyttle in Longholme and William Bell yr.

16. The sd. day Thomas Hope, *s.* to John Hope in Over-Crage. *Wit.* George Talepher in Over-Crage and Matthew Lyttle yr.

30. The sd. day Matthew Lyttle, *s.* to William Lyttle in Steenholme. *Wit.* John Hope in Holmehead and Andrew Irving, yr. ∞

Feb. 20. The sd. day Jeane Lyttle, *d.* to John Lyttle in Overdowgland. *Wit.* John Battie in Dowglandholme and John Lyttle yr.

20. The sd. day likeways Margaret Hislope, *d.* to John Hislope in Hole. *Wit.* John Allet in Bombie and Matthew Lyttle in Over-Crage.

27. The sd. day Robert Hope, *s.* to John Hope in Longholme. *Wit.* James Oliver in Longholme and James Johnston, yr.

Mar. 6. The sd. day Besse Wright, *d.* to George Wright in Longholme. *Wit.* John Pasley in Longholme and Adam Glendining, yr.

6. The sd. day likewise Jane Bettie, *d.* to John Battie in Calfield in Wawchope. *Wit.* Thomas Irving in Carlsgill and John Irving yr.

10. The sd. day Magdalen Scott, *d. natural* to John Scot in Bankhowse. *Wit.* Thomas Hope and William Bell both in Wawchope P.

13. The sd. day Adam Gowenloke, *s.* to Thomas Gowenloke in Whichshields. *Wit.* Andrew Irving in Holmehead and John Scott yr.

13. The sd. day likewise Isabel Lyttle, *d.* to John Lyttle in Dowglandholme. *Wit* Matthew Lyttle in Over-Crage and George Talpher, yr.

15. The sd. day Jean Armstrong, *d.* to John Armstrong in Longholme. *Wit.* John Hope in Longholme and Hugh Alexander yr.

31. The sd. day Margaret Clarke, *d.* to William Clark in Longholm. *Wit.* James Pasley in Long. and James Reid yr.

April 28. The sd. day Besse Scott, *d.* to Adam Scott in Longholme. *Wit.* George Thomson in Longholme and Thomas Aitchison yr. ∞

28. The sd. day Margaret Murray, *d.* to David Murray in Timpen. *Wit.* John Murray in Timpen and Thomas Murray yr. ∞

May	26.	The sd. day John Irving, *s.* to David Irving in Coldtown in Wawchope. *Wit.* Gaving Armstrong in Cold-town and George Irving yr.
June	5.	The sd. day Isabel Battie, *d.* to Walter Battie in Burnfoot. *Wit.* Edward Lyttle in Overdowgland and John Lyttle yr.
June	9.	The sd. day Adam Reid, *s.* to James Reid in Longholme. *Wit.* John Pasley in Longholme and William Aitchison, yr.
July	15.	The sd. day Janet Scot, *d.* to Adam Scot in Todshaw-hill in the P. of Westerkirk.
	17.	The sd. day Adam Scot *s.* to John Scot in Holme-head. *Wit.* George Scott in Holm-head and John Murray yr.
Aug.	28.	The sd. day William Reid, *s.* to David Reid in Longholme. *Wit.* John Pasley in Longholme and John Scot yr.
Sept.	25.	The sd. day John Dixon, *s.* to David Dixon in Longholme. *Wit.* James Edgar in Longholme and John Lyttle yr
Oct.	9.	The sd. day John Byres, *s.* to Thomas Byres in Longholme. *Wit.* Andrew Wright in Longholme and ffergus Bell yr.
Oct.	20.	The sd. day Thomas Lindsay, *s.* to John Lindsay in Longholme. *Wit.* John fforsythe in Longholme and Robert Blacloake yr.
Nov.	6.	The sd. day John Wilson, *s.* to James Wilson in Broomholme. *Wit.* John Murray in Broomholm and Adam Glendining in Longholm.
	13.	The sd. day Margaret Irving, *d.* to John Irving in Carlesgill. *Wit.* George Talpher in Over-Crage and Thomas Lyttle yr.
Dec.	8.	The sd. day Margaret Dalgliesh, *d.* to Walter Dalgliesh in Longholme. *Wit.* George Thomson in Longholme and George Wright yr.
	10.	The sd. day Anna Allet, *d.* to Robert Allet in Longholme. *Wit.* John Lindsay in Longholme and James Oliver yr. ∞
	18.	The sd. day Margaret Wright, *d.* to Andrew Wright in Longholme. *Wit.* William Wright in Longholme and James Oliver yr.
	20.	The sd. day James Grive, *s.* to John Grive in Glendining. *Wit.* Sir James Johnston of Wester-hall and William Aitchison in Longholme.

1671

Jan.	15.	The sd. day Bessie Alexander, *d.* to Heugh Alexander in Longholme. *Wit.* William Wright in Longholme and James Reid yr.
Feb.	1.	The sd. day Grissel Palmer, *d.* to William Palmer in Nether Crage. *Wit.* Thomas Armstrong of Nether Crage and John Armstrong yr.
	14.	The sd. day Archbald Irving, *s.* to Thomas Irving in Carlesgill. *Wit.* William Irving in Carlesgill and Andrew Irving, yr
	14.	The sd. day likewise James Irving, *s.* to William Irving in Carlsgill. *Wit.* Thomas Irving in Carlsgill and Archbald Irving yr.
	28.	The sd. day Andrew Lyttle, *s.* to Andrew Lyttle in Chappelknowe in the half P. of Morton. *Wit*…….
	28.	The sd. day also Margaret Scot, *d. naturall* to John Scot in Longholme. *Wit.* George Wilson in Walls and William Huggon yr. ∞
Mar.	12.	The sd. day Archbald Thomson, *s.* to Archbald Thomson in Knoks. *Wit.* George Dixon in Lineholme and William Dixon, yr.
	17.	The sd. day Mary Gibson, *d.* to Mr. Thomas Gibson in Longholme. *Wit.* George Thomson in Longholme and Jo. Pasley, yr.
April	5.	The sd. day Andrew Glendining, *s.* to William Glendining at Castle. *Wit.* John Glendining at Castle and Thomas Glendining yr.

April	15.	The sd. day William Wilson, *s.* to Thomas Wilson in Pottholme. *Wit.* Thomas Scott in Bankhouse and William Hislope in Pottholme.
	16.	The sd. day Jane Aitchison, *d.* to Thomas Aitchison in Longholme. *Wit.* James Oliver in Longholme and David Dixon, yr.
	30.	The sd. day John Wilson, *s. natural* to George Wilson in Walls in the P. of Waughope. *Wit.* John Pasley in Longholme and James Pasley, yr.
May	28.	The sd. day Margaret Lyttl, *d. natural* to John Lyttle in Hole. *Wit.* Edward Lyttle in Dowgland and Thomas Lyttle in Overcrage.
June	15.	The sd. day George Maxwell, *s. natural* to John Maxwell of Broomholme. *Wit.* Adam Glendining in Longholme and John Wright yr.
	19.	The sd. day Besse Scot, *d.* to John Scot in Longholme. *Wit.* Patrick Scoon at Miltown and John Hope in Longholme.
	19.	The sd. day likewise Margaret and Helen Lambe, *drs.* to James Lambe in Pottholme. *Wit.* Thomas Wilson in Pottholme and William Hislop yr.
July	6.	The sd. day John Scot, *s.* to Walter Scot in Dryclewghside in the P. of Wauchope. *Wit.* Thomas Wilson in Pottholme and James Lamb[me] yr.
	13.	The sd. day Margaret Johnston, *d.* to James Johnston in Longholme. *Wit.* James Oliver in Longholme and David Reid yr.
	16.	The sd. day William Forsythes, *s.* to John Forsythes in Longholme. *Wit.* Heugh Alexander in Longholme and John Scot yr.
	23.	The sd. day John ffletcher, *s.* to Thomas ffletcher in Longholme. *Wit.* John Allet in Longholme and George Thomson yr.
	24.	The sd. day James Irving, *s.* to John Irving in the P. of Lochmabene. *Wit.* John Lermond in the P. of Westerkirk and William Whals yr.
Oct.	8.	The sd. day Thomas Armstrong, *s. natural* to John Armstrong of Over-Crage. *Wit.* Thomas Hope in Over-Crage and John Hope yr. ∞
	12.	The sd. day Janet Wright, *d.* to Robert Wright in Longholme. *Wit.* Adam Glendining in Longholme and Richard Irving yr.
	15.	The sd. day Walter Thomson, *s.* to John Thomson in Carlesgill. *Wit.* Thomas Irving in Carlesgill and Archbald Irving, yr.
Nov.	19.	The sd. day Jenet Beattie, *d.* to Walter Beattie in Burnfoot. *Wit.* Edward Lyttle in Overdowgland and John Lyttle, yr.
	28.	The sd. day Thomas Clark, *s.* to Walter Clark in Milholme. *Wit*........∞
Dec.	8.	The sd. day Isabel Lyttle, *d.* to Archbald Lyttle in Middowgland. *Wit.* John Lyttle in Overdowgland and William Lyttle, yr.
	31.	The sd. day William Scott, *s.* to John Scott in Bank-howse. *Wit.* James Lambe in Pott-holme, and William Hislope, yr.

1672

Jan.	7.	The sd. day ffrancis Scot, *s.* to Adam Scot in Longholme. *Wit.* William Wright in Longholme and John Hope yr.
	28.	The sd. day Helen Gowenlocke, *d.* to Thomas Gowenlocke in Whichsheels. *Wit.* Andrew Gowenlocke at Castle and John Hope, yr.
Feb.	15.	The sd. day Hugh Reid, *s.* to David Reid in Longholme. *Wit.* Thomas Lyttle in Longholme and James Johnston, yr.
	17.	The sd. day Francis Scot, *s. natural* to Thomas Scot in Bankhowse. *Wit.* John Scot in Bankhowse and David Scot, yr.

Mar.	1.	The. sd. day William Bell, *s. natural* to John Bell in Galaside. *Wit.* John Pasley in Longholme and John Hope, yr.

Mar.   1.   The. sd. day William Bell, *s. natural* to John Bell in Galaside. *Wit.* John Pasley in Longholme and John Hope, yr.

      2.   The sd. day Francis Scot, *s.* to John Scot of Rennelburn. *Wit.* Walter Scot in Brekenwray and John Scot Bankhowse. ∞

    21.   The sd. day James Dixon, *s.* to David Dixon in Longholme. *Wit.* William Atchison in Longholme and James Oliver yr

    21.   The sd. day likeways Elizabeth Grahame, *d. natural* to Robert Grahame in the P. of Kirkandrews. *Wit.* John Glendining at Castle and William Glendining yr.

April 19.   The sd. day Isibell Blakloke, *d. natural* to George Boocklocks in the P. of Kirkandrews. *Wit.* George Ferguson at Miltown and John Glendining yr.

    21.   The sd. day Jeane Lyttle, *d.* to John Lyttle in Dowglandholme. *Wit.* Edward Lyttle in Over-dowgland and William Lyttle yr

May 16.   The sd. day Walter Allet, s. to Robert Allet in Longholme. *Wit.* John Pasley in Longholme and William Atchison yr. ∞

26.   The sd. day......*s.* to.......in the P. of Middlebie. *Wit.* George Bell in Middlebie and John Bell, yr.

June 6.   The sd. day Nans Oliver, *d.* to James Oliver in Longholme. *Wit.* Adam Glendining in Longholme and George Wright, yr. ∞

    26.   The sd. day Andrew Macvitie, *s.* to Archbald Macvitie in the P. of Wauchope. *Wit.* John Macvitie in Stubholme and John Purves, yr.

July 5.   The sd. day Thomas Scot, *s. natural* to Walter Scot in the P. of Canobie. *Wit.* William Dixon in Blough and Alexander Armstrong.

    18.   The sd. day Thomas Lyttle, *s. natural* to William Lyttle in Dowgland. *Wit.* John Scott in Bankhowse and Thomas Scot, yr.

    28.   The sd. day Mary Lyttle, *d* to Thomas Lyttle in Rushill. *Wit.* John Pasley younger in Longholme and David Dixon, yr.

    30.   The sd. day Walter Hope, *s.* to John Hope in Over-Grage. *Wit.* George Talpher in Over-Crage and Matthew Lyttle younger yr.

Aug. 15.   The sd. day Margaret Bettie, *d.* to John Bettie in Burnfoot. *Wit.* John Lyttle in Over-Dowgland and William Lyttle, yr.

Sept. 3.   The sd. day Margaret Lyttle, *d.* to John Lyttle in Over-dowgland. *Wit.* John Bettie in Dowglandholme and John Lyttle yr.

    22.   The sd. day Bessie Glendining, *d.* to Adam Glendining in the P. of Hutton. *Wit.* William Scot in Bankhowse and John Scot, yr.

Oct 6.   The sd. day William Wright, *s.* to Andrew Wright in Longholme. *Wit.* John Hope in Longholme and William Bell, yr.

    12.   The sd. day Margaret Crage, *d.* to John Crage at Castle. *Wit.* William Dixon at Castle and Andrew Lyttle, yr. ∞

    20.   The sd. day Margaret Tod, *d.* to Michaell Tod in Hole. *Wit.* William Irving in Carlesgill and John Irving yr

Nov. 14.   The sd. day Janat Reid *d* to James Reid in Longholme. *Wit.* James Pasley in Longholme and ffrancis Bell yr.

1673

Jan. 11.   The sd. day Elspeth Jarden, *d.* to Robert Jarden in Milnholme. *Wit.* William Palmer in Nethercrage and Adam Hislope yr.

    12.   The sd. day William Bettie, *s.* to William Bettie at Castle. *Wit.* Thomas Glendining at Castle and Andrew Lyttle yr.

Feb.	6.	The sd. day Margaret Lyttle, *d.* to John Lyttle in Longholme. *Wit.* Simeon Fletcher in Longholme and Robert Wright yr.
	22.	The sd. day Helen Dalglish, *d.* to Walter Dalglish in Longholme. *Wit.* Charles Wright in Longholme and John Hope yr.
	27.	The sd. day William Scot, *s.* to Walter Scot in Miln-holme. *Wit.* John Scot in Bankhouse and William Thomson yr.
Mar.	17.	The sd. day Janet Maxwell, *d. naturall* to John Maxwell of Broomholme. *Wit.* George Thomson in Longholme and John Pasley, yr
	23.	The sd. day John Wright, *s.* to Robert Wright in Long. *Wit.* James Reid in Longholme and David Dixon, yr.
	30.	The sd. day John Glendining, *s.* to William Glendining at Castle. *Wit.* William Dixon at Castle and William Bettie yr.
April	1.	The sd. day Margaret Fletcher, *d.* to Thomas Fletcher in Longholme. *Wit.* William Cranston in Longholme and David Dixon, yr.
	6.	The said day Margaret Armstrong, *d.* to John Armstrong in Longholme. *Wit.* William Bell in Longholme and David Reid yr.
	17.	The sd. day Thomas Wilson, *s.* to James Wilson in Longholme. *Wit.* David Dixon in Longholme and David Reid yr.
	22.	The sd. day John Bell, *s.* to William Bell in the P. of Kirkpatricke. *Wit.* George Bell in Carruthers and Richard Bell yr.
June	22.	The sd. day James Lindsay, *s.* to John Lindsay in Longholme. *Wit.* George Thomson in Longholme and John Forsyth, yr.
	23.	The sd. day Mary Reid, *d.* to William Reid in Longholme. *Wit.* Robert Wright in Longholme and John Armstrong yr.
	29.	The sd. day John Mair, *s.* to John Mair in Pottholme. *Wit.* Thomas Murray in Holme-head and John Scot yr.
July	27.	The sd. day Janet Irving, *d.* to William Irving in Carlesgill. *Wit.* John Lyttle in Overdowgland and Andrew Lyttle yr
Aug.	17.	The sd. day Helen Hope, *d.* to John Hope in Longholme. *Wit.* John Wright in Longholme and William Bell yr.
Sept.	7.	The sd. day Margaret Lyttle, *d.* to Archbald Lyttle in Longholme. *Wit.* Thomas Fletcher in Long. and George Wright, yr
Oct.	5.	The sd. day Margaret Allet, *d.* to Robert Allet, proportioner of Long. *Wit.* William Aitchison in Long. and John Hope yr. ∞
	15.	The sd. day Francis Johnston, *s.* to James Johnston in Long. *Wit.* John Johnston in Longholme and David Reid, yr.
Nov.	8.	The sd. day William Allet, *s. naturall* to John Allet in Longholme. *Wit.* George Thomson in Long. and John Hope, yr.
	30.	The sd. day Elspeth Aitchison, *d.* to Thomas Atchison in Long. *Wit.* James Johnston in Longholme and William Bell, yr.
Dec.	25.	The sd. day Janet Byres, *d.* to Thomas Byres in Long. *Wit.* William Reid in Long. and Robert Macgill yr.

1674

Jan.	5.	The sd. day Helen Lyttle, *d.* to John Lyttle in the P. of Kirkpatrick. *Wit.* David Harkness and John Lyttle.
	27.	The sd. day Janet Anderson, *d.* to Robert Anderson at Milltown. *Wit.* Andrew Lyttle at Castle and Andrew Scot, yr.

Feb.	4.	The sd. day Walter Dalglish, *s.* to Walter Dalglish in Long. *Wit.* John Johnston in Longholme and James Oliver, yr.
	15.	The sd. day William Lyttle, *s. naturall* to Matthew Lyttle in Over-crage. *Wit.* Thomas Murray in Holmehead and James Oliver in Lough.
	26.	The sd. day James Reid, *s.* to David Reid in Long. *Wit.* William Reid in Long. and James Reid, yr.
Mar.	11.	The sd. day William Aitchison, s. to Thomas Aitchison in Long. *Wit.* Robert Wright in Long. and David Dixon yr.
April	2.	The sd. day Elizabeth Thomson, *d.* to George Thomson in Long. *Wit.* John Hope in Long. and John Allet yr.
	12.	The sd. day Jeane Allet, *d.* to James Allet in Long. *Wit.* James Pasley in Long. and David Reid yr.
	12.	The sd. day likways Janet Wilson, *d.* to Thomas Wilson in Hole. *Wit.* Edward Lyttle in Dowgland and William Lyttle yr.
	19.	The sd. day Matthew Irving, *s.* to . . . . Irving in Carlesgill. *Wit.* Edward Lyttle in Overdowgland and John Lyttle, yr.
May	1	The sd. day James Lyttle *s. naturall* to William Lyttle in Dowgland. *Wit.* Edward Lyttle in Overdowgland and John Lyttle yr.
	10.	The sd. day Blench Lyttle, *d.* to Archbald Lyttle in Mid-dowgland. *Wit.* John Bettie in Dowgland and William Lyttle yr.
June	24.	The sd. day Mary Dixon, *d.* to George Dixon in Broomholme. *Wit.* John Murray in Broomholme and David Murray, yr.
July	19.	The sd. day Isabel Scot, *d.* to John Scot in Dowglandholme. *Wit.* John Bettie in Dowgland and Archbald Lyttle yr.
Aug.	2.	The sd. day Thomas Wright, *s.* to Andrew Wright in Lough. *Wit.* Archbald Lyttle in Long. and William Bell, yr.
	9.	The sd. day Matthew Dixon, *s.* to David Dixon in Longh. *Wit.* William Irving in Long. and William Bell yr.
Sept.	15.	The sd. day Anna Clarke, *d.* to Walter Clarke in Miln-holme. *Wit.* Walter Scot in Brekenwray and Andrew Lyttle yr. ∞
	26.	The sd. day Janet Armstrong, *d.* to John Armst. in Longh. *Wit* Charles Wright in Longholme and John Lindsay, yr.
Nov.	1.	The sd. day Nans Wright, *d.* to Robert Wright in Longh. *Wit.* George Thomson in Long. and James Pasley yr.
	21.	The sd. day Besse Bell, *d. naturall* to Francis Bell in Longh. *Wit.* Thomas Atchison in Longh. and George Wright, yr.
Dec.	27.	The sd. day Isabel Lindsay, *d.* to John Lindsay in Long. *Wit.* John Pasley in Longholme and David Dixon, yr.

1675

Jan.	3.	The sd. day Heugh Alexander, *s.* to Heugh Alexander in Lon. *Wit.* John Wright in Longholme and Thomas Atchison yr.
	3.	The sd. day likewise Janet Scot, *d.* to Walter Scot in Longh. *Wit.* John Allet in Longholme and William Bell yr.
	31.	The sd day John Lyttle, *s.* to William Lyttle in Overdowgland. *Wit.* John Bettie in Dowglandholme and John Scott yr.
Feb.	28.	The sd. day Margaret Oliver, *d.* to James Oliver in Long. *Wit.* Thomas Murray in Holmhead and Andrew Irving yr.

435

Mar.	28.	The sd. day John Lyttle, *s.* to John Lyttle in Overdowgland. *Wit.* John Bettie in Dowglandholme and John Scott yr.
April	22.	The sd. day Isabel Pasley, *d.* to John Pasley in Long. *Wit.* James Pasley in Longholme and Robert Wright yr.
	25.	The sd. day Thomas Davison *s. naturall* to John Davison in the P. of Middlebie. *Wit.* James Nicholl and William Bell, both in the same P.
May	2.	The sd. day John Smyth, *s.* to George Smyth in the P. of Kirkpatrick. *Wit.* William Irving in Mossknow and William Scott yr.
	9.	The sd. day Helen Lyttle, *d.* to the deceased Andrew Lyttle in Whichsheels. *Wit.* Andrew. Gowenloke in Whichsheels and Thomas Gowenloke yr
June	3.	The sd. day Mary Scot, *d.* to John Scot in Dryclewgh-side in the P. of Wawchope. *Wit.* John Moffat and Archbald Lyttle, in the foresd. P.
July	4.	The sd. day Walter Irving, s. to William Irving in Carlesgill. *Wit.* Edward Lyttle in Over-dowgland and William Lyttle yr.
	11.	The sd. day Isabel Armstrong, *d.* to Robert Armst. in Whichsheels. Wit. Andrew Gowenlocke in Whichsheels and Thomas Gowenloke yr.
Sept.	19.	The sd. day John Pasley *s. natural* to James Pasley in Long. *Wit.* John Pasley in Longholme and William Bell yr.
Oct.	7.	The sd. day John Thomson, *s.* to George Thomson in Long. *Wit.* James Reid in Longholme and Thomas Byres yr.
	12.	The sd. day Andrew Bettie, s. to John Bettie in Nether-Craige. *Wit.* John Armstrong Over-craige and John Hope yr. ∞

1676

Feb.	11	The sd. day Isabel Scot, *d.* to John Scot at Castle. *Wit.* William Glendñing at Castle and Thomas Waddel at Milntown.
April	11.	The sd. day Agnis Hope, *d.* to John Hope in Over-craige. *Wit.* Walter Armstrong in Craigburn and John Bettie in Over-craige.
	23.	The sd. day Ewphan Waddel, *d.* to Thomas Waddel at Milntown. *Wit.* John Glendñing at Castle and William Glendñing yr.
	28.	The sd. day Jeane Atchison, *d.* to Thomas Atchison in Long. *Wit.* Robert Wright in Longholme and Thomas Fletcher yr. ∞
May	2.	The sd. day Margaret Armstrong, *d.* to John Armst. fiar of Over-Craige. *Wit.* John Hope in Over Craige and John Bettie yr.
Aug.	13.	The sd. day Mary Allet, *d.* to Robert Allet in Long. *Wit.* John Pasley in Longholme and James Johnston yr.
Oct.	22.	The sd. day Nans Alexander, *d.* to Hewgh Alexander in Longh. *Wit.* William Bell in Longh. and James Johnston yr.
	22.	The sd. day Richard Glendñing, *s. naturall* Adam Glendñing in Longh. *Wit.* John Brown in Longh. and James Reid yr.
Nov.	12.	The sd. day Adam Dalglish, *s.* to Walter Dalglish in Tailend. *Wit.* John Scot in Holmehead and John Hope yr.
Dec.	14.	The said Janet Byres, *d.* to Thomas Byres in Long. *Wit.* Robert Pasley in Lough. and James Reid yr. ∞
	27.	The sd. day Adam Purves in Bigholms in the P. of Waughope, *s.* to John Purves yr. *Wit.* John Moffat in Irving and William Armst. yr.
	31.	The sd. day Isabel Wright, *d.* to Robert Wright in Longh. *Wit.* George Thomson in Longh. and Robert Kirkup yr.

Jan.	21.	The sd. day Mary Lyttle, *d.* to John Lyttle in Long. *Wit.* William fforsyths in Longholme and William Brown yr
Feb.	11.	The sd. day Margaret Gowenloke, *d.* to Thomas Gowenloke Whichsheels. *Wit.* James Synton in Whichsheels and Andrew Gowenloke yr.
Mar.	1.	The sd. day William Irving, *s.* to John Irving in Carlesgill. *Wit.* William Irving in Carlesgill and Archbald Irvinge yr.
	25.	The sd. day John Armstrong, *s.* to John Armst. in Longholme. *Wit.* George Thomson in Longholme and James Johnston yr.
April	22.	The sd. day Thomas Glendñing, *s.* to William Glendñing at Castle. *Wit.* John Glendñing at Castle and Andrew Scott yr.
	24.	The sd. day Janet Thomson, *d.* to George Thomson in Long. *Wit.* Robert Wright in Longh. and John Hope yr. ∞
	24.	The sd. day likways Margaret Reid, *d.* to James Reid in Long. *Wit.* William fforsyths in Longholme and James ohnston yr. ∞
May	10	The sd. day Janet Reid, *d.* to William Reid in Longh. *Wit.* Robert Wright in Longh. and David Reid yr.
June	6.	The sd. day Jeane Reid, *d.* to David Reid in Longh. *Wit.* Robert Wright in Longholme and Thomas Byres yr
	12.	The sd. day Janet Lyttle, *d.* to William Lyttle Overdowgland. *Wit.* John Armstrong of Over- Craige and John Hope yr.
	12.	The sd. day likwise Susanna Johnston, *d.* to James Johnston in Longh. *Wit.* Robert Wright in Longh. and James Oliver yr.
	22.	The sd. day Robert and Walter Waylie *sons* to George Wylie at Milntown. *Wit.* John Atchison at Milntown and Thomas Waddel yr.
	24.	The sd. day Isabel Bell, *d.* to William Bell at Milntown. *Wit.* John Scot in Holmehead and George Scot yr.
	29.	The sd. day Thomas Allet, *s. naturall* to John Allet in Longh. *Wit.* William Glendñining at Castle and John Murray yr
July	15.	The sd. day William Lyttle, *s. naturall* to Thomas Lyttlr in Bombie. *Wit.* John Scot in Holmehead and John Hope yr.
	16.	The sd. day Thomas Macvitie, *s.* to Archbald Macvitie in the P. of Wauchope. *Wit.* John Scot in Mikleholme and William Bell yr.
Aug.	15.	The sd. day Mary Wright, *d.* to Andrew Wright in Longholme. *Wit.* Thomas Byres in Longh. and David Reid yr.
Sept.	9.	The sd. day William Irving, *s.* to William Irving in Carlesgill. *Wit.* Thomas Armstrong of Over-craige and William Armst. yr.
Oct.	12.	The sd. day John Pasley, *s.* to Robert Pasley in Longh. *Wit.* John Hope in Longholme and Robert Mackgill yr.
Dec.	16.	The sd. day John Millen, *s.* to James Millen in Longh. *Wit.* George Thomson in Longholme and William fforsythes yr.

Feb.	14.	The sd. day John Lawson, *s.* to William Lawson in Rush-hill. *Wit.* Robert Wright in Longholme and John Scot yr.
	15.	The sd. day Nans Bettie, *d.* to John Bettie in Dowgland. *Wit.* John Scot in Bankhows and William Scot yr.
Mar.	14.	The sd. day Walter Blacke, *s.* to William Blacke in the P. of Westerkirk.

Mar.	14.	The sd. day likewise Margaret Atchison, *d. naturall* to Walter Atchison in the sd. P. *Wit.* William River and Simeon Johnst. both in the foresd. P.
	21.	The sd. day John Reid, *d.* [sic] to James Reid in Longh. *Wit.* Robert Mackill in Longholme and James Johnston yr.
	28.	The sd. day John Hwnam, *s. naturall* to John Hwnam in Longh. *Wit.* George Thomson in Longh. and Robert Wright yr
April	7.	The sd. day Bessie Oliver, *d.* to James Oliver in Longholme. *Wit.* Thomas ffletcher in Longh. and James Brown, yr.
May	9.	The sd. day Mary Armstrong, *d.* to John Armst. fiar of Over-Craige. *Wit.* John Hope of Over- Craige and William Lyttle yr.
Aug.	8.	The sd. day John Atchison *s.* to Thomas Atchison in Longh. *Wit.* George Thomson in Longh. and Robert Mackgill yr.
	16.	The sd. day David Hope, *s.* to John Hope in Carlesgill. The sd. day and at the same time Besse Lyttle, *d.* to William in Carlesgill. *Wit.* Thomas Armstrong of Craige and Matthew Lyttle yr.
Sept	15	The sd. day Jeane Wright, *d.* to Robert Wright in Longh. *Wit.* John Hope in Longh. and Robert Pasley yr.
Oct.	13.	The sd. day James Scot, *s.* to John Scot in Bankhowse. *Wit.* Adam Glendñining in Longh. and Andrew Wright, yr.
Dec.	1.	The sd. day George Lyttle in Longh., *s.* to John Lyttle yr. *Wit.* William fforsyths in Longh. and John Wright yr.
	1.	The sd. day also Isabel Dalglish, *d.* to Walter Dalglish in Milnholme. *Wit.* John Longlands in Bank-hows and Michael Tod in Pottholme
	29.	The sd. day Thomas Lyttle, *s.* to Archbald Lyttle in the P. of Wauchope. Wit. John Scot in Mikleholme and Jasper Hay yr.
	29.	The sd. day likewise John Beattie, *s.* to William Bettie in the half P. of Mortown. *Wit.* Andrew Huietson in Blowgh and Robert Hewetson yr.

1679

Jan.	6.	The sd. dy. Besse Bell, *d.* to Patrick Bell in the P. of Waughope. *Wit.* John Bell in Galaside and Adam Bettie, yr.
	10.	The sd. day Sibell Lyttle, *d.* to Matthew Lyttle in Over-Craige. *Wit.* John Armstrong fiar of Over-Craige and William Irving, yr.
	12.	The sd. day Sibell Lyttle, *d. naturall* to William Scot in Bankhowse. *Wit.* John Langlands in Bankhowse and Andrew Irving yr.
	13.	The sd. day Adam Story, *s.* to John Story in Whichsheels. *Wit.* Thomas Gowenloke in Whichsheels and John Armstrong yr.
Feb.	2.	The sd. day Rosina Lawson, *d.* to William Lawson in Rush-hill. *Wit.* David Reid in Longh. and Andrew Wright yr.
	11.	The sd. day Besse Macvitie, *d.* to Andrew Macvitie in Stubholme in the P. of Wawchope. *Wit.* John Scott, Mikleholme and William Bell yr.
	11.	The sd. day likewayes Janet Allet, *d.* to Robert Allet in the same P. *Wit.* the foresd. persons.
	14.	The sd. day Richard Byrs, *s.* to Thomas Byres in Longh. *Wit.* William fforsyths in Longh. and Thomas Sinclar yr.
	20.	The sd. day Nans Thomson, *d.* to George Thomson in Long. *Wit.* William fforsyths in Long. and Thomas Byrs yr.

Mar.	25.	The sd. day Robert Wright, *s.* to Andrew Wright in Longh. *Wit.* John Scot in Longholme and David Reid yr.
April	2.	The sd. day Mary Wright, *d.* to Robert Wright in Longh. *Wit.* James Pasley in Longholme and Thomas Sinclar yr.
	27.	The sd. day Margaret Scot, *d.* to William Scott in Graystownlee in the P. of Westerkirk. *Wit.* Sir James Johnston of Westerhall and John Johnston his son.
May	3.	The sd. day John, *s.* to William Bell at Milntown. *Wit.* John Atchison at Milntown and George Wylie yr.
	28.	The sd. day Adam, *s.* to John Scot in Longh. *Wit* John Scot in Mikle-holme and Robert Wright in Longh.
July	8.	The sd. day John Glendñning, *s. naturall* to John Glendñining at Castle. *Wit.* Thomas Murray of Castle and John Murray yr.
Aug.	4.	The sd. day Patrick Johnston, *s.* to James Johnston in Longh. *Wit.* William fforsythes in Longh. and James Johnston yr.
	10.	The sd. day Janet Scot, *d. naturall* to Walter Scot in the P. of Ewes. *Wit.* Thomas Armstrong of Nether-Craige and Thomas Nicol yr.
	25.	The sd. day Gilbert Atchison, *s. naturall* to John Atchison in the P. of Westerkirk. *Wit.* Andrew Lyttle and Adam Warricke both in the sd. P.
	31.	The sd. day Walter Hope, *s.* to John Hope in Longh. *Wit.* Thomas ffletcher in Longh. and John fforsythes yr.
Sept.	29.	The sd. day John Grahame, *s.* to ffrancis Grahame in the P. of Westerkirk. *Wit…*
Oct.	15.	The sd. day Helen, *d.* to John Thomson in Burn. *Wit.* William Armstrong in Burn and Walter Armstrong yr.
Oct.	16.	The sd. day Besse Reid, *d.* to James Reid in Longh. *Wit.* George Thomson in Longh. and John Hwnam yr.
	30.	The sd. day Janet *d.* to John Irving in Over-Craige. *Wit.* Thomas Armstrong of Over-Craig and Thomas Armstrong of Nether-Craig.
Nov.	8.	The sd. day Janet, *d.* to David Reid in Longh. *Wit.* Adam Glendining in Longholme and William Brown yr.
	14.	The sd. day Helen and Janet, *drs.* to George fferguson at Miltown. *Wit.* William Bell at Milntown and Thomas Waddel yr.
	18.	The sd. day Adam Hislope, *s.* to Robert Hislope in Broomholme. *Wit.* John Maxwell of Broomholme and Robert Hwetson.
	18.	The sd. day likways George Hwnan, *s.* to John Hwnam in Long. *Wit.* James Reid in Longh. and George Thomson yr.
	30.	The sd. day William, *s.* to James Thomson in the P. of Westerkirk. *Wit.* Thomas Armstrong of Nether-Craige and John Hope in Holmhead.

1680

Jan.	4.	The sd. day Isabel, *d.* to Thomas Gowenlocke, Whichsheels. *Wit.* John Scot in Holmehead and and John Hope yr.
	9.	The sd. day Jane Warroch, *d.* to John Warroch in the P. of Waughope. *Wit.* John Scot, Mikleholme and William Bell yr.
	25.	The sd. day John, *s.* to John Lyttle in Hole. *Wit.* John Armst. in Over-Craige and John Irving, yr.
	29.	The sd. day Janet, *d.* to John Hislope in the P. of Wawchope. *Wit* Andrew Lyttle, Nishill and William Lyttle yr.

Feb.	22.	The sd. day Jeane, *d.* to William Irving in Over-Craige. *Wit.* John Armst. of Over-Craige and John Irving yr.
Mar.	5.	The sd. day Simon, *s.* to James Millen in Longh. *Wit.* George Thomson in Longh. and Thomas ffletcher yr.
	13.	The sd. day Andrew, *s.* to William Lyttle in Kirk-gill in Westerkirk P. *Wit.* John Johnston of Westerhall and John Atchison.
	14.	The sd. day William, *s.* to Adam Thomson in the P. of West. *Wit.* Thomas Armstrong of Over- Craige and Thomas Armstrong of Nether-Craige.
	18.	The sd. day William Pasley, *s.* to Robert Pasley in Longh. *Wit.* Robert Allet proportioner of Longholme and Robert Wright yr.
April	18.	The sd. day Isabel, *d.* to George Corry in P. of Hutton. *Wit.* Robert Scott of Gillesbie and William Graham of Shawes.
	18.	The sd. day likways Andrew Lyttle in Hooke in the P. of Applegirth. *Wit.* the foresaid persons.
	29.	The sd. day John Maxwell, *s.* to John Maxwell of Broomholme. *Wit.* Sir Patrick Maxwell of Springkell and John Scott of Rennelburn.
	30.	The sd. day John Armst., s. to John Armst. fiar of Over-Craige. *Wit.* John Irving in Over-Craige and William Irving yr.
May	9.	The sd. day Besse Armstrong, *d.* to Lansolat Armstrong in Whichsheels. *Wit.* William fforsyths in Longholme and Thomas Atchison yr.
	15.	The sd. day William Gilaspie, *s.* to John Gilaspie in the P. of Applegirth.
	16.	The sd. day William Glendñning, *s.* to William Glendñning at Castle. *Wit.* John Cranston at Castle and Thomas Glend. yr.
	25.	The sd. day John Scot, *s.* to ffrancis Scot of Davington. *Wit.*
June	17.	The sd. day Robert, *s.* to Thomas Aitchison in Longhol. *Wit.* Mr. Walter Maxwell and John Maxwell of Broomholme.
	27	The sd. day Janet, *d. naturall* to Matthew Lyttle in Bombie. *Wit.* John Hope in Longholme and Robert Pasley yr.
	30.	The sd. day John, *s.* to Matthew Lyttle in Mid-dowgland. *Wit.* Walter Bettie in Over-dowgland and John Bettie yr.
	30.	The sd. day likwise Grissel, *d.* to John Bettie in Over-dowgland.
July	13.	The sd. day Jean Lyttle *d.* to Christopher Lyttle in Mikleholme in the P. of Wauchope.
Aug.	21.	The sd. day John Fisher, *s.* to John Fisher in the P. of Cavers. *Wit.* Robert Purdom, in the sd. P. and...................
Sept.	1.	The sd. day Janet Lyttle, *d.* to John Lyttle in Longh. *Wit.* William fforsythes in Longh. and Thomas Sinclar yr.
Oct.	3.	The sd. day Jean Byres *d.* to James Byres in Hole. *Wit*.................
	7.	The sd. day Jean, *d.* to John Glendñning at Castle. *Wit* John Chranston at Castle and Thomas Glendñning yr.
	7.	The sd. day likwise George Armstrong, *s.* to John Armst. in Longh. *Wit.* Robert Pasley in Longh. and John Pasley yr.
	7.	The sd. day also Janet Bell, *d.* to ffrancis Bell in Longh. *Wit.* John Wright in Longholme and and Thomas Atchison yr.
Oct.	17.	The sd. day Elizabeth, *d.* to Thomas Byres in Longh. *Wit.* James Johnston in Longh. and James Oliver yr.
	28.	The sd. day George Wright, *s.* to Andrew Wright in Long. *Wit.* Alexander Allen in Long. and David Reid yr.

Nov.	10.	The sd. day Mary, *d.* to John Scot in Long. *Wit.* Walter Maxwell in Longh. and John Wright yr.
Dec.	20.	The sd. day Janet Lyttle, *d.* to Archbald Lyttle in the P. of Wawchope. *Wit.* John Scott in Mikleholme and Will Bell yr.
	21.	The sd. day Margaret, *d.* to George Thomson in Longh. *Wit.* Walter Maxwell in Longh. and Alexander Allen yr.

1681

Jan.	9.	The sd. day Jean Lawson, *d.* to William Lawson in Rushhill. *Wit.* John fforsythes in Longh. and Thomas Atchison yr.
	14.	The sd. day William, *s.* to Walter Dalglish in Milnholme. *Wit.* John Armstrong in Nether-Craige and Thomas Nicol yr.
Feb.	2.	The sd. day Margaret, *d.* to Thomas Waddell at Milntown. *Wit.* John Atchison at Milntown and William Scot at Castle.
	20.	The sd. day Walter, *s.* to James Oliver in Longh. *Wit.* James Pasley in Longh. and James Reid yr.
Mar.	6.	The sd. day Helen, *d.* to William Scot at Castle. *Wit.* John Cranston at Castle and Thomas Gowenlocke yr.
	13.	The sd. day William, *s.* to Thomas Armstrong of Nether-Craige bapt. on Sabbath-day. *Wit.* Thomas Armstrong of Over-Craig and John Armstrong yr.
	29.	The sd. day Robert, *s.* to William Scot in Longh. *Wit.* William fforsythes in Longh. and Thomas Sinclar yr.
April	26.	The sd. day Jean, *d.* to Thomas Murray in Holmehead. *Wit.* John Hope in Holmehead and Archbald Lyttle yr.
May	19.	The sd. day James, *s.* to John Cranston at Castle. *Wit.* Thomas Waddel at Milntown and John Atchison there.
July	10.	The sd. day John ffletcher, *s.* to Simon ffletcher in Longholme. *Wit.* James Miller in Longholme and David Reid yr.
Aug.	7.	The sd. day Andrew Hewetson, *s.* to Robert Hewetson in Broomholme. *Wit.* Robert Pasley in Long. and James Oliver yr.
	7.	The sd. day also Helen Bryden, *d.* to Robert Bryden in Hole. *Wit.* John Irving in Over-Craige and William Irving, yr.
	12.	The sd. day Helen Warroch, *d.* to John Warroch in the P. of Wawchope. *Wit.* Mr. Thomas Allen in Walls and John Johnston yr.
Sept.	11.	The sd. day Andrew Hislop, *s.* to Robert Hislope in Broomholme. *Wit.* John Scot of Rennelburn and John Maxwell of Broomholme. The sd. day likewise, Janet, *d.* to John Armstrong in Broomeholme. *Wit.* James Johnston in Long-holme and James Pasley yr.

Thursday December 8

Dec.	8.	The foresd. day Elizabeth Allen, *d.* to Mr. Robert Allen Minister at Staplegor-town Baptized in the foresd Kirk be Mr. David Layng Minister at Canobie. *Wit.* Mr. Thomas Henderson Minister at Gretney, Mr. Patrick Inglish Minister at Annan, Thomas Armstrong of Over-Craig, John Armstrong, fiar yrof and severals others. She was born about five hours in the forenoon, on the Wednesday immediatly before, being the seventh of the sd. Month. ∞

441

The following notes, evidently made by the Rev. Robert Allan, minister of Stapelgortoun, appear at the end of the Register:—

My second son was born at Staplegortown *alias* Pott-holme in Eskdale on Mun. the 24 of Oct. 1687 about 4 hours in the forenoon and was baptized Robert in the Kirk of Staplegortown on Thurs. the 27 of the foresd. month & that by Mr. John Brown minister at Westerkirk with Mr. Simon Merp* minister at Wauchope Mr. John Mahill† minister at Ewes Mr. Robert Pitcarn Robert Scot at Castle & severall others.

*The name given in the Wauchope Session Records is Wyld or Wool.
†The unusual spelling leads us to believe this refers to John Melvill, minister at Ewes.
‡The minister at Westerkirk at this time was in fact John Browne.

Item my third son was born at Staplegortown *alias* Pott-holme on Mund. Nov. 18 1689 about 10 hours in the fore-noon and bapt. Walter by Mr. John Home‡ minister at Westerkirk in the Kirk of Staplegortown on thurs. following being the 21 of the foresd. month Bap. Wit. John Scot in Stubholme David Dixson in Longholme and some others. My foresd. son Walter was weaned at Wauchope about the begining of Jun. 1691, his mother most carefully & tenderly nurssing him (& all of them) at the foresd. time.

Then on Mund. March 13 1694 my third daughter was born the foresd. day about 9 hours in the forenoon in the manssion houss at Wauchope Walls and was bapt. in the meeting house yr on thurs. the 17 of the foresd. month by Mr. John Halyburton minister at Graitney and was named Margaret. She was weaned about the 13 of Sept. 1695 her mother nursing her just one year and a half.

Item at Overstub-holme on thurs. April 23 1696 my fourth son & seventh child was born about ....hours in the forenoon of the foresd. day and was bapt William at the foresd. place on Sat. the 2 day of June 1696 and yt by Mr. Robert Gardener, Curat. at Arthuret Kirk in the Kingdome of England the nat. minister before the sad & bad [?] revolution at Rerrick in the bishoprick and Sherifdome of Galloway in Scotland & before these witnesses Mr. Walter Gladstone messenger in Hawick Thomas Grahame Schoolm^r. in longholme Michael Tod in Pott-holme William Murray yr.

List of subscribers for the building of a stone and lime-wash wall around Wauchope Burial Ground. The original list was in the possession of John Hyslop, then Robert Hyslop and finally with Robert's daughter Hilda McVittie Cooper. She kept a copy which is detailed below. In l964 she sent the original list to Edward Armstrong, Town Clerk of Langholm, for safe keeping in Langholm Archives.

		£ s d
His Grace the Duke of		
Buccleuch		3 . 0 . 0
Arthur Rea	Langholm	1 . 0 . 0
Simon Hyslop	New Langholm	1 . 0 . 0
James Stothard	Blough	1 . 0 . 0
Walter Nicol	Porterburn	1 . 0 . 0
Simon Hyslop	The Kerr	1 . 0 . 0
William Scott	Herd in Irvine	10 . 0.
Adam Armstrong	Cronksbankhead	10 . 0
William Warwick		12 . 0
James Murray	Kirtleton	10 . 0
James Stothard	Linbridgeford	3 . 0
Robert Nicol	Joiner in New Langholm	10 . 0
Andrew Hope	Loophill	10 . 0
Thomas Stothard	Linbridgeford	10 . 6
John Telfer	Mason in New Langholm	5 . 0
John Hyslop	Crofthead	10 . 6
Peter Kerr	Hagg	10 . 6
John Summervail	Glenzierholm	10 . 6
Col. Murray	Langholm	1 . 1 . 0
Adam Park	Westwater	6 . 0
John Thomson	Hakshole	10 . 0
George Warwick	Auchenrivock	10 . 6
James Summervail	Glenzierholm	7 . 6
William Warwick		10 . 6
David Laing	Westerhall	10 . 0
Alexander Epsom		5 . 0
John Coorthwaite		5 . 0
John Hyslop	Potholm	5 . 0
Mrs. Julia Murray		2 . 6
William Rea		2 . 6
William Park		2 . 0

ACTA. PARL. SCOT.

"Act in favors of James & Anna Duke and Dutches of Buccleugh and Monmouth for fairs at Dalkeith, Langholm, and Casiltoun.

Apud Edinburgh August 23, 1672

Anent a Suplication presented to the Kings Majestie and Estates of Parlia^t be James and Anna Duke and Dutches of Buccleuch and Monmouth. Mentioning that the toune of Dalkeith lying in the shirrefdome of Edinburgh and the toune of Langholme lying in the Lordship & Regallitie of Eskdaill and shirrefdome of Dumfreis. And lykwise the toune of Cassiltoun lying in the lordship and regallitie of Liddisdaill & shirrefdome of Roxburgh pertaining to the Petitioners ly in such places of the Countrey as that it would be advantageous not onlie to these tounes bot also to the nixt adjacent places of the rexive* Countreys where they ly. That there should be ane convenient number of fairs appointed therin. Humblie therefor Desireing that some fairs may be added to the saids tounes of Dalkeith and Langholme and uther fair and ane weiklie mercat appointed to be kept at Cassiltoun. As the supplication at length Beirs Which being taken into consideration The Kings Majestie with advice and consent of his Estates of Parlia^t Doe heirby Give and Grant to the said James and Anna Duke and Dutches of Buccleugh and Monmouth and their successors two yeirlie frie faires to be kept and holden at the said toune of Dalkeith (besides the other fairs formerlie holdin there) the one upon the last tuisday of Aprile and the other upon the second tewsday of Jully yeirlie. As also two fairs yeirlie to be holden and kept at the sd. toune of Langholme (besides the other fair kept therat) the one upon the fyft day of Aprile and the other upon the fyftein of Jully yeirlie. As lykwayes thrie frie yeirlie fairs to be keipt at the said toune of Cassiltoun. One upon the eightein day of Junij the second upon the fourth day of September and the Thrid upon the tenth day of October yeirlie in all tyme comeing. Togidder with ane weiklie mercat to be holdin at the said toune of Cassiltoune upon fryday. And incaice any of the saids faires shall happin to fall upon ane sunday That the samyn be holdin the day imediatlie following for buying and Selling of horse nolt sheip meil malt and all sort of merchandice and other Comodities necessar and usefull for the Cuntrie With Power to the said Duke and Dutches and their forsaids or such as they shall appoint to collect and uptake the tolls customes and dewties belonging to the saids yeirlie faires and weiklie mercat. And to enjoy all other freedomes liberties priviledges and imunities ficlyke and als frielie as any other hes done or may doe in the lyke caices."

"Act in favors of Ann Dutches of Buceleugh and James Earl of Dalkeith her Son for two yearly fairs at the Toun of Langholm.   A.D. 1701

OUR SOVERAIGN LORD and Estates of Parliament Considering that fairs and mercats in convenient places tend to the good and advantadge of the Inhabitants thereof and of all his Majesties other Leidges dwelling near thereto and likewayes to increase trade and commerce in the nation and that it is very fit for these ends to Authorize two yearly fairs upon the dayes following at the Toun of Langholme belonging to Ann Dutches of Buccleugh and James Earl of Dalkeith her son and lying within the parochine of Staple Gordon of old within the shire ot Dumfreis and now by annexation within the shire of Roxburgh Do therefore by these presents Appoint two fairs to be kept and holden yearly at the said toun of Langholme One upon the last Tuesday of May and the other upon the first Tuesday of September in all time comeing for every kind of merchandize And have Given and Granted and hereby Give and Grant to the said Ann Dutchess of Buceleugh and James Earl of Dalkeith and their heirs and successors for ever the right and priviledge of keeping and holding the said fairs yearly the haill tolls customes profites and casualties thereof and competent to pertain thereto and all other advantadges used and wont With full power to them to exact uplift dispose upon and enjoy the samen and to cause proclaim and ride the said fairs and make such orders thereanent as they think fit and to do all other things concerning the same which any haveing the priviledge of keeping fairs within the Kingdom lawfully do or may do."

LIST OF CORNETS AT THE COMMON-RIDING

1817	W. Pasley, Manufacturer	1853	T. Dalgliesh, Horse Dealer
1818	John Elliot, Butcher	1854	William Anderson, Blacksmith
1819	John Elliot, Butcher	1855	James Scott, Carter
1820	William Beattie, Crown Inn	1856	Joseph Park, Draper
1821	James Murray, Farmer	1857	John Hotson, Mason
1822	Robert Brown, Milntown	1858	John Reid, Scourer
1823	Robert Brown, Milntown	1859	Andrew Smith, Shepherd
1824	John Glendinning, Merchant	1860	James Lauder, Blacksmith
1825	James Irving, Baker	1861	William Keir, Joiner
1826	John Thomson, Innkeeper	1862	Thomas Saunders, Draper
1827	William Foster, Joiner	1863	Walter Scoon, Blacksmith
1828	Thomas Veitch, Meal Dealer	1864	Matthew Irving, Woolsorter
1829	John Sibson, Saddler	1865	Andrew Johnstone, Spinner
1830	Walter Chalmers, Brewer	1866	William Beattie, Mason
1831	William Telford, Cooper	1867	John Beattie, Warehouseman
1832	Walter Scoon, Blacksmith	1868	Thomas Anderson, Blacksmith
1833	James Dalgliesh, Surgeon	1869	Lawrence Ewart, Blacksmith
1834	James Hope, Candlemaker	1870	William McVittie, Finisher
1835	W. Warwick, Horse Dealer	1871	James Tait, Skinner
1836	John Kershaw, Shoemaker	1872	Andrew Beattie, Millwright
1837	James Clark, Saddler	1873	Alexander McVittie, Joiner
1838	Richard Wood, Surgeon	1874	William Douglas, Painter
1839	William Hyslop, Baker	1875	James Latimer, Joiner
1840	Matthew Murray, Carter	1876	James Turnbull, Slater
1841	Walter Hotson, Shoemaker	1877	George Little, Weaver
1842	David Irving, Joiner	1878	James Reid, Woolsorter
1843	Robert Anderson, Blacksmith	1879	John Anderson, Blacksmith
1844	Robert Lunn, Butcher	1880	James Reid, Warehouseman
1845	William Millar, Miller	1881	Christopher Weatherstone, Baker
1846	Thomas Little, Stone Dyker	1882	Robert McVittie, Joiner
1847	Robert Scoon, Blacksmith	1883	Robert Thomson, Skinner
1848	Aitchison Grieve, Blacksmith	1884	John Fletcher, Painter
1849	Walter Clark, Blacksmith	1885	John T. Burnet, Ewesbank
1850	John W. J. Paterson, Terrona	1886	James Smith, Painter
1851	James Veitch, Carter	1887	John Irving, Langholm Mill
1852	John Young, Salutation Inn	1888	John Murray, Baker

1889	James Irving, Whitshiels	1926	Robert Irving, Dairyman
1890	James Fletcher, Warehouseman	1927	N. H. Copeland, Postman
1891	William Trotter, Draper	1928	John Goodfellow, Painter
1892	William B. Scott, Ashley Bank	1929	Alexander McVittie, Dairyman
1893	Archibald Irving, Painter	1930	L. Ewart, Motor Mechanic
1894	Harry A. Scott, Ashley Bank	1931	James Ewart, Law Clerk
1895	Robert Stewart, Baker	1932	Andrew Beattie, Yarnman
1896	Robert W. Reid, Blacksmith	1933	J. T. Armstrong, Groom
1897	David Irving, Joiner	1934	Robert Graham, Plumber
1898	John W. Church, Grocer	1935	C. Stewart Paisley, Tanner
1899	Thomas Ellis, Groom	1936	R. I. Borthwick, Dairyman
1900	John Payne, Tailor	1937	W. W. Robinson, Engineer
1901	George Scoon, Mason	1938	W. N.Calwell, Farmer
1902	John V. Goodfellow, Jr., Painter	1939	A. Irving, Pattern Weaver
1903	John Ewart, Blacksmith	1940	*J. J. Paterson, Terrona
1904	Robert D. Hyslop, Postal Clerk	1941	*James J. Paterson
1905	Simon L. Irving, Langholm Mill	1942	*James J. Paterson
1906	William Douglas, Groom	1943	*James J. Paterson
1907	John Wallace, Butcher	1944	*James J. Paterson
1908	James Young, Vanman	1945	*James J. Paterson
1909	James J. Paterson, Terrona	1946	John Murray, Baker
1910	Arthur Irving, Painter	1947	Alex. S. Morrison, Baker
1911	William Thomson, Vanman	1948	Edgar Morrison, Motor Mechanic
1912	Adam Grieve, Stationer	1949	James Robinson, Joiner
1913	Robert Rae, Coal Agent	1950	J. M. Young, Trans. Driver
1914	*John Wilson, Baker	1951	William Park, Painter
1915	*John Wilson, Baker	1952	J. J. Paterson, Terrona
1916	*John Wilson, Baker	1953	John Paterson, Terrona
1917	*Robert Stewart, Baker	1954	W. H. M. Reid, Painter
1918	*T. G. Elliot, Pattern Weaver	1955	J. M. Maxwell, Plasterer
1919	Frederick Scott, Powerloom Tuner	1956	J. T. Donaldson, Painter
1920	W. A. Lightbody, Manufacturer	1957	Ian Murray, Plasterer
1921	Alfred A. Bell, Glenlea	1958	W. P. Bell, Farmer
1922	Arthur W. Bell, Manufacturer	1959	A. J. Jeffrey, Engineer
1923	Robert Fletcher, Painter	1960	A. G. Morgan, Skinner
1924	Gilbert F. Bell, Manufacturer	1961	G. Ian McVittie, Pattern Weaver
1925	James Laidlaw, Lorryman	1962	W. H. Harkness, Carder

446

1963	George Ellwood, Weaver	1982	R. J. M. Maxwell, Bricklayer
1964	R. Irving Edgar, Builder	1983	C. A. Irving, Ceramic Painter
1965	David P. McVittie, Joiner	1984	Wm. S. Young, Medical Technologist
1966	R. Hudson, Y'store Foreman	1985	J. Kenneth Donaldson, Pattern Weaver
1967	C. Barnfather, Pattern Weaver	1986	Iain C. Park, Warehouseman
1968	Cyril Johnstone, Butcher	1987	Robert J. Rae, Plumber
1969	W. C. Laidlaw, Baker	1988	Andrew J. Jeffrey, Electrician
1970	Neil Davidson, Shepherd	1989	Andrew Johnstone, Textile Weaver
1971	Robert S. Nixon, Driver	1990	Kevan J. Hotson, Bricklayer
1972	S. H .Morrison, Tweed Finisher	1991	Alan Donaldson, Computer Progarmmer
1973	M. Bell, Forestry Worker	1992	Stephen Rae, Carpet Fitter
1974	Graham Cubbon, Bricklayer	1993	Andrew W. Walton, Textile Weaver
1975	J. R. Reid, Textile Dyer	1994	Ian L. Ewart, Dyer
1976	J. E. Murray, Motor Mechanic	1995	Stephen Ellwood, Mill Warper
1977	C. J. Erskine, Shop Assistant	1996	David J. McVittie, Textile Worker
1978	M. T. Borthwick, Joiner	1997	Simon P. Wood, Mill Warper
1979	T. Morrison, Motor Mechanic	1998	Malcolm M. Devlin, Warehouse Operative
1980	David H. Pool, Textile Designer	1999	Darren G. Irving, Resin Caster
1981	A. R. Currie, Woodcutter	2000	Steven Hotson, Builder

*War Years.

Note in 1952 and again in 2001 the Common-Riding was curtailed owing to Foot-and-Mouth Disease.

In 2001 John Murray, in his semi-julilee year, accepted the position of flag carrier.

This list of names from 1817 to 1911 was in the first edition of this book. It has been updated from the Official Programme of the Common-Riding and from information in the Eskdale and Liddesdale Advertiser.

ESKDALE KILWINNING LODGE OF FREEMASONS

LIST OF PAST MASTERS OF THE CRAFT

1747	John Maxwell	1820	John Irving
1748-50	No records	1821	William Nichol
1751	John Maxwell	1822	William Johnstone
1752-53	John Little	1823	John Irving
1754-64	No records	1824-30	John Young
1765-66	John Cragie	1831	William Johnstone
1767	Gilbert Richardson	1832	Ninian Wilson
1768-69	John Little	1833-34	John Young
1770	John Armstrong	1835	Ninian Wilson
1771	Gilbert Richardson	1836	William Johnstone
1772-76	John Little	1837	John Young
1777	John Armstrong	1838	William Johnstone
1778	William Yeoman	1839-42	John Young
1779-80	Gilbert Richardson	1843-53	William Johnstone
1781-83	No records	1854-60	John Irving
1784	William Yeoman	1871-72	Joseph Clark Lyall
1785-93	John Little	1873	William Byers
1794-95	John Graham	1874	Joseph Clark Lyall
1796	William Johnston	1875-87	John Scott
1797-99	John Graham	1888-89	Henry Sanders
1800	William Johnstone	1890-93	William Alex. Conn
1801	Thomas Douglas	1894-96	Henry Graham
1802	John Young	1897-1901	Thomas Moses
1803-6	William Johnstone	1902-04	William E. Elton
1807	Francis Beattie	1905-08	E. J. Bell
1808	William Johnstone	1909-11	The Rev. J. A. Seaton
1809	William Yeoman	1912-15	James Petrie
1810-11	William Johnstone	1916-19	Thomas R. Easton
1812	Alexander Hotson	1920	Thomas Lightbody
1813	John Irving	1921	Alexander Sharp
1814-15	William Johnstone	1922-23	Martin Beattie
1816	John Young	1924-25	W. A. Lightbody
1817	William Johnstone	1925-26	William Murray
1818-19	John Young	1926-27	John Hyslop

1927-29	William B. McVittie	1964-65	Francis H. H. Johnston
1929-32	E. Ashley Cochrane	1965-66	Alexander Pool
1932-33	Thomas Hyslop	1966-67	William Elliot
1933-34	William Kerr	1967-68	John I. Millar
1934-35	Archibald A Oliver	1968-69	John E. Bell
1935-36	David Edgar	1969-70	John E.Bell
1936-37	John H. Tolson	1970-71	John D. Cameron
1937-38	John Wright	1972-73	Richard A. Irving
1938-39	John Goodfellow	1973-74	Arthur J. Tolson
1939-40	David Mitchell	1974-75	Peter Irving Stuart
1940-41	Charles Constable	1975-76	Lawrence B. M. Martin
1941-42	Simon Grieve	1976-77	Anthony Anderson
1942-44	Charles Constable	1977-79	John I. Hotson
1944-46	James Maxwell	1979-80	Brian L. Porteous
1946-47	James M. Inglis	1980-81	George Beattie
1947-48	John T. Jeffrey	1981-82	John Hetherington
1948-49	Charles S. Paisley	1982-83	R. W. Raymond Clemmett
1949-50	David Maxwell	1983-84	William M. Hotson
1950-51	Lawrence Ewart	1984-85	David Yarrow
1951-52	James Veitch	1985-86	David A. Cooper
1952-53	Henry Erskine	1986-87	Joseph Graham
1953-54	Andrew J. Jeffrey	1987-88	W. K. Braithwaite, Snr.
1954-55	James A. Irving	1988-89	Kenneth MacQueen
1955-56	James Dinwoodie	1989-90	Thomas J. Martin
1956-57	Jas. G. Barnfather	1990-91	Wm. K. Braithwaite, Snr.
1957-58	William W. Barrow	1991-92	Ian J. McGuigan
1958-59	Matthew Borthwick	1992-94	David W. Hogg
1959-60	John Cowan	1994-95	Iain W. Logan
1960-61	M. J. C. Dinwoodie	1995-96	Hamilton Smith
1962-63	D. I. Anderson	1996-97	Thomas J. Martin
1963-64	Jack Hetherington	1997-98	Wm. K. Braithwaite, Jnr.

INDEX

E

F